Get the eBooks FREE!

(PDF, ePub, Kindle, and liveBook all included)

We believe that once you buy a book from us, you should be able to read it in any format we have available. To get electronic versions of this book at no additional cost to you, purchase and then register this book at the Manning website.

Go to https://www.manning.com/freebook and follow the instructions to complete your pBook registration.

That's it!
Thanks from Manning!

HTTP/2 in Action

HTTP/2 in Action

BARRY POLLARD

MANNING

SHELTER ISLAND

Manning Publications Co.
20 Baldwin Road
PO Box 761
Shelter Island, NY 11964

Development editor: Kevin Harreld
Technical development editor: Thomas McKearney
Review editor: Ivan Martinovic
Project editor: Vincent Nordhaus
Copy editor: Kathy Simpson
Proofreader: Alyson Brener
Technical proofreader: Lokeshwar Vangala
Typesetter: Dennis Dalinnik
Cover designer: Marija Tudor

ISBN: 9781617295164
Printed in the United States of America
1 2 3 4 5 6 7 8 9 10 – SP – 24 23 22 21 20 19

In memory of Ronan Rafferty (1977–2018),
web developer and friend

brief contents

contents

preface

I became interested in HTTP/2 at an early stage. The emergence of a new technology that promised almost free performance gains while potentially removing the need for some of the messy workarounds web developers had to use was definitely intriguing. The reality was a little more complicated, however, and after spending some time figuring out how to deploy it on my Apache server and then struggling to explain the impact on performance that I was seeing, I got frustrated with the lack of documentation. I wrote a couple of blog posts on how to set it up, and those posts proved to be popular. At the same time, I started getting involved with some of the HTTP/2 projects on GitHub, as well as lurking around the topic on Stack Overflow and helping out those who had similar issues to my own. When Manning came calling, looking for someone to write a book about HTTP/2, I jumped at the chance. I hadn't been involved in its genesis, but I felt that I could speak to the many struggling web developers out there like me who had heard about this technology but lacked the knowledge to get it deployed.

In the year and a half that it's taken to write this book, HTTP/2 has become mainstream and is used by more and more websites. Some of the deployment issues have gotten easier as software has updated, and I hope that some of the issues described in this book will soon be problems of the past, but I suspect that for a few more years at least, HTTP/2 will require some effort to enable it.

When you're able to switch it on, HTTP/2 should give you an instant performance boost with little configuration or understanding required. Nothing comes for free in this life, however, and subtleties and nuances in the protocol and in deployments of it mean that deeper understanding will serve website owners well. Web performance optimization is a flourishing industry, and HTTP/2 is another tool that should lead to interesting techniques and opportunities both now and in the future.

An enormous amount of information is available on the web, and for those who have the time and the willingness to seek it out, filter it, and understand it, it's immensely satisfying to read all the varied opinions and even communicate directly with the protocol designers and implementers. For a topic as big as HTTP/2, however, the scope and depth of a book gives me the opportunity to explain the technology fully while touching on related topics and giving you references to follow up on if I pique your interest in something. I hope I've achieved that goal with this book.

acknowledgments

First and foremost, I'd like to thank my incredibly understanding wife, Aine, who has spent the past year and a half doing most of the minding of our two young children (that became "three young children" during the writing of this book!) while I've been locked away furiously tapping on my keyboard. She may be the one person in the world who is happier than I to see this book finally published! A special shout-out also needs to go to my in-laws (the Buckleys), who helped Aine entertain our children far away from my home study so I could concentrate.

The Manning team was hugely supportive throughout this process. In particular, I'd like to thank Brian Sawyer, who first got in touch and offered me the chance to write this book. His help in guiding me through the proposal process ensured that the book was picked up by the publisher. Kevin Harreld did a great job as the development editor, gently pushing me in the right direction while patiently answering my many questions. Thomas McKearney provided terrific technical oversight as the technical development editor, giving detailed feedback on all the chapters. The three rounds of reviews organized by Ivan Martinovic provided invaluable feedback and guidance on what was working and what needed improvement as the book progressed. Similarly, the Manning Early Access Program (MEAP) is a fantastic way of getting feedback from real readers, and Matko Hrvatin did great work in organizing that.

I'd also like to thank the whole Manning marketing team who helped get out the word of the book from the beginning, but special thanks to Christopher Kaufman, who put up with my seemingly endless requests for edits of the promotional material. Getting the book ready for production was a daunting task, so thanks to Vincent

Nordhaus for shepherding my precious output through that process. Kathy Simpson and Alyson Brener made the book immeasurably more readable during copy editing and proofreading and both had the unenviable task of dealing with my questioning their (much better!) wording and grammar on too many occasions. Thanks also to the other proofreaders, graphics, layout, and typesetting teams who took this book through the final stages. My name may be on the cover, but all these people, among others, helped craft my meandering thoughts into a professional publication. Any mistakes that managed to still make it in are undoubtedly my own fault, not theirs.

I received feedback from many people outside Manning, from the proposal reviewers to the manuscript reviewers (thanks in particular to those of you who made it through all three reviews!) to MEAP readers. In particular, I'd like to thank Lucas Pardue and Robin Marx, who painstakingly reviewed the whole manuscript and provided valuable HTTP/2 expertise throughout this process. Other reviewers include Alain Couniot, Anto Aravinth, Art Bergquist, Camal Cakar, Debmalya Jash, Edwin Kwok, Ethan Rivett, Evan Wallace, Florin-Gabriel Barbuceanu, John Matthews, Jonathan Thoms, Joshua Horwitz, Justin Coulston, Matt Deimel, Matthew Farwell, Matthew Halverson, Morteza Kiadi, Ronald Cranston, Ryan Burrows, Sandeep Khurana, Simeon Leyzerzon, Tyler Kowallis, and Wesley Beary. Thanks to you all.

On the technology side, I have to give thanks to Sir Tim Berners-Lee for kicking this whole web thing off all those years ago, and to Mike Belshe and Robert Peon for inventing SPDY and then formalizing it as HTTP/2 with the help of Martin Thompson, acting as editor. Standardization was possible only thanks to the hard-working volunteers of the Internet Engineering Task Force (IETF) and in particular the HTTP Working Group, chaired by Mark Nottingham and Patrick McManus. Without all of them—and without their employers' permission to spend time on this work—there'd be no HTTP/2, and, therefore, no need for this book.

I'm continually amazed by the amount of time and effort the technology community puts into volunteer work. From open source projects to community sites such as Stack Overflow, GitHub, and Twitter to blogs and presentations, many people give so much of their time for no apparent material reward other than helping others and stretching their own knowledge. I'm thankful and proud to be part of this community. This book wouldn't have been possible without learning from the teachings of web performance experts Steve Sounders, Yoav Weiss, Ilya Grigorik, Pat Meehan, Jake Archibald, Hooman Beheshti and Daniel Stenberg, all of whom are referenced in this book. Particular thanks to Stefan Eissing, who did tremendous work on the Apache HTTP/2 implementation that first piqued my interest, and Tatsuhiro Tsujikawa, who created the underlying nghttp2 library that it uses (along with many other HTTP/2 implementations). On a similar note, freely available tools such as WebPagetest, The HTTP Archive, W3Techs, Draw.io, TinyPng, nghttp2, curl, Apache, nginx, and Let's Encrypt are a big part of why this book is possible. I'd like to extend extra special thanks to those companies that gave permission to use images of their tools in this book.

Finally, I'd like to thank you, the reader, for showing an interest in this book. Although many people helped produce it in one way or another, they do it only because of people like you who help keep books alive and make them worthwhile to publish. I hope that you gain valuable insights and understanding from this book.

about this book

HTTP/2 in Action was written to explain the protocol in an easy-to-follow, practical manner, using real-world examples. Protocol specifications can be dry and difficult to understand, so this book aims to ground the details in easy-to-understand examples that are relevant to all users of the internet.

Who should read this book?

This book was written for web developers, website administrators, and those who simply have an interest in understanding how internet technology works. The book aims to provide complete coverage of HTTP/2 and all the subtleties involved in it. Although plenty of blog posts on the topic exist, most are at a high level or a detailed level on a specific topic. This book aims to cover the entire protocol and many of the complexities involved in it, which should prepare the reader to read and understand the spec and specific blog posts, should they wish to read even further. HTTP/2 was created primarily to improve performance, so anyone who's interested in web performance optimization is sure to gain useful understanding and insights. Additionally, the book contains many references for further reading.

How this book is organized

The book is 10 chapters divided into 4 parts.

Part 1 explains the background of, need for, and ways of upgrading to HTTP/2:

- Chapter 1 provides the background needed to understand the book. Even those with only a basic understanding of the internet should be able to follow along.

- Chapter 2 looks at the problems with HTTP/1.1 and why HTTP/2 was needed.
- Chapter 3 discusses the upgrade options that enable HTTP/2 for your website and some of the complications involved with this process. This chapter is supplemented by the appendix, which provides installation instructions for the popular web servers Apache, nginx, and IIS.

The pace picks up in part 2, as I teach the protocol and what it means for web development practices:

- Chapter 4 describes the basics of the HTTP/2 protocol, how an HTTP/2 connection is established, and the basic format of HTTP/2 frames.
- Chapter 5 covers HTTP/2 push, which is a brand-new part of the protocol, allowing website owners to proactively send resources that browsers haven't yet asked for.
- Chapter 6 looks at what HTTP/2 means for web development practices.

Part 3 gets into the advanced parts of the protocol, which web developers and even web server administrators may not currently have much ability to influence:

- Chapter 7 covers the remainder of the HTTP/2 specification—including state, flow control, and priorities—and looks at the differences in HTTP/2 conformance in the implementations.
- Chapter 8 takes a deep dive into the HPACK protocol, which is used for HTTP header compression in HTTP/2.

Part 4 looks at the future of HTTP:

- Chapter 9 looks at TCP, QUIC, and HTTP/3. Technology never sleeps, and now that HTTP/2 is available, developers are already looking at ways to improve it. This chapter discusses the inefficiencies that weren't solved by HTTP/2 and how they may be improved in its successor: HTTP/3.
- Chapter 10 looks beyond HTTP/3 at other ways that HTTP can be improved, including a reflection on the problems that were raised during HTTP/2 standardization and whether these problems have proved to be issues in the real world.

After reading this book, readers should have an excellent understanding of HTTP/2 and related technologies, and they should have gained greater understanding of web performance optimization. They will also be ready for QUIC and HTTP/3 when it comes out in the future.

About the code

Unlike most technical books, *HTTP/2 in Action* doesn't have a huge amount of code, because the book is about a protocol rather than a programming language. It tries to teach you high-level concepts that apply to any web server or programming language used to serve pages on the web. The book has some examples in NodeJS and Perl, however, as well as web-server configuration snippets.

Source code and configuration snippets are formatted in a `fixed-width font` `like this` to separate them from ordinary text. Sometimes, code is also in bold to highlight code that has changed from previous steps in the chapter, such as when a new feature adds to an existing line of code.

The source code is available to download from the publisher's website at https://www.manning.com/books/http2-in-action or from GitHub at https://github.com/bazzadp/http2-in-action.

liveBook discussion forum

Purchase of *HTTP/2 in Action* includes free access to a private web forum run by Manning Publications, where you can make comments about the book, ask technical questions, and receive help from the author and from other users. To access the forum go to https://livebook.manning.com/#!/book/http2-in-action/discussion. You can also learn more about Manning's forums and the rules of conduct at https://livebook.manning.com/#!/discussion.

Manning's commitment to our readers is to provide a venue where a meaningful dialogue between individual readers and between readers and the author can take place. It is not a commitment to any specific amount of participation on the part of the author, whose contribution to the forum remains voluntary (and unpaid). We suggest you try asking the author some challenging questions lest his interest stray! The forum and the archives of previous discussions will be accessible from the publisher's website as long as the book is in print.

Online resources

Need additional help?

- The HTTP/2 home page is at https://http2.github.io/. The page includes links to the HTTP/2 and HPACK specifications, HTTP/2 implementations, and FAQs.
- The HTTP Working Group home page is at https://httpwg.org/. Most of the group's work is publicly available at the GitHub page https://github.com/httpwg/ and the group's mailing lists (https://lists.w3.org/Archives/Public/ietf-http-wg/).
- Stack Overflow also has an HTTP/2 tag (https://stackoverflow.com/questions/tagged/http2), and the author often answers questions there.

about the author

BARRY POLLARD is a professional software developer who has nearly two decades of industry experience developing and supporting software and infrastructure. He has a keen interest in web technologies, performance tuning, security, and the practical use of technology. You can find him blogging at https://www.tunetheweb.com or as @tunetheweb on Twitter.

about the cover illustration

The figure on the cover of *HTTP/2 in Action* is captioned "Habit of a Russian Market Woman in 1768." The illustration is taken from Thomas Jefferys' *A Collection of the Dresses of Different Nations, Ancient and Modern* (four volumes), London, published between 1757 and 1772. The title page states that these are hand-colored copperplate engravings, heightened with gum arabic. Thomas Jefferys (1719–1771) was called "Geographer to King George III." He was an English cartographer who was the leading map supplier of his day. He engraved and printed maps for government and other official bodies and produced a wide range of commercial maps and atlases, especially of North America. His work as a map maker sparked an interest in local dress customs of the lands he surveyed and mapped, which are brilliantly displayed in this collection. Fascination with faraway lands and travel for pleasure were relatively new phenomena in the late eighteenth century, and collections such as this one were popular, introducing both the tourist as well as the armchair traveler to the inhabitants of other countries. The diversity of the drawings in Jefferys' volumes speaks vividly of the uniqueness and individuality of the world's nations some 200 years ago. Dress codes have changed since then, and the diversity by region and country, so rich at the time, has faded away. It's now often hard to tell the inhabitants of one continent from another. Perhaps, trying to view it optimistically, we've traded a cultural and visual diversity for a more varied personal life—or a more varied and interesting intellectual and technical life. At a time when it's difficult to tell one computer book from another, Manning celebrates the inventiveness and initiative of the computer business with book covers based on the rich diversity of regional life of two centuries ago, brought back to life by Jefferys' pictures.

Part 1

Moving to HTTP/2

To understand why HTTP/2 is creating such a buzz in the web performance industry, you first need to look at why it's needed and what problems it looks to solve. Therefore, the first part of this book introduces HTTP/1 to those readers who aren't familiar with exactly what it is or how it works; then it explains why a version 2 was needed. I talk at a high level about how HTTP/2 works, but leave the low-level details until later in the book. Instead, I close this part by talking about the various methods you can use to deploy HTTP/2 to your site.

Web technologies
and HTTP

This chapter covers

- How a web page is loaded by the browser
- What HTTP is and how it evolved up to HTTP/1.1
- The basics of HTTPS
- Basic HTTP tools

This chapter gives you background on how the web works today and explains some key concepts necessary for the rest of this book to make sense; then it introduces HTTP and the history of the previous versions. I expect many of the readers of this book to be at least somewhat familiar with a lot of what is discussed in this first chapter, but I encourage you not to skip it; use this chapter as an opportunity to refresh yourself on the basics.

1.1 How the web works

The internet has become an integral part of everyday life. Shopping, banking, communication, and entertainment all depend on the internet, and with the growth of the Internet of Things (IoT), more and more devices are being put online, where they can be accessed remotely. This access is made possible by several technologies, including Hypertext Transfer Protocol (HTTP), which is a key method of requesting access to remote web applications and resources. Although most people understand how to use a web browser to surf the internet, few truly understand how this technology works, why HTTP is a core part of the web, or why the next version (HTTP/2) is causing such excitement in the web community.

1.1.1 The internet versus the World Wide Web

For many people, the internet and the World Wide Web are synonymous, but it's important to differentiate between the two terms.

The *internet* is a collection of public computers linked through the shared use of the Internet Protocol (IP) to route messages. It's made up of many services, including the World Wide Web, email, file sharing, and internet telephony. The World Wide Web (or the web), therefore, is but one part of the internet, though it's the most visible part, and as people often look at email through web-mail front ends (such as Gmail, Hotmail, and Yahoo!), some of them use *the web* interchangeably with *the internet.*

HTTP is how web browsers request web pages. It was one of the three main technologies defined by Tim Berners-Lee when he invented the web, along with unique identifiers for resources (which is where Uniform Resource Locators, or URLs, came from) and Hypertext Markup Language (HTML). Other parts of the internet have their own protocols and standards to define how they work and how their underlying messages are routed through the internet (such as email with SMTP, IMAP, and POP). When examining HTTP, you're dealing primarily with the World Wide Web. This line is getting more blurred, however, as services built on top of HTTP, even without a traditional web front end, mean that defining the web itself is trickier and trickier! These services (known by acronyms such as REST or SOAP) can be used by web pages and non-web pages (such as mobile apps) alike. The IoT simply represents devices that expose services that other devices (computers, mobile apps, and even other IoT devices) can interact with, often through HTTP calls. As a result, you can use HTTP to send a message to a lamp to turn it on or off from a mobile phone app, for example.

Although the internet is made up of myriad services, a lot of them are being used proportionally less and less while use of the web continues to grow. Those of us who recall the internet in the earliest days recall acronyms such as BBS and IRC that are practically gone today, replaced by web forums, social media websites, and chat applications.

All this means that although the term *World Wide Web* was often incorrectly used interchangeably with *the internet,* the continued rise of the web—or at least of HTTP, which was created for it—may mean that soon, that understanding may not be as far from the truth as it once was.

1.1.2 What happens when you browse the web?

For now, I return to the primary and first use of HTTP: to request web pages. When you open a website in your favorite browser, whether that browser is on a desktop or laptop computer, a tablet, a mobile phone, or any of the myriad other devices that

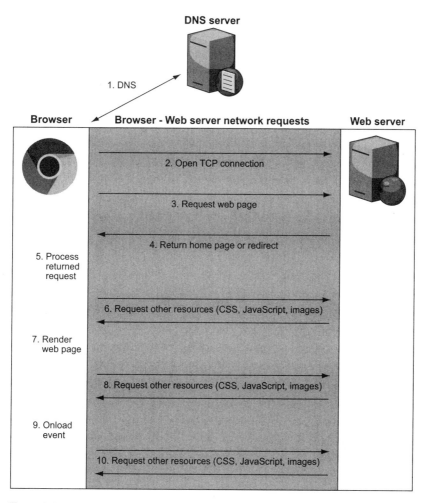

Figure 1.1 Typical interaction when browsing to a web page

allow internet access, an awful lot is going on. To get the most out of this book, you need to understand exactly how browsing the web works.

Suppose that you fire up a browser and go to www.google.com. Within a few seconds, the following will have happened, as illustrated in figure 1.1:

1 The browser requests the real address of www.google.com from a Domain Name System (DNS) server, which translates the human-friendly name www.google.com to a machine-friendly IP address.

   If you think of an IP address as a telephone number, DNS is the telephone book. This IP address is either an older-format IPv4 address (such as 216.58.192.4, which is nearly human-usable) or a new-format IPv6 address (such as 2607:f8b0:4005:801:0:0:0:2004, which is definitely getting into "machines-only" territory). Much as telephone area codes are occasionally redesignated when a city starts to run out of phone numbers, IPv6 is needed to deal with the explosion of devices connecting to the internet now and in the future.

Be aware that due to the global nature of the internet, larger companies often have several servers around the globe. When you ask your DNS for the IP address, it often provides the IP address of the nearest server to make your internet browsing faster. Someone based in America will get a different IP address for www.google.com than someone based in Europe, for example, so don't worry if you get different values of IP addresses for www.google.com than those I've given here.

Whatever happened to IPv5?

If Internet Protocol version 4 (IPv4) was replaced with version 6 (IPv6), what happened to version 5? And why have you never heard of IPv1 through IPv3?

The first 4 bits of an IP packet give the version, in theory limiting it to 15 versions. Before the much-used IPv4, there were four experimental versions starting at 0 and going up to 3. None of these versions was formally standardized until version 4, however.[a] After that, version 5 was designated for Internet Stream Protocol, which was intended for real-time audio and video streaming, similar to what Voice over IP (VoIP) became later. That version never took off, however, not least because it suffered the same address limitations of version 4, and when version 6 came along, work on it was stopped, leaving version 6 as the successor to IPv4. Apparently, it was initially called version 7 under the incorrect assumption that version 6 was already assigned.[b] Versions 7, 8, and 9 have also been assigned but are similarly not used anymore. If there ever is a successor to IPv6, it will likely be IPv10 or later, which no doubt will lead to questions similar to the ones that open this sidebar!

---

[a]   See https://tools.ietf.org/html/rfc760. This protocol was later updated and replaced (https://tools.ietf.org/ html/rfc791).

[b]   See https://archive.is/QqU73#selection-417.1-417.15.

---

2   The web browser asks your computer to open a Transmission Control Protocol (TCP) connection[1] over IP to this address on the standard web port (port 80)[2] or over the standard secure web port (port 443).

IP is used to direct traffic through the internet (hence, the name Internet Protocol!), but TCP adds stability and retransmissions to make the connection reliable ("Hello, did you get that?" "No, could you repeat that last bit, please?").

---

[1]   Google has started experimenting with QUIC, so if you're connecting from Chrome to a Google site, you may use that. I discuss QUIC in chapter 9.

[2]   Some websites, including Google, use a technology called HSTS to automatically use a Secure HTTP connection (HTTPS), which runs on port 443, so even if you try to connect over HTTP, the connection automatically upgrades to HTTPS before the request is sent.

As these two technologies are often used together, they're usually abbreviated as TCP/IP, and, together, they form the backbone of much of the internet.

A server can be used for several services (such as email, FTP, HTTP, and HTTPS [HTTP Secure] web servers), and the port allows different services to sit together under one IP address, much as a business may have a telephone extension for each employee.

3 When the browser has a connection to the web server, it can start asking for the website. This step is where HTTP comes in, and I examine how it works in the next section. For now, be aware that the web browser uses HTTP to ask the Google server for the Google home page.

NOTE At this point, your browser will have automatically corrected the shorthand web address (www.google.com) to the more syntactically correct URL address of http://www.google.com. The actual full URL includes the port and would be http://www.google.com:80, but if standard ports are being used (80 for HTTP and 443 for HTTPS), the browser hides the port. If nonstandard ports are being used, the port is shown. Some systems, particularly in development environments, use port 8080 for HTTP or 8443 for HTTPS, for example.

If HTTPS is being used (I go into HTTPS in a lot more detail in section 1.4), extra steps are required to set up the encryption that secures the connection.

4 The Google server responds with whatever URL you asked for. Typically, what gets sent back from the initial page is the text that makes up the web page in HTML format. HTML is a standardized, structured, text-based format that makes up the text content of a page. It's usually divided into various sections defined by HTML tags and references other bits of information needed to make the media-rich web pages you're used to seeing (Cascading Style Sheets [CSS], JavaScript code, images, fonts, and so on).

Instead of an HTML page, however, the response may be an instruction to go to a different location. Google, for example, runs only on HTTPS, so if you go to http://www.google.com, the response is a special HTTP instruction (usually, a 301 or 302 response code) that redirects to a new location at https://www.google.com. This response starts some or all of the preceding steps again, depending on whether the redirect address is a different server/port combination, a different port in the same location (such as a redirect to HTTPS), or even a different page on the same server and port.

Similarly, if something goes wrong, you get back an HTTP response code, the best-known of which is the 404 Not Found response code.

5 The web browser processes the returned request. Assuming that the returned response is HTML, the browser starts to parse the HTML code and builds in memory the Document Object Model (DOM), which is an internal representation of the page. During this processing, the browser likely sees other resources that it needs to display the page properly (such as CSS, JavaScript, and images).

6   The web browser requests any additional resources it needs. Google keeps its web page fairly lean; at this writing, only 16 other resources are needed. Each of these resources is requested in a similar manner, following steps 1–6, and yes, that includes this step, because those resources may in turn request other resources. The average website isn't as lean as Google and needs 75 resources,[3] often from many domains, so steps 1–6 must be repeated for all of them. This situation is one of the key things that makes web browsing slow and one of the key reasons for HTTP/2, the main purpose of which is to make requesting these additional resources more efficient, as you'll see in future chapters.

7   When the browser has enough of the critical resources, it starts to render the page onscreen. Choosing when to start rendering the page is a challenging task and not as simple as it sounds. If the web browser waits until all resources are downloaded, it would take a long time to show web pages, and the web would be an even slower, more frustrating place. But if the web browser starts to render the page too soon, you end up with the page jumping around as more content downloads, which is irritating if you're in the middle of reading an article when the page jumps down. A firm understanding of the technologies that make up the web—especially HTTP and HTML/CSS/JavaScript—can help website owners reduce these annoying jumps while pages are being loaded, but far too many sites don't optimize their pages effectively to prevent these jumps.

8   After the initial display of the page, the web browser continues, in the background, to download other resources that the page needs and update the page as it processes them. These resources include noncritical items such as images and advertising tracking scripts. As a result, you often see a web page displayed initially without images (especially on slower connections), with images being filled in as more of them are downloaded.

9   When the page is fully loaded, the browser stops the loading icon (a spinning icon on or near the address bar for most browsers) and fires the `OnLoad` JavaScript event, which JavaScript code may use as a sign that the page is ready to perform certain actions.

10 At this point, the page is fully loaded, but the browser hasn't stopped sending out requests. We're long past the days when a web page was a page of static information. Many web pages are now feature-rich applications that continually communicate with various servers on the internet to send or load additional content. This content may be user-initiated actions, such as when you type requests in the search bar on Google's home page and instantly see search suggestions without having to click the Search button, or it may be application-driven actions, such as your Facebook or Twitter feed's automatically updating without your having to click a refresh button. These actions often happen in the background and are

---

[3] https://httparchive.org/reports/page-weight#reqTotal

invisible to you, especially advertising and analytics scripts that track your actions on the site to report analytics to website owners and/or advertising networks.

As you can see, a *lot* happens when you type a URL, and it often happens in the blink of an eye. Each of these steps could form the basis for a whole book, with variations in certain circumstances. This book, however, concentrates on (and delves a little deeper into) steps 3–8 (loading the website over HTTP). Some later chapters (particularly chapter 9) also touch on step 2 (the underlying network connection that HTTP uses).

1.2   *What is HTTP?*

The preceding section is deliberately light on the details of how HTTP works so you can get an idea of how HTTP fits into the wider internet. In this section, I briefly describe how HTTP works and is used.

As I mentioned earlier, *HTTP* stands for *Hypertext Transfer Protocol*. As the name suggests, HTTP was initially intended to transfer hypertext documents (documents that contain links to other documents), and the first version didn't support anything but these documents. Quickly, developers realized that the protocol could be used to transfer other file types (such as images), so now the *Hypertext* part of the HTTP acronym is no longer too relevant, but given how widely used HTTP is, it's too late to rename it.

HTTP depends on a reliable network connection, usually provided by TCP/IP, which is itself built on some type of physical connection (Ethernet, Wi-FI, and so on). Because communication protocols are separated into layers, each layer can concentrate on what it does well. HTTP doesn't concern itself with the lower-level details of how that network connection is established. Although HTTP applications should be mindful of how to handle network failures or disconnects, the protocol itself makes no allowances for these tasks.

The Open Systems Interconnection (OSI) model is a conceptual model often used to describe this layered approach. The model consists of seven layers, though these layers don't map exactly to all networks and in particular to internet traffic. TCP spans at least two (and possibly three) layers, depending on how you define the layers. Figure 1.2 shows roughly how this model maps to web traffic and where HTTP fits into this model.

There's some argument about the exact definition of each layer. In complex systems like the internet, not everything can be classified and separated as easily as developers would like. In fact, the Internet Engineering Task Force (IETF) warns against getting too hung up on layering.[4] But it can be helpful to understand at a high level where HTTP fits in this model and how it depends on lower-level protocols to work. Many web applications are built on top of HTTP, so the Application layer, for example, refers more to networking layers than to JavaScript applications.

HTTP is, at heart, a request-and-response protocol. The web browser makes a request, using HTTP syntax, to the web server, which responds with a message containing the requested resource. The key to the success of HTTP is its simplicity. As

---

[4] https://tools.ietf.org/html/rfc3439#section-3

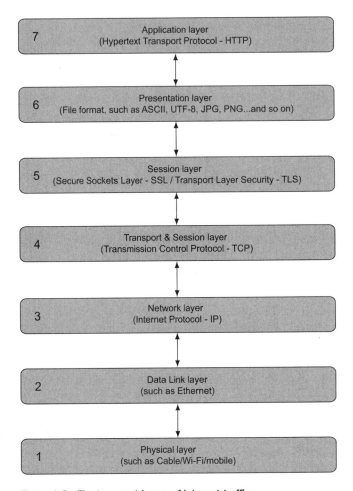

Figure 1.2   The transport layers of internet traffic

you'll see in later chapters, however, this simplicity can be a cause of concern for HTTP/2, which sacrifices some of that simplicity for efficiency.

The basic syntax of an HTTP request, after you open a connection, is as follows:

```
GET /page.html↵
```

The ↵ symbol represents a carriage return/newline (Enter or Return key). In its basic form, HTTP is as simple as that! You provide one of the few HTTP methods (GET, in this case) followed by the resource you want (/page.html). Remember that at this point, you've already connected to the appropriate server, using a technology such as TCP/IP, so you're simply requesting the resource you want from that server and don't need to be concerned with how that connection happens or is managed.

The first version of HTTP (0.9) allowed only this simple syntax and had only the GET method. In this case, you might ask why you needed to state GET for an HTTP/0.9

request, because it's superfluous, but future versions of HTTP introduced other methods, so kudos to the inventors of HTTP for having the foresight to see that more methods would come. In the next section, I discuss the various versions of HTTP, but this syntax is still recognizable as the format of an HTTP GET request.

Consider a real-life example. Because the web server needs only a TCP/IP connection to receive HTTP requests, you can emulate the browser by using a program such as Telnet. Telnet is a simple program that opens a TCP/IP connection to a server and allows you to type text commands and view text responses. This program is exactly what you need for HTTP, though I cover much better tools for viewing HTTP near the end of the chapter. Unfortunately, some technologies are becoming less prevalent, and Telnet is one of them; many operating systems no longer include a Telnet client by default. It may be necessary for you to install a Telnet client to try some simple HTTP commands, or you can use an equivalent like the nc command. This command is short for netcat and is installed in most Linux-like environments, including macOS, and for the simple examples I show here, it's almost identical to Telnet.

For Windows, I recommend using the PuTTY software[5] over the default client bundled with Windows (which usually isn't installed anyway and must be added manually), as the default client often has display issues, such as not displaying what you're typing or overwriting what's already on the terminal. When you install and launch PuTTY, you see the configuration window, where you can enter the host (www.google.com), port (80), and connection type (Telnet). Make sure that you click the Never option for closing the window on exit; otherwise, you won't see the results. All these settings are shown in figure 1.3. Note also that if you have trouble entering any of the following commands and receive a message about a badly formatted request, you may want to change Connection > Telnet > Telnet Negotiation Mode to Passive.

If you're using an Apple Macintosh or a Linux machine, you may be able to issue the Telnet command directly from a shell prompt if Telnet is already installed:

```
$ telnet www.google.com 80
```

Or, as I mentioned earlier, use the nc command in the same way:

```
$ nc www.google.com 80
```

When you have a Telnet session and make the connection, you see a blank screen, or, depending on your Telnet application, some instructions like the following:

```
Trying 216.58.193.68...
Connected to www.google.com.
Escape character is '^]'.
```

---

[5] https://www.putty.org/

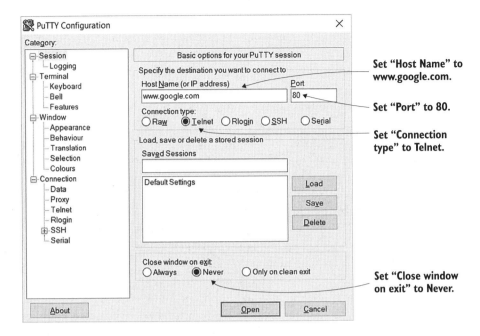

Figure 1.3 PuTTY details for connecting to Google

Whether or not this message is displayed, you should be able to type your HTTP commands, so type GET / and then press the Return key, which tells the Google server that you're looking for the default page (/) and (because you haven't specified an HTTP version) that you want to use the default HTTP/0.9. Note that some Telnet clients don't echo back what you're typing by default (especially the default Telnet client bundled with Windows, as I mentioned earlier), so it can be difficult to see exactly what you're typing. But you should still send the commands.

> **Using Telnet behind company proxies**
>
> If your computer doesn't have direct internet access, you won't be able to connect to Google directly by using Telnet. This scenario is often the case in corporate environments that use a proxy to restrict direct access. (I cover proxies in chapter 3.) In this case, you may be able to use one of your internal web servers (such as your intranet site) as an example rather than Google. In section 1.5.3, I discuss other tools that can work with a proxy, but for now, you can read along without following the instructions.

The Google server will respond, most likely using HTTP/1.0, despite the fact that you sent a default HTTP/0.9 request (no server uses HTTP/0.9 anymore). The response is an HTTP response code of 200 (to state that the command was a success) or 302 (to state that the server wants you to redirect to another page), followed by a closing of the connection. I go into more detail on this process in the next section, so don't get too concerned about these details now.

Following is one such response from a command-line prompt on a Linux server with the response line in bold. Note that the HTML content returned isn't shown in full for the sake of brevity:

```
$ telnet www.google.com 80
Trying 172.217.3.196...
Connected to www.google.com.
Escape character is '^]'.
GET /
HTTP/1.0 200 OK
Date: Sun, 10 Sep 2017 16:20:09 GMT
Expires: -1
Cache-Control: private, max-age=0
Content-Type: text/html; charset=ISO-8859-1
P3P: CP="This is not a P3P policy! See
    https://www.google.com/support/accounts/answer/151657?hl=en for more info."
Server: gws
X-XSS-Protection: 1; mode=block
X-Frame-Options: SAMEORIGIN
Set-Cookie:
    NID=111=QIMb1TZHhHGXEPjUXqbHChZGCcVLFQOvmqjNcUIejUXqbHChZKtrF4Hf4x4DVjTb01R
    8DWShPlu6_aQ-AnPXgONzEoGOpapm_VOTW0Y8TWVpNap_1234567890-p2g; expires=Mon,
    12-Mar-2018 16:20:09 GMT; path=/; domain=.google.com; HttpOnly
Accept-Ranges: none
Vary: Accept-Encoding

<!doctype html><html itemscope="" itemtype="http://schema.org/WebPage"
    lang="en"><head><meta content="Search the world's information, including
    webpages, images, videos and more. Google has many special features to help
    you find exactly what you're looking for." name="description

…etc.

</script></div></body></html>Connection closed by foreign host.
```

If you're based outside the United States, you may see a redirect to a local Google server instead. If you're based in Ireland, for example, Google sends a 302 response and advises the browser to go to Google Ireland (http://www.google.ie) instead, as shown here:

```
GET /
HTTP/1.0 302 Found
Location: http://www.google.ie/?gws_rd=cr&dcr=0&ei=BWe1WYrf123456qpIbwDg
Cache-Control: private
Content-Type: text/html; charset=UTF-8
P3P: CP="This is not a P3P policy! See
    https://www.google.com/support/accounts/answer/151657?hl=en for more info."
Date: Sun, 10 Sep 2017 16:23:33 GMT
Server: gws
Content-Length: 268
```

```
X-XSS-Protection: 1; mode=block
X-Frame-Options: SAMEORIGIN
Set-Cookie: NID=111=ff1KAwIMjt3X4MEg_KzqR_9eAG78CWNGEF1DG0XIf7dLZsQeLerX-
    P8uSnXYCWNGEF1DG0dsM-8V8X8ny4nbu2w96GRTZtzXWOHvWS123456dhd0LpD_123456789;
    expires=Mon, 12-Mar-2018 16:23:33 GMT; path=/; domain=.google.com; HttpOnly

<HTML><HEAD><meta http-equiv="content-type" content="text/html;charset=utf-8">

    <TITLE>302 Moved</TITLE></HEAD><BODY>
                                <H1>302 Moved</H1>
                                            The document has moved
                                                            <A
    HREF="http://www.google.ie/?gws_rd=cr&amp;dcr=0&amp;ei=BWe1WYrfIojUgAbqpIbw
    Dg">here</A>.
</BODY></HTML> Connection closed by foreign host.
```

As shown at the end of each example, the connection is closed; to send another HTTP command, you need to reopen the connection. To avoid this step, you can use HTTP/1.1 (which keeps the connection open by default, as I discuss later) by entering HTTP/1.1 after the requested resource:

```
GET / HTTP/1.1↵↵
```

Note that if you're using HTTP/1.0 or HTTP/1.1, you must press Return twice to tell the web server that you're finished sending the HTTP request. In the next section, I discuss why this double return/blank line is required for HTTP/1.0 and HTTP/1.1 connections.

After the server responds, you can reissue the GET command to get the page again. In reality, web browsers usually use this open connection to get other resources rather than the same resource again, but the concept is the same.

Technically, to abide by the HTTP/1.1 specification, HTTP/1.1 requests also require you to specify the host header, for reasons that I (again) discuss later. For these simple examples, however, don't worry about this requirement too much, because Google doesn't seem to insist on it (although if you're using websites other than www.google.com, you may see unexpected results).

As you can see, the basic HTTP syntax is simple. It's a text-based request-and-response format, although this format changes under HTTP/2 when it moves to a binary format.

If you're requesting nontext data such as an image, a program like Telnet won't be sufficient. Gobbledygook will appear in the terminal session as Telnet tries and fails to convert the binary image format to meaningful text, as in this example:

```
$ telnet www.google.com 80
Trying 172.217.3.164...
Connected to www.google.com.
Escape character is '^]'.
GET /images/branding/googlelogo/2x/googlelogo_color_120x44dp.png
▒.k▒
```

```
I   ¥&   ] S   y 8           .K?F [I   iH g  ?Sk    "   f>#U p I  7E^T    ~n EG I  ^
    +. `x  \w      CR╫     U3V   O>6b y8 S   CHj ^ .      F   4=xw
( F Bc  ] Zu    -Hj i   R   G mH . |       <     xH궈
      . l fH 5 л    %WH 7's/ÿ wʌ
 b @ 4       { :$  .  (O    ÿ  ÿ -  !i        \ DˠM   9

. $I $I $I $I      ~ T LC
 IEND B  Connection closed by foreign host.
```

I no longer use Telnet, because much better tools are available for viewing the details of an HTTP request, but this exercise is useful for explaining the format of an HTTP message and showing how simple the initial versions of the protocol were.

As I mention earlier, the key to the success of HTTP is its simplicity, which makes it relatively easy to implement at a service level. Therefore, almost any computer with network abilities, from complex servers to light bulbs in the IoT world, can implement HTTP and immediately provide useful commands across a network. Implementing a fully HTTP-compliant web server is a much more arduous task. Similarly, web browsers are hugely complex and have myriad other protocols to contend with after a web page has been fetched over HTTP (including HTML, CSS, and JavaScript used to display the page it has fetched). But creating a simple service that listens for an HTTP GET request and responds with data isn't difficult. The simplicity of HTTP has also led to the boom in the microservices architectural style, in which an application is broken into many independent web services, often based on lighter application servers such as Node.js (Node).

1.3 The syntax and history of HTTP

HTTP was started by Tim Berners-Lee and his team at the CERN research organization in 1989. It was intended to be a way of implementing a web of interconnecting computers to provide access to research and link them so they could easily reference one another in real time; a click of a link would open an associated document. The idea for such a system had been around for a long time, and the term *hypertext* was coined in the 1960s. With the growth of the internet during the 1980s, it was possible to implement this idea. During 1989 and 1990, Berners-Lee published a proposal[6] to build such a system; he went on to build the first web server based on HTTP and the first web browser to request HTML documents and display them.

1.3.1 HTTP/0.9

The first published specification for HTTP was version 0.9, issued in 1991. The specification[7] is small at fewer than 700 words. It specifies that a connection is made over TCP/IP (or a similar connection-oriented service) to a server and optional port (80 to be used if no port is specified). A single line of ASCII text should be sent, consisting

---

[6] https://www.w3.org/History/1989/proposal.html
[7] https://www.w3.org/Protocols/HTTP/AsImplemented.html

of GET, the document address (with no spaces), and a carriage return and line feed (the carriage return being optional). The server is to respond with a message in HTML format, which it defines as "a byte stream of ASCII characters." It also states, "The message is terminated by the closing of the connection by the server," which is why the connection was closed after each request in previous examples. On handling errors, the specification states: "Error responses are supplied in human-readable text in HTML syntax. There is no way to distinguish an error response from a satisfactory response except for the content of the text." It ends with this text: "Requests are idempotent. The server need not store any information about the request after disconnection." This specification gives us the stateless part of HTTP, which is both a blessing (in its simplicity) and a curse (due to the way that technologies such as HTTP cookies had to be tacked on to allow state tracking, which is necessary for complex applications).

Following is the only possible command in HTTP/0.9:

```
GET /section/page.html↵
```

The requested resource (/section/page.html) can change, of course, but the rest of the syntax is fixed.

There was no concept of HTTP header fields (herein known as HTTP headers) or any other media, such as images. It's amazing to think that from this simple request/response protocol, intended to provide easy access to information in a research institute, quickly spawned the media-rich World Wide Web that is so ingrained in the world today. Even from an early stage, Berners-Lee called his invention the World-WideWeb (without the spaces that we use today), again showing his foresight of the scope of the project and plans for it to be a global system.

1.3.2 *HTTP/1.0*

The WorldWideWeb was an almost-instant success. According to NetCraft,[8] by September 1995 there were 19,705 hostnames on the web. A month later, this figure jumped to 31,568 and has grown at a furious rate ever since. At this writing, we're approaching 2 billion websites. By 1995, the limitations of the simple HTTP/0.9 protocol were apparent, and most web servers had already implemented extensions that went way beyond the 0.9 specification. The HTTP Working Group (HTTP WG), headed by Dave Raggett, started working on HTTP/1.0 in an attempt to document the "common usage of the protocol." The document was published in May 1996 as RFC 1945.[9] An RFC (Request for Comments) document is published by the IETF; it can be accepted as a formal standard or be left as an informal documentation.[10] The HTTP/1.0 RFC is the latter and is not a formal specification. It describes itself as a "memo" at the top,

---

[8] https://news.netcraft.com/archives/category/web-server-survey/
[9] https://tools.ietf.org/html/rfc1945
[10] An excellent post on reading and understanding RFCs is at https://www.mnot.net/blog/2018/07/31/read_rfc.

stating, "This memo provides information for the internet community. This memo does not specify an internet standard of any kind."

Regardless of the formal status of the RFC, HTTP/1.0 added some key features, including

- More request methods: HEAD and POST were added to the previously defined GET.
- Addition of an optional HTTP version number for all messages. HTTP/0.9 was assumed by default to aid in backward compatibility.
- HTTP headers, which could be sent with both the request and the response to provide more information about the resource being requested and the response being sent.
- A three-digit response code indicating (for example) whether the response was successful. This code also enabled redirect requests, conditional requests, and error status (404 – Not Found being one of the best known).

These much-needed enhancements of the protocol happened organically through use, and HTTP/1.0 was intended to document what was already happening with many web servers in the real world, rather than define new options. These additional options opened a wealth of new opportunities to the web, including the ability to add media to web pages for the first time by using response HTTP headers to define the content type of the data in the body.

HTTP/1.0 METHODS

The GET method stayed much the same as under HTTP/0.9, though the addition of headers allowed a conditional GET (an instruction to GET only if this resource has changed since the last time the client got it; otherwise, tell the client that the resource hasn't changed and to carry on using that old copy). Also, as I mentioned earlier, users could GET more than hypertext documents and use HTTP to download images, videos, or any sort of media.

The HEAD method allowed a client to get all the meta information (such as the HTTP headers) for a resource without downloading the resource itself. This method is useful for many reasons. A web crawler like Google, for example, can check whether a resource has been modified and download it only if it has, thus saving resources for both it and the web server.

The POST method was more interesting, allowing the client to send data to a web server. Rather than put a new HTML file directly on the server by using standard file-transfer methods, users could POST the file by using HTTP, provided that the web server was set up to receive the data and do something with it. POST isn't limited to whole files; it can be used for much smaller parts of data. Forms on websites typically use POST, with the contents of the form being sent as field/value pairs in the body of the HTTP request. The POST method, therefore, allowed content to be sent from the client to the server as part of an HTTP request, representing the first time that an HTTP request could have a body, like HTTP responses.

In fact, GET allows data to be sent in query parameters that are specified at the end of a URL, after the ? character. https://www.google.com/?q=search+string, for example, tells Google that you're searching for the term search string. Query parameters were in the earliest Uniform Resource Identifier (URI) specification,[11] but they were intended to provide additional parameters to clarify the URI rather than to serve as a way of uploading data to a web server. URLs are also limited in terms of length and content (binary data can't be sent here, for example), and some confidential data (passwords, credit card data, and so on) shouldn't be stored in a URL, as it is easily visible on the screen and in browser history, or may be included if the URL is shared. POST, therefore, is often a better way of sending data, and data isn't as visible (though care should still be taken with this data when sent over plain HTTP rather than secure HTTPS, as I discuss later). Another difference is that a GET request is *idempotent* whereas a POST request is not, meaning that multiple GET requests to the same URL should always return the same result, whereas multiple POST requests to the same URL requests may not. If you refresh a standard page on a website, for example, it should show the same thing. If you refresh a confirmation page from an e-commerce website, your browser may ask whether you're sure that you want to resubmit the data, which may result in your making an additional purchase (though e-commerce sites should write their applications to ensure that this situation doesn't happen!).

HTTP REQUEST HEADERS
Whereas HTTP/0.9 had a single line to GET a resource, HTTP/1.0 introduced HTTP headers. These headers allowed a request to provide the server additional information, which it could use to decide how to process the request. HTTP headers are provided on separate lines after the original request line. An HTTP GET request changed from this

```
GET /page.html↵
```

to this

```
GET /page.html HTTP/1.0↵
Header1: Value1↵
Header2: Value2↵
↵
```

or (without headers) to

```
GET /page.html HTTP/1.0↵
↵
```

That is, an optional *version* section was added to the initial line (default was HTTP/0.9 if not specified), and an optional HTTP header section was followed by two carriage return/newline characters (henceforth called *return characters* for brevity) at the end

---

[11] https://tools.ietf.org/html/rfc1630

instead of one. The second newline was necessary to send a blank line, which was used to indicate that the (optional) request header section was complete.

HTTP headers are specified with a header name, a colon, and then the header content. The header name (though not the content) is case-insensitive, per the specification. Headers can span multiple lines when you start each new line with a space or tab, but this practice isn't recommended; few clients or servers use this format and may fail to process them correctly. Multiple headers of the same type may be sent; they're semantically identical to sending comma-separated versions. As a result

```
GET /page.html HTTP/1.0↵
Header1: Value1↵
Header1: Value2↵
```

should be treated the same way as

```
GET /page.html HTTP/1.0↵
Header1: Value1, Value2↵
```

Although HTTP/1.0 defined some standard headers, this example also demonstrates that HTTP/1.0 allows custom headers (Header1, in this example) to be provided without requiring an updated version of the protocol. The protocol was designed to be extensible. The specification, however, explicitly states that "these fields cannot be assumed to be recognizable by the recipient" and may be ignored, whereas the standard headers should be processed by an HTTP/1.0-compliant server.

A typical HTTP/1.0 GET request is

```
GET /page.html HTTP/1.0↵
Accept: text/html,application/xhtml+xml,image/jxr/,*/*↵
Accept-Encoding: gzip, deflate, br↵
Accept-Language: en-GB,en-US;q=0.8,en;q=0.6↵
Connection: keep-alive↵
Host: www.example.com↵
User-Agent: MyAwesomeWebBrowser 1.1↵↵
```

This example tells the server what formats you can accept the response in (HTML, XHTML, XML, and so on), that you can accept various encodings (such as gzip, deflate, and brotli, which are compression algorithms used to compress data sent over HTTP), and what languages you prefer (GB English, followed by US English, followed by any other form of English), and what browser you're using (MyAwesomeWebBrowser 1.1). It also tells the server to keep the connection open (a topic that I return to later). The whole request is completed with the two return characters. From here on, I exclude the return characters for readability reasons. You can assume the last line in the request is followed by two return characters.

HTTP RESPONSE CODES

A typical response from an HTTP/1.0 server is

```
HTTP/1.0 200 OK
Date: Sun, 25 Jun 2017 13:30:24 GMT
```

```
Content-Type: text/html
Server: Apache

<!doctype html>
<html>
<head>
…etc.
```

The rest of the HTML provided follows. As you see, the first line of the response is the HTTP version of the response message (HTTP/1.0), a three-digit HTTP status code (200), and a text description of that status code (OK). Status codes and descriptions were new concepts under HTTP/1.0; under HTTP/0.9, there was no such concept as a response code; errors could be given only in the returned HTML itself. Table 1.1 shows the HTTP response codes defined in the HTTP/1.0 specification.

Table 1.1 HTTP/1.0 response codes

Category	Value	Description	Details
1xx (informational)	N/A	N/A	HTTP/1.0 doesn't define any 1xx status codes, but does define the category.
2xx (successful)	200	OK	This code is the standard response code for a successful request.
	201	Created	This code should be returned for a POST request.
	202	Accepted	The request is being processed but hasn't completed processing yet.
	204	No content	The request has been accepted and processed, but there's no BODY response to send back.
3xx (redirection)	300	Multiple choices	This code isn't used directly. It explains that the 3xx category implies that the resource is available at one (or more) locations, and the exact response provides more details on where it is.
	301	Moved permanently	The Location HTTP response header should provide the new URL of the resource.
	302	Moved temporarily	The Location HTTP response header should provide the new URL of the resource.
	304	Not modified	This code is used for conditional responses in which the BODY doesn't need to be sent again.
4xx (client error)	400	Bad request	The request couldn't be understood and should be changed before resending.
	401	Unauthorized	This code usually means that you're not authenticated.
	403	Forbidden	This code usually means that you're authenticated, but your credentials don't have access.
	404	Not found	This code is probably the best-known HTTP status code, as it often appears on error pages.

Table 1.1   HTTP/1.0 response codes *(continued)*

Category	Value	Description	Details
5xx (server error)	500	Internal server error	The request couldn't be completed due to a server-side error.
	501	Not implemented	The server doesn't recognize the request (such as an HTTP method that hasn't yet been implemented).
	502	Bad gateway	The server is acting as a gateway or proxy and received an error from the downstream server.
	503	Service unavailable	The server is unable to fulfill the request, perhaps because the server is overloaded or down for maintenance.

Astute readers may notice some missing codes (203, 303, 402) from earlier drafts of the HTTP/1.0 RFC. Some additional codes were excluded from the final published RFC. Some of these codes returned in HTTP/1.1, though often with different descriptions and meanings. The Internet Assigned Numbers Authority (IANA) maintains the full list of HTTP status codes across all versions of HTTP, but the status codes in table 1.1, first defined in HTTP/1.0,[12] represent most typically used status codes.

It may also be apparent that some of the responses could overlap. You may wonder, for example, whether an unrecognized request is a 400 (bad request) or a 501 (not implemented). The response codes are designed to be broad categories, and it's up to each application to use the status code that fits best. The specification also stated that response codes were extensible, so new codes could be added as needed without changing the protocol. This is another reason why the response codes are categorized. A new response code (such as 504) may not be understood by an existing HTTP/1.0 client, but it would know that the request failed for some reason on the server side and could handle it the way it handles other 5xx response codes.

HTTP RESPONSE HEADERS

After the first return line are zero or more HTTP/1 header response lines. Request headers and response headers follow the same format. They're followed by two return characters and then the body content, as shown in bold:

```
GET /
HTTP/1.0 302 Found
Location: http://www.google.ie/?gws_rd=cr&dcr=0&ei=BWe1WYrf123456qpIbwDg
Cache-Control: private
Content-Type: text/html; charset=UTF-8
Date: Sun, 10 Sep 2017 16:23:33 GMT
Server: gws
Content-Length: 268
X-XSS-Protection: 1; mode=block
X-Frame-Options: SAMEORIGIN
```

---

[12] https://www.iana.org/assignments/http-status-codes/http-status-codes.xhtml

```
<HTML><HEAD><meta http-equiv="content-type" content="text/html;charset=utf-8
">
    <TITLE>302 Moved</TITLE></HEAD><BODY>
                                <H1>302 Moved</H1>
                                            The document has moved
<A HREF="http://www.google.ie/?gws_rd=cr&amp;dcr=0&amp;ei=BWe1WYrfIojUgAbqpI
bwDg">here</A>.</BODY></HTML> Connection closed by foreign host.
```

With the publication of HTTP/1.0, the HTTP syntax was greatly expanded to make it capable of creating dynamic, feature-rich applications beyond the simple document repository fetching that the initial published version HTTP/0.9 allowed. HTTP was also getting more complicated, expanding from the approximately 700-word HTTP/0.9 specification to the nearly 20,000-word HTTP/1.0 RFC. Even as this specification was published, however, the HTTP Working Group saw it as a stopgap to document current use and was already working on HTTP/1.1. As I mentioned earlier, HTTP/1.0 was published mostly to bring some standards and documentation to HTTP as it was being used in the wild, rather than to define any new syntax for clients and servers to implement. In addition to the new response codes, other methods (such as PUT, DELETE, LINK, and UNLINK) and additional HTTP headers in use at the time were listed in the appendices of the RFC, some of which would be standardized in HTTP/1.1. The success of HTTP was such that the working group struggled to keep up with the implementations only five short years after it was launched to the world.

1.3.3   *HTTP/1.1*

As you've seen, HTTP was launched as version 0.9 as a basic way of fetching text-based documents. This version was expanded beyond text to a more fully fledged protocol 1.0, which was further standardized and refined in 1.1. As the versioning suggests, HTTP/1.1 was more a tweak of HTTP/1.0 that didn't contain radical changes to the protocol. Moving from 0.9 to 1.0 was a much bigger change, with the addition of HTTP headers. HTTP/1.1 made some further improvements to allow optimal use of the HTTP protocol (such as persistent connections, mandatory server headers, better caching options, and chunked encoding). Perhaps more important, it provided a formal standard on which to base the future of the World Wide Web. Although the basics of HTTP are simple enough to understand, there are many intricacies that could be implemented in slightly different ways, and the lack of a formal standard makes it difficult to scale.

The first HTTP/1.1 specification was published in January 1997[13] (only nine months after the HTTP/1.0 specification was published). It was replaced by an update specification in June 1999[14] and then enhanced for a third time in June 2014.[15] Each version made the previous ones obsolete. The HTTP specification now spanned 305

---

[13] https://tools.ietf.org/html/rfc2068
[14] https://tools.ietf.org/html/rfc2616
[15] https://tools.ietf.org/html/rfc7230 and https://tools.ietf.org/html/rfc7235

pages and nearly 100,000 words, which shows how much this simple protocol grew and how important it was to clarify the intricacies of how HTTP should be used. In fact, at this writing the specification is being updated again,[16] and this update is expected to be published early in 2019. Fundamentally, HTTP/1.1 isn't too different from HTTP/1.0, but the explosion of the web in the first two decades of its existence gave rise to additional features and required documentation showing exactly how to use it.

Describing HTTP/1.1 would take a book in itself, but I attempt here to discuss the main points, to provide background and context for some of the HTTP/2 discussions later in this book. Many of the additional features of HTTP/1.1 were introduced through HTTP headers, which themselves were introduced in HTTP/1.0, meaning that the fundamental structure of HTTP didn't change between the two versions, although making the host header mandatory and adding persistent connections were two notable changes in the syntax from HTTP/1.0.

MANDATORY HOST HEADER

The URL provided with HTTP request lines (such as a GET command) isn't an absolute URL (such as http://www.example.com/section/page.html) but a relative URL (such as /section/page.html). When HTTP was created, it was assumed that a web server would host only one website (though possibly many sections and pages on that site). Therefore, the host part of the URL was obvious, because a user had to be connected to that web server before making HTTP requests. Nowadays, many web servers host several sites on the same server (a situation known as *virtual hosting*), so it's important to tell the server *which site* you want as well as *which relative URL* you want on that site. This feature could have been implemented by changing the URL in the HTTP requests to the full, absolute URL, but it was thought this change would have broken many existing web servers and clients. Instead, the feature was implemented by adding a Host header in the request:

```
GET / HTTP/1.1
Host: www.google.com
```

This header was optional in HTTP/1.0, but HTTP/1.1 made it mandatory. The following request is technically badly formed, as it specifies HTTP/1.1 but doesn't provide a Host header:

```
GET / HTTP/1.1
```

According to the HTTP/1.1 specification,[17] this request should be rejected by the server (with a 400 response code), though most web servers are more forgiving than they should be and have a default host that is returned for such requests.

Making the Host header mandatory was an important step in HTTP/1.1, allowing servers to make more use of virtual hosting and therefore allowing the enormous

---

[16] https://github.com/httpwg/http-core
[17] https://tools.ietf.org/html/rfc7230#section-5.4

growth of the web without the complexity of adding individual web servers for each site. Additionally, the relatively low limit of IPv4 IP addresses would have been reached much sooner without this change. On the other hand, if that limit had not been implemented, perhaps it would have helped forced the move to IPv6 much earlier; instead, it's in the process of being rolled out at this writing despite having been around for more than 20 years!

Specifying a mandatory `Host` header field instead of changing the relative URL to an absolute URL involved some contention.[18] HTTP proxies, introduced with HTTP/1.1, allowed connection to an HTTP server via an intermediary HTTP server. The syntax for proxies was already set to require full absolute URLs for all requests, but actual web servers (also called *origin servers*) were mandated to use the `Hosts` header. As I mentioned earlier, this change was necessary to avoid breaking existing servers, but making it mandatory left no doubt that HTTP/1.1 clients and servers must use virtual-hosting-style requests to be fully compliant HTTP/1.1 implementations. It was thought that in some future version of HTTP, this situation would be dealt with better. The HTTP/1.1 specification states, "To allow for transition to the absolute-form for all requests in some future version of HTTP, a server MUST accept the absolute-form in requests, even though HTTP/1.1 clients will only send them in requests to proxies." Nevertheless, as you'll see later, HTTP/2 didn't resolve this problem cleanly, instead replacing the `Host` header with the `:authority` pseudoheader field (see chapter 4).

PERSISTENT CONNECTIONS (AKA KEEP-ALIVES)

Another important change introduced in HTTP and supported by many HTTP/1.0 servers, even though it wasn't included in the HTTP/1.0 specification, was the introduction of persistent connections. Initially, HTTP was a single request-and-response protocol. A client opens the connection, requests a resource, gets the response, and the connection is closed. As the web became more media-rich, this closing of the connection proved to be wasteful. Displaying a single page required several HTTP resources, so closing the connection only to reopen it caused unnecessary delays. This problem was resolved with a new `Connection` HTTP header that could be sent with an HTTP/1.0 request. By specifying the value `Keep-Alive` in this header, the client is asking the server to keep the connection open to allow the sending of additional requests:

```
GET /page.html HTTP/1.0
Connection: Keep-Alive
```

The server would respond as usual, but if it supported persistent connections, it included a `Connection: Keep-Alive` header in the response:

---

[18] See https://lists.w3.org/Archives/Public/ietf-http-wg-old/1999SepDec/0014.html for some discussions on this subject.

```
HTTP/1.0 200 OK
Date: Sun, 25 Jun 2017 13:30:24 GMT
Connection: Keep-Alive
Content-Type: text/html
Content-Length: 12345
Server: Apache

<!doctype html>
<html>
<head>
…etc.
```

This response tells the client that it can send another request on the same connection as soon as the response is completed, so the server doesn't have to close the connection to the client only to reopen it. It can be more complicated to know when the response is complete when you use persistent connections; the connection closing is a pretty good sign that the server has finished sending for a nonpersistent connection! Instead, the Content-Length HTTP header must be used to define the length of the response body, and when the entire body has been received, the client is free to send another request.

An HTTP connection can be closed at any point by either the client or the server. Closing may occur accidentally (perhaps due to network connectivity errors) or deliberately (if, for example, a connection isn't used for a while and a server decides to close the connection to regain some resources for other connections). Therefore, even with persistent connections, both clients and servers should monitor the connections and be able to handle unexpectedly closed connections. The situation becomes more complicated with certain requests. If you're checking out on an e-commerce website, for example, you may not want to resend the request without checking whether the server processed the initial request.

HTTP/1.1 not only added this persistent-connection process to the documented standard, but also went one step further and changed it to the default. Any HTTP/1.1 connection could be assumed to be using persistent connections even without the presence of the Connection: Keep-Alive header in the response. If the server did want to close the connection, for whatever reason, it had to explicitly include a Connection: close HTTP header in the response:

```
HTTP/1.1 200 OK
Date: Sun, 25 Jun 2017 13:30:24 GMT
Connection: close
Content-Type: text/html; charset=UTF-8
Server: Apache

<!doctype html>
<html>
<head>
…etc.
Connection closed by foreign host.
```

I touched on this topic in the Telnet examples earlier in this chapter. Now you can use Telnet again to send the following:

- An HTTP/1.0 request without a `Connection: Keep-Alive` header. You should see that the connection is automatically closed by the server after the response is sent.
- The same HTTP/1.0 request, but with a `Connection: Keep-Alive` header. You should see that the connection is kept open.
- An HTTP.1.1 request, with or without a `Connection: Keep-Alive` header. You should see that the connection is kept open by default.

It's not unusual to see HTTP/1.1 clients include this `Connection: Keep-Alive` header for HTTP/1.1 requests, despite the fact that it's the default and should be assumed. Similarly, servers sometimes include the header in HTTP/1.1 responses despite this being unnecessary.

On a similar topic, HTTP/1.1 added the concept of pipelining, so it should be possible to send several requests over the same persistent connection and get the responses back in order. If a web browser is processing an HTML document, for example, and sees that it needs a CSS file and a JavaScript file, it should be able to send the requests for these files together and get the responses back in order rather than waiting for the first response before sending the second request. Here's an example:

```
GET /style.css HTTP/1.1
Host: www.example.com

GET /script.js HTTP/1.1
Host: www.example.com

HTTP/1.1 200 OK
Date: Sun, 25 Jun 2017 13:30:24 GMT
Content-Type: text/css; charset=UTF-8
Content-Length: 1234
Server: Apache

.style {
…etc.

HTTP/1.1 200 OK
Date: Sun, 25 Jun 2017 13:30:25 GMT
Content-Type: application/x-javascript; charset=UTF-8
Content-Length: 5678
Server: Apache

Function(
…etc.
```

For several reasons (which I go into in chapter 2), pipelining never took off, and support for it in both clients (browsers) and servers is poor. So, although persistent connections allow the TCP connection to be reused for multiple requests, which was a good performance improvement, HTTP/1.1 is still fundamentally a request-and-response protocol for most implementations. While that one request is being handled, the HTTP connection is blocked from being used for other requests.

OTHER NEW FEATURES

HTTP/1.1 introduced many other features, including

- New methods in addition to the GET, POST, and HEAD methods defined in HTTP/1.0. These methods are PUT, OPTIONS, and the less-used CONNECT, TRACE, and DELETE.
- Better caching methods. These methods allowed the server to instruct the client to store the resource (such as a CSS file) in the browser's cache so it could be reused later if required. The Cache-Control HTTP header introduced in HTTP/1.1 had more options than the Expires header from HTTP/1.0.
- HTTP cookies to allow HTTP to move from being a stateless protocol.
- The introduction of character sets (as shown in some examples in this chapter) and language in HTTP responses.
- Proxy support.
- Authentication.
- New status codes.
- Trailing headers (discussed in chapter 4, section 4.3.3).

HTTP has continually added new HTTP headers to further expand capabilities, many for performance or security reasons. The HTTP/1.1 specification doesn't claim to be the definitive end for HTTP/1.1 and actively encourages new headers, even dedicating a section[19] on how headers should be defined and documented. As I mention earlier, some of these headers are added for security reasons and are used to allow the website to tell the web browser to turn on certain optional security protections, so they require no implementation on the server side (other than the ability to send the header). At one time, there was a convention to include an X- in these headers to show that they weren't formally standardized (X-Content-Type, X-Frame-Options, X-XSS-Protection), but this convention has been deprecated,[20] and new experimental headers are difficult to differentiate from headers in the HTTP/1.1 specification. Often, these headers are standardized in their own RFCs (Content-Security-Policy,[21] Strict-Transport-Security,[22] and so on).

---

[19] https://tools.ietf.org/html/rfc7231#section-8.3.1
[20] https://tools.ietf.org/html/rfc6648
[21] https://tools.ietf.org/html/rfc7762
[22] https://tools.ietf.org/html/rfc6797

1.4   *Introduction to HTTPS*

HTTP was originally a plain-text protocol. HTTP messages are sent across the internet unencrypted and therefore are readable by any party that sees the message as it's routed to its destination. The internet, as the name suggests, is a network of computers, not a point-to-point system. The internet provides no control of how messages are routed, and you, as an internet user, have no idea how many other parties will see your messages as they're sent across the internet from your internet service provider (ISP) to telecom companies and other parties. Because HTTP is plain-text, messages can be intercepted, read, and even altered en route.

HTTPS is the secure version of HTTP that encrypts messages in transit by using the Transport Layer Security (TLS) protocol, though it's often known by its previous incarnation as Secure Sockets Layer (SSL), as discussed in the sidebar below.

HTTPS adds three important concepts to HTTP messages:

- *Encryption*—Messages can't be read by third parties while in transit.
- *Integrity*—The message hasn't been altered in transit, as the entire encrypted message is digitally signed, and that signature is cryptographically verified before decryption.
- *Authentication*—The server is the one you intended to talk to.

SSL, TLS, HTTPS, and HTTP

HTTPS uses SSL or TLS to provide encryption. SSL (Secure Sockets Layer) was invented by Netscape. SSLv1 was never released outside Netscape, so the first production version was SSLv2, released in 1995. SSLv3, released in 1996, addressed some insecurities.

As SSL was owned by Netscape, it wasn't a formal internet standard, though it was subsequently published by the IETF as a *historic document*.[a] SSL was standardized as TLS (Transport Layer Security). TLSv1.0[b] was similar to SSLv3, though not compatible. TLSv1.1[c] and TLSv1.2[d] followed in 2006 and 2008, respectively, and were more secure. TLSv1.3 was approved as a standard in 2018;[e] it's more secure and performant,[f] though it will take time to become widespread.

Despite the availability of these newer, more secure, standardized versions, SSLv3 was considered to be good enough by many people, so it was the de facto standard for a long time, even though many clients supported TLSv1.0 as well. In 2014, however, major vulnerabilities were discovered in SSLv3,[g] which must no longer be used[h] and is no longer supported by browsers. This situation started a major move toward TLS. After similar vulnerabilities were found in TLSv1.0, security guidelines insisted that TLSv1.1 or later be used.[i]

The net effect of all this history is that people use these acronyms in different ways. Many people still refer to encryption as SSL because it was the standard for so long; others use SSL/TLS or TLS. Some people try to avoid the debate by referring to it as HTTPS, even though this term isn't strictly correct.

In general in this book, I refer to encryption as HTTPS (rather than SSL or SSL/TLS) unless I'm specifically talking about specific parts of the TLS protocol. On a similar note, I refer to the core semantics of HTTP as HTTP, whether it's used over an unencrypted HTTP connection or an encrypted HTTPS connection.

---

a   https://tools.ietf.org/html/rfc6101
b   https://tools.ietf.org/html/rfc2246
c   https://tools.ietf.org/html/rfc4346
d   https://tools.ietf.org/html/rfc5246
e   https://tools.ietf.org/html/rfc8446
f   https://blog.cloudflare.com/rfc-8446-aka-tls-1-3/
g   https://www.us-cert.gov/ncas/alerts/TA14-290A
h   https://tools.ietf.org/html/rfc7568
i   https://www.pcisecuritystandards.org/documents/Migrating-from-SSL-Early-TLS-Info-Supp-v1_1.pdf

HTTPS works by using public key encryption, which allows servers to provide public keys in the form of digital certificates when users first connect. Your browser encrypts messages by using this public key, which only the server can decrypt, as only it has the corresponding private key. This system allows you to communicate securely with a website without having to know a shared secret key in advance, which is crucial for a system like the internet, where new websites and users come and go every second of every day.

The digital certificates are issued, and digitally signed, by various certificate authorities (CAs) trusted by the browser, which is why it's possible to authenticate that the public key is for the server you're connecting to. One big problem with HTTPS is that it indicates only that you're connecting to that server—not that the server is trustworthy. Fake phishing sites can be set up easily with HTTPS for a different but similar domain (exmplebank.com instead of examplebank.com). HTTPS sites are usually shown with a green padlock in web browsers, which many users take to mean *safe*, but it merely means *securely encrypted*.

Some CAs do some extra vetting on websites when they issue certificates and provide an Extended Validation certificate (known as an EV certificate), which encrypts the HTTP traffic the same way as a normal certificate but also displays the company name in most web browsers, as shown in figure 1.4.

Many people dispute the benefits of EV certificates,[23] mostly because the vast majority of users don't notice the company name and don't act any differently on sites that use EV or standard Domain Validated (DV) certificates. A middle ground of Organizational Validated (OV) certificates do some of the checks but don't give extra notification in browsers, making them largely pointless at a technical level (though CAs may include extra support commitments as part of purchasing them).

---

[23] https://www.tunetheweb.com/blog/what-does-the-green-padlock-really-mean/

	HTTP	HTTPS DV and OV certificates	HTTPS EV certificates
Chrome	ⓘ Not secure | bbc.com	🔒 tunetheweb.com	🔒 Twitter, Inc. [US] | twitter.com
Firefox	ⓘ www.bbc.com	🔒 https://www.tunetheweb.com	🔒 Twitter, Inc. (US) | https://twitter.com
Opera	🌐 www.bbc.com	🔒 www.tunetheweb.com	🔒 Twitter, Inc. [US] | twitter.com
IE 11	▬ http://www.bbc.com/	🔒 https://www.tunetheweb.com/ ⌕ ▾ 🔒 ↻	🔒 https://twitter.com/ ⌕ ▾ 🔒 Twitter, Inc. [US]
EDGE	bbc.com	🔒 tunetheweb.com	🔒 Twitter, Inc. [US] twitter.com

Figure 1.4   HTTPS web browser indicators

The Google Chrome team is researching and experimenting with these security indicators at the time of this writing,[24] trying to remove what it sees as unnecessary information, including the scheme (http and https), any www prefix, and possibly even the padlock itself (instead assuming that HTTPS is the norm and that HTTP should be explicitly marked as not secure). The team is also considering whether to remove EV.[25]

HTTPS is built around HTTP and is almost seamless to the HTTP protocol itself. It's hosted on a different port by default (port 443 as opposed to port 80 for standard HTTP), and it has a different URL scheme (https:// as opposed to http://), but it doesn't fundamentally alter the way HTTP is used in terms of syntax or message format except for the encryption and decryption itself.

When the client connects to an HTTPS server, it goes through a negotiation stage (or *TLS handshake*). In this process, the server provides the public key, client and server agree on the encryption methods to use, and then client and server negotiate a shared encryption key to use in the future. (Public key cryptography is slow, so public encryption keys are used only to negotiate a shared secret, which is used to encrypt future messages with better performance). I discuss the TLS handshake in detail in chapter 4 (section 4.2.1).

After the HTTPS session is set up, standard HTTP messages are exchanged. The client and server encrypt these messages before sending and decrypt upon receipt, but to the average web developer or server manager, there's no difference between HTTPS and HTTP after it's configured. Everything happens transparently unless you're looking at the raw messages sent across the network. HTTPS wraps up standard HTTP requests and responses rather than replacing them with another protocol.

HTTPS is a huge topic that's well beyond the scope of this book. I touch on it again briefly in future chapters, as HTTP/2 does bring in some changes. But for now, it's important only to know that HTTPS exists and that it works at a lower level than HTTP (between TCP and HTTP). Unless you're looking at the encrypted messages themselves, you won't see any real difference between HTTP and HTTPS.

---

[24] https://blog.chromium.org/2018/05/evolving-chromes-security-indicators.html
[25] https://groups.google.com/forum/#!topic/mozilla.dev.security.policy/szD2KBHfwl8%5B1-25%5D

For web servers using HTTPS, you need a client that can understand HTTPS and do the encryption and decryption, so you can no longer use Telnet to send example HTTP requests to those servers. The OpenSSL program provides an `s_client` command that you can use to send HTTP commands to an HTTPS server, similar to the way Telnet is used:

```
openssl s_client -crlf -connect www.google.com:443 -quiet
GET / HTTP/1.1
Host: www.google.com

HTTP/1.1 200 OK
…etc.
```

We're reaching the end of the usefulness of command-line tools to examine HTTP requests, however. In the next section, I take a brief look at browser tools, which provide a much better way to see HTTP requests and responses.

1.5 Tools for viewing, sending, and receiving HTTP messages

Although it was helpful to use tools like Telnet to understand the basics of HTTP, command-line tools like the ones discussed here have limitations, not least of which is dealing with the enormous size of most web pages. Several tools allow you to see and send HTTP requests in a better way than Telnet. Many of these tools can be used from the main tool you use to interact with the web: your web browser.

1.5.1 Using developer tools in web browsers

All web browsers come with so-called *developer tools*, which allow you to see many details behind websites, including HTTP requests and responses.

You launch developer tools by pressing a keyboard shortcut (F12 on Windows for most browsers, or Option+Command+I on Apple computers) or by right-clicking a bit of HTML and choosing Inspect from the contextual menu. Developer tools have various tabs showing the technical details behind the page, but the one you're most interested in for the purposes of this discussion is the Network tab. If you open the developer tools and then load the page, the Network tab shows all the HTTP requests, and clicking on one of them produces more details, including the request and response headers. Figure 1.5 shows the Chrome developer tools that you get when loading https://www.google.com.

The URL is entered at the top in the address bar (1) as usual. Note the padlock, and `https://` scheme, showing that Google is using HTTPS successfully (though, as mentioned, Chrome may be changing this). The web page is returned below the address bar, again as usual. If you loaded this page with developer tools open, however, you see a new section with various tabs. Clicking the Network tab (2) shows the HTTP requests (3), including information such as the HTTP method (`GET`), the response status (200), the protocol (`http/1.1`), and the scheme (`https`). You can change the columns shown by right-clicking the column headings. The Protocol,

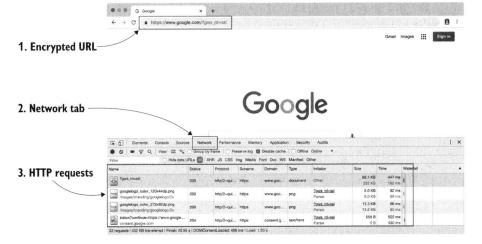

Figure 1.5   Developer tools Network tab in Chrome

Scheme, and Domain columns aren't shown by default, for example, and for some sites (such as Twitter), you see `h2` in this column for HTTP/2 or perhaps even `http/2+quic` (Google) for an even newer protocol that I discuss in chapter 9.

Figure 1.6 shows what happens when you click the first request (1). The right section is replaced by a tabbed view where you can see the response headers (2) and the request headers (3). I've discussed many but not all of these headers in this chapter.

HTTPS is handled by the browser, so developer tools show only the HTTP request messages before they're encrypted and the response messages after they've been

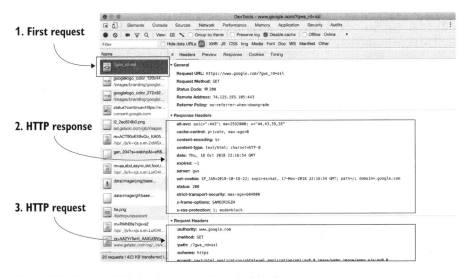

Figure 1.6   Viewing HTTP headers in developer tools in Chrome

decrypted. For the most part, HTTPS can be ignored after it's set up, provided that you have the right tools to handle encryption and decryption for you. Additionally, most browsers' developer tools show media correctly, so images display properly, and code (HTML, CSS, and JavaScript) can often be formatted for easier reading.

I return to developer tools throughout the book. You should familiarize yourself with your browser's developer tools for your site, or for popular sites you use, if you're not familiar with them.

1.5.2 Sending HTTP requests

Although web browsers' developer tools are the best way to *see* raw HTTP requests and responses, they're surprisingly poor at allowing you to *send* raw HTTP requests. Other than the address bar, which can be used only to send simple GET requests, and whatever functionality a website has built (to POST via HTML forms, for example), the tools rarely offer you the ability to send any other raw HTTP messages.

The Advanced REST client application[26] gives you a way of sending raw HTTP messages and seeing the responses. Send a GET request (1) for the URL https://www.google .com (2) and click Send (3) to get the response (4), as shown in figure 1.7. Note that the application handles HTTPS for you.

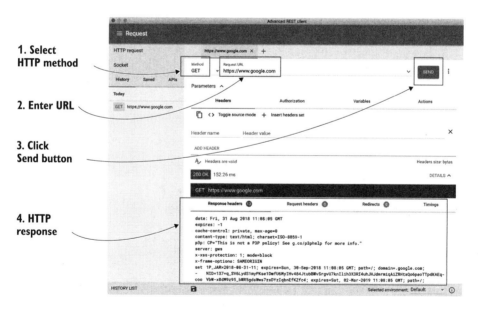

Figure 1.7 Advanced REST client application

---

[26] https://install.advancedrestclient.com (Note: this must be opened in Chrome.)

Using this application is no different from using the browser, but the Advanced REST Client also allows you to send other types of HTTP requests (such as POST and PUT) and to set the header or body data to send. Advanced REST Client started life as a Chrome browser extension[27] but has since been moved to a separate application. Similar browser extension tools act like Advanced REST Client, including Postman (Chrome), Rested,[28] RESTClient[29] (Firefox), and RESTMan[30] (Opera), all of which have comparable functionality.

1.5.3   *Other tools for viewing and sending HTTP requests*

You can use many other tools to send or view HTTP requests outside the browser. Some of these work from the command line (such as curl,[31] wget,[32] and httpie[33]), and some work with desktop clients (such as SOAP-UI[34]).

If you're looking to view the traffic at a lower level, you may want to consider Chrome's net-internals page or network sniffer programs such as Fiddler[35] and Wireshark.[36] I look at some of these tools in later chapters when I look at the details of HTTP/2, but for now the tools mentioned in this section should suffice.

Summary

- HTTP is one of the core technologies of the web.
- Browsers make multiple HTTP requests to load a web page.
- The HTTP protocol started as a simple text-based protocol.
- HTTP has grown more complex, but the basic text-based format hasn't changed in the past 20 years.
- HTTPS encrypts standard HTTP messages.
- Various tools are available for viewing and sending HTTP messages.

---

[27] https://chrome.google.com/webstore/detail/advanced-rest-client/hgmloofddffdnphfgcellkdfbfbjeloo
[28] https://addons.mozilla.org/en-US/firefox/addon/rested/
[29] https://addons.mozilla.org/en-US/firefox/addon/restclient/
[30] https://addons.opera.com/en/extensions/details/restman/
[31] https://curl.haxx.se/
[32] https://www.gnu.org/software/wget/
[33] https://httpie.org/
[34] https://www.soapui.org/
[35] https://www.telerik.com/fiddler
[36] https://www.wireshark.org/

The road to HTTP/2

Why do we need HTTP/2? The web works fine under HTTP/1, doesn't it? What is HTTP/2 anyway? In this chapter, I answer these questions with real-world examples and show why HTTP/2 is not only necessary, but also well overdue.

HTTP/1.1 is what most of the internet is built upon and has been functioning reasonably well for a 20-year-old technology. During that time, however, web use has exploded, and we've moved from simple static websites to fully interactive pages that cover online banking, shopping, booking holidays, watching media, socializing, and nearly every other aspect of our lives.

Internet availability and speed are increasing with technologies such as broadband and fiber for offices and homes, which means that speeds are many times better than the old dial-up speeds that users had to deal with when the internet was launched. Even mobile has seen technologies such as 3G and 4G bring broadband-level speeds on the move at reasonable, consumer-level prices.

Although the increase in download speeds has been impressive, the need for faster speeds has outpaced this increase. Broadband speeds will probably continue to increase for some time, but other limitations can't be fixed as easily. As you shall see, latency is a key factor in browsing the web, and latency is fundamentally limited by the speed of light—a universal constant that physics says can't increase.

2.1   *HTTP/1.1 and the current World Wide Web*

In chapter 1, you learned that HTTP was a request-and-response protocol originally designed for requesting a single item of plain-text content and that ended the connection upon completion. HTTP/1.0 introduced other media types, such as allowing images on a web page, and HTTP/1.1 ensured that the connection wasn't closed by default (on the assumption that the web page would need more requests).

These improvements were good, but the internet has changed considerably since the last revision of HTTP (HTTP/1.1 in 1997, though the formal spec was clarified a few times and is being clarified again at the time of this writing, as mentioned in chapter 1). The HTTP Archive's trends site at https://httparchive.org/reports/state-of-the-web allows you to see the growth of websites in the past eight years, as shown in figure 2.1. Ignore the slight dip around May 2017, which was due to measurement issues at HTTP Archive.[1]

As you can see, the average website requests 80 to 90 resources and downloads nearly 1.8 MB of data—the amount of data transported across the network, including text resources compressed with gzip or similar applications. Uncompressed websites are now more than 3 MB, which causes other issues for constrained devices such as mobile.

There is a wide variation in that average, though. Looking at the Alexa Top 10 websites[2] in the United States, for example, you see the results shown in table 2.1.

The table shows that some websites (such as Wikipedia and Google) are hugely optimized and require few resources, but others load hundreds of resources and many megabytes of data. Therefore, looking at the average website or even the value of these average stats has been questioned before.[3] Regardless, it's clear that the trend is for an increasing amount of data across an increasing number of resources. The growth of websites is driven primarily by becoming more media-rich, with images and

---

[1]   https://github.com/HTTPArchive/legacy.httparchive.org/issues/98#issuecomment-301641938
[2]   https://www.alexa.com/topsites/countries/US
[3]   https://speedcurve.com/blog/web-performance-page-bloat/

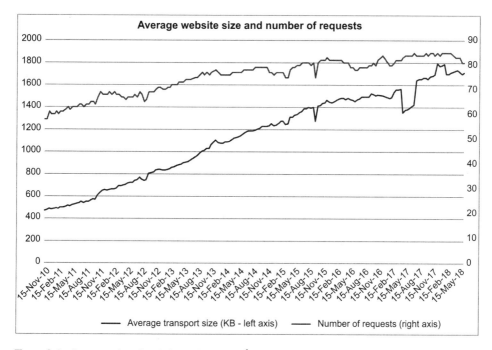

Figure 2.1   Average size of websites 2010–2018[4]

Table 2.1   The top 10 websites in the United States ordered by popularity

Popularity	Site	Number of requests	Size
1	https://www.google.com	17	0.4 MB
2	https://www.youtube.com	75	1.6 MB
3	https://www.facebook.com	172	2.2 MB
4	https://www.reddit.com	102	1.0 MB
5	https://www.amazon.com	136	4.46 MB
6	https://www.yahoo.com	240	3.8 MB
7	https://www.wikipedia.org	7	0.06 MB
8	https://www.twitter.com	117	4.2 MB
9	https://www.ebay.com	160	1.5 MB
10	https://www.netflix.com	44	1.1 MB

---

[4] https://httparchive.org/reports/state-of-the-web

videos being the norm on most websites. Additionally, websites are becoming more complex, with multiple frameworks and dependencies needed to display their content correctly.

Web pages started out as static pages, but as the web became more interactive, web pages started to be generated dynamically on the server side, such as Common Gateway Interface (CGI) or Java Servlet/Java Server Pages (JSPs). The next stage moved from full pages generated server-side to basic HTML pages supplemented by AJAX (Asynchronous JavaScript and XML) calls made from client-side JavaScript. These AJAX calls make extra requests to the web server to allow the contents of the web page to change without necessitating a full page reload or requiring the base image to be generated dynamically server-side. The simplest way to understand this is to look at the change in web search. In the early days of the web, before the advent of search engines, directories of websites and pages were the primary ways of finding information on the web, and they were static and updated only occasionally. Then the first search engines arrived, allowing users to submit a search form and get the results back from the server (dynamic pages generated server-side). Nowadays, most search sites make suggestions in a drop-down menu as you type before you even click Search. Google went one step further by showing results as users typed (though it reversed that function in the summer of 2017, as more searches moved to mobile, where this functionality made less sense).

All sorts of web pages other than search engines also make heavy use of AJAX requests, from social media sites that load new posts to news websites that update their home pages as news comes in. All these extra media and AJAX requests allow websites to be more interesting web *applications*. The HTTP protocol wasn't designed with this huge increase in resources in mind, however, and the protocol has some fundamental performance problems in its simple design.

2.1.1 *HTTP/1.1's fundamental performance problem*

Imagine a simple web page with some text and two images. Suppose that a request takes 50 milliseconds (ms) to travel across the internet to the web server and that the website is static, so the web server picks the file up from the file server and sends it back—say, in 10 ms. Similarly, the web browser takes 10 ms to process the image and send the next request. These figures are hypotheticals; if you have a content management system (CMS) that creates pages on the fly (WordPress runs PHP to process a page, for example), the 10 ms server time may not be accurate, depending on what processing is happening on the server and/or database. Additionally, images can be large and take longer to send than an HTML page. We'll look at real examples later in this chapter, but for this simple example, the flow under HTTP would look like figure 2.2.

The boxes represent processing at the client or server end, and the arrows represent network traffic. What's immediately apparent in this hypothetical example is how much time is spent sending messages back and forth. Of the 360 ms needed to draw

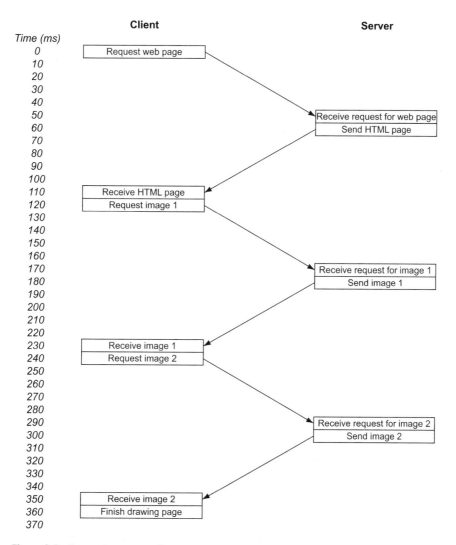

Figure 2.2 Request–response flow over HTTP for a basic example website

the complete page, only 60 ms was spent processing the requests at the client or browser side. A total 300 ms, or more than 80% of the time, was spent waiting for messages to travel across the internet. During this time, neither the web browser nor the web server does much in this example; this time is wasted and is a major problem with the HTTP protocol. At the 120 ms mark, after the browser has asked for image 1, it *knows* that it needs image 2, but waits for the connection to be free before sending the request for it, which doesn't happen until the 240 ms mark. This process is inefficient, but there are ways around it, as you'll see later. Most browsers open multiple connections, for example. The point is that the basic HTTP protocol is quite inefficient.

Most websites aren't made up of only two images, and the performance issues in figure 2.2 increase with the number of assets that need to be downloaded—particularly for smaller assets with a small amount of processing on either side relative to the network request and response time.

One of the biggest problems of the modern internet is latency rather than bandwidth. *Latency* measures how long it takes to send a single message to the server, whereas *bandwidth* measures how much a user can download in those messages. Newer technologies increase bandwidth all the time (which helps address the increase in the size of websites), but latency isn't improving (which prevents the number of requests from increasing). Latency is restricted by physics (the speed of light). Data being transmitted through fiber-optic cables is traveling pretty close to the speed of light already; there's only a little to be gained here, no matter how much the technology improves.

Mike Belshe of Google did some experiments[5] that show we're reaching the point of diminishing returns for increasing bandwidth. We may now be able to stream high-definition television, but our web surfing hasn't gotten faster at the same rate, and websites often take several seconds to load even on a fast internet connection. The internet can't continue to increase at the rate it has without a solution for the fundamental performance issues of HTTP/1.1: too much time is wasted in sending and receiving even small HTTP messages.

2.1.2   *Pipelining for HTTP/1.1*

As stated in chapter 1, HTTP/1.1 tried to introduce *pipelining*, which allows concurrent requests to be sent before responses are received so that requests can be sent in parallel. The initial HTML still needs to be requested separately, but when the browser sees that it needs two images, it can request them one after the other. As shown in figure 2.3, pipelining shaves off 100 ms, or a third of the time in this simple, hypothetical example.

Pipelining should have brought huge improvements to HTTP performance, but for many reasons, it was difficult to implement, easy to break, and not well supported by web browsers or web servers.[6] As a result, it's rarely used. None of the main web browsers uses pipelining, for example.[7]

Even if pipelining were better supported, it still requires responses to be returned in the order in which they were requested. If Image 2 is available, but Image 1 has to be fetched from another server, the Image 2 response waits, even though it should be possible to send this file immediately. This problem is known as *head-of-line (HOL) blocking* and is common in other networking protocols as well as HTTP. I discuss the TCP HOL blocking issue in chapter 9.

---

[5]   https://docs.google.com/a/chromium.org/viewer?a=v&pid=sites&srcid=Y2hyb21pdW0ub3JnfGRldnxneDox-MzcyOWI1N2I4YzI3NzE2

[6]   https://tools.ietf.org/html/draft-nottingham-http-pipeline-01#section-3

[7]   https://en.wikipedia.org/wiki/HTTP_pipelining#Implementation_in_web_browsers

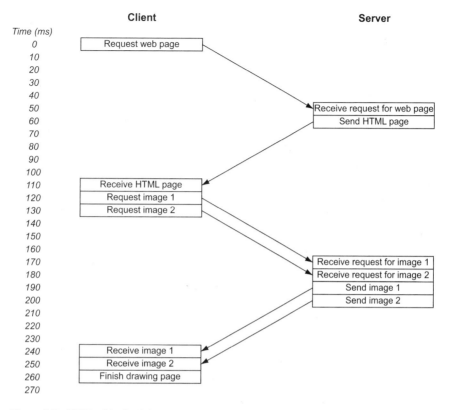

Figure 2.3   HTTP with pipelining for a basic example website

2.1.3   *Waterfall diagrams for web performance measurement*

The flows of requests and responses shown in figures 2.2 and 2.3 are often shown as waterfall diagrams, with assets on the left and increasing time on the right. These diagrams are easier to read than the flow diagrams used in figures 2.2 and 2.3 for large numbers of resources. Figure 2.4 shows a waterfall diagram for our hypothetical example site, and figure 2.5 shows the same site when pipelining is used.

Figure 2.4   Waterfall diagram of example website

In both examples, the first vertical line represents when the initial page can be drawn (known as *first paint time* or *start render*), and the second vertical line shows when the page is finished. Browsers often try to draw the page before the images have been

Figure 2.5 Waterfall diagram of example website with pipelining

downloaded, and the images are filled in later, so images often sit between these two times. These examples are simple, but they can get complex, as I show you in some real-life examples later in this chapter.

Various tools, including WebPagetest[8] and web-browser developer tools (introduced briefly at the end of chapter 1), generate waterfall diagrams, which are important to understand when reviewing web performance. Most of these tools break the total time for each asset into components such as Domain Name Service (DNS) lookup and TCP connection time, as shown in figure 2.6.

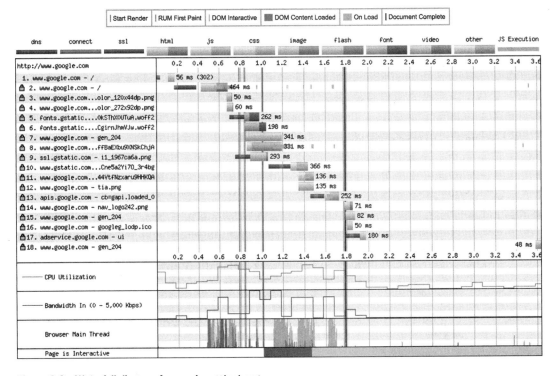

Figure 2.6 Waterfall diagram from webpagetest.org

---

8 https://www.webpagetest.org

This diagram provides a lot more information than simple waterfall diagrams do. It breaks each request into several parts, including

- The DNS lookup
- The network connection time
- The HTTPS (or SSL) negotiation time
- The resource requested (and also splits the resource load into two pieces, with the lighter color for the request and the darker color for the response download)
- Various vertical lines for the various stages in loading the page
- Other graphs that show CPU use, network bandwidth, and what the browser's main thread is working on

All this information is useful for analyzing the performance of a website. I make heavy use of waterfall diagrams throughout this book to explain the concepts.

2.2 *Workarounds for HTTP/1.1 performance issues*

As stated earlier, HTTP/1.1 isn't an efficient protocol because it blocks on a send and waits for a response. It is, in effect, synchronous; you can't move on to another HTTP request until the current request is finished. If the network or the server is slow, HTTP performs worse. As HTTP is intended primarily to request resources from a server that's often far from the client, network slowness is a fact of life for HTTP. For the initial use case of HTTP (a single HTML document), this slowness wasn't much of a problem. But as web pages grew more and more complex, with more and more resources required to render them properly, slowness became a problem.

Solutions for slow websites led to a whole *web performance optimization* industry, with many books and tutorials on how to improve web performance being published. Although overcoming the problems of HTTP/1.1 wasn't the only performance optimization, it was a large part of this industry. Over time, various tips, tricks, and hacks have been created to overcome the performance limitations of HTTP/1.1, which fall into the following two categories:

- Use multiple HTTP connections.
- Make fewer but potentially larger HTTP requests.

Other performance techniques, which have less to do with the HTTP protocol, involve ensuring that the user is requesting the resources in the optimal manner (such as requesting critical CSS first), reducing the amount downloaded (compression and responsive images), and reducing the work on the browser (more efficient CSS or JavaScript). These techniques are mostly beyond the scope of this book, though I return to some of them in chapter 6. The Manning book *Web Performance in Action*, by Jeremy Wagner,[9] is an excellent resource for learning more about these techniques.

---

[9] https://www.manning.com/books/web-performance-in-action

2.2.1 *Use multiple HTTP connections*

One of the easiest ways to get around the blocking issue of HTTP/1.1 is to open more connections, allowing parallelization to have multiple HTTP requests on the go. Additionally, unlike with pipelining, no HOL blocking occurs, as each HTTP connection works independently of the others. Most browsers open six connections per domain for this reason.

To increase this limit of six further, many websites serve static assets such as images, CSS, and JavaScript from subdomains (such as `static.example.com`), allowing web browsers to open a further six connections for each new domain. This technique is known as *domain sharding* (not to be confused with database sharding by those readers who come from a nonweb background, though the performance reasons are similar). Domain sharding can also be handy for reasons other than increasing parallelization, such as reducing HTTP headers such as cookies (see section 2.3). Often, these shared domains are hosted on the same server. Sharing the same resources but using different domain names fools the browser into thinking that the server is separate. Figure 2.7 shows that stackoverflow.com uses multiple domains: loading JQuery from a Google domain, scripts and stylesheets from `cdn.static.net`, and images from `i.stack.imgur.com`.

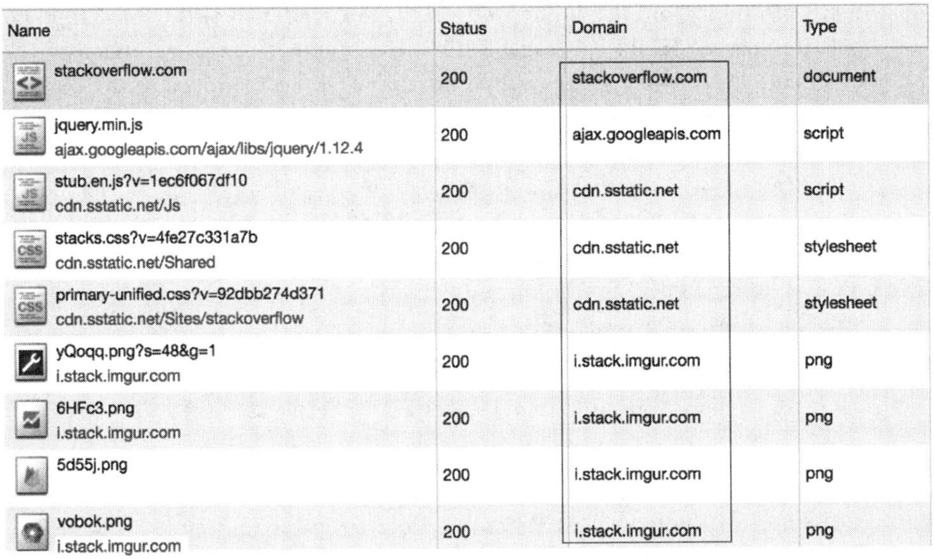

Name	Status	Domain	Type
stackoverflow.com	200	stackoverflow.com	document
jquery.min.js ajax.googleapis.com/ajax/libs/jquery/1.12.4	200	ajax.googleapis.com	script
stub.en.js?v=1ec6f067df10 cdn.sstatic.net/Js	200	cdn.sstatic.net	script
stacks.css?v=4fe27c331a7b cdn.sstatic.net/Shared	200	cdn.sstatic.net	stylesheet
primary-unified.css?v=92dbb274d371 cdn.sstatic.net/Sites/stackoverflow	200	cdn.sstatic.net	stylesheet
yQoqq.png?s=48&g=1 i.stack.imgur.com	200	i.stack.imgur.com	png
6HFc3.png i.stack.imgur.com	200	i.stack.imgur.com	png
5d55j.png	200	i.stack.imgur.com	png
vobok.png i.stack.imgur.com	200	i.stack.imgur.com	png

Figure 2.7 Multiple domains for stackoverflow.com

Although using multiple HTTP connections sounds like a simple fix to improve performance, it isn't without downsides. There are additional overheads for both the client and server when multiple HTTP connections are used: starting a TCP connection takes time, and maintaining the connection requires extra memory and processing.

The main issue with multiple HTTP connections, however, is significant inefficiencies with the underlying TCP protocol. TCP is a guaranteed protocol that sends packets with a unique sequence number and rerequests any packets that got lost on the way by checking for missing sequence numbers. TCP requires a three-way handshake to set up, as shown in figure 2.8.

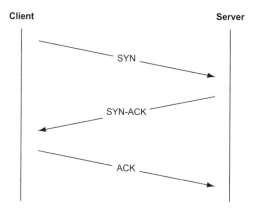

Figure 2.8   TCP three-way handshake

I'll explain these steps in detail:

1 The client sends a synchronization (SYN) message that tells the server the sequence number it should expect all future TCP packets from this request to be based on.

2 The server acknowledges the sequence numbers from the client and sends its own synchronization request, telling the client what sequence numbers it will use for its messages. Both messages are combined into a single SYN-ACK message.

3 Finally, the client acknowledges the server sequence numbers with an ACK message.

This process adds 3 network trips (or 1.5 round trips) before you send a single HTTP request!

In addition, TCP starts cautiously, with a small number of packets sent before acknowledgement. The congestion window (CWND) gradually increases over time as the connection is shown to be able to handle larger sizes without losing packets. The size of the TCP congestion window is controlled by the TCP *slow-start* algorithm. As TCP is a guaranteed protocol that doesn't want to overload the network, TCP packets in the CWND must be acknowledged before more packets can be sent, using increments of the sequence numbers set up in the three-way handshake. Therefore, with a small CWND, it may take several TCP acknowledgements to send the full HTTP request messages. HTTP responses, which are often much larger than HTTP requests, also suffer from the same congestion window constraints. As the TCP connection is used more, it increases the CWND and gets more efficient, but it always starts artificially throttled, even on the fastest, highest-bandwidth networks. I return to TCP in chapter 9, but for now, even this quick introduction should show that multiple TCP connections have a cost.

Finally, even without any issues with TCP setup and slow start, using multiple independent connections can result in bandwidth issues. If all the bandwidth is used, for example, the result can be TCP timeouts and retransmissions on other connections. There's no concept of prioritization between the traffic on those independent connections to use the available bandwidth in the most efficient manner.

When the TCP connection has been made, secure websites require the setup of HTTPS. This setup can be minimized on subsequent connections by reusing many of the parameters used in the main connection rather than starting from scratch, but the process still takes further network trips, and, therefore, time. I won't discuss the HTTPS handshake in detail now, but we'll examine it in more detail in chapter 4.

Therefore, it's inefficient, at a TCP and HTTPS level, to open multiple connections, even if doing so is a good optimization at an HTTP level. The solution for the latency problems of HTTP/1.1 requires multiple extra requests and responses; therefore, the solution is prone to the very latency problems it's supposed to resolve!

Additionally, by the time these additional TCP connections have reached optimal TCP efficiency, it's likely that the bulk of the web page will have loaded and the additional connections are no longer required. Even browsing to subsequent pages may not require many resources if the common elements are cached. Patrick McManus of Mozilla states that in Mozilla's monitoring for HTTP/1, "74 percent of our active connections carry just a single transaction." I present some real-life examples later in this chapter.

Multiple TCP connections, therefore, aren't a great solution to the problems of HTTP/1, though they can improve performance when no better solution is available. Incidentally, this explains why browsers limit the number of connections to six per domain. Although it's possible to increase this number (as some browsers allow you to), there are diminishing returns, given the overhead required for each connection.

2.2.2   *Make fewer requests*

The other common optimization technique is to make fewer requests, which involves reducing unnecessary requests (such as by caching assets in the browser) or requesting the same amount of data over fewer HTTP requests. The former method involves using HTTP caching headers, discussed briefly in chapter 1 and revisited in more detail in chapter 6. The latter method involves bundling assets into combined files.

For images, this bundling technique is known as *spriting*. If you have a lot of social media icons on your website, for example, you could use one file for each icon. But this method would lead to a lot of inefficient HTTP queuing, as the images will be small, so a relatively large proportion of the time needed to fetch them will be spent on the overheads of downloading them. Instead, you can bundle them into one large

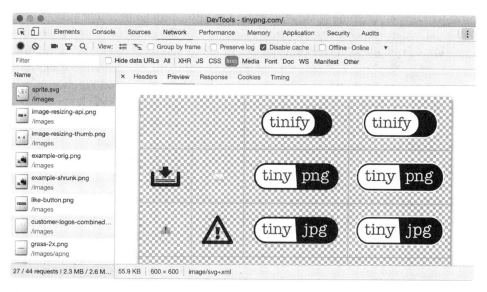

Figure 2.9   Sprite image for TinyPNG

image file and then use CSS to pull out sections of the image to effectively re-create the individual images. Figure 2.9 shows one such sprite image used by TinyPNG, which has common icons in one file.

For CSS and JavaScript, many websites concatenate multiple files so that fewer files are produced, though with the same amount of code in the combined files. This concatenation is often done while minimizing the CSS or JavaScript to remove whitespace, comments, and other unnecessary elements. Both of these methods produce performance benefits but require effort to set up.

Other techniques involve inlining the resources into other files. Critical CSS is often included directly in the HTML with <style> tags, for example. Or images can be included in CSS as inline *Scalable Vector Graphic (SVG)* instructions or base 64-encoded binary files, which saves additional HTTP requests.

The main downside to this solution is the complexity it introduces. Creating image sprites takes effort; it's easier to serve images as separate files. Not all websites use a build step in which optimizations such as concatenating CSS files can be automated. If you use a *Content Management System (CMS)* for your website, it may not automatically concatenate JavaScript, or sprite images.

Another downside is the waste in these files. Some pages may be downloading large sprite image files and using only one or two of those images. It's complicated to track how much of your sprite file is still used and when to trim it. You also have to rewrite all your CSS to load the images correctly from the right locations in the new sprite file. Similarly, JavaScript can become bloated and much larger than it needs to be if you concatenate too much and download a huge file even when you need only to use a small amount of it. This technique is inefficient in terms of both the network layer (particularly at the beginning, due to TCP slow start) and processing (as the web browser needs to process data it won't use).

The final issue is caching. If you cache your sprite image for a long time (so that site visitors don't download it too often) but then need to add an image, you have to make the browsers download the whole file again, even though the visitor may not need this image. You can use various techniques such as adding a version number to the filename or using a query parameter,[10] but these techniques are still wasteful. Similarly, on the CSS or JavaScript side, a single code change requires the whole concatenated file to be redownloaded.

2.2.3 HTTP/1 performance optimizations summary

Ultimately, HTTP/1 performance optimizations are hacks to get around a fundamental flaw in the HTTP protocol. It would be much better to fix this flaw at the protocol level to save everyone time and effort here, and that's exactly what HTTP/2 aims to do.

2.3 Other issues with HTTP/1.1

HTTP/1.1 is a simple text-based protocol. This simplicity introduces problems. Although the bodies of HTTP messages can contain binary data (such as images in whatever format the client and server can agree on), the requests and the headers themselves must still be in text. Text format is great for humans but isn't optimal for machines. Processing HTTP text messages can be complex and error-prone, which introduces security issues. Several attacks on HTTP have been based on injecting newline characters into HTTP headers, for example.[11]

The other issue with HTTP being a text format is that HTTP messages are larger than they need to be, due to not encoding data efficiently (such as representing the `Date` header as a number versus full human-readable text) and repeating headers. Again, for the initial use case of the web with single requests, this situation wasn't much of a problem, but the increasing number of requests makes this situation quite inefficient. The use of HTTP headers has grown, which leads to a lot of repetition. Cookies, for example, are sent with every HTTP request to the domain, even if only the main page request requires cookies. Usually, static resources such as images, CSS, and JavaScript don't need cookies. Domain sharding, as described earlier in this chapter, was brought in to allow extra connections, but it was also used to create so-called cookieless domains that wouldn't need cookies sent to them for performance and security reasons. HTTP responses are also growing, and with security HTTP headers such as `Content-Security-Policy` producing extremely large HTTP headers, the deficiencies of the text-based protocol are becoming more apparent. With many websites being made up of 100 resources or more, large HTTP headers can add tens or hundreds of kilobytes of data transferred.

---

[10] https://css-tricks.com/strategies-for-cache-busting-css/
[11] https://www.owasp.org/index.php/Testing_for_HTTP_Splitting/Smuggling_(OTG-INPVAL-016)

Performance limitations are only one aspect of HTTP/1.1 that could be improved. Other issues include the security and privacy issues of a plain-text protocol (addressed pretty successfully by wrapping HTTPS around it) and the lack of state (addressed less successfully by the addition of cookies). In chapter 10, I explore these issues more. To many, however, the performance issues are problems that aren't easy to address without implementing workarounds that introduce their own issues.

2.4 Real-world examples

I've shown that HTTP/1.1 is inefficient for multiple requests, but how bad is that situation? Is it noticeable? Let's look at a couple of real-world examples.

> ### Real-world websites and HTTP/2
>
> When I originally wrote this chapter, both of the example websites I used didn't support HTTP/2. Both sites have since enabled it, but the lessons shown here are still relevant as examples of complex websites that suffer under HTTP/1.1, and many of the details discussed here are likely similar to those of other websites. HTTP/2 is gaining in popularity, and any site chosen as an example may be upgraded at some point. I prefer to use real, well-known sites to demonstrate the issues that HTTP/2 looks to solve rather than using artificial example websites created purely to prove a point, so I've kept the two example websites despite the fact that they're now on HTTP/2. The sites are less important than the concepts they show.
>
> To repeat these tests at webpagetest.org, you can disable HTTP/2 by specifying `--disable-http2` (Advanced Settings > Chrome > Command-Line Options). There are similar options if you're using Firefox as your browser.[a] These are also helpful ways to test your own HTTP/2 performance changes after you go live with HTTP/2.
>
> ---
> [a] https://www.webpagetest.org/forums/showthread.php?tid=14162

2.4.1 Example website 1: amazon.com

I've talked theoretically up until now, but now I look at real-world examples. If you take www.amazon.com and run it through www.webpagetest.org, you get the waterfall diagram shown in figure 2.10. This figure demonstrates many of the problems with HTTP/1.1:

- The first request is for the home page, which I've repeated in a larger format in figure 2.11.

  It requires time to do a DNS lookup, time to connect, and time to do the SSL/TLS HTTPS negotiation before a single request is sent. The time is small (slightly more than 0.1 second in figure 2.11), but it adds up. Not much can be done about that for this first request. This result is part and parcel of the way the web works, as discussed in chapter 1, and although improvements to HTTPS ciphers and protocols might reduce the SSL time, the first request is

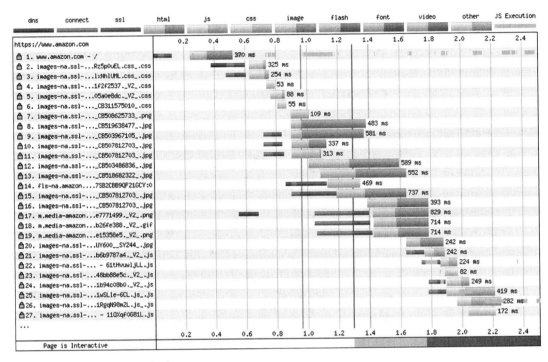

Figure 2.10   Part of the results for www.amazon.com

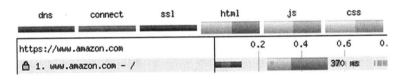

Figure 2.11   The first request for the home page

going to be subject to these delays. The best you can do is ensure that your servers are responsive, and, ideally, close to the users to keep round-trip times as low as possible. In chapter 3, I discuss content delivery networks (CDNs), which can help with this problem.

After this initial setup, a slight pause occurs. I can't explain this pause, which could be due to slightly inaccurate timings or an issue in the Chrome browser. I didn't see the same gap when repeating the test with Firefox. Then the first HTTP request is made (light color), and the HTML is downloaded (slightly darker color), parsed, and processed by the web browser.

- The HTML makes references to several CSS files, which are also downloaded, as shown in figure 2.12.

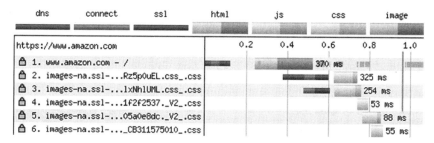

Figure 2.12 The five requests for the CSS files

- These CSS files are hosted on another domain (`images-na.ssl-images-amazon.com`), which has been sharded from the main domain for performance reasons, as discussed earlier. As this domain is separate, you need to start over from the beginning for the second request and do another DNS lookup, another network connection, and another HTTPS negotiation before using this domain to download the CSS. Although the setup time for request 1 is somewhat unavoidable, this second setup time is wasted; the domain name sharding is done to work around HTTP/1.1 performance issues. Note also that this CSS file appears early in the processing of the HTML page in request 1, causing request 2 to start slightly before the 0.4-second mark despite the fact that the HTML page doesn't finish downloading until slightly after 0.5 of a second. The browser didn't wait for the full HTML page to be downloaded and processed; instead, it requested the extra HTTP connection as soon as it saw the domain referenced (even if the resource itself doesn't start to be downloaded until after the HTML has been fully received in this example due to the connection setup delays).

- The third request is for another CSS file on the same sharded domain. As HTTP/1.1 allows only a single request in flight at the same time, the browser creates another connection. You don't need the DNS lookup this time (because you know the IP address for that domain from request 2), but you do need the costly TCP/IP connection setup and HTTPS negotiating time before you can request this CSS. Again, the only reason for this extra connection is to work around HTTP/1.1 performance issues.

- Next the browser requests three more CSS files, which are loaded over the two connections already established. Not shown in the diagram is why the browser didn't request these other CSS files immediately, which would have necessitated creating even more connections and the costs associated with them. I looked at the Amazon source code, and there's a `<script>` tag before these CSS files request that blocks the later requests until the script is processed, which explains why requests 4, 5, and 6 aren't requested at the same time as requests 2 and 3. This point is an important one that I return to later: although HTTP/1.1 inefficiencies are a problem for the web and could be solved by improvements to

HTTP (like those in HTTP/2), they're far from being the only reasons for slow performance on the web.

- After the CSS has been dealt with in requests 2 to 6, the browser decides that the images are next, so it starts downloading them, as shown in figure 2.13.

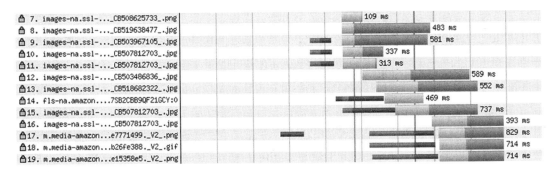

Figure 2.13   Image downloads

- The first .png file is in request 7, which is a sprite file of multiple images (not shown in figure 2.13), and another performance tweak that Amazon implemented. Next, some .jpg files are downloaded from request 8 onward.
- When two of these image requests are in flight, the browser needs to make more costly connections to allow other files to load in parallel in requests 9, 10, 11, and 15 and then again for new domains in requests 14, 17, 18, and 19.
- In some cases (requests 9, 10, and 11), the browser guessed that more connections are likely to be needed and set up the connections in advance, which is why the connect and SSL parts happen earlier and why it can request the images at the same time as requests 7 and 8.
- Amazon added a performance optimization to do a DNS prefetch[12] for m.media-amazon.com well before it needs it, though oddly not for fls-na.amazon.com. This is why the DNS lookup for request 17 happens at the 0.6 second mark, well before it's needed. I return to this topic in chapter 6.

The loading continues past these requests, but even looking at only these first few requests identifies problems with HTTP/1.1, so I won't belabor the point by continuing through the whole site load.

Many connections are needed to prevent any queuing, and often, the time taken to make this connection doubles the time needed to download the asset. Web Page Test has a handy connection view[13] (shown in figure 2.14 for this same example).

---

[12] https://css-tricks.com/prefetching-preloading-prebrowsing/
[13] https://www.webpagetest.org/result/170820_NR_53c5bf9ca1e67301a933947d80a32a53/1/details/#connectionView_fv_1

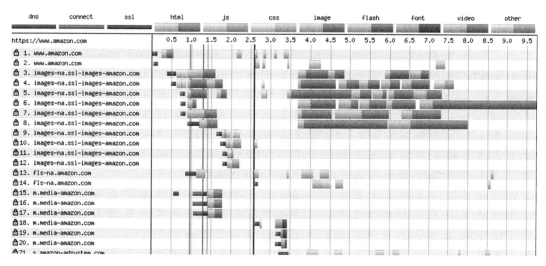

Figure 2.14 Connection view of loading amazon.com

You can see that loading amazon.com requires 20 connections for the main site, ignoring the advertising resources, which add another 28 connections (not shown in figure 2.14). Although the first six `images-na.ssl-images-amazon.com` connections are fairly well used (connections 3–8), the other four connections for this domain (connections 9–12) are less well used; like many other connections (such as 15, 16, 17, 18, 19, and 20), they're used to load only one or two resources, making the time needed to create that connection wasteful.

The reason why these four extra connections are opened for `images-na.ssl-images-amazon.com` (and why Chrome appears to break its limit of six connections per domain) is interesting and took a bit of investigation. Requests can be sent with credentials (which usually means cookies), but requests can also be sent without them and handled by Chrome over separate connections. For security reasons, due to how cross-origin requests are handled in the browser,[14] Amazon uses `setAttribute` (`"crossorigin"`, `"anonymous"`) in some of these requests for JavaScript files, without credentials, which means that the existing connections aren't used. Instead, more connections are created. The same isn't necessary for direct JavaScript requests with the `<script>` tag in HTML. The workaround also isn't needed for resources hosted on the main domain being loaded, which again shows that sharding can be inefficient at an HTTP level.

The Amazon example shows that even when a site is well optimized with the workarounds necessary to boost performance under HTTP/1.1, there is a still a performance penalty to using these performance workarounds. These performance workarounds are also complicated to set up. Not every site wants to manage multiple

---

[14] https://developer.mozilla.org/en-US/docs/Web/HTTP/CORS

domains or sprite images or merge all their JavaScript (or CSS) into one file, and not every site has the resources of Amazon to create these optimizations or is even aware of them. Smaller sites are often much less optimized and therefore suffer the limitations of HTTP/1 even more.

2.4.2   *Example website 2: imgur.com*

What happens if you don't make these optimizations? As an example, look at imgur.com. Because it's an image sharing site, imgur.com loads a huge number of images on the home page, but doesn't sprite them into single files. A subsection of the WebPagetest waterfall diagram is shown in figure 2.15.

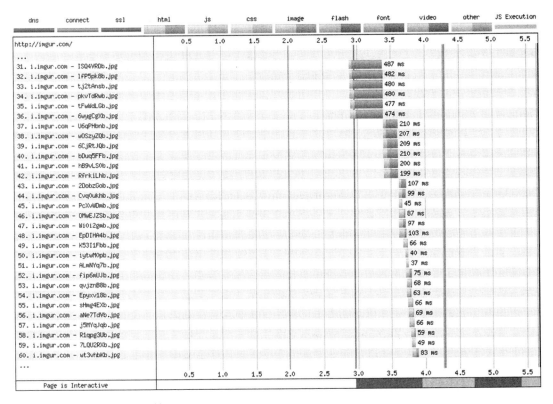

Figure 2.15   Waterfall view of imgur.com

I skipped the first part of the page load (before request 31), which repeats a lot of the amazon.com example. What you see here is that the maximum six connections are used to load requests 31–36; the rest are queued. As each of those six requests finishes, another six can be fired off, followed by another six, which leads to the telltale waterfall shape that gives these charts their name. Note that the six resources are unrelated and could finish at different times (as they do farther down the waterfall chart), but if they're similar size resources, it's not unusual for them to finish at around the same time. This fact gives the illusion that the resources are related, but on the HTTP level, they're not (though they share network bandwidth and go to the same server).

The waterfall diagram for Chrome, shown in figure 2.16, makes the problem more apparent, as it also measures the delay from when the resource could have been requested. As you can see, for later requests, a long delay occurs before the image is requested (highlighted by the rectangle), followed by a relatively short download time.

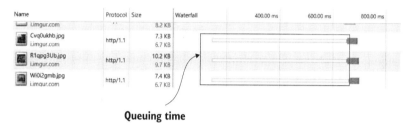

Figure 2.16   Chrome developer tools waterfall view of imgur.com

2.4.3   How much of a problem is this really?

Although this chapter identifies inefficiencies in HTTP, workarounds are available. These workarounds, however, take time, money, and understanding to implement and to maintain going forward, and they add their own performance problems. Developers aren't cheap, and having them spend time working around an inefficient protocol is necessary but costly (not to mention the many sites that don't realize the impact of poor performance on their traffic). Multiple studies show that slower websites lead to abandonment and to loss of visitors and sales.[15, 16]

You must also consider how serious this problem is in relation to other performance problems. There are any number of reasons why a website is slow, from the quality of the internet connection to the size of the website to the ridiculous amounts of JavaScript that some websites use, to the proliferation of poorly performing ads and tracking networks. Although being able to download resources quickly and efficiently is certainly one part of the problem, many websites would still be slow. Clearly, many websites are worried about this aspect of performance, which is why they implement the HTTP/1.1 workarounds, but many other sites don't because of the complexity and understanding that these workarounds require.

The other problem is the limitations of these workarounds. These workarounds generate their own inefficiencies, but as websites continue to grow in both size and

---

[15] https://developers.google.com/web/fundamentals/performance/why-performance-matters/
[16] https://developer.akamai.com/blog/2016/09/14/mobile-load-time-user-abandonment

complexity, at some point even the workarounds will no longer work. Although browsers open six connections per domain and could increase this number, the overhead of doing so versus the gains is reaching the point of diminishing returns, which is why browsers limited the number of connections to six in the first place, even though site owners have tried to work around this limit with domain sharding.

Ultimately, each website is different, and each website owner or web developer needs to spend time analyzing the site's own resource bottlenecks, using tools such as waterfall diagrams, to see whether the site is being badly affected by HTTP/1.1 performance problems.

2.5   *Moving from HTTP/1.1 to HTTP/2*

HTTP hadn't really changed since 1999, when HTTP/1.1 came on the scene. The specification was clarified in the new Request for Comments (RFCs) published in 2014, but this specification was more a documentation exercise than any real change in the protocol. Work had started on an updated version (HTTP-NG), which would have been a complete redesign of how HTTP worked, but it was abandoned in 1999. The general feeling is that the change was overly complex, with no path to introduce it in the real world.

2.5.1   *SPDY*

In 2009, Mike Belshe and Robert Peon at Google announced that they were working on a new protocol called SPDY (pronounced "speedy" and not an acronym). They had been experimenting on this protocol in laboratory conditions and saw excellent results, with up to 64% improvement in page load times. The experiments were run on copies of the top 25 websites, not hypothetical websites that may not represent the real world.

SPDY was built on top of HTTP, but doesn't fundamentally change the protocol, in much the same way that HTTPS wrapped around HTTP without changing its underlying use. The HTTP methods (GET, POST, and so on) and the concept of HTTP headers still exist in SDPY. SPDY worked at a lower level, and to web developers, server owners, and (crucially) users, the use of SPDY was almost transparent. Any HTTP request was simply converted to a SPDY request, sent to the server, and then converted back. This request looked like any other HTTP request to higher-level applications (such as JavaScript applications on the client side and those configuring web servers). Additionally, SPDY was implemented only over secure HTTP (HTTPS), which allowed the structure and format of the message to be hidden from all the internet plumbing that passes messages between client and server. All existing networks, routers, switches, and other infrastructure, therefore, could handle SPDY messages without any changes and without even knowing that they were handling SPDY messages rather than HTTP/1 messages. SPDY was essentially backward-compatible and could be introduced with minimal changes and risk, which is undoubtedly a big reason why it succeeded and HTTP-NG failed.

Whereas HTTP-NG tried to address multiple issues with HTTP/1, the main aim of SPDY was to tackle the performance limitations of HTTP/1.1. It introduced a few important concepts to deal with the limitations of HTTP/1.1:

- *Multiplexed streams*—Requests and responses used a single TCP connection and were broken into interleaved packets grouped into separate streams.
- *Request prioritization*—To avoid introducing new performance problems by sending all requests at the same time, the concept of prioritization of the requests was introduced.
- *HTTP header compression*—HTTP bodies had long been compressed, but now headers could be compressed too.

It wasn't possible to introduce these features with the text-based request-and-response protocol that HTTP was up until then, so SPDY became a binary protocol. This change allowed the single connection to handle small messages, which together formed the larger HTTP messages, much the way that TCP itself breaks larger HTTP messages into many smaller TCP packets that are transparent to most HTTP implementations. SPDY implemented the concepts of TCP at the HTTP layer so that multiple HTTP messages could be in flight at the same time.

Additional advanced features such as server push allowed the server to tag on extra resources. If you requested the home page, server push could provide the CSS file needed to display it, in response to that request. This process saves the need to suffer the performance delay of the round trip asking for that CSS file and the complication and effort of inlining critical CSS.

Google was in the unique position of being in control of both a major browser (Chrome) and some of the most popular websites (such as www.google.com), so it could do much larger real-life experiments with the new protocol by implementing it at both ends of the connection. SPDY was released to Chrome in September 2010, and by January 2011, all Google services were SPDY-enabled[17]—an incredibly quick rollout by any measure.

SPDY was an almost-instant success, with other browsers and servers quickly adding support. Firefox and Opera added support in 2012. On the server side, Jetty added support, followed by others, including Apache and nginx. The vast majority of websites that supported SPDY were on the latter two web servers. Websites that introduced SPDY (including Twitter, Facebook, and WordPress) saw the same performance gains as Google, with little downside apart from initial setup. SPDY reached up to 9.1% of all websites, according to w3techs.com,[18] though browsers have started removing support for it now that HTTP/2 is here. Since early 2018, use of SPDY has plummeted, as shown in figure 2.17.

---

[17] https://groups.google.com/d/msg/spdy-dev/TCOW7Lw2scQ/T2kM5aPDydwJ
[18] https://w3techs.com/technologies/details/ce-spdy/all/all

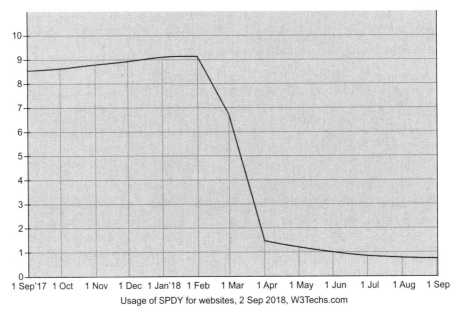

Usage of SPDY for websites, 2 Sep 2018, W3Techs.com

Figure 2.17   SPDY support on websites has dropped since the launch of HTTP/2.

2.5.2   *HTTP/2*

SPDY proved that HTTP/1.1 could be improved, not in a theoretical manner, but with examples of it working on major sites in the real world. In 2012, the HTTP Working Group of the Internet Engineering Task Force (IETF) noted the success of SPDY and asked for proposals for the next version of HTTP.[19] SPDY was the natural basis for this next version, as it had been proved in the wild, though the working group explicitly avoided saying so, preferring to be open to any proposals (though some people dispute this position, as covered in chapter 10).

After a short period, during which other proposals were considered, SPDY formed the basis of HTTP/2 in the first draft, published in November 2012.[20] This draft was modified slightly over the next two years to improve it (particularly its use of streams and compression). I go into the technical details of the protocol in chapters 4, 5, 7, and 8, so I'm covering this topic lightly here.

By the end of 2014, the HTTP/2 specification was submitted as a proposed standard for the internet, and in May 2015, it was formally approved as RFC 7450.[21] Support followed quickly, especially because the specification was heavily based on SPDY, which many browsers and servers had already implemented. Firefox supported

---

[19] https://lists.w3.org/Archives/Public/ietf-http-wg/2012JanMar/0098.html
[20] https://tools.ietf.org/html/draft-ietf-httpbis-http2-00
[21] https://tools.ietf.org/html/rfc7540

HTTP/2 from February 2015, and Chrome and Opera from March 2015. Internet Explorer 11, Edge, and Safari followed later in the year.

Web servers quickly added support, with many implementing the various versions as they went through standardization. LiteSpeed[22] and H2O[23] were some of the first web servers with support. By the end of 2015, the main three web servers used by the vast majority of internet users (Apache, IIS, and nginx) had implementations, though they were initially marked as experimental and not switched on by default.

As of September 2018, HTTP/2 is available on 30.1% of all websites, according to w3tech.com.[24] This reach is in large part due to content delivery networks and larger sites enabling HTTP/2, but it's still impressive for a three-year-old technology. As you will see in chapter 3, enabling HTTP/2 on the server side currently requires a fair bit of effort; otherwise, use might be even higher.

The takeaway point is that HTTP/2 is here and is available. It has been proved in real life and has been shown to improve performance significantly precisely because it addresses the problems with HTTP/1.1 raised in this chapter.

2.6 *What HTTP/2 means for web performance*

You've seen the inherent performance problems with HTTP/1 and now have the solution with HTTP/2, but are all web performance problems solved with HTTP/2, and how much faster should owners expect their websites to be if they upgrade to HTTP/2?

2.6.1 *Extreme example of the power of HTTP/2*

Many examples show the performance improvements of HTTP/2. I have one on my site at https://www.tunetheweb.com/performance-test-360/. This page is available over HTTP 1.1, HTTP 1.1 over HTTPS, and HTTP/2 over HTTPS. As discussed in chapter 3, browsers support HTTP/2 only over HTTPS; hence, there's no HTTP/2 without the HTTPS test. This test is based on a similar test at https://www.httpvshttps .com/ that excludes the HTTPS-without-HTTP/2 test and loads a web page with 360 images over the three technologies, using a bit of JavaScript to time the loads. The result is shown in figure 2.18.

This test shows that the HTTP version took 10.471 seconds to load the page and all the images. The HTTPS version took about the same time at 10.533 seconds, showing that HTTPS doesn't cause the performance penalty it once did and the difference is barely noticeable from plain-text HTTP. In fact, rerunning this test several times often showed HTTPS being marginally faster than HTTP, which makes no sense (because HTTPS involves extra processing), but this extra processing is within the margin of error for this test site.

---

[22] https://blog.litespeedtech.com/2015/04/17/lsws-5-0-is-out-support-for-http2-esi-litemage-cache/

[23] https://h2o.example.net/

[24] https://w3techs.com/technologies/details/ce-http2/all/all

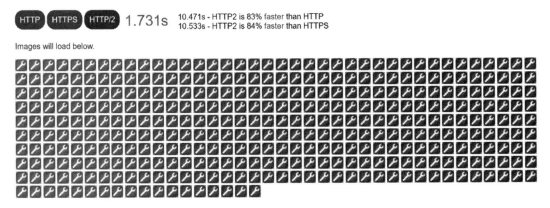

Figure 2.18   HTTP versus HTTPS versus HTTP/2 performance test

The real surprise is HTTP/2, which loaded the site in 1.731 seconds—83% faster than the other two technologies! Looking at the waterfall diagrams shows the reason. Compare the HTTPS and HTTP/2 diagrams in figures 2.19 and 2.20.

Under HTTPS, you see the familiar delay of setting up multiple connections and then loading the images in batches of six. Under HTTP/2, however, the images are requested together, so there's no delay. For brevity's sake, I've shown only the first 21 requests rather than all 360 requests, but this figure illustrates the massive performance benefits of HTTP/2 for loading this kind of site. Note also in figure 2.19 that after the maximum number of connections for the page are used, the browser chooses to load Google Analytics in request 10. That request is for a different domain

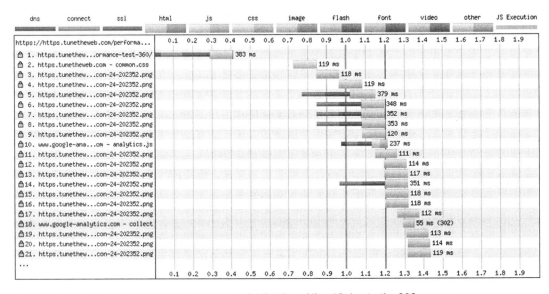

Figure 2.19   Waterfall of HTTPS test. Ignore the highlighting of line 18 due to the 302 response.

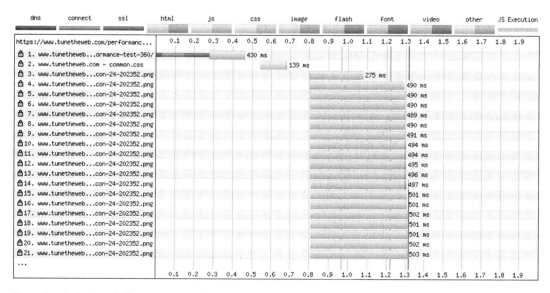

Figure 2.20 Waterfall diagram of HTTP/2 test

that hasn't reached its maximum connection limit. Figure 2.20 shows a much higher simultaneous-request limit, so many more of the images are requested at the beginning, and the Google Analytics request isn't shown in the first 21 requests but farther down this waterfall chart.

Astute readers may have noticed that the images take longer to download under HTTP/2: around 490 ms compared with around 115 ms under HTTP/1.1 (ignoring the first six, which took longer when you include connection setup time). Assets can appear to take longer to download under HTTP/2 because of the different way of measuring them. Waterfall diagrams typically measure from when the request is sent to when the response is received and may not measure queuing time. Taking request 16 as an example, under HTTP/1, this resource is requested at about the 1.2-second mark and is received 118 ms later, at approximately 1.318 ms. The browser, however, knew it needed the image after it processed the HTML and made the first request at 0.75 second, which is exactly when the HTTP/2 example requested it (not by coincidence!). Therefore, the 0.45-second delay isn't accurately reflected in HTTP/1 waterfall diagrams, and arguably, the clock should start at the 0.75-second mark. As noted in section 2.4.2, Chrome's waterfall diagram includes waiting time; so, it shows the true overall download time, which is longer than HTTP/2.

Requests *can* take longer under HTTP/2, however, due to bandwidth, client, or server limitations. The need to use multiple connections under HTTP/1 creates a natural queuing mechanism of six requests at the same time. HTTP/2 uses a single connection with streams, in theory removing that restriction, though implementations are free to add their own limitations. Apache, which I use to host this page, has a limit of 100 concurrent requests per connection by default, for example. Sending many requests at the same time leads to the requests sharing the available resources and taking longer to download. The images take progressively longer in figure 2.20 (from 282 ms in request line 4 to 301 ms in request line 25). Figure 2.21 shows the same results at lines 88–120. You can see that the image requests take up to 720 ms (six times as long as under HTTP/1). Also, when the 100-request limit is reached, a pause occurs until the first requests are downloaded; then the remaining resources are requested. This effect is identical to the waterfall effect due to HTTP/1 connection limitations but happens less and later due to the much-increased limits. Note also that during this pause, Google Analytics is requested as request 104. A similar thing happened during the pause in HTTP/1.1 in figure 2.19, but it happened much earlier, at request 10.

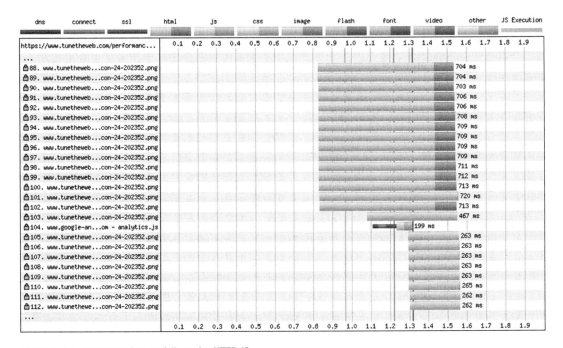

Figure 2.21   Delays and waterfalls under HTTP/2

The important point that's easy to miss when you're looking at waterfall diagrams under HTTP/2 is that they intrinsically measure different things. Instead, you should look at the overall time, and here, HTTP/2 clearly wins in the overall page load time.

2.6.2   *Setting expectations of HTTP/2 performance gains*

The example in section 2.6.1 shows the enormous gains that HTTP/2 can give a website; 83% performance improvements are vey impressive. This example isn't realistic, however, and most websites struggle to see anything near this result. This example illustrates the conditions under which HTTP/2 performs best (another reason why I prefer to use real, well-known websites in the examples in this book). Some websites may not see any performance improvement by switching to HTTP/2 if they have other performance problems, which means that the HTTP/1 deficiencies aren't much of a problem.

There are two reasons why HTTP/2 may make little difference to some existing websites. The first reason is that the websites may be so tuned, using the workarounds discussed in section 2.2, that they see little slowness due to the problems inherent in HTTP/1. But even well-tuned sites still suffer some performance drawbacks from these techniques, not to mention the significant effort needed to use and maintain these performance techniques. In theory, HTTP/2 allows every website to be even better than a domain-sharded, concatenated website making great use of sprites and inline CSS, JavaScript, and images with zero effort as long as the server supports HTTP/2!

The other reason why HTTP/2 may not improve sites is if other performance problems far eclipse the issues due to HTTP/1. Many websites have massive print-quality images, which take a long time to download. Other websites load far too much JavaScript, which takes time to download (HTTP/2 may be able to help) and process (HTTP/2 won't help). Websites that are slow even after loading or that suffer from jank (when the browser struggles to keep up with the user's scrolling around the website) aren't improved by HTTP/2, which looks only at the networking side of performance. Other, mostly edge cases also make HTTP/2 slower in certain instances of high packet loss, which I discuss in chapter 9.

Having said all that, I strongly believe that HTTP/2 will lead to more-performant websites and reduce the need to use some of the complicated workarounds that website owners have had to use up until now. At the same time, HTTP/2 advocates must set expectations as to what HTTP/2 can solve and what it can't; otherwise, people will only be disappointed when they move their sites to HTTP/2 and don't immediately see a huge performance increase. At this writing, we're probably at the peak of inflated expectations (for those who are familiar with the Gartner hype cycle),[25] and the expectation that a new technology will solve all problems is common before reality sets in. Sites need to understand their own performance problems, and HTTP/1 bottlenecks are only one part of those performance problems. In my experience, however, typical websites will see good improvement from moving to HTTP/2, and it will be extremely rare (though not impossible) for HTTP/2 to be slower than HTTP/1. One example would be a bandwidth-bound website (such as a site with many print-quality images), which may be slower under HTTP/2 if the natural ordering, enforced by the limited number of connections in HTTP/1.1, resulted in critical resources being downloaded faster. One graphic-design company published an interesting example,[26] but even this example can be made faster under HTTP/2 with the right tuning, as discussed in chapter 7.

---

[25] https://www.gartner.com/technology/research/methodologies/hype-cycle.jsp

[26] https://99designs.ie/tech-blog/blog/2016/07/14/real-world-http-2-400gb-of-images-per-day/

To return to real-world examples, I took a copy of Amazon's website, altered all references to make them local references, loaded the copy over HTTP/1 and HTTP/2 (both over HTTPS), and measured the different load times with the typical results shown in table 2.2.

Table 2.2 Improvements HTTP/2 might give Amazon

Protocol	Load time	First byte	Start render	Visually complete	Speed index
HTTP/1	2.616	0.409s	1.492s	2.900s	1692
HTTP/2	2.337	0.421s	1.275s	2.600s	1317
Difference	*11%*	*-3%*	*15%*	*10%*	*22%*

This table introduces a few terms that are common in web performance circles:

- *Load time* is the time it takes for the page to send the `onload` event—typically, after all CSS and blocking JavaScript are loaded.
- *First byte* is how long it takes to get the first response from the website. Usually, this response is the first real response, ignoring any redirects.
- *Start render* is when the page starts painting. This metric is a key performance metric, as users are likely to give up on a website if it doesn't give a visual update that it's loading the website.
- *Visually complete* is when the page stops changing, often long after load time, if asynchronous JavaScript is still changing the page after the initial onload time.
- *Speed index* is a WebPagetest calculation that indicates the average time for each part of the web page to be loaded, in milliseconds.[27]

Most of these metrics show good improvement with HTTP/2. First-byte time has worsened slightly, but repeating the tests showed the opposite to be true for some tests, so this result looks to be within the margin of error.

I admit, however, that these improvements are somewhat artificial because I haven't implemented the site exactly as Amazon did. I used only one domain (so no domain sharding occurred) and saved each asset as a static file rather than the dynamically generated content, as Amazon would do, which might be subject to other delays. Nonetheless, these limitations occurred in both the HTTP/1 and HTTP/2 versions of the test, so within these limitations, you can see clear improvements with HTTP/2.

Comparing the waterfall diagrams between the two loads in figures 2.22 and 2.23 shows the expected improvements under HTTP/2: no additional connections and less of a stepped waterfall load at the beginning, when many resources are needed.

---

[27] https://sites.google.com/a/web pagetest.org/docs/using-web pagetest/metrics/speed-index

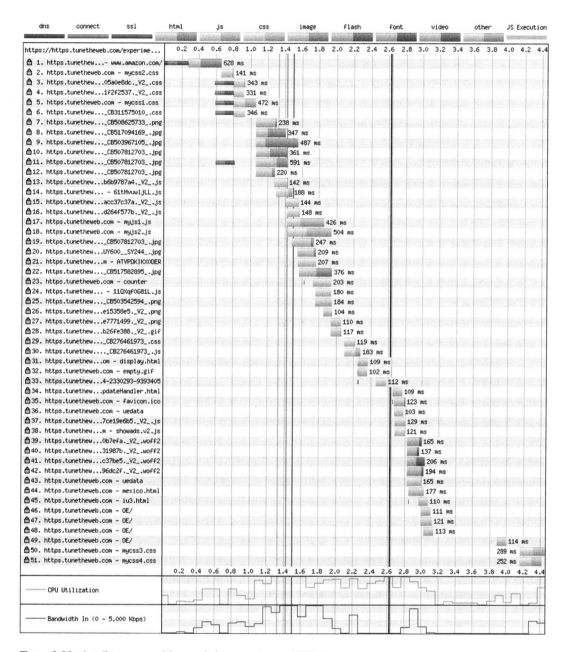

Figure 2.22 Loading a copy of Amazon's home page over HTTP/1

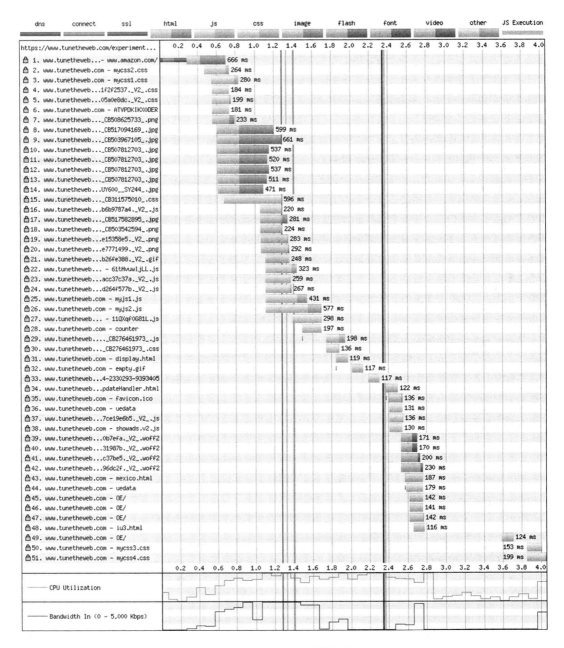

Figure 2.23   Loading a copy of amazon.com's home page over HTTP/2

No code has been changed on the website between the two request types; this result is simply the improvement due to HTTP/2. There's still a waterfall aspect to the loading of the site under HTTP/2 due to the dependent nature of web technologies: web pages load CSS, which loads images, for example. But less time is wasted setting up connections and queues, so the waterfall effect due to HTTP constraints is gone. The numbers may seem to be small, but a 22% improvement is a huge gain, especially considering that this improvement didn't require any changes beyond the web server itself.

Sites that are truly optimized for HTTP/2 and that use some of the new features available within HTTP/2 (which I cover later in this book) should see much bigger improvements. At the moment, we have 20 years of experience in optimizing sites under HTTP/1 but almost no experience optimizing for HTTP/2.

I'm using Amazon as an example of a well-known website that (when I wrote this chapter) hadn't yet moved to HTTP/2 and was highly (though not perfectly!) optimized for HTTP/1. To be clear, I'm not saying that Amazon is badly coded or not performant; I'm showing the performance improvements that HTTP/2 can potentially give a website immediately, and, perhaps more importantly, the effort that can be saved by not having to do the HTTP/1.1 workarounds to get great performance.

Since I originally wrote this chapter, Amazon has moved to HTTP/2, which has shown some similar results. The point, however, is to see Amazon as an example of a real-world, complicated website that has already implemented some HTTP/1 performance optimizations but still can improve dramatically with HTTP/2.

2.6.3 *Performance workarounds for HTTP/1.1 as potential antipatterns*

Because HTTP/2 fixed the performance problems in HTTP/1.1, in theory, there should be no need to deploy the performance workarounds discussed in this chapter anymore. In fact, many people believe that these workarounds are becoming antipatterns in the HTTP/2 world, because they could prevent you from getting the full benefits of HTTP/2. The benefits of a single TCP connection to load a website, for example, are negated if the website owner uses domain sharding and therefore forces several connections (though I discuss connection coalescing, which is designed to address this problem, in chapter 6). HTTP/2 makes it much simpler to create a performant website by default.

The reality is never that simple, though, and as I state in subsequent chapters (particularly chapter 6), it may be too soon to drop these techniques completely until HTTP/2 gets more bedded in. On the client side, some users will still be using HTTP/1.1 despite strong browser support. They may be using older browsers or connecting via a proxy that doesn't yet support HTTP/2 (including antivirus scanners and corporate proxies).

Additionally, on both the client and server sides, implementations are still changing while people learn how best to use this new protocol. For 20 years after HTTP/1.1 was launched, a thriving web performance optimization industry grew, teaching developers how best to optimize their websites for the HTTP protocol. Although I hope that HTTP/2 won't require as much web optimization as HTTP/1.1 did, and it should give most of the same performance benefits those optimizations give under HTTP/1.1 without any effort, developers are still getting used to this new protocol, and undoubtedly, some best practices and techniques will require learning.

By now, you're presumably eager to get HTTP/2 up and running. In chapter 3, I show you how to do this. I return to performance optimization later to show how you can measure improvements and best use HTTP/2 to your advantage. This chapter has given you a taste of what HTTP/2 can bring to the web, and I hope that it makes you eager to understand how you can deploy it on your website.

Summary

- HTTP/1.1 has some fundamental performance problems, particularly with fetching multiple resources.
- Workarounds exist for these performance problems (multiple connections, sharding, spriting, and so on), but they have their own downsides.
- Performance issues are easy to see in waterfall diagrams that can be generated by tools such as WebPagetest.
- SDPY was designed to address these performance issues.
- HTTP/2 is the standardized version of SPDY.
- Not all performance problems can be solved by HTTP/2.

Upgrading to HTTP/2

This chapter covers

- HTTP/2 support in browsers and servers
- Different options to enable HTTP/2 for your website
- Reverse proxies and CDNs and how they affect HTTP/2
- Troubleshooting why HTTP/2 isn't being used

In the first two chapters, I introduced HTTP and showed where it fits on the web today; then I explained why HTTP/2 was a necessary upgrade that should be faster than HTTP/1 for most sites. Now it's time to get HTTP/2 working on your site so that you can see how much it will benefit you.

3.1 HTTP/2 support

HTTP/2 was formally approved as an internet standard in May 2015, so it's still a relatively recent technology. As with all new technologies, implementers must decide when is the right time to embrace. Implement too soon, and the technology will be considered to be bleeding-edge and risky to implement, as the technology is likely to change considerably and may even be dropped if it turns out to be unsuccessful. Additionally, the ability to use the technology will be hampered by other parties that don't support it, meaning that there's potentially little to gain from being one of the first movers. On the flip side, the first movers prove the technology and pave the way for it to go mainstream.

Luckily, for the most part HTTP/2 doesn't fit into the usual technology cycle, because it was proved in real life in its earlier, nonstandardized incarnation as SPDY (as discussed in chapter 2). At this writing, more than 30% of websites already use HTTP/2, according to w3tech.com.[1] This figure will likely have increased further by the time you read this book. HTTP/2 is already proven and is already in use on many sites. Whether you can use a new web technology on your site comes down to three considerations:

- Do web browsers support the technology?
- Does your infrastructure support it?
- Is a robust fallback available if the technology isn't supported?

On the whole, HTTP/2 fares well in all categories. It has good support in nearly all browser and server software, and a seamless fallback to HTTP/1.1 is available if HTTP/2 isn't supported. A few subtleties and nuances make this seemingly strong support less clear, however.

3.1.1   *HTTP/2 support on the browser side*

HTTP/2 support on the browser side is strong. Nearly every modern browser supports it, as shown by the caniuse.com page for HTTP/2[2] (figure 3.1).

Android was the last major platform to add support in its native browser for the Western world, but the UC browser (which is popular in China, India, Indonesia, and other Asian countries) still doesn't support HTTP/2 at this writing. The Opera Mini browser renders the page server side, so the page is served from Opera's servers and can mostly be ignored for this discussion.

Switching to Usage Relative view, as shown in figure 3.2, changes the size of each box relative to the percentage of users of that version. This figure illustrates the strong use of the UC browser (version 11.8 at this writing), which is the main holdout on HTTP/2 at this time.

Support isn't universal in browsers yet, but is strong, at 83.21% of global browser use at this writing, so it will only improve in time. Additionally, if you're primarily serving users in one country, caniuse.com allows you to see statistics per country to give you even more accurate statistics on your user base (which may not use the UC browser much). These statistics have a few important subtleties, however.

---

[1] https://w3techs.com/technologies/details/ce-http2/all/all
[2] https://caniuse.com/#feat=http2

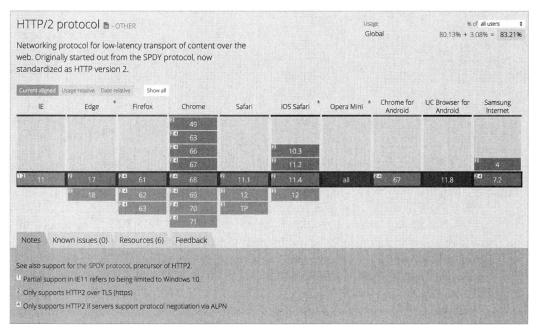

Figure 3.1   caniuse.com page for HTTP/2

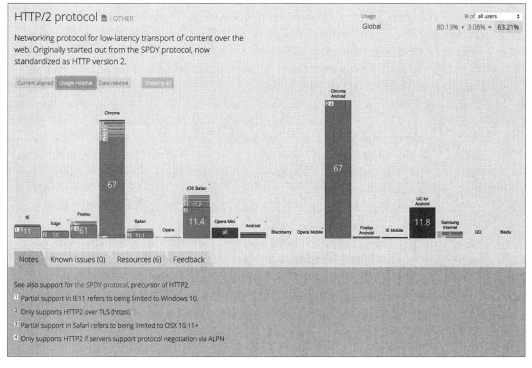

Figure 3.2   caniuse.com Usage Relative page for HTTP/2

HTTP/2 AND HTTPS FOR BROWSERS

The little 2 by each browser that supports HTTP/2 in the preceding figures is explained at the bottom as "Only supports HTTP2 over TLS (https)," so websites that don't use HTTPS can't benefit from HTTP/2. A similar restriction was in place for SPDY, and this restriction was discussed at length when HTTP/2 was standardized, with many parties pushing for HTTPS to be mandated as part of the specification. In the end, this requirement was left out of the formal specification of HTTP/2, but all browser vendors have stated that they'll support only HTTP/2 over HTTPS, making it the de facto standard. Demanding HTTPS will undoubtedly upset owners of HTTP-only sites, but there are two good reasons for this demand.

The first reason is purely practical. Using HTTP/2 only through HTTPS means that it's less likely there will be compatibility issues. Many HTTP-aware pieces of infrastructure on the internet wouldn't know how to handle HTTP/2 messages until they're upgraded. By wrapping the messages in HTTPS, you hide the HTTP messages themselves and therefore prevent compatibility issues. (An HTTPS message can be read only by the receiver, although I discuss the special case of intercepting proxies in the next section.)

The second reason is more ideological in nature. Many browser vendors (and others, including me) strongly believe in moving away from unencrypted HTTP and further believe that all websites should move to HTTPS. Therefore, newer features are often restricted to HTTPS as a form of encouraging that move.

HTTPS adds security, privacy, and integrity to communications with websites. These features are no longer important only for e-commerce sites, where payment details need to be protected, but should be important for *all* sites.[3] Search terms and the pages you're looking at contain personal data that could be sensitive. A sign-up form asking for your email address to register interest is collecting private information, so it should be secured. Although intercepting and altering data may sound unlikely for a blog, for example, data providers such as mobile operators and airplane Wi-Fi operators regularly inject advertisements if users are browsing the internet through them and HTTPS isn't used on the site to prevent this situation. More malicious parties can inject more dangerous content, such as crypto-currency mining JavaScript code or malware.

It will be harder for website owners to avoid HTTPS, and HTTP/2 requiring it is another reason to move to it.

Even if you have HTTPS on your site, you may still run into problems. HTTP/2 requires *strong* HTTPS. The little 4 by some of the browsers (Chrome, Firefox, and Opera) means "Only supports HTTP2 if servers support protocol negotiation via ALPN." I discuss this topic in section 3.1.2, but for now, be aware that *Application Layer Protocol Negotiation (ALPN)* is supported only by newer HTTPS servers and that certain browsers won't use HTTP/2 if ALPN isn't available. Additionally, many browsers

---

[3] https://tools.ietf.org/html/rfc7258

require certain newer, more secure cipher suites before they use HTTP/2.[4] Again, I discuss this topic in section 3.1.2.

INTERCEPTING PROXIES

To be able to use HTTP/2, both the browser and the server must support HTTP/2. If users use a proxy that effectively breaks the HTTP connection in two, however, that might prevent the use of HTTP/2 if the proxy doesn't support HTTP/2.

In many corporate environments, it's common to use a proxy and restrict direct internet access. This allows scanning for threats, and prevents access to certain sites (such as personal email accounts). Similarly, for the home user, many antivirus products create a proxy through which web traffic flows for scanning purposes.

For HTTPS traffic (as required by HTTP/2 for all web browsers, for example), this situation is a problem, as these proxies can't read this encrypted traffic. Therefore, when you use a proxy that needs to read HTTPS traffic, your browser is configured to create one HTTPS connection to the proxy, and the proxy creates a separate HTTPS connection to the real website. So your web browser is making an HTTPS connection only to the proxy and sends a fake HTTPS certificate to the browser, pretending to be the real site. Normally, this condition would be a big warning sign in browsers, as part of the point of HTTPS is to validate the authenticity of the HTTPS certificate issuer. Installing these proxies, however, involves setting up the proxy software as a recognized certificate issuer on that computer, so the web browser will accept these fake certificates.

Splitting the traffic into two parts allows the proxy to read the traffic, but, unfortunately, your browser is no longer connecting directly to the website, so your ability to use HTTP/2 depends on whether the proxy supports HTTP/2. If the proxy doesn't support HTTP/2, it effectively downgrades your connection to HTTP/1.1. In addition to not benefiting from HTTP/2, you may be confused about why the downgrade is happening when both browser and server seem to support HTTP/2 (see section 3.3).

Many people in the security industry think that intercepting proxies cause more problems than they solve, because browser makers generally are strong and proactive about ensuring good HTTPS connections, and breaking this connection in two means that the browser can no longer verify the final connection. Regardless, proxies are being used and need to be considered in trying to understand HTTP/2 support. Studies have shown anywhere from 4% to 9% of internet traffic is being intercepted this way, with 58% of that traffic being intercepted by antivirus software and 35% being intercepted by corporate proxies.[5] The easiest way to see whether the computer you're using is using an intercepting proxy is to view the HTTPS certificate and see whether it was issued by a real certificate authority (there are many, so this may not be obvious) or a local piece of software. Figure 3.3 shows the difference in Internet Explorer when the Avast virus scanner is creating the certificates.

---

[4] https://tools.ietf.org/html/rfc7540#appendix-A
[5] https://jhalderm.com/pub/papers/interception-ndss17.pdf

Certificate issuer

Figure 3.3   Viewing the HTTPS certificate for a direct connection with Google and one that's being intercepted by an antivirus product

On the positive side, intercepting proxies usually are used in home or corporate environments where the connection is typically fast anyway and HTTP/2 is less beneficial. It's much rarer to intercept mobile traffic this way, and low-latency networks (such as mobile) are some of the primary beneficiaries of improvements in HTTP/2.

SUMMARY OF BROWSER SUPPORT OF HTTP/2

As this section has shown, browser support for HTTP/2 is generally strong, and the advent of *evergreen browsers* that automatically update (see the sidebar below) has meant that the rollout of HTTP/2 happened pretty seamlessly on the browser side. There are several reasons why HTTP/2 may not be used, however, including the need for strong HTTPS setup on the server side and the use of intercepting proxies.

The requirement for HTTPS, and especially the strict nature of the type of HTTPS, is an added complication in enabling HTTP/2 and does cause confusion. This complication mostly requires the server to be set up correctly, however, as I discuss in section 3.1.2. The web is moving toward HTTPS, and the penalties for unencrypted HTTP sites will continue to grow, with more visible warnings and fewer features available. At this writing, more than 75% of internet traffic is served over HTTPS.[6] Although that figure is undoubtedly skewed by high use of several large sites, the reality is that if you run a website that doesn't use HTTPS, you should be making plans to move to it as soon as possible.

> ### Evergreen browsers
>
> Browsers such as Chrome and Firefox update silently in the background without prompting the user and are known as *evergreen browsers*. As a result, users of these browsers are likely to be running the latest versions of these browsers, which have HTTP/2 support.
>
> This situation was not always common. Web development history is full of frustrated developers having to detect browser versions and implement hacks if some users were still using Internet Explorer 5 or the like.

---

[6] https://letsencrypt.org/stats/

The picture isn't quite as rosy as it seems, however. Although Chrome, Firefox, and Opera on the desktop do a pretty good job of staying evergreen, the other browsers and platforms don't autoupgrade as seamlessly. Safari upgrades are often linked to the underlying operating system, in particular on mobile devices, and although the rate of uptake of the latest version of iOS is always fast, major upgrades are released only annually, and features such as HTTP/2 usually are part of major upgrades. Android moved to the evergreen Webview Chromium from Android 5 (Lollipop), but often still requires users to choose to install upgrades via the Play Store. Edge is another apparent evergreen browser that doesn't live up to its name, due to being tied to operating-system upgrades,[a] though Microsoft has recently committed to improving this[b].

Finally, some people switch off automatic upgrades. Corporate environments like control of when updates roll out, so many of them switch off automatic updates and then don't make as much time as they should to roll out the upgrades manually.

---

[a] https://www.scirra.com/blog/173/just-how-evergreen-is-microsoft-edge
[b] https://blogs.windows.com/windowsexperience/2018/12/06/microsoft-edge-making-the-web-better-through-more-open-source-collaboration/

3.1.2 HTTP/2 support for servers

Server support of HTTP/2 has lagged behind browser support, but now nearly all servers have added support. The HTTP/2 GitHub site has a page tracking HTTP/2 implementations on both the client and the server side,[7] which allows a quick check of which servers support HTTP/2. According to Netcraft,[8] the four most popular web servers, which account for more than 80% of active internet sites, use Apache, nginx, Google, or Microsoft IIS, all of which support HTTP/2.

The problem on the server side lies not in whether the latest version of server software supports HTTP/2, but in whether that support is in the version that websites are running. Most implementations don't update automatically or as easily as browsers do, so servers are often running older versions from before HTTP/2 support was added. Often, the version is tied to the operating system (Microsoft IIS support was added only in IIS 10.0 and Windows Server 2016, for example) or to that operating system's package manager (such as `yum` for Red Hat/CentOS/Fedora, which hasn't installed a version of Apache or nginx with HTTP/2 support at this writing).

Although it's often possible to upgrade the version of your server software, the process may be complicated. On Linux-based systems, upgrading may involve downloading source code and compiling it, which requires some level of skill and understanding, as well as an ongoing commitment to keep the software up-to-date or at least to apply security patches. The benefit of letting the operating system or package manager handle this process is that staying on top of security issues becomes a simple matter of running updates periodically (or even automatically). By stepping outside that process,

---

[7] https://github.com/http2/http2-spec/wiki/Implementations
[8] https://news.netcraft.com/archives/category/web-server-survey/

you take on more work or introduce more risk, or both. Depending on your operating system, it may be possible to use a third-party repository (repo) that provides HTTP/2 versions of the software, but then you're trusting that third party rather than the official repos.

HTTPS LIBRARIES AND SUPPORT

One of the biggest issues on the server side, particularly on the Linux side, is the strict HTTPS requirements that I mentioned earlier in this chapter. Most web servers delegate the SSL/TLS intricacies needed for HTTPS to a separate library—usually OpenSSL, although variants exist, including LibreSSL and BoringSSL. This cryptographic library is often part of the operating system, and although upgrading the web server can be tricky, upgrading the SSL/TLS libraries is often even more difficult, because it potentially affects all other software on the server.

In section 3.1.1, you saw that Chrome and Opera support HTTP/2 only over the ALPN extension to SSL/TLS rather than the older NPN (Next Protocol Negotiation) extension. ALPN, like NPN before it, allows the web server to state which application protocols the server supports as part of the HTTPS negotiation; I look at this topic in more detail in chapter 4. The problem is that ALPN support is included only in recent versions of OpenSSL (1.0.2 and later) and isn't available as part of standard builds on many platforms. RedHat and CentOS added support for OpenSSL 1.0.2 only in August and September 2017, respectively, but the packaged versions of web-server software such as Apache are often compiled against the older 1.0.1 version, which doesn't support ALPN, so doesn't allow HTTP/2 for Chrome and Opera. Similarly, Ubuntu added OpenSSL support in version 16, not in the widely used version 14, and Debian didn't add OpenSSL with ALPN support until version 9 (Stretch). Even if there is a modern OpenSSL and the web server is compiled against it, the HTTP/2 code may not be included by default, as summarized in table 3.1.

Table 3.1 ALPN support in various Linux operating systems

Operating system and version	ALPN in default OpenSSL	ALPN in default Apache/nginx	HTTP/2 in default Apache/nginx
RHEL/CentOS < 7.4	N (1.0.1)	N	N
RHEL/CentOS 7.4 & 7.5	Y (1.0.2)	N/Y	N/Y
Ubuntu 14.04 LTS	N (1.0.1)	N	N
Ubuntu 16.04 LTS	Y (1.0.2)	Y	N/Y
Ubuntu 18.04 LTS	Y (1.1.0)	Y	Y
Debian 7 ("Wheezy")	N (1.0.1)	N	N
Debian 8 ("Jessie")	N (1.0.1)	N	N
Debian 9 ("Stretch")	Y (1.1.0)	Y	Y

As you can see in table 3.1, of the common Linux distributions, only Ubuntu 18.04 and Debian 9 give you HTTP/2 out of the box for Apache (though it needs to be turned on during web-server configuration). For RHEL/CentOS, Apache needs to be installed from source or from another nondefault repo if you want to use HTTP/2.

For nginx, HTTP/2 can be installed via the nginx repo,[9] so HTTP/2 is usually configured for nginx as long as you're using the latest version, but it still depends on the underlying OpenSSL version.

SUMMARY OF SERVER SUPPORT

Although server-side support of HTTP/2 is theoretically as good as browser-side support, the reality is that for some time, most people will be running older versions of server software that don't support HTTP/2. These versions need to be upgraded to support HTTP/2, and the upgrades may be simple or complicated. This situation will change as newer versions of operating systems become the norm, but it's a challenge to HTTP/2 adoption. The good news is that upgrading should be in the control of website owners, who can take on the hassle of upgrading their software to HTTP/2 on the server side, and when they do, they can assume that most client-side software will support it. If support on the server side were strong and support on the client side were relatively weak, website owners could do little but wait until their users upgraded. Should you not want to or be able to upgrade your web-server software, other implementations are possible, as I discuss in section 3.2.

3.1.3 *Fallback when HTTP/2 isn't supported*

The other good news is that when HTTP/2 isn't supported, websites still work, as they fall back to using HTTP/1.1. HTTP/1.1 is a long way from being disabled (if it ever is). In theory, there are no real downsides to enabling HTTP/2 if you can, in terms of supportability.

The situation becomes interesting, however, when you want to start taking advantage of HTTP/2 features and changing your website, which may disadvantage HTTP/1.1 users. The site will still work, but it may be slower if you don't shard, combine, and inline assets. How much of an issue this situation is for you depends on the amount of HTTP/1.1 traffic you have. I return to this topic in chapter 6.

More difficult to measure are implementation issues on the client or server side. HTTP/2 is still relatively young, and despite being actively used in real life, it's still in the early stages of adoption. Undoubtedly, bugs will be found in implementations that may affect the loading of your website over HTTP/2. In my experience so far, these bugs usually result in HTTP/2's not being as fast as you expect rather than causing any real harm. But you should test any major upgrade (such as HTTP/2) thoroughly before switching it on for your production website.

---

[9] http://nginx.org/en/download.html

3.2 Ways to enable HTTP/2 for your website

The most obvious way to move to HTTP/2 is to enable HTTP/2 on your web server, but this process may require an upgrade. Enabling HTTP/2 on your web server isn't the only way to enable it, however, and you may want to consider other options. These options involve adding an infrastructure in front of your web server: another piece of software or a service such as a content delivery network (CDN) to handle the HTTP/2 part of the connection. Which method is right for you depends on several factors, including whether your web server supports HTTP/2, how difficult it is to turn on HTTP/2 support, and whether you want to complicate your environment by implementing some of the other options.

After you enable HTTP/2, you may notice that your traffic is still using HTTP/1.1, so in section 3.3, I discuss troubleshooting. Skip to that section if you've already implemented HTTP/2 but are struggling to get HTTP/2 working in your environment.

3.2.1 HTTP/2 on your web server

Enabling HTTP/2 on your web server allows HTTP/2-aware clients to use this new protocol. Figure 3.4 shows this simple setup.

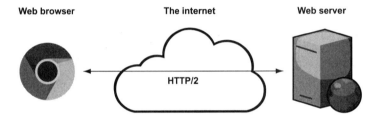

Web browser   **The internet**   **Web server**

HTTP/2

Figure 3.4   HTTP/2 on your web server

The main issue with this option is that it may not be readily available to you. As discussed in section 3.1.2, you may have to upgrade your web server to a new version, which may require upgrading the operating system of the server on which your web server runs. Or perhaps your web server software doesn't support HTTP/2 even in the latest version. Table 3.2 shows the versions of some common web and application servers in which HTTP/2 support was added.

Table 3.2   When HTTP/2 support was added to popular web servers

Web server	Version HTTP/2 added
Apache HTTPD	2.4.17 (though marked as experimental until 2.4.26)
IIS	10.0
Jetty	9.3
Netty	4.1

Table 3.2   When HTTP/2 support was added to popular web servers *(continued)*

Web server	Version HTTP/2 added
nginx	1.9.5
Node.JS	8.4.0 (though not enabled by default until 9.0 and still marked as experimental until 10.10)
Tomcat	8.5

Linux software typically is installed through package managers (such as yum and apt-get) with a set of official software repos, which allows ease of installation and patching. Many of these environments prioritize stability over new features, and with HTTP/2 being relatively new (at least in server release terms), the default versions of the web servers often don't include HTTP/2 support. If your operating system doesn't provide a straightforward way of enabling HTTP/2 on your preferred web server (many do not), and you want to enable new features such as HTTP/2 on your server, you're left with little choice but to install applications from alternative locations. This decision isn't without risk, and you should understand the consequences before venturing down this path (see the sidebar below).

Risks of installing applications from alternative locations

Installing from an alternative location means downloading a prepackaged version of your web server directly from another site, adding a repository from which the package manager can download the package, or installing from source code.

Downloading a prebuilt package from a third party means that you're trusting this provider of your software for a key part of your infrastructure and one that runs as root (as web servers usually do). Additionally, many of these packages statically compile against a version of OpenSSL, so if a vulnerability is discovered in OpenSSL, you need to update your web server to include any fix. Many companies aren't comfortable with either of these restrictions. If you're comfortable with using a third party's prebuilt package, CodeIt[a] is a site that provides a repo with prebuilt packages of Apache and nginx and gives good instructions on how to install them.

Another alternative is to run your web server in a container such as Docker. Images of containers with complied versions of common web servers are available. You have the same issue of putting your trust in the provider of that container, but you run the application in its own container, which may have restricted access to the rest of the server. As container software is a topic in itself, I don't discuss it further in this book.

Those who prefer not to trust a third party can install the software from the original source code. The source code should be downloaded from a reputable source (ideally, the original vendor) and verified after download, either by checking the download against a signature or by calculating and checking a hash of the download.

Even if you're installing from the vendor's official site, you're managing this software outside the package manager tools, so you won't benefit from security patches that

Risks of installing applications from alternative locations (continued)

the package manager makes easy to install; you need to take on the responsibility of upgrading manually yourself. RHEL 7 and CentOS 7, for example, supply Apache 2.4.6 in the standard repo. This version is not the original Apache 2.4.6, however; it's continually patched by Red Hat to include all the relevant security updates since that version. By running a version outside a package manager, you won't get these security patches and need to upgrade the software yourself to get any security fixes; otherwise, you risk running insecure software that's vulnerable to attack.

Yet another option is to use an alternative semiofficial repo. Many operating system vendors provide an alternative software collection repo (such as Red Hat Software Collections), or the vendor may supply an official repo (as nginx does). The advantages are ease of installation and continued ease of patching.

Ultimately, you need to decide which method you're most comfortable with when it comes to installing third-party software on your servers.

---
[a]   https://codeit.guru/en_US/

The appendix provides instructions on installing and upgrading some common web servers and platforms to enable HTTP/2 support. Depending on your operating system and web server users, this process can be quite complicated. As time goes by, this process will become easier as the default installations are upgraded to versions that have HTTP/2 support; then enabling HTTP/2 support should involve a simple configuration change, or the protocol may be enabled by default. For the next few years, however, many people will struggle to enable HTTP/2 support in their web-server software.

Other options are available, however, as you'll see in the next two sections. In certain setups, with a load balancer in front of your web server, for example, enabling HTTP/2 on your web server may not provide HTTP/2 to your users if the load balancer itself doesn't support HTTP/2.

If you're looking to set up a simple web server to experiment with HTTP/2 and perhaps to follow some of the examples in this book, I recommend that you choose the web server you're most comfortable with. If you have no particular preference, Apache is the most fully featured of the popular web servers due to its availability on many platforms and also to its support of HTTP/2 push and HTTP/2 proxy (both of which I cover later in this book).

3.2.2   *HTTP/2 with a reverse proxy*

Another option for implementing HTTP/2 is putting a reverse proxy server in front of your main web server that does speak HTTP/2; then it can translate requests in HTTP/1.1 and proxy them to your existing web server, as shown in figure 3.5.

Reverse proxies, as the name suggests, do the opposite of standard intercepting proxies. A standard proxy shields the network from the outside world and provides a

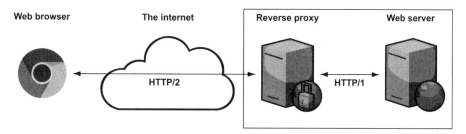

Figure 3.5   Implementing HTTP/2 with a reverse proxy

path for outbound traffic that needs to talk to the internet. A reverse proxy handles incoming traffic from the internet, allowing access to servers that aren't directly available to the outside world. Reverse proxies are already common and are used primarily for one of two reasons:

- To act as a *load balancer*
- To offload functionality such as HTTPS or HTTP/2

A *load* balancer sits in front of at least two web servers and sends traffic to either web server, depending how it's configured (live-live or live-standby). Live-live load balancers use an algorithm to decide how to split the traffic (based on the source IP address or by round robin, for example). This setup is shown in figure 3.6.

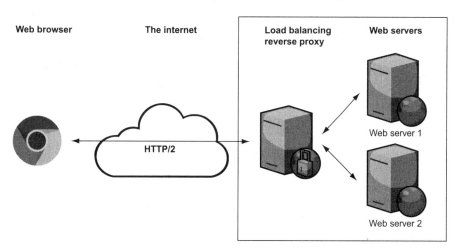

Figure 3.6   Load-balancing reverse proxy

If you already have this setup, it may be possible to enable HTTP/2 on the *load balancer* and not have to enable it on your web servers at all. In fact, as I've already mentioned, enabling HTTP/2 on the web server may have no effect if all traffic speaks to the *load balancer* as the first point of contact. Some of the load-balancer products (such as F5, Citrix Netscaler, and HAProxy) already support HTTP/2, and those that don't are expected to add support soon.

Do you need to speak HTTP/2 all the way through?

When you implement HTTP/2 on the reverse proxy, the HTTP/2 connection is terminated at the reverse proxy, and from then on, a separate connection (possibly using HTTP/1.1) is used. This process is similar to terminating HTTPS at a reverse proxy and then talking HTTP to the rest of your infrastructure, which is a common use case to ease the configuration of HTTPS (certificates need to be set up and managed only at the entry point) and because of the resources HTTPS required in the past (though these requirements are negligible nowadays with the increase in compute power).

So do you need to speak HTTP/2 all the way through, and what do you lose by making backend connections over HTTP/1.1?

The primary benefit of HTTP/2 is the speed improvements over high-latency, low-bandwidth connections, such as end users to your edge server (reverse proxy in this case). Traffic from your reverse proxy to the rest of your web infrastructure will likely have to travel short distances (often to the same data center, if not the same machine) over low-latency, high-bandwidth network links, so the performance problems of HTTP/1.1 are often less of an issue.

The use of a single connection for HTTP/2 traffic is also less of a benefit from reverse proxies to real servers because they're not limited to the six connections that browsers set. There's even some concern that using a single connection may cause performance issues, depending on how this connection is implemented on the reverse proxy and the destination server. nginx has stated that it will not implement HTTP/2 for proxy pass connections partly for this reason.[a]

Therefore, as with HTTPS, there's potentially no need to talk HTTP/2 all the way through your infrastructure for basic HTTP/2 support. Even HTTP/2-only features such as HTTP/2 push can still be implemented over this setup, as I discuss in chapter 5.

---

[a] http://mailman.nginx.org/pipermail/nginx/2015-December/049445.html

---

Even without using a reverse proxy for a *load balancer*, it's quite common (and, in my opinion, recommended) to have a web server such as Apache or nginx in front of backend application servers such as Tomcat or Node.js and for the web server to proxy pass some (or all) of the requests to the backend server, as shown in figure 3.7.

This technique has several advantages, the main one being that you offload functionality and load to the web server, such as serving static assets (images, CSS files, JavaScript libraries, and so on) from the web server, offloading HTTPS, and—yes—offloading HTTP/2. By lightening the load for the application server, you allow it to concentrate on what it does best: serving dynamic assets that take a bit of processing and possibly database lookups to decide what to return.

This option also has security benefits, as the first point of contact is the web server, which may be able to prevent bad requests from reaching the more delicate application

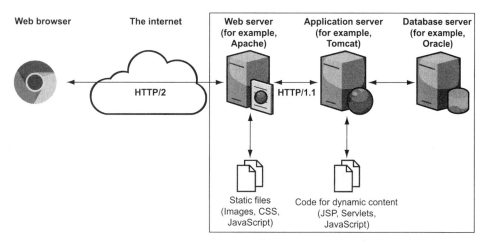

Figure 3.7 Web server in front of application server/database server

server and definitely any backend database. Therefore, if you're using an application server on which it's difficult to enable HTTP/2, it may be possible (and even recommended) to get HTTP/2 support by placing another web server that supports HTTP/2 in front of it.

A reverse proxy can also be an effective way of testing HTTP/2 and its effect on your website. Simply host a reverse proxy close to your server under a different server name (http2.example.com or test.example.com) and proxy requests back to the main web server, using HTTP/1.1 over the fast local connection, as shown in figure 3.8.

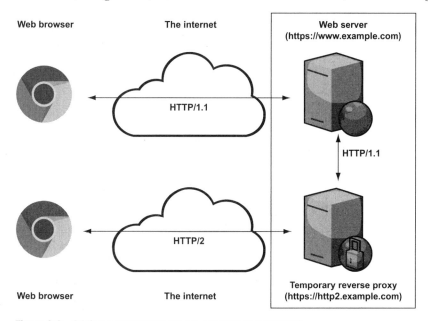

Figure 3.8 Adding a temporary reverse proxy to test HTTP/2

You may not need a separate proxy server if your web server already supports HTTP/2 but you haven't switched it on yet. By setting up a virtual host with HTTP/2 enabled and a separate hostname, you can have both HTTP/1.1 and HTTP/2 sites running; therefore, you can test HTTP/2 before enabling it on the main virtual host that your visitors are using.

3.2.3   *HTTP/2 through a CDN*

A CDN is a series of servers spread around the world that act as a local point of contact for your website. Visitors to your website connect to the nearest CDN server by having different DNS entries globally. Requests are routed back to your web server (called the *origin server*), and a copy may be cached in the CDN to allow for quicker serving the next time an identical request comes in. Most CDNs already support HTTP/2, so you can switch on HTTP/2 by using a CDN and leaving your origin server on HTTP/1.1. This method is similar to the reverse proxy method except that CDNs have many reverse proxies and manage this infrastructure for you. This setup is shown in figure 3.9.

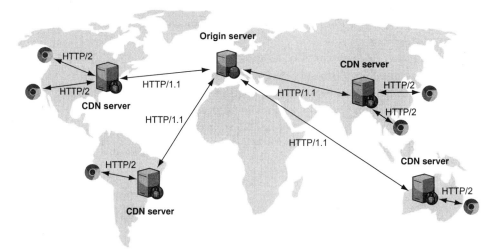

Figure 3.9   Enabling HTTP/2 through a CDN

Despite adding extra infrastructure to your setup, using a CDN may be considerably faster than connecting directly, because the local server can handle some of the connection setup requests for the client (such as the initial TCP connection and HTTPS negotiation). The benefit of having these client setup requests handled by a server closer to the users outweighs the negatives of having an additional server hop involved in the requests. Also, responses can be cached at each CDN server so that additional requests are served directly by the local server and not by the origin server, saving time for the user and load and bandwidth for the origin server.

CDNs are supercharged reverse proxies. CDNs were used primarily for performance reasons before HTTP/2 came along, but now they also offer an easy upgrade option for HTTP/2.

A CDN can handle the HTTPS requirements necessary for HTTP/2. But if HTTPS isn't implemented at the origin server, web traffic will be encrypted only for some of its journey across the internet. Although many of the reasons to use HTTPS are to mitigate risks at the client side (connecting to an unknown Wi-Fi network, for example, involves risks that only HTTPS can mitigate), it's still preferred to use HTTPS for the full end-to-end connection. Many people say that it's disingenuous to offload HTTPS at a CDN while talking HTTP for the rest of the journey through the internet, because your website visitors won't know that their passwords are potentially traveling across the website unsecured. But if it isn't easy to get the strict HTTPS setup required for HTTP/2 on your server (such as ALPN support), at least you can let the CDN handle this process and revert to an older HTTPS configuration over HTTP/1.1 for the connection to the origin server.

CDNs offer many benefits, and ease of HTTP/2 support is yet another reason to consider using them. CDNs were quick to implement HTTP/2, and some even offer a free tier that provides an easy route to HTTP/2 for smaller sites. The CDN will be able to unencrypt the traffic, however, so you must be comfortable with such a third party having access to your traffic.

3.2.4 *Implementing HTTP/2 summary*

You have several ways to enable HTTP/2 for your website, depending on what infrastructure you use to serve your web traffic. Unfortunately, the most obvious method of implementing HTTP/2 on your web server is currently difficult and can require a lot of manual effort for older versions. This situation will improve as the technology becomes more common and as server software gets upgraded, but for the moment, the process is far more painful than it should be.

Other options exist for adding HTTP/2 support, and website owners looking to implement HTTP/2 should be aware of them. Reverse proxies can be owned and managed on site or as a service, such as by using a CDN. These methods can be simple ways to implement HTTP/2 until server-side support becomes widespread in common server distributions.

At this point, you should be able to choose the best upgrade option to HTTP/2 for your website and start experimenting to see what difference it makes on your website. The rest of this book will make more sense if you have an HTTP/2-enabled server to try the examples on, though some items can be shown with public websites.

3.3 *Troubleshooting HTTP/2 setup*

The easiest way to see whether HTTP/2 is being used is to look at the developer tools in your browser. Even though HTTP/2 is seemingly enabled on the web server, many people struggle to get HTTP/2 working due to some of the many subtleties mentioned throughout this chapter. Following are some of the common reasons I've seen since getting involved with HTTP/2:

- *HTTP/2 isn't supported on your web server.* Obviously, your server needs to support HTTP/2. As discussed in this chapter, most of the default installations on servers currently don't support HTTP/2. Check what version of your server software you're running and when HTTP/2 support was added. Please note that installing the latest updates (such as with `yum update` or `apt-get`) alone won't necessarily update your web server to a version that supports HTTP/2.

- *HTTP/2 isn't enabled on your web server.* Even if your web server supports HTTP/2, it may not be enabled. Some servers (such as IIS) enable HTTP/2 support by default. On other servers (such as Apache), HTTP support depends on the configuration or build you use. ApacheHaus Windows builds enable HTTP/2 by default, for example, but installing from source doesn't enable it by default. Additionally, since version 2.4.27, Apache no longer supports HTTP/2 when using the `prefork` mpm.[10]

  Also, some compile options (such as `--enable-http2` for Apache and `--with-http_v2_module` for nginx) are needed to allow HTTP/2 to be switched on, but don't switch it on by default. If HTTP/2 isn't working, check the documentation for your web server to see how to turn it on.

- *HTTPS isn't enabled on your web server.* As discussed in section 3.1.1, web browsers support HTTP/2 only over HTTPS, so if your site is HTTP-only and not HTTPS, you won't be able to use HTTP/2 from browsers until you switch your site to HTTPS.

- *ALPN support isn't enabled on your web server.* ALPN is an extension to the TLS protocol used to create the HTTPS session, which allows the server to advertise that it supports HTTP/2. Some web browsers (Safari, Edge, and Internet Explorer at this writing) allow you to use HTTP/2 over the older NPN as well as the newer ALPN method. Other browsers (such as Chrome, Firefox, and Opera) use only the newer ALPN method.

  The easiest way to test ALPN support is to use an online tool such as SSL-Labs[11] (which runs a comprehensive test for HTTPS setup but takes a few minutes to run) or KeyCDN HTTP/2 Test[12] (which is quicker, as it tests only for HTTP/2 and ALPN support). If your web server isn't publicly accessible, you can't use a web tool to test for this support and must use a command-line tool such as OpenSSL's s_client (assuming that your version of OpenSSL supports ALPN):

```
openssl s_client -alpn h2 -connect www.example.com:443 -status
```

---

[10] https://github.com/icing/mod_h2/releases/tag/v1.10.7
[11] https://www.ssllabs.com/ssltest/
[12] https://tools.keycdn.com/http2-test

Alternatively, download the testssl tool,[13] which performs most of the same tests as SSLLabs. But it requires a version of OpenSSL that supports ALPN to fully test for HTTP/2 support.

Similar to the web browsers, some web servers (such as Apache) use only ALPN; others (such as nginx) use ALPN or NPN. Whether your server supports ALPN depends on the version of the TLS library you're using. Table 3.3 shows ALPN support in common libraries. If you're unsure what TLS library you're using, it's likely that you're on OpenSSL for Linux, LibreSSL for macOS, or SChannel for Windows.

Table 3.3 **ALPN support in common TLS libraries**

TLS library	Version that added ALPN support
OpenSSL	1.0.2
LibreSSL	2.5.0
SChannel (used by Microsoft applications)	8.1 / 2012 R2
GnuTLS	3.2.0

Even if your TLS library supports ALPN, your server software may not have been built with that version of the TLS library. RHEL/CentOS 7.4 added OpenSSL 1.0.2, for example, but the versions of Apache and nginx installed by default are still built with OpenSSL 1.0.1, so they don't have ALPN support.

Apache normally adds a line to the error log on restart, detailing the OpenSSL version it's running with:

```
[mpm_worker:notice] [pid 19678:tid 140217081968512] AH00292:
Apache/2.4.27 (Unix) OpenSSL/1.0.2k-fips configured -- resuming normal
operations
```

Alternatively, you can run ldd against the mod_ssl module and see what version it links against:

```
$ ldd /usr/local/apache2/modules/mod_ssl.so | grep libssl
        libssl.so.10 => /lib64/libssl.so.10 (0x00007f185b829000)
$ ls -la /lib64/libssl.so.10
lrwxrwxrwx. 1 root root 16 Oct 15 16:07 /lib64/libssl.so.10 ->
libssl.so.1.0.2k
```

For nginx, you can use the -V option to show the build:

```
$ nginx -V
nginx version: nginx/1.13.6
built by gcc 4.8.5 20150623 (Red Hat 4.8.5-16) (GCC)
```

---

[13] https://testssl.sh/

```
built with OpenSSL 1.0.2k-fips  26 Jan 2017
TLS SNI support enabled
configure arguments: --with-http_ssl_module --with-http_v2_module
```

For other servers, refer to your support documentation.

- *Strong HTTPS ciphers aren't enabled on your web server.* The HTTP/2 specification lists several ciphers that a client must not use for an HTTP/2 connection.[14] Some browsers (such as Chrome) don't use HTTP/2 with these ciphers, so your server must be set up with better ciphers if you want to use HTTP/2 (which at this writing means using ECDHE GCM or POLY ciphers). Most default installations include stronger ciphers that usually are used in preference to weaker ciphers, but if you ported old cipher configurations from a previous installation, these ciphers may not be enabled.

  To check out your HTTPS cipher setup, use the SSLLabs online testing tool. This tool can be complicated to understand initially but gives you complete information on your HTTPS setup, including whether HTTP/2 is supported for common clients.

  The Mozilla SSL Configuration Generator[15] is also a useful tool for providing the HTTPS config necessary for common web browsers. Most sites should use the Modern settings, though you may need to use the Intermediate settings if you need to support older clients.

- *An intercepting proxy is being used and downgrading you to HTTP/1.1.* If you're using a proxy (in a corporate environment, for example) or antivirus software, these elements may be downgrading your connection to HTTP/1.1 as they intercept the HTTPS connection. I discuss this topic in section 3.1.1. Look at the HTTPS certificate for the website to see whether it was issued by a real certificate authority.

  If your website is public-facing, you can use online tools such as SSLLabs or KeyCDN HTTP/2 Test[16] to see whether your website supports HTTP/2. If so, the problem may be a local issue for you, possibly caused by an intercepting proxy.

  For virus software, it's usually possible to turn off HTTPS interception or to whitelist certain websites.

- *An upgrade header was incorrectly forwarded.* A backend server (such as Apache) may use an Upgrade: h2 header to suggest switching to HTTP/2. If that header is blindly forwarded by a reverse proxy, even though it doesn't understand HTTP/2, this header can cause problems. The browser tries to upgrade to HTTP/2 (as the header suggests that it should) and fails because the reverse proxy doesn't understand HTTP/2. The reverse proxy shouldn't forward the

---

[14] https://httpwg.org/specs/rfc7540.html#BadCipherSuites
[15] https://mozilla.github.io/server-side-tls/ssl-config-generator/
[16] https://tools.keycdn.com/http2-test

Upgrade header in such a case. I discuss this topic further in chapter 4. Safari handles this situation particularly badly, often with a nsposixerrordomain:100 error.

- *HTTPS headers are invalid.* Chrome returns an ERR_SPDY_PROTOCOL_ERROR message for invalid HTTP headers (such as spaces in the header name or double colons),[17] even though it's more forgiving of identical errors in HTTP/1.1. Safari can return a nsposixerrordomain:100 error for the same reason.
- *Cached items report the original download protocol.* If you upgrade your server to HTTP/2 and try to test it, you may still be using the cached resources if you don't clear the cache first. The cached items show the HTTP version that was originally used to download the request (which may be HTTP/1.1 if they were downloaded before the upgrade). Similarly, if the server sends a 304 Not Modified response, the browser uses the cached resource and displays whatever protocol was used to download it.

Summary

- HTTP/2 support on the client side is strong, with nearly all major browsers supporting it.
- HTTP/2 support on the server side is available in newer versions, but, often, these versions aren't easy to install without a full server upgrade and/or manual installation.
- Various options to enable HTTP/2 are available, including using third-party infrastructure such as CDNs to provide this support.
- There are several reasons why HTTP/2 may not be used even after it has been enabled.

---

[17] https://www.michalspacek.com/chrome-err_spdy_protocol_error-and-an-invalid-http-header

Part 2

Using HTTP/2

In the first part of the book, I covered the need and motivation for a new version of HTTP, introduced HTTP/2, and described the ways to set up HTTP/2 for your website. For many people, this information is sufficient, and most sites should start seeing the benefits of upgrading to HTTP/2 even without making any other changes. HTTP/2 was designed to be easy to migrate to and to give most sites immediate benefits without requiring any changes.

To truly benefit from all that HTTP/2 has to offer, however, it's useful to have a deeper understanding of the protocol and how it works. This part of the book describes the core aspects of this protocol. Chapters 4 and 5 cover the technical details of the protocol that allow website owners and developers to make the most of HTTP/2. Chapter 6 takes a break from the protocol itself to discuss what it means for web performance and what practices developers should change to optimize for this new HTTP/2 world.

HTTP/2 protocol basics

This chapter covers

- The basics of HTTP/2: what it is and how it differs from HTTP/1.1
- How client and server agree to use HTTP/2 instead of HTTP/1.1
- HTTP/2 frames and how to debug them

This chapter covers the basics of HTTP/2 (frames, streams, and multiplexing). I discuss more advanced parts of the protocol (in particular, stream prioritization and flow control) in chapters 7 and 8. The HTTP/2 specification[1] is the ultimate reference point for the protocol and can be referred to after or in conjunction with this chapter, but the added detail and examples in this chapter will (I hope) make learning the protocol easier.

---

[1] https://tools.ietf.org/html/rfc7540

4.1   *Why HTTP/2 instead of HTTP/1.2?*

I touched on the differences between HTTP/1 and HTTP/2 in chapter 2. HTTP/2 was created specifically to address performance problems in HTTP/1, and the new version of the protocol differs by adding the following concepts:

- Binary rather than textual protocol
- Multiplexed rather than synchronous
- Flow control
- Stream prioritization
- Header compression
- Server push

These concepts (described in more detail in this chapter) are fundamental, breaking changes to the protocol in that they aren't backward-compatible; although an HTTP/1.0 web server could understand HTTP/1.1 messages and ignore the extra functionality that the later version introduced, this isn't true for HTTP/2 messages, which have a different structure and format. For this reason, HTTP/2 was viewed as being a major version upgrade.

Most of these differences deal with how HTTP/2 is sent on the wire between client and server. At a higher level than most web developers will deal with (the HTTP semantics),[2] HTTP/2 acts a lot like HTTP/1. It has the same methods (GET, POST, PUT, and so on); it uses the same URLs, the same response status codes (200, 404, 301, 302), and the same HTTP headers (mostly). HTTP/2 is a more efficient way to make those same HTTP requests.

In many ways, HTTP/2 is like HTTPS in that it effectively wraps standard HTTP messages in a special format before sending and unwraps them after receiving. Therefore, although the client (web browser) and server (web server) need to know the exact details to send messages back and forth, higher-level applications don't need to treat these versions too differently, because the underlying concepts of HTTP that they use are similar. Unlike HTTPS, however, HTTP/2 should lead to different ways of developing websites. In the same way that a strong understanding of HTTP/1 led to the web optimizations discussed in chapter 2, a strong understanding of HTTP/2 leads to different optimizations that can make web developers better and help make websites faster. Therefore, it's important to understand these core differences.

> **HTTP/2.0 or HTTP/2?**
> HTTP/2 was originally called HTTP/2.0, but the HTTP Working Group decided to drop the minor version number (.0) and use HTTP/2 instead. HTTP/2 defines the major parts of this new version of HTTP as I mentioned earlier (binary, multiplexed, and so

---

[2] https://tools.ietf.org/html/draft-ietf-httpbis-semantics

on), and any future implementation or change (such as HTTP/2.1) will be expected to be compatible. The same thing happened with HTTP/1 (a term that never caught on but that I use throughout this book to mean HTTP/1.0 and HTTP/1.1), which was a text-based protocol with headers followed by bodies.

Additionally, unlike in HTTP/1 messages, the version number isn't explicitly stated in the request. There's no GET /index.html HTTP/1.1-style request in HTTP/2, for example. Many implementations use the minor version in log files, however. In Apache log files, for example, the version number is shown as HTTP/2.0, and the files even dummy up an HTTP/1-style request:

```
78.1.23.123 - - [14/Jan/2018:15:04:45 +0000] 2 "GET / HTTP/2.0" 200 1797
"-" "Mozilla/5.0 (Windows NT 10.0; Win64; x64) AppleWebKit/537.36
(KHTML, like Gecko) Chrome/63.0.3239.132 Safari/537.36"
```

Therefore, you see HTTP/1-type messages in the logs despite my earlier statement to the contrary. This request, however, isn't a real request and is mocked up by the web server for ease of parsing log messages rather than something sent directly by the protocol. In fact, HTTP/2.0 is referenced in only one place in the specification: the preface message (discussed in section 4.2.5).

4.1.1 Binary rather than textual

One of the main differences between HTTP/1 and HTTP/2 is that HTTP/2 is a binary, packet-based protocol, whereas HTTP/1 is entirely text-based. Text-based protocols are easy for humans to understand but more difficult for computers to parse. This situation was acceptable for the simple request-and-response protocol that HTTP started out as, but is increasingly limiting the use of the protocol for the modern internet.

With the text-based protocol, requests need to be sent and responses received in full before another request can be processed. On the whole, HTTP worked this way for the past 20 years, though small enhancements were made. HTTP/1.0 introduced binary HTTP bodies, for example, where images and other media could be sent in response, and HTTP/1.1 introduced pipelining (see chapter 2) and chunked encoding. Chunked encoding allowed part of the message body to be sent first, with the rest to follow as it became available. The HTTP body is split into chunks, and the client receiving the chunked response (or the server receiving the chunked request) could start processing the message before it was fully received. This technique is often used when the length of data that's generated dynamically isn't known in advance. Both chunked encoding and pipelining have head-of-line (HOL) blocking issues whereby the message at the top of the queue prevents subsequent responses from being sent, not to mention the fact that pipelining was not well supported in the real world.

HTTP/2 moves to a full binary protocol, in which HTTP messages are split and sent in clearly defined frames. All HTTP/2 messages effectively use chunked encoding as standard, and this doesn't need to be set explicitly. In fact, the HTTP/2 specification states

> *The chunked transfer encoding defined in Section 4.1 of RFC7230 MUST NOT be used in HTTP/2.*

These frames are similar to the TCP packets that underlie most HTTP connections. When all the frames are received, the full HTTP message can be reconstructed. Despite being like TCP in many ways, HTTP/2 is still usually layered on top of TCP rather than replacing it (though Google is experimenting with replacing TCP with QUIC and having a lighter implementation of HTTP/2 over it, as I discuss in chapter 9). An underlying protocol such as TCP is used to guarantee that the messages arrive, and in order, without needing to add such handling to the HTTP/2 protocol.

The binary representation of HTTP/2 is for the sending and receiving of messages, but the messages themselves are similar to older HTTP/1 messages. The binary framing usually is handled by the lower-level client or libraries (web browser or web server). As mentioned earlier, higher-level applications such as JavaScript applications need not care how the messages are sent, and can, for the most part, treat an HTTP/2 connection exactly like an HTTP/1.1 connection. It can be helpful, however, to understand and even view HTTP/2 frames to debug unexpected errors—particularly relevant during this early stage of adoption, when you may need to debug implementation issues in certain (I hope rare!) scenarios.

4.1.2   *Multiplexed rather than synchronous*

HTTP/1 was a synchronous, single request-and-response protocol. The client sent an HTTP/1 message, and the server got an HTTP/1 response back. Chapter 2 discusses why this protocol was inefficient, especially given the modern World Wide Web, where a website is often made up of hundreds of resources. The main workarounds in HTTP/1 were to open multiple connections or to send fewer large requests instead of many small requests, but both workarounds introduce their own problems and inefficiencies. Figure 4.1 shows how three TCP connections can be used to send and receive three HTTP/1 requests in parallel. Note that request 1 for the initial page isn't shown, because only after this initial request do multiple resources need to be requested in parallel in requests 2–4.

HTTP/2 allows multiple requests to be in progress at the same time, on a single connection, using different streams for each HTTP request or response. This concept of multiple independent requests happening at the same time was made possible by moving to the binary framing layer, where each frame has a stream identifier. The receiving party can reconstruct the full message when all frames for that stream have been received.

Frames are the key to allowing multiple messages to be sent at the same time. Each frame is labeled to indicate which message it belongs to (the stream), which allows two, three, or a hundred messages to be sent or received at the same time on the same

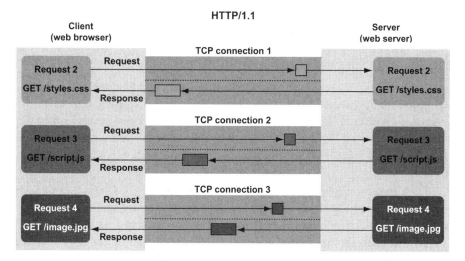

Figure 4.1   Multiple HTTP/1 requests in parallel require multiple TCP connections.

multiplexed connection, as opposed to the six parallel HTTP/1 connections that
most browsers allow. Figure 4.2 shows the same three requests as in figure 4.1, but the
requests are sent one after the other on the same connection (similar to HTTP/1.1
pipelining), and the responses are sent back intermingled (which isn't possible in
HTTP/1.1 *pipelining*).

This example shows that requests aren't sent at exactly the same time, as, ultimately, each frame needs to be sent after another on the same HTTP/TCP connection. This is also true of HTTP/1.1, because even though requests appear to be

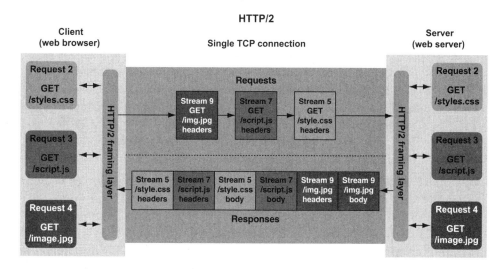

Figure 4.2   Requesting three resources across a multiplexed HTTP/2 connection

parallel on multiple connections, there is (at least usually!) only one network connection, so each request would be queued to be sent at a network level. The main point is that the HTTP/2 connection isn't blocked after sending a request until the response is received, as it is in HTTP/1.1 (as discussed in chapter 2).

Similarly, responses can be sent back intermingled (streams 5 and 7 in figure 4.2), or sequentially (stream 9 in figure 4.2). The order in which the server sends back responses is entirely up to the server, though the client can indicate priorities. If multiple responses can be sent, the server can prioritize the important resources (such as CSS and JavaScript) over less important resources (such as images). I cover this topic in chapter 7.

Each request is given a new, incremental stream ID (5, 7, and 9 in figure 4.2), and responses are sent back on the same stream ID, so streams are bidirectional, as HTTP connections were. Streams are closed when the response is finished. An HTTP/2 stream isn't directly analogous to an HTTP/1.1 connection, because streams are discarded and not reused, whereas HTTP/1.1 keeps the connection open and it can be reused to send another request.

To prevent a clash of stream IDs, client-initiated requests are given odd stream IDs (which is why I used stream IDs 5, 7, and 9 in the preceding figures, assuming that streams 1 and 3 were already used on this connection), and server-initiated requests are given even stream IDs. Note that the server can't technically initiate a stream at this writing except in specific use cases, which are still ultimately in response to a client stream, as I discuss in chapter 5. Responses to requests are marked with the same stream ID, as mentioned earlier. Stream ID 0 (not shown in the figures) is a control stream used by both client and server to manage the connection.

Understanding figure 4.2 is the key to understanding HTTP/2. If you get that concept and see why it differs from HTTP/1, you've gone a long way toward understanding HTTP/2. Intricacies and subtleties exist, but this figure demonstrates two fundamentals of HTTP/2:

- HTTP/2 uses multiple binary frames to send HTTP requests and responses across a single TCP connection, using a multiplexed stream.
- HTTP/2 is mostly different at the message-sending level, and at even a slightly higher level, the core concepts of HTTP remain the same. Requests have a method (such as GET), a resource you want to get (such as /styles.css), headers, body, status codes (such as 200, 404), caching, cookies, and so on, which stay the same.

The first point means that HTTP/2 could have been depicted as in figure 4.3, in which each stream acts like a separate connection in the HTTP/1 world. But figure 4.3 is perhaps open to misinterpretation by those who are familiar with HTTP/1, as HTTP/2 streams aren't reused (as connections are in HTTP/1) and HTTP/2 streams aren't completely independent—for good reason, as you'll see in chapter 7.

This second point is why HTTP/2 has been able to make so much headway already. As long as the web browser and the web server know HTTP/2 and can handle

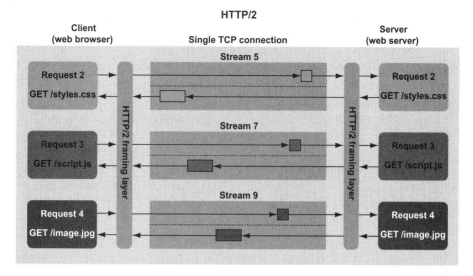

Figure 4.3 HTTP/2 streams are similar to HTTP/1 connections.

the low-level details, the users (end users and web developers) don't need to know about HTTP/2 or treat it differently from the way they treat any other website. HTTP/2 doesn't even need a new scheme (the https:// bit at the beginning of URLs), as I discuss in section 4.2. In fact, most people have been using HTTP/2 for some time without knowing it. Google, Twitter, and Facebook all use HTTP/2, so if you've used these sites, you likely have already used HTTP/2 even if you weren't aware of it.

But much as having a good understanding of HTTP/1 has enabled web developers to create better, more performant websites, those of you who take time to understand how HTTP/2 works will be much better placed to allow your websites to benefit from the protocol.

4.1.3 Stream prioritization and flow control

Before HTTP/2, HTTP was a single request-and-response protocol, so there was no need for prioritization within the protocol. The client (typically, the web browser) decided the priority outside of HTTP by deciding what order to send the messages in, using the limited number of HTTP/1 connections (typically, six). This prioritization usually required requesting critical resources (HTML, render blocking CSS, and critical JavaScript) first and requesting non-blocking items (such as images and asynchronous JavaScript) later. Requests were queued, awaiting a free HTTP/1 connection, and the queuing, managed by the browser, decided the priority.

HTTP/2 now has a much higher limit on the number of requests in flight at any time (typically, 100 active streams by default in many implementations), so many requests no longer need to be queued by the browser and can be sent immediately. This fact could lead to bandwidth being wasted on lower-priority resources (such as images) and therefore cause the page to appear to load slower over HTTP/2. Stream prioritization is needed so that the most critical resources can be sent with higher priority. Stream prioritization is implemented by the server sending more frames for higher-priority requests than for lower-priority requests when a queue of frames is waiting to be sent. Stream prioritization also allows greater control than under HTTP/1, in which the separate connections are independent. In HTTP/1, other than not using a connection, it wasn't possible to prioritize certain connections. If you have five critical resources and a sixth noncritical one, under HTTP/1, all the resources can be sent with the same priority on the six separate connections, or the first five can be sent while the sixth is held back. Under HTTP/2, all six requests can be sent with the appropriate priority, and this priority is used to decide how much resource to allocate to sending each response.

Flow control is another necessary consequence of using multiple streams over the same connection. If the receiver is unable to process the incoming messages as fast as the sender is sending, a backlog exists, which must be buffered and eventually leads to packets being dropped and needing to be resent. TCP allows the connection to be throttled back in such a scenario at a connection level, but HTTP/2 requires it to happen at a stream level. Take the example of a web page with a live video on it. If the video is paused by the user, it may be prudent to pause the download for that HTTP/2 stream only, but to allow any other resources used by the website to continue to download at full capacity through other streams.

In chapter 7, I return to stream prioritization and flow control and provide more details on how they work. These processes usually are controlled by the browser and server, so users and web developers have little control of them at this writing, which is why I discuss them later in the book.

4.1.4   *Header compression*

HTTP headers are used to send additional information about requests and responses from client to server, and vice versa. There's a lot of repetition in these headers, as they're often sent identically for every resource. Consider the following headers, which are sent with every request and often repeat values sent previously:

- `Cookie`—Cookies are sent with every request to that domain (except for uncredentialed requests that Amazon uses [see chapter 2], but these are somewhat specialized and not the norm). Cookie headers can get particularly large and often are needed only for the HTML document resources, but get sent for every request.
- `User-Agent`—This header typically states the web browser being used. It never changes during the session, but it is still sent with every request.
- `Host`—This header is used to fully qualify the request URL and is always the same for each request to the same host.
- `Accept`—This header defines the format of the response it expects (acceptable image formats that the browser knows how to display, and so on). Because the

formats that a browser supports typically don't change without a browser upgrade, this header changes per request type (image, document, font, and so on), but is the same for each instance of these types.

- `Accept-Encoding`—This header defines the compression formats (typically, `gzip`, `deflate`, and increasingly `br` for browsers that accept the newer brotli compression). Similar to the `Accept` header, this header doesn't change throughout the session.

These response headers can be duplicated and are wasteful. Some specialized response headers (such as Content Security Policy headers) can be large and similarly repetitious—especially bad for smaller requests, in which the HTTP headers will be proportionally larger parts of the download.

HTTP/1 allows compressing HTTP bodies (hence, the `Accept-Encoding` header mentioned earlier), but not compressing HTTP headers. HTTP/2 brings in the concept of header compression, but as I discuss in chapter 8, it uses a technique other than body compression to allow cross-request compression and prevent some security issues with the algorithms used for HTTP body compression.

4.1.5   *Server push*

Another important difference between HTTP/1 and HTTP/2 is that HTTP/2 adds the concept of *server push*, which allows the server to respond to a request with more than one response. Under HTTP/1, when the home page is returned, the browser must read it and then request the other resources (such as CSS and JavaScript) before it starts rendering the page. With HTTP/2 server push, those resources can be sent with the initial response and should be available when the browser looks to use them.

HTTP/2 server push is a new concept in HTTP, but if care isn't taken, it can easily cause wasted bandwidth, when resources that a browser doesn't need are pushed anyway, particularly if the resources being pushed were sent with a previous request and are already available in the browser cache. Deciding when and how to push is key to making the most of this feature. For that reason, HTTP/2 server push gets a chapter of its own (chapter 5) in this book.

4.2   *How an HTTP/2 connection is established*

Given that HTTP/2 is so different from HTTP/1 at a connection level, both the client web browser and the server need to be able to talk and understand HTTP/2 to be able to use it. As two independent parties are involved, there needs to be a process in which each party can say that it's willing and able to use HTTP/2.

The move to HTTPS was the last similar change, which was made possible with a new URL scheme (https://) and was served over a different default port (443 for HTTPS as opposed to 80 for HTTP). This change allowed a clear separation of the protocols, and, therefore, a clear indication of which protocol to use to communicate.

There are several downsides to moving to a new scheme, port, or both, however, including

- Until adoption is near universal, the default needs to remain the existing http:// (or https:// if it ever becomes the default, as many people hope). Therefore, adding a new scheme, as HTTPS did, would require a redirect to use HTTP/2, which would introduce slowness—the very thing that HTTP/2 was supposed to solve!
- Sites have to change links to the new scheme. Although internal links could be fixed with relative links on the website itself (/images/image.png rather than https://example.com/images/image.png, for example), external links would need to include the full URL, including the scheme. The adoption of HTTPS has often been complicated, in part, by the need for sites to change every URL to the new scheme.
- Compatibility issues occur with existing network infrastructure (such as firewalls blocking any new nonstandard ports).

For these reasons and to make any transition to HTTP/2 more seamless, HTTP/2 (and SPDY, on which it's based) decided not to use a new scheme, but looked at alternative methods to establish the HTTP/2 connection. The HTTP/2 specification[3] provides three ways to create the HTTP/2 connection (though a fourth way has since been added, as described in section 4.2.4):

- Use HTTPS negotiation.
- Use the HTTP Upgrade header.
- Use prior knowledge.

In theory, HTTP/2 is available over unencrypted HTTP, in which it is known as h2c, and over encrypted HTTPS, in which it is known as h2. In practice, all web browsers support HTTP/2 only over HTTPS (h2), so option 1 is used to negotiate HTTP/2 by web browsers. Server-to-server HTTP/2 communication can be over unencrypted HTTP (h2c) or HTTPS (h2), so it can use all these methods, depending on which scheme is used.

4.2.1   *Using HTTPS negotiation*

HTTPS connections go through a protocol-negotiation stage to set up the connection, as they need to agree on the SSL/TLS protocol, cipher, and various other settings to use before the connection is established and HTTP messages are exchanged. This stage is flexible, allowing new HTTPS protocols and ciphers to be introduced and used only when both client and server agree to use them. HTTP/2 support can be part of that HTTPS handshake, saving any upgrade redirection that would need to have been done at connection establishment and before the first HTTP message was sent.

---

[3]   https://tools.ietf.org/html/rfc7540#section-3

HTTPS HANDSHAKE

Using HTTPS means using SSL/TLS to encrypt a standard HTTP connection, whether HTTP/1 or HTTP/2. See the "SSL, TLS, HTTPS, and HTTP" sidebar in chapter 1 for the differences between these acronyms and the naming conventions used in this book.

Public-private key encryption is known as *asymmetric encryption* because it uses different keys to encrypt and unencrypt messages. This type of encryption is needed to allow secure communication to a server you've never connected to before, but it's slow, so it's used to agree on a symmetric encryption key to be used for encrypting the rest of the connection. This agreement happens during the TLS handshake, which occurs at the beginning of the connection. Under TLSv1.2, which is the main version in use now, it uses the handshake shown in figure 4.4 to set up the encrypted connection. This handshake changes slightly in the newly standardized TLSv1.3, as discussed in chapter 9.

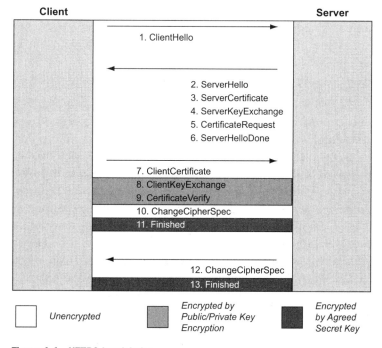

Figure 4.4   HTTPS handshake

The handshake involves four sets of messages:

- The client sends a `ClientHello` message detailing its cryptographic capabilities. This message is sent unencrypted because the encryption method hasn't been agreed on yet.

- The server sends a similar `ServerHello` message back, choosing the HTTPS protocol (such as TLSv1.2) based on what it knows the client supports. It also sends the cipher it will use for this connection (such as `ECDHE-RSA-AES128-GCM-SHA256`), again by choosing one based on those advertised in the `ClientHello` message and on what it supports itself. Then it provides the server HTTPS certificate (`ServerCertificate`). The secret key details depend on the cipher selected (`ServerKeyExchange`) and whether a client HTTPS certificate is needed (`CertificateRequest`, not needed for most websites). Finally, the server says that it's done (`ServerHelloDone`).
- The client verifies the server certificate and sends a client certificate if requested (`ClientCertificate`, not needed for most sites). Then it sends its secret key details (`ClientKeyExchange`). These details are sent encrypted by the public key in the server certificate so that only the server can decrypt the message with the private key. If client certificates are being used, a `CertificateVerify` message is sent, signed with the private key, to prove ownership of the client certificate. The client uses the `ServerKeyExchange` and `ClientKeyExchange` details to define an encrypted symmetric key and sends a `ChangeCipherSpec` message to inform the client that encryption is beginning; then it sends an encrypted `Finished` message.
- The server also switches to an encrypted connection (`ChangeCipherSpec`) and sends an encrypted `Finished` message.

In addition to being used to agree on the symmetric encryption key to be used, public-private key cryptography is used to confirm identity, as there's little point in using strong encryption if you're securely talking to the wrong party! Identity is confirmed as messages are signed by the server's hidden private key, which can be unlocked with the public key in the certificate. Each SSL/TLS certificate is also cryptographically signed by a recognized certificate authority that the computer trusts. If client certificates are being used, a similar process works in reverse. With regard to identity, all that can be confirmed is that the server domain it is part of signed the SSL/TLS certificate. If the server domain is wrong (www.amaz0n.com rather than www.amazon.com), you're securely talking to the wrong server and may be talking to a party different from the one you thought you were talking to. As I mentioned when I introduced HTTPS in chapter 1, this situation causes much confusion. A green padlock doesn't mean that a site is legitimate or safe—only that communication to it is securely encrypted.

After all these steps, the HTTPS session is set up, and all future communications are secured with the agreed key(s). This setup adds at least two round trips before you can send a single request. HTTPS was traditionally viewed as slow, but although advances in computers make encryption and decryption of messages not really noticeable, the initial connection delay is noticeable, as shown in the waterfall figures in chapter 2. When this initial HTTPS setup is done, future HTTP messages on the same connection don't need to go through this negotiation. Similarly, future connections (whether they're extra connections in parallel or reconnections at a later time) can skip some of these steps if they reuse the key that was used the last time, in a process known as TLS *session resumption*.

You can do little about this initial slowness except try to limit creating new connections (as HTTP/2 does). Most people agree that the benefits of HTTPS outweigh the performance costs of the initial connection. TLSv1.3,[4] finalized at the time of this writing, introduces extra efficiencies to drop this negotiation to one round trip (or even zero round trips when picking up from a previous negotiation), but it will take some time to be adopted and still leaves one round trip in many cases.

APPLICATION-LAYER PROTOCOL NEGOTIATION

ALPN[5] added an additional extension to the `ClientHello` message, where clients could advertise application protocol support ("Hey, I support h2 and http/1. If you want to, use either of them."), and also to the `ServerHello` message, where servers could confirm which application protocol to use after HTTPS negotiation ("OK, let's use h2"). I demonstrate this process in figure 4.5.

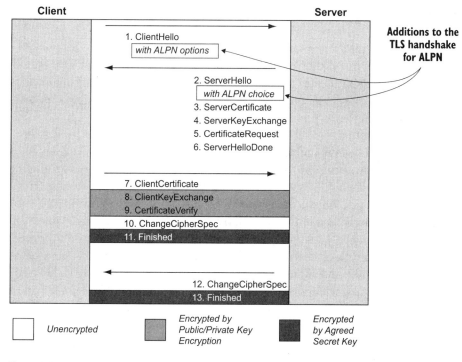

Figure 4.5   HTTPS handshake with ALPN

[4] https://tools.ietf.org/html/draft-ietf-tls-tls13
[5] https://tools.ietf.org/html/rfc7301

ALPN is simple and can be used to agree whether or not to use HTTP/2 for the existing HTTPS negotiation messages without adding any further round trips, redirects, or other upgrade delays. The only problem with ALPN lies in its being relatively new, with support not being universal, particularly on the server side, where older versions of TLS libraries are common (see chapter 3). If ALPN isn't supported, the server usually assumes that the client doesn't support HTTP/2 and uses HTTP/1.1.

ALPN can be used for other protocols besides HTTP/2, but at this writing it's used only for HTTP/2 and the SPDY protocol on which it's based, although other ALPN applications have been registered, including the original three versions of HTTP: HTTP/0.9, HTTP/1.0, and HTTP/1.1.[6] In fact, ALPN was finalized in July 2014, before HTTP/2 came along, and the RFC for ALPN[7] defines the extension only for HTTP/1.1 and SPDY. The HTTP/2 ALPN extension (h2) was registered later, as part of finalizing the HTTP/2 specification.[8]

NEXT PROTOCOL NEGOTIATION

NPN, the predecessor to ALPN, worked in a similar manner. Despite being used by a lot of browsers and web servers, it was never formalized as an internet standard (though a draft specification was worked on).[9] ALPN, which was formalized, is based heavily on NPN, which is like HTTP/2 being the formalized version of SPDY.

The main difference is that with NPN, the client decides the protocol being used, whereas with ALPN, the server decides (the way the rest of the TLS parameters are decided). With NPN, the ClientHello message declares that the client is happy to use NPN, the ServerHello message includes all the NPN protocols supported by the server, and after encryption is enabled, the client picks the NPN protocol (such as h2) and sends another message with this choice. Figure 4.6 illustrates this process, with the three extra pieces highlighted in steps 1, 2, and 11.

NPN is a three-step process, whereas ALPN is a two-step process, though both processes reuse existing HTTPS steps and don't add round trips (though NPN does add one message to confirm the protocol to use). Additionally, with NPN, the chosen application protocol is encrypted (step 11 in figure 4.6), whereas in ALPN, it's sent in the unencrypted ServerHello message. Because the protocols supported by the server are sent unencrypted in the ServerHello message in NPN, and because some network solutions may want to know the application that's going to be used, the TLS Working Group decided to change this process in ALPN so that the server choses the application protocol (as it does for the other HTTPS parameters).

NPN has been deprecated in favor of ALPN, and as discussed in chapter 3, many web browsers have stopped supporting NPN for HTTP/2 connections; some web servers (such as Apache) never supported it in the first place. Other implementations are

---

[6] https://www.iana.org/assignments/tls-extensiontype-values/tls-extensiontype-values.xhtml#alpn-protocol-ids
[7] https://tools.ietf.org/html/rfc7301
[8] https://tools.ietf.org/html/rfc7540#section-11.1
[9] https://tools.ietf.org/html/draft-agl-tls-nextprotoneg-04

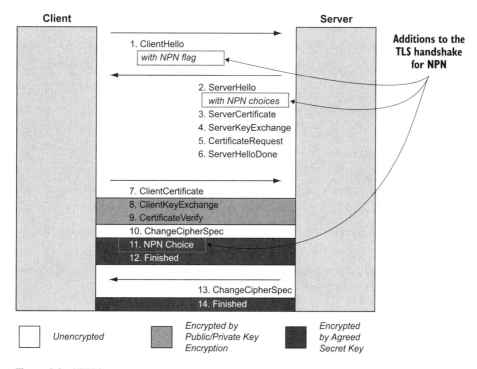

Figure 4.6   HTTPS handshake with NPN

expected to deprecate use of it over time. The HTTP/2 specification states that ALPN should be used[10] and makes no mention of NPN, so technically, implementations that still use NPN aren't following the specification.

Deprecation of NPN causes problems for servers that don't yet support ALPN. NPN was older and was therefore supported by more servers (or at least the TLS libraries that they use). Although newer versions support ALPN, older versions, which are common even at this writing (such as OpenSSL 1.0.1), support only the older NPN extension. This situation is one reason why HTTP/2 may not be used even when a server is configured for it (see chapter 3).

EXAMPLE OF AN HTTPS HANDSHAKE WITH ALPN

You can use a few tools to see the HTTPS handshake, but curl[11] is one of the easiest, and is available to many environments, though it may be a version without ALPN support. For those of you who use Git Bash, for example, it includes a version with ALPN support. The following output shows what happens when you connect to Facebook with HTTP/2 by using curl, with the ALPN- and HTTP/2-specific parts in bold:

---

[10] https://tools.ietf.org/html/rfc7540#section-3.3
[11] https://curl.haxx.se/

```
$ curl -vso /dev/null --http2 https://www.facebook.com
* Rebuilt URL to: https://www.facebook.com/
*   Trying 31.13.76.68...
* TCP_NODELAY set
* Connected to www.facebook.com (31.13.76.68) port 443 (#0)
* ALPN, offering h2
* ALPN, offering http/1.1
* successfully set certificate verify locations:
*   CAfile: /etc/pki/tls/certs/ca-bundle.crt
  CApath: none
} [5 bytes data]
* TLSv1.2 (OUT), TLS handshake, Client hello (1):
} [214 bytes data]
* TLSv1.2 (IN), TLS handshake, Server hello (2):
{ [102 bytes data]
* TLSv1.2 (IN), TLS handshake, Certificate (11):
{ [3242 bytes data]
* TLSv1.2 (IN), TLS handshake, Server key exchange (12):
{ [148 bytes data]
* TLSv1.2 (IN), TLS handshake, Server finished (14):
{ [4 bytes data]
* TLSv1.2 (OUT), TLS handshake, Client key exchange (16):
} [70 bytes data]
* TLSv1.2 (OUT), TLS change cipher, Client hello (1):
} [1 bytes data]
* TLSv1.2 (OUT), TLS handshake, Finished (20):
} [16 bytes data]
* TLSv1.2 (IN), TLS handshake, Finished (20):
{ [16 bytes data]
* SSL connection using TLSv1.2 / ECDHE-ECDSA-AES128-GCM-SHA256
* ALPN, server accepted to use h2
* Server certificate:
*   subject: C=US; ST=California; L=Menlo Park; O=Facebook, Inc.;
      CN=*.facebook.com
*   start date: Dec  9 00:00:00 2016 GMT
*   expire date: Jan 25 12:00:00 2018 GMT
*   subjectAltName: host "www.facebook.com" matched cert's "*.facebook.com"
*   issuer: C=US; O=DigiCert Inc; OU=www.digicert.com; CN=DigiCert SHA2 High
      Assurance Server CA
*   SSL certificate verify ok.
* Using HTTP2, server supports multi-use
* Connection state changed (HTTP/2 confirmed)
```

Here, you can see that the client states that it will use ALPN to state support of HTTP/2 (h2) and also HTTP/1.1 (http/1.1). Then it goes through the various handshake steps (not all the details are shown, but enough to give you a taste of what's going on), and, finally, a connection is established with the TLSv1.2, ECDHE-ECDSA-AES128-GCM-SHA256 cipher suite, and h2 ALPN setting. Next the server certificate is displayed, and curl switches to HTTP/2. Using curl is a good way to test for ALPN support on a server (provided that your version of curl supports ALPN, of course). If you're curious, you can test NPN by using the --no-alpn flag, but this test doesn't show as much information and excludes all the ALPN lines shown in the preceding example without substituting any NPN equivalents, though the last two lines are identical:

```
$ curl -vso /dev/null --http2 https://www.facebook.com --no-alpn
...
*  SSL certificate verify ok.
* Using HTTP2, server supports multi-use
* Connection state changed (HTTP/2 confirmed)
```

4.2.2 *Using the HTTP upgrade header*

A client can request to upgrade an existing HTTP/1.1 HTTP connection to HTTP/2 by sending an `Upgrade` HTTP header. This header should be used only for unencrypted HTTP connections (h2c). Encrypted HTTPS HTTP/2 connections (h2) shouldn't use this method to negotiate HTTP/2 and must use ALPN as part of HTTPS negotiation. As I've stated several times, web browsers support HTTP/2 only over encrypted connections, so they won't use this method. Those of you who are working with outside browsers (on APIs, for example) may be interested to learn more details on how this process works.

When a client sends an `Upgrade` header is entirely up to the client. The header could be sent with every request, with the initial request only, or only if the server has advertised HTTP/2 support via the `Upgrade` header in an HTTP response. The following examples describe how the `Upgrade` header works.

EXAMPLE 1: AN UNSUCCESSFUL UPGRADE REQUEST

An HTTP/1.1 request is made with an `Upgrade` header, as this client supports HTTP/2 and therefore prefers to use it:

```
GET / HTTP/1.1
Host: www.example.com
Upgrade: h2c
HTTP2-Settings: <will be discussed later>
```

Such a request must include an `HTTP-Settings` header, which is a base-64 encoding of the HTTP/2 settings message, which I discuss later.

A server that doesn't understand HTTP/2 can respond as normal with an HTTP/1.1 message, as though the `Upgrade` header hadn't been sent:

```
HTTP/1.1 200 OK
Date: Sun, 25 Jun 2017 13:30:24 GMT
Connection: Keep-Alive
Content-Type: text/html
Server: Apache

<!doctype html>
<html>
<head>
…etc.
```

EXAMPLE 2: A SUCCESSFUL UPGRADE REQUEST

Instead of ignoring the upgrade request and sending back an HTTP/1.1 200 response, a server that understands HTTP/2 can respond with an HTTP/1.1 101 response, saying that it will switch the protocol:

```
HTTP/1.1 101 Switching Protocols
Connection: Upgrade
Upgrade: h2c
```

Then the server immediately switches to HTTP/2, sending a SETTINGS frame (see section 4.3.3) and then sending the response to the original message in HTTP/2 format.

EXAMPLE 3: A SERVER-SUGGESTED UPGRADE

An HTTP/1.1 request is made, but the client assumes that the server doesn't support HTTP/2, so it doesn't send an Upgrade header:

```
GET / HTTP/1.1
Host: www.example.com
```

A server that understands HTTP/2 can respond with a 200 response code but tell the client that it also supports HTTP/2 by advertising support in the Upgrade HTTP header in the response. In this case, it's an upgrade *suggestion* as opposed to an upgrade *request*, as all upgrade requests must be initiated from the client. Following is an example in which the server advertises h2 (HTTP/2 over HTTPS) and h2c (HTTP/2 over HTTP) support:

```
HTTP/1.1 200 OK
Date: Sun, 25 Jun 2017 13:30:24 GMT
Connection: Keep-Alive
Content-Type: text/html
Server: Apache
Upgrade: h2c, h2

<!doctype html>
<html>
<head>
…etc.
```

The client can use this information to initiate the upgrade by sending the Upgrade header in the next request, as in the preceding two examples:

```
GET /styles.css HTTP/1.1
Host: www.example.com
Upgrade: h2c
HTTP2-Settings: <will be discussed later>
```

The server responds with a 101 response and upgrades the connections as described earlier. Note that the Upgrade header and negotiation method can't be used for h2 connections—only for h2c connections. Here, the server has advertised both h2 and h2c connections, but if the client wants to use h2, it should switch to HTTPS and use ALPN to negotiate this connection.

ISSUES WITH SENDING AN UPGRADE HEADER

Because all web browsers at this writing support HTTP/2 only over HTTPS, the upgrade option will likely never be used by browsers, which can cause problems.

Consider this scenario. You have a web browser that supports HTTP/2 on one side of the connection, and on the other side, you have a web server that supports only HTTP/1.1 (such as an older Apache version) in front of an application server (such as Tomcat) that supports HTTP/2. In this case, the web server is acting as a reverse proxy and is likely sending all requests between the client (web browser) and the ultimate server (Tomcat application server), both of which talk HTTP/2. The application server may try to be helpful and send the Upgrade header to suggest moving to the better HTTP/2 protocol. The web server may blindly forward this header. The client will see this upgrade suggestion and decide that upgrading would be a good idea. But the web server, which the client connects to, doesn't support HTTP/2.

In a similar scenario, the web server is already talking HTTP/2 to the web browser, but proxying requests using HTTP/1.1 to the backend application server. The application server may send the upgrade suggestion, and if this suggestion is forwarded to the browser, it may get confused, as the suggestion is to upgrade an HTTP/2 connection to h2, which it's already using.

These problems aren't theoretical; they've caused real issues while HTTP/2 has been rolled out. Safari used to return errors when it saw an h2 upgrade header on an HTTP/2 connection (see chapter 3).

At this writing, the nginx team has been asked to stop passing on the Upgrade header blindly[12] when it's sitting in front of an Apache server that advertises HTTP/2 support via this header, for example. Removing this header can be achieved with some configuration (proxy_hide_header Upgrade), but few people know to add it until they run into problems. Additionally, some clients or servers may not implement the Upgrade header properly. While experimenting with HTTP/2, I noticed a problem with NodeJS disconnecting after Apache started advertising the Upgrade header.[13] This problem has been fixed but is still present in older versions of NodeJS that are still in use.

Although these problems may well be fixed by the time this book is published, similar issues will undoubtedly arise. All in all, I prefer that server implementations *not* advertise the upgrade option (at least, by default). In my opinion, this option won't be used much and will cause more problems than it solves. For most implementations (and all browsers), HTTPS negotiation is more likely to be used. The prior-assumption method may be used for backend servers if HTTPS isn't supported or necessary. Apache is one of the main offenders and has been requested to stop

---

[12] https://trac.nginx.org/nginx/ticket/915
[13] https://github.com/nodejs/node/issues/4334

including the Upgrade header by default,[14] but in the meantime, you can use the following mod_headers Apache configuration to turn off sending of this header, which I recommend doing if you're running Apache with HTTP/2 support (though this solution could cause problems with other protocols that need to use the Upgrade header, such as WebSockets, so it can't be used in those scenarios):

```
Header unset Upgrade
```

4.2.3   *Using prior knowledge*

The third and final way that the HTTP/2 specification states that a client can use HTTP/2 is if it already knows that a server understands HTTP/2. In that case, it can start talking HTTP/2 right away, avoiding any upgrade request.

How the client has prior knowledge that the server is able to understand HTTP/2 could be through different methods. If you're running a reverse proxy to offload HTTPS, you may want to talk HTTP/2 over HTTP (h2c) to your backend servers because you know they speak HTTP/2. Alternatively, prior knowledge can be assumed based on alternative support advertised by the Alt-Svc Header (HTTP/1.1) or the ALTSVC frame (see section 4.2.4).

This option is the riskiest one because it makes certain assumptions that the server can speak HTTP/2. Clients using prior knowledge must take care to handle any rejection messages appropriately in case the prior knowledge turns out to be incorrect. The server response to the HTTP/2 preface message, which I discuss later in this chapter, is of huge importance in this way of choosing to use HTTP/2. This method should be used only when you're in control of both the client and server.

4.2.4   *HTTP Alternative Services*

A fourth way, not included in the original HTTP/2 specification, is to use HTTP Alternative Services,[15] added as a separate standard after HTTP/2 was released. This standard allows the server to inform the client using HTTP/1.1 (via an Alt-Svc HTTP header) that the requested resource is available in another location (such as another server or port) using a different protocol. This protocol could be used to start HTTP/2 with prior knowledge.

Alternative Services aren't only for HTTP/1 and can be communicated over an existing HTTP/2 connection (via a new ALTSVC frame, covered later in the chapter), in case the client wants to switch to a different connection (one located close to the client, for example, or one that's less busy). This standard is fairly new and not in widespread use. It still incurs starting on one connection and then switching, which is slower than starting HTTP/2 through ALPN or prior knowledge. It introduces some interesting possibilities that are beyond the scope of this book, but at least one content delivery network seems to be intent on taking full advantage of it.[16]

---

[14] https://bz.apache.org/bugzilla/show_bug.cgi?id=59311
[15] https://tools.ietf.org/html/rfc7838
[16] https://blog.cloudflare.com/cloudflare-onion-service/

4.2.5 The HTTP/2 preface message

The first message that must be sent on an HTTP/2 connection (no matter which method is used to establish HTTP/2 support) is the HTTP/2 connection preface, or "magic" string. This message is sent by the client as the first message on the HTTP/2 connection. This message is a sequence of 24 octets and looks like this in hex notation:

```
0x505249202a20485454502f322e300d0a0d0a534d0d0a0d0a
```

This sequence translates to the following message in ASCII:

```
PRI * HTTP/2.0\r\n\r\nSM\r\n\r\n
```

This message may seem to be an odd one to send, but not coincidentally, it's almost an HTTP/1-style message:

```
PRI * HTTP/2.0↵
↵
SM↵
↵
```

That is, the HTTP method is `PRI` (instead of `GET` or `POST`), the resource is `*`, and the HTTP version number is `HTTP/2.0`. Next is a double return (so no request headers), followed by a request body of `SM`.

The intention of this nonsensical, HTTP/1-like message is for when a client tries to speak HTTP/2 to a server that doesn't understand HTTP/2. Such a server tries to parse this message as it would any other HTTP message and fails because it doesn't recognize the nonsense method (`PRI`) or the HTTP version (`HTTP/2.0`), and it should reject the message. Note this preface message is the only part of the official specification that still refers to HTTP/2.0 with the minor version number; it's HTTP/2 everywhere else, as discussed in the "HTTP/2.0 or HTTP/2?" sidebar in section 4.1. The server, which knows that the client speaks HTTP/2 based on the incoming message, doesn't send this magic message; it must send a `SETTINGS` frame as its first message (which can be empty).

> **Why PRI and SM?**
> The original HTTP/2 preface in the early drafts of the HTTP/2 specifications used FOO and BAR[a] or BA[b], which are well-known placeholder names in programming. But in version 4 of the draft spec, this placeholder changed to PRI SM,[c] with no comment in the specification as to why.
>
> This change apparently was made in response to the Edward Snowden revelations[d] that came out during this time about the PRISM program used to gather internet traffic from various companies. The revelations upset proponents of the free internet (some of whom also help decide on the standards of the internet) and who thought that it would be humorous to start every HTTP/2 connection with a little reminder.

Why PRI and SM? *(continued)*

The contents of this message weren't important; the message was intended to be a nonsense message that shouldn't be recognized as valid HTTP. Other suggestions included STA RT, but ultimately, PRI SM made it into the final spec in a change commit labeled "Exercising editorial discretion regarding magic."[e]

[a]   https://tools.ietf.org/html/draft-ietf-httpbis-http2-02#section-3.2
[b]   https://tools.ietf.org/html/draft-ietf-httpbis-http2-03#section-3.2
[c]   https://tools.ietf.org/html/draft-ietf-httpbis-http2-04#section-3.5
[d]   https://blog.jgc.org/2015/11/the-secret-message-hidden-in-every.html
[e]   https://github.com/http2/http2-spec/commit/ac468f3fab9f7092a430eedfd69ee1fb2e23c944

4.3   *HTTP/2 frames*

When you've set up the HTTP/2 connection, you can start sending HTTP/2 messages. As you've seen, HTTP/2 messages are made up of frames of data that are sent on streams on a single multiplexed connection. Frames are a low-level concept that many web developers don't need to know about, but it's always worthwhile to understand the building blocks of a technology. Many of the errors at the end of chapter 3 are easier to debug by looking at HTTP/2 at frame level, so looking at the frame level has practical as well as theoretical uses. I explain the main parts of HTTP/2 by using a real-world example.

In this section, I look at and explain the frame types, which can seem a little daunting and confusing at first and is a lot to take in. I encourage readers not to fixate too much on first reading but to understand the overall concept of HTTP/2 frames and have a high-level understanding of each frame type. The sections on the individual frames and settings for each frame can serve as references later, as can the HTTP/2 specification itself, but you don't need to memorize them to understand the remainder of this book or HTTP/2 in the real world.

4.3.1   *Viewing HTTP/2 frames*

A few tools are available for viewing HTTP/2 frames, including Chrome's net-export page, nghttp, and Wireshark. Your web server may also be able to increase logging to show the individual frames, but with potentially lots of users, that technique can quickly get messy, so the preceding tools are easier to use unless you're trying to debug a potential issue on your web server.

CHROME NET-EXPORT

The easiest way to view HTTP/2 frames without installing additional software is to use Chrome's net-export page. This used to be available in the net-internals page, but from Chrome 71 this moved to net-externals for a number of reason[17], and

---

[17] https://docs.google.com/document/d/1Ll7T5cguj5m2DqkUTad5DWRCqtbQ3L1q9FRvTN5-Y28/

requires a bit more effort to view. Open a Chrome browser, and type the following in the URL bar:

```
chrome://net-export/
```

Click "Start Logging to Disk" and choose a file location for the log file. In another tab, open an HTTP/2 site (such as https://www.facebook.com) and after it has loaded, click on "Stop Logging". At this point you can use the NetLog viewer (https://netlog-viewer .appspot.com) to open and examine the log file created (note: this tool only views the file locally and does not upload it to a server). Click on the HTTP/2 option on the left, and then the site (such as www.facebook.com), and you should see the underlying HTTP/2 messages as shown in figure 4.7.

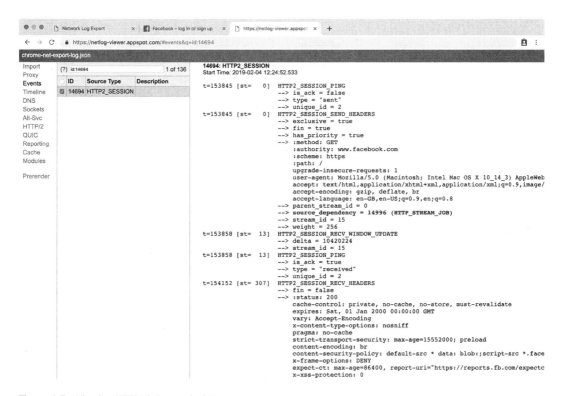

Figure 4.7   Viewing HTTP/2 frames in Chrome

Chrome adds a lot of its own detail to this screen and often splits frames across multiple lines. The following output is from one SETTINGS frame:

```
t=   1646 [st=      1]    HTTP2_SESSION_RECV_SETTINGS
t=   1647 [st=      2]    HTTP2_SESSION_RECV_SETTING
                          --> id = "1 (SETTINGS_HEADER_TABLE_SIZE)"
                          --> value = 4096
```

```
t=    1647 [st=      2]    HTTP2_SESSION_RECV_SETTING
                          --> id = "5 (SETTINGS_MAX_FRAME_SIZE)"
                          --> value = 16384
t=    1647 [st=      2]    HTTP2_SESSION_RECV_SETTING
                          --> id = "6 (SETTINGS_MAX_HEADER_LIST_SIZE)"
                          --> value = 131072
t=    1647 [st=      2]    HTTP2_SESSION_RECV_SETTING
                          --> id = "3 (SETTINGS_MAX_CONCURRENT_STREAMS)"
                          --> value = 100
t=    1647 [st=      2]    HTTP2_SESSION_RECV_SETTING
                          --> id = "4 (SETTINGS_INITIAL_WINDOW_SIZE)"
                          --> value = 65536
```

It can be a bit more difficult to read the individual frames when you use this Chrome screen than when you use the other two tools, but the screen contains most of the same information. On the other hand, it's handy to have this level of detail in the browser without having to install other tools, and you can use various tools to format the output better.[18] At this writing, I'm not aware of other browsers that show this level of detail, although Opera, which has the same code base as Chrome, has similar functionality.

USING NGHTTP

nghttp is a command-line tool developed on top of the nghttp2 C library, used by many web servers and clients to handle the underlying HTTP/2 complexities. If you have the nghttp2 library installed for your server (Apache requires nghttp2 libraries, for example), you may have this tool installed. You can use it to view the HTTP/2 messages in a similar manner to the Chrome net-export tool, though I find the output clearer:

```
$ nghttp -v https://www.facebook.com
[  0.042] Connected
The negotiated protocol: h2
[  0.109] recv SETTINGS frame <length=30, flags=0x00, stream_id=0>
         (niv=5)
         [SETTINGS_HEADER_TABLE_SIZE(0x01):4096]
         [SETTINGS_MAX_FRAME_SIZE(0x05):16384]
         [SETTINGS_MAX_HEADER_LIST_SIZE(0x06):131072]
         [SETTINGS_MAX_CONCURRENT_STREAMS(0x03):100]
         [SETTINGS_INITIAL_WINDOW_SIZE(0x04):65536]
[  0.109] recv WINDOW_UPDATE frame <length=4, flags=0x00, stream_id=0>
         (window_size_increment=10420225)
[  0.109] send SETTINGS frame <length=12, flags=0x00, stream_id=0>
         (niv=2)
         [SETTINGS_MAX_CONCURRENT_STREAMS(0x03):100]
         [SETTINGS_INITIAL_WINDOW_SIZE(0x04):65535]
…etc.
```

USING WIRESHARK

Wireshark[19] allows you to sniff all the traffic being sent and received by your computer. This tool can be handy for some hardcore low-level debugging, as you get to see the raw messages sent and received. Unfortunately, it's also rather complicated to use!

---

[18] https://github.com/rmurphey/chrome-http2-log-parser
[19] https://www.wireshark.org/

One of the complications is the fact that Wireshark isn't the client; it sniffs traffic sent from your browser to the server. All browsers use HTTP/2 over HTTPS, though, so unless you know the SSL/TLS keys being used to encrypt and decrypt these messages, you won't be able to read the traffic, which is the very point of HTTPS. Chrome and Firefox developers thought of this use case, and those browsers allow you to save your HTTPS keys to a separate file so you can use tools like Wireshark to debug. Obviously, you should turn this tool off when you're using it for debugging. All you do is tell Chrome or Firefox the file to save the keys in, by setting the SSLKEYLOGFILE environment file or by passing the following code in the command line to start Chrome:

```
"C:\Program Files (x86)\Google\Chrome\Application\chrome.exe" --ssl-key-log-
file=%USERPROFILE%\sslkey.log
```

> **NOTE** Make sure to use the correct hyphens. Many applications, such as those in Microsoft Office, like to automatically change short hyphens (-) to en dashes (–) or em dashes (—), which are three separate characters and which the command line doesn't recognize as passing arguments. The results are an empty file with the SSL keys never being added to it and much confusion and frustration.

For macOS, set the SSLKEYLOGFILE environment variable:

```
$ export SSLKEYLOGFILE=~/sslkey.log
$ /Applications/Google\ Chrome.app/Contents/MacOS/Google\ Chrome
```

or provide it directly as a command-line argument:

```
$ /Applications/Google\ Chrome.app/Contents/MacOS/Google\ Chrome--ssl-key-
log-file=/Users/barry/sslkey.log
```

Next, launch Wireshark and set the same file location by choosing Edit > Preferences > Protocols > SSL and setting the (Pre)-Master-Secret log filename, as shown in figure 4.8.

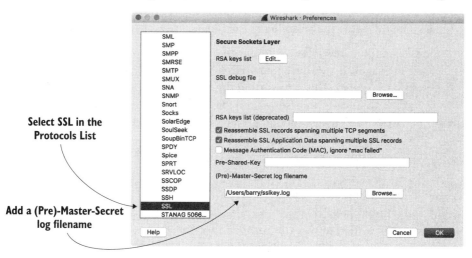

Figure 4.8 Setting a Wireshark HTTPS secret key file

At this point, you should be able to read all the HTTPS data used by Chrome, so if you visit https://www.facebook.com and filter in Wireshark on http2, you should be able to see the messages, including the preface message discussed in section 4.1.5 (available in Wireshark), as shown in figure 4.9.

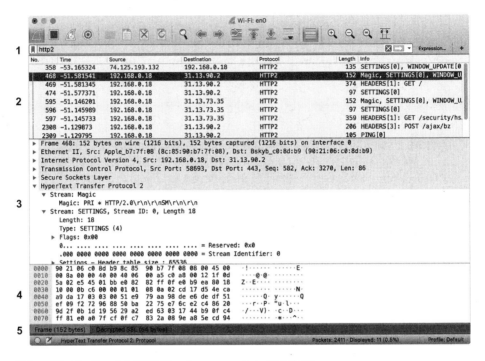

Figure 4.9   The "magic" HTTP/2 preface message in Wireshark

A lot is going on in figure 4.9, so if you're not used to Wireshark, it can be intimidating. The following list describes the various sections labeled 1–5:

1   The filter view allows you to type various filter options. Here, I filtered for `http2` messages. If you have many HTTP/2 connections open, you may want to use a more specific filter, including the IP address of the server you're connected to. The following filter shows only HTTP/2 messages sent to and from IP address 31.13.90.2 (the Facebook server I was connected to in this example; get it from your browser's developer tools):

```
http2 && (ip.dst==31.13.90.2 || ip.src==31.13.90.2)
```

2   Next is a list of messages that match your filter. If you click these messages, you get more details.

3   This section shows the full detail of the message. If Wireshark recognizes the protocol (and I've yet to find one that it doesn't!), it displays each protocol that the message applies to in an easy-to-read format.

This example, reading from the top down, starts with Wireshark's own base format, which it calls a frame (not to be confused with HTTP/2 frames). The base frames are sent as Ethernet messages, which are wrapped up into IPv4 messages, sent over TCP, sent over SSL/TLS, and finally, you see the HTTP/2 messages. Wireshark allows you to view the messages for any of these levels. In the screenshot, I expanded the HTTP/2 section and then further expanded the "magic" HTTP/2 preface message, but you could similarly expand the other levels if you're more interested in looking at messages at an Ethernet, IP, TCP, or SSL/TLS level.

4   The section near the bottom shows the raw data, usually displayed in hex and ASCII format.

5   The tabs at the bottom of the raw data allow you to decide how raw to display the data. You'll almost certainly be interested only in decompressed header format (or decrypted SSL for the magic message, which doesn't have any compressed headers), not the raw frame format.

You can even use Wireshark to look at the HTTPS negotiation messages (including ALPN extension requests in the `ClientHello` message and responses in the `Server-Hello` messages). In figure 4.10, the arrows indicate that the client prefers h2 first and `http/1.1` next.

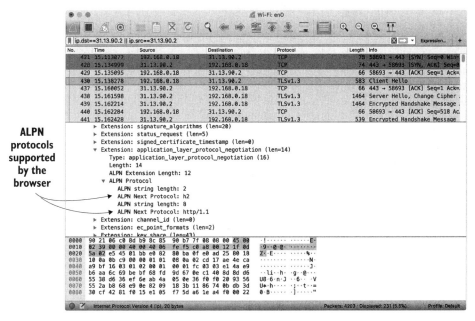

Figure 4.10   ALPN extensions as part of `ClientHello` message in Wireshark

Having problems getting Wireshark to decrypt traffic?

Unfortunately, using Wireshark to decrypt HTTPS traffic can be a little flaky, to say the least, so you may have to try several times to get it right.

One of the reasons is that this process works only for a new HTTPS session with a full TLS handshake. The problem is that if you connect to the same site again, the site may reuse some of the old encryption settings, and only a partial handshake may be completed—not enough for Wireshark to decrypt the traffic. To see whether HTTPS session resumption is being used in Wireshark, filter for `ssl`, rather than `http2`. Look at the first `ClientHello` message to see whether the `Session ID` or `SessionTicket TLS` is nonzero. If so, you're rejoining an old session, and Wireshark won't be able to decrypt the messages (unless it was running after the original session was established).

Worse, none of the browsers offers a reliable way to remove the SSL/TLS session keys/session tickets and enforce a full handshake. Some requests have been made to add this functionality to Chrome[a] and Firefox,[b] but they've been open for some time.

I've found Wireshark generally harder to get working in macOS. The latest version of Firefox no longer seems to be logging the SSL key information all the time, for example.

The best advice I can offer is to ensure you're running the latest version of Wireshark. Taking a break and returning when the session is expired also seems to help, though is not satisfying. Alternatively, you could try an alternative browser, which shouldn't have a previous session stored.

---

[a]   https://bugs.chromium.org/p/chromium/issues/detail?id=90454
[b]   https://bugzilla.mozilla.org/show_bug.cgi?id=285440

WHICH TOOL TO USE

Use whichever tool you feel most comfortable with or an alternative tool if you prefer. Wireshark gives the most detail, so if you want to get to know message structures and formats well, it has no equal. But this level of detail can be too much in many cases. Also, setting it up is complicated. Unless you're familiar with Wireshark, it may be better to use one of the other two tools.

For the remainder of this chapter, I use nghttp in examples, because it's the easiest tool to capture and format for the purposes of this book. The messages should be similar no matter what tool you use, though there may be differences in the order in which they display data or in some settings.

These tools can be useful for low-level debugging or looking at the detail of the protocol, but most people won't need to use them day to day. Certainly, most developers will get enough out of the standard developer tools in browsers that they don't need to delve into the lower level net-export or Wireshark's level of detail. All three are great tools to have in your back pocket, however, because they help you cement your understanding of the protocol.

4.3.2 HTTP/2 frame format

Before you start looking at some example frames, it may help to understand what makes up an HTTP/2 frame. Each HTTP/2 frame is made up of a fixed-length header (detailed in table 4.1), followed by the payload.

Table 4.1 HTTP/2 frame header format

Field	Length	Description
Length	24 bits	Length of the frame, not including all the header fields detailed in this table with a maximum size of $2^{24} - 1$ octets; limited by SETTINGS_MAX_FRAME_SIZE, which defaults to the smaller size of 2^{14} octets
Type	8 bits	Currently, 14 frame types have been defined:[a] • DATA (0x0) • HEADERS (0x1) • PRIORITY (0x2) • RST_STREAM (0x3) • SETTINGS (0x4) • PUSH_PROMISE (0x5) • PING (0x6) • GOAWAY (0x7) • WINDOW_UPDATE (0x8) • CONTINUATION (0x9) • ALTSVC (0xa), added through RFC 7838[b] • (0xb), not used at present but used in the past[c] • ORIGIN (0xc), added through RFC 8336[d] • CACHE_DIGEST, proposed[e]
Flags	8 bits	Frame-specific flags
Reserved Bit	1 bit	Not currently used and must be set to 0
Stream Identifier	31 bits	An unsigned 31-byte integer identifying the frame

[a] https://www.iana.org/assignments/http2-parameters/http2-parameters.xhtml
[b] https://tools.ietf.org/html/rfc7838
[c] https://github.com/httpwg/http-extensions/pull/323
[d] https://tools.ietf.org/html/rfc8336
[e] https://datatracker.ietf.org/doc/draft-ietf-httpbis-cache-digest/?include_text=1

The fact that the frames are so explicitly defined is what makes HTTP/2 a binary protocol. HTTP/2 frames are different from variable-length HTTP/1 text messages, which had to be parsed by scanning for line breaks and spaces—an inefficient and error-prone process. The much stricter, well-defined format of HTTP/2 frames allows for easier parsing and smaller messages, as particular codes can be used (such as 0x01 for a HEADERS frame type rather than the full wording).

> **Octets versus bytes**
>
> The HTTP/2 specification, like many protocol definitions, uses *octet* rather than the ambiguous byte. An octet is exactly 8 bits, whereas a byte is mostly understood to be 8 bits, depending on the system architecture in use.

The Length field is (I hope) self-explanatory. The following sections will look at each message Type in detail. The Flags field is frame-specific and described with each frame type. The Reserved Bit field current isn't used. The Stream Identifier field should also be self-explanatory. Apparently, one reason to limit this field to 31 bits was for Java interoperability, because it has no 32-bit unsigned integer.[20]

The meaning of the flags and the makeup of the payload depend on the frame type. HTTP/2 has been written to be extensible. The original HTTP/2 specification[21] defined only frame types 0–9, but three more have been added and more will undoubtedly be added in the future.

4.3.3   *Examining HTTP/2 message flow by example*

The easiest way to understand frames is to view real-world use of them. Use nghttp, for example, to connect to www.facebook.com (one of the many sites that support HTTP/2). The output follows:

```
$ nghttp -va https://www.facebook.com | more
[  0.043] Connected
The negotiated protocol: h2
[  0.107] recv SETTINGS frame <length=30, flags=0x00, stream_id=0>
          (niv=5)
          [SETTINGS_HEADER_TABLE_SIZE(0x01):4096]
          [SETTINGS_MAX_FRAME_SIZE(0x05):16384]
          [SETTINGS_MAX_HEADER_LIST_SIZE(0x06):131072]
          [SETTINGS_MAX_CONCURRENT_STREAMS(0x03):100]
          [SETTINGS_INITIAL_WINDOW_SIZE(0x04):65536]
[  0.107] recv WINDOW_UPDATE frame <length=4, flags=0x00, stream_id=0>
          (window_size_increment=10420225)
[  0.107] send SETTINGS frame <length=12, flags=0x00, stream_id=0>
          (niv=2)
          [SETTINGS_MAX_CONCURRENT_STREAMS(0x03):100]
          [SETTINGS_INITIAL_WINDOW_SIZE(0x04):65535]
[  0.107] send SETTINGS frame <length=0, flags=0x01, stream_id=0>
          ; ACK
          (niv=0)
[  0.107] send PRIORITY frame <length=5, flags=0x00, stream_id=3>
          (dep_stream_id=0, weight=201, exclusive=0)
[  0.107] send PRIORITY frame <length=5, flags=0x00, stream_id=5>
          (dep_stream_id=0, weight=101, exclusive=0)
```

---

[20] https://stackoverflow.com/questions/39309442/why-is-the-stream-identifier-31-bit-in-http-2-and-why-is-it-preceded-with-a-rese

[21] https://tools.ietf.org/html/rfc7540

```
[  0.107] send PRIORITY frame <length=5, flags=0x00, stream_id=7>
         (dep_stream_id=0, weight=1, exclusive=0)
[  0.107] send PRIORITY frame <length=5, flags=0x00, stream_id=9>
         (dep_stream_id=7, weight=1, exclusive=0)
[  0.107] send PRIORITY frame <length=5, flags=0x00, stream_id=11>
         (dep_stream_id=3, weight=1, exclusive=0)
[  0.107] send HEADERS frame <length=43, flags=0x25, stream_id=13>
         ; END_STREAM | END_HEADERS | PRIORITY
         (padlen=0, dep_stream_id=11, weight=16, exclusive=0)
         ; Open new stream
         :method: GET
         :path: /
         :scheme: https
         :authority: www.facebook.com
         accept: */*
         accept-encoding: gzip, deflate
         user-agent: nghttp2/1.28.0
[  0.138] recv SETTINGS frame <length=0, flags=0x01, stream_id=0>
         ; ACK
         (niv=0)
[  0.138] recv WINDOW_UPDATE frame <length=4, flags=0x00, stream_id=13>
         (window_size_increment=10420224)
[  0.257] recv (stream_id=13) :status: 200
[  0.257] recv (stream_id=13) x-xss-protection: 0
[  0.257] recv (stream_id=13) pragma: no-cache
[  0.257] recv (stream_id=13) cache-control: private, no-cache, no-store,
must-revalidate
[  0.257] recv (stream_id=13) x-frame-options: DENY
[  0.257] recv (stream_id=13) strict-transport-security: max-age=15552000;
preload
[  0.257] recv (stream_id=13) x-content-type-options: nosniff
[  0.257] recv (stream_id=13) expires: Sat, 01 Jan 2000 00:00:00 GMT
[  0.257] recv (stream_id=13) set-cookie: fr=0m7urZrTka6WQuSGa..BaQ42y.61.A
AA.0.0.BaQ42y.AWXRqgzE; expires=Tue, 27-Mar-2018 12:10:26 GMT; Max-Age=7776
000; path=/; domain=.facebook.com; secu
re; httponly
[  0.257] recv (stream_id=13) set-cookie: sb=so1DWrDge9fIkTZ7e-i5S2To; expi
res=Fri, 27-Dec-2019 12:10:26 GMT; Max-Age=63072000; path=/; domain=.facebo
ok.com; secure; httponly
[  0.257] recv (stream_id=13) vary: Accept-Encoding
[  0.257] recv (stream_id=13) content-encoding: gzip
[  0.257] recv (stream_id=13) content-type: text/html; charset=UTF-8
[  0.257] recv (stream_id=13) x-fb-debug: yrE7eqv05dkxF8R1+i4VlIZmUNInVI+AP
DyG7HCW6t7NCEtGkIIRqJadLwj87Hmhk6z/N3O212zTPFXkT2GnSw==
[  0.257] recv (stream_id=13) date: Wed, 27 Dec 2017 12:10:26 GMT
[  0.257] recv HEADERS frame <length=517, flags=0x04, stream_id=13>
         ; END_HEADERS
         (padlen=0)
         ; First response header
<!DOCTYPE html>
<html lang="en" id="facebook" class="no_js">
<head><meta charset="utf-8" />
…etc.
[  0.243] recv DATA frame <length=1122, flags=0x00, stream_id=13>
…
```

```
[  0.243] recv DATA frame <length=2589, flags=0x00, stream_id=13>
...
[  0.264] recv DATA frame <length=13707, flags=0x00, stream_id=13>
...
[  0.267] send WINDOW_UPDATE frame <length=4, flags=0x00, stream_id=0>
          (window_size_increment=33706)
[  0.267] send WINDOW_UPDATE frame <length=4, flags=0x00, stream_id=13>
          (window_size_increment=33706)
...
[416.688] recv DATA frame <length=8920, flags=0x01, stream_id=13>
          ; END_STREAM
[417.226] send GOAWAY frame <length=8, flags=0x00, stream_id=0>
          (last_stream_id=0, error_code=NO_ERROR(0x00), opaque_data(0)=[])
```

I show some of the DATA frames but cut most of them, replacing them with ...etc. text. You can also pass the -n flag to hide the data and show only the frame headers:

```
$ nghttp -nv https://www.facebook.com | more
```

Even with the data truncated, this code looks complicated, so I'll walk you through it bit by bit.

First, you connect and negotiate the HTTP/2 over HTTPS (h2). nghttp doesn't output the HTTPS setup or the HTTP/2 preface/magic message, so you receive a SETTINGS frame first:

```
$ nghttp -v https://www.facebook.com | more
[  0.043] Connected
The negotiated protocol: h2
[  0.107] recv SETTINGS frame <length=30, flags=0x00, stream_id=0>
          (niv=5)
          [SETTINGS_HEADER_TABLE_SIZE(0x01):4096]
          [SETTINGS_MAX_FRAME_SIZE(0x05):16384]
          [SETTINGS_MAX_HEADER_LIST_SIZE(0x06):131072]
          [SETTINGS_MAX_CONCURRENT_STREAMS(0x03):100]
          [SETTINGS_INITIAL_WINDOW_SIZE(0x04):65536]
```

SETTINGS FRAME

The SETTINGS frame (0x4) is the first frame that must be sent by the server and also by the client (after the HTTP/2 preface/magic message). The frame consists of either an empty payload or several field/value pairs, as shown in table 4.2.

The SETTINGS frame defines only one flag that can be set in the common frame header: ACK (0x1). Set the flag to 0 if the settings are being advertised by this side of the HTTP/2 connection; set it to 1 for an acknowledgment of settings already sent by the other side of the HTTP/2 connection. If it's an acknowledgment (the flag is set to 1), no other settings should be set in the payload.

Table 4.2 `HEADERS` **frame format**

Field	Length	Description
`Identifier`	16 bits	Six settings are defined in the specification, and two more have been added recently (with more likely to be added in the future). Proposed settings aren't formally standardized: ■ `SETTINGS_HEADER_TABLE_SIZE` (0x1) ■ `SETTINGS_ENABLE_PUSH` (0x2) ■ `SETTINGS_MAX_CONCURRENT_STREAMS` (0x3) ■ `SETTINGS_INITIAL_WINDOW_SIZE` (0x4) ■ `SETTINGS_MAX_FRAME_SIZE` (0x5) ■ `SETTINGS_MAX_HEADER_LIST_SIZE` (0x6) ■ `SETTINGS_ACCEPT_CACHE_DIGEST` (0x7)[a] ■ `SETTINGS_ENABLE_CONNECT_PROTOCOL` (0x8)[b] *Note:* the `SETTINGS_ACCEPT_CACHE_DIGEST` is a proposed setting, not formally standardized yet and subject to change.
`Value`	32 bits	This field is the value of the setting. Note that if a setting isn't defined, the default values are used. Proposed settings aren't formally standardized yet: ■ 4096 octets ■ 1 ■ No limit ■ 65,535 octets ■ 16,384 octets ■ No limit ■ 0 – No ■ 0 – No *Note:* the `SETTINGS_ACCEPT_CACHE_DIGEST` is a proposed setting, not formally standardized yet and subject to change, including its default value.

[a]   https://tools.ietf.org/html/draft-ietf-httpbis-cache-digest
[b]   https://tools.ietf.org/html/rfc8441

With this knowledge in mind, look again at the first message:

```
[  0.107] recv SETTINGS frame <length=30, flags=0x00, stream_id=0>
        (niv=5)
        [SETTINGS_HEADER_TABLE_SIZE(0x01):4096]
        [SETTINGS_MAX_FRAME_SIZE(0x05):16384]
        [SETTINGS_MAX_HEADER_LIST_SIZE(0x06):131072]
        [SETTINGS_MAX_CONCURRENT_STREAMS(0x03):100]
        [SETTINGS_INITIAL_WINDOW_SIZE(0x04):65536]
```

The received `SETTINGS` frame has a payload 30 octets long, with no flags set (so not an acknowledgement frame), and uses the stream ID `0`. Stream ID `0` is reserved for control messages (`SETTINGS` and `WINDOW_UPDATE` frames), so it's correct for the server to use stream `0` to send this `SETTINGS` frame.

Next you get the settings themselves, of which there are 5 (niv=5) in this example, each of which is 16 bits (identifier) + 32 bits (value). This example is 48 bits or 6 octets in total, which makes up the 30-octet length given in the header (5 headers x 6 octets = 30 octets). So far, so good. Now look at the individual settings sent:

1 Facebook is using a SETTINGS_HEADER_TABLE_SIZE of 4,096 octets. This setting is used for HPACK HTTP header compression, which I discuss in chapter 8, so ignore it for now.

2 Facebook also uses a SETTINGS_MAX_FRAME_SIZE of 16,384 octets, so your client (nghttp) must not send any larger payloads on this connection.

3 Next Facebook sets the SETTINGS_MAX_HEADER_LIST_SIZE to 131,072 octets, so you're not allowed to send any uncompressed headers larger than that.

4 Facebook sets the SETTINGS_MAX_CONCURRENT_STREAMS to 100 streams. Chapter 2 shows an example in which an attempt was made to load more than 100 images from a server with a 100-stream limit. In that case, requests were queued, waiting for a free stream, similar to the way that requests queue in HTTP/1, but with a lower connection limit than the six connections most browsers use. HTTP/2 dramatically increases the number of parallel requests that can be performed, but the number is often limited by the server (typically, to 100 or 128 streams) rather than left unlimited (the default).

5 Finally Facebook sets the SETTINGS_INITIAL_WINDOW_SIZE to 65,536 octets. This setting is used for flow control, which I cover in chapter 7.

A few things in this seemingly simple frame are worth noting. For a start, the settings can be in any order, such as SETTINGS_MAX_CONCURRENT_STREAMS, which is defined in the specification as setting 3 (0x03) but is given after SETTINGS_MAX_HEADER_LIST_SIZE, which is setting 6 (0x06). Also, many of the settings are using the default initial values, so the server could have sent this reduced SETTINGS frame for the same effect with only three settings:

```
[  0.107] recv SETTINGS frame <length=18, flags=0x00, stream_id=0>
         (niv=3)
         [SETTINGS_MAX_HEADER_LIST_SIZE(0x06):131072]
         [SETTINGS_MAX_CONCURRENT_STREAMS(0x03):100]
         [SETTINGS_INITIAL_WINDOW_SIZE(0x04):65536]
```

There's no harm, however, in being more explicit about the values you want to use.

This example shows that Facebook is using a SETTINGS_INITIAL_WINDOW_SIZE 1 octet larger than the default (65,535 octets), which seems to be odd, as it's hardly worth changing the default for.

Finally, note that the Facebook server isn't setting SETTINGS_ENABLE_PUSH. This setting is intended for the server to push to the client, so it's for the client to use. It doesn't make sense for the server to set this setting, although I guess it could be used to advertise whether push support is possible on this server (if the spec authors decided to use it for this purpose). It's more important for the client SETTINGS frame to turn this setting off if the client doesn't support *HTTP/2 push* or doesn't want it enabled.

Moving back to the example, I'll skip the WINDOW_UPDATE frame for a moment and look at the next three SETTINGS frames instead:

```
[  0.107] recv SETTINGS frame <length=30, flags=0x00, stream_id=0>
          (niv=5)
          [SETTINGS_HEADER_TABLE_SIZE(0x01):4096]
          [SETTINGS_MAX_FRAME_SIZE(0x05):16384]
          [SETTINGS_MAX_HEADER_LIST_SIZE(0x06):131072]
          [SETTINGS_MAX_CONCURRENT_STREAMS(0x03):100]
          [SETTINGS_INITIAL_WINDOW_SIZE(0x04):65536]
[  0.107] send SETTINGS frame <length=12, flags=0x00, stream_id=0>
          (niv=2)
          [SETTINGS_MAX_CONCURRENT_STREAMS(0x03):100]
          [SETTINGS_INITIAL_WINDOW_SIZE(0x04):65535]
[  0.107] send SETTINGS frame <length=0, flags=0x01, stream_id=0>
          ; ACK
          (niv=0)
  ...
[  0.138] recv SETTINGS frame <length=0, flags=0x01, stream_id=0>
          ; ACK
          (niv=0)
```

nghttp receives the initial server SETTINGS frame (already discussed), followed by the client's sending a SETTINGS frame with a couple of settings. Next the client acknowledges the server's SETTINGS frame. The acknowledgment SETTINGS frame is a simple one, with the ACK (0x01) flag set, 0 length, and therefore 0 settings (niv=0). A bit farther down is the server's acknowledgement of the client's SETTINGS frame in an identical simple format.

This example shows that a period exists during which one side has sent a SETTINGS frame but hasn't received any acknowledgment. During this time, these nondefault settings can't be used. But because all HTTP/2 implementations must be able to process the default values, and because the SETTINGS frame must be sent first, this situation shouldn't cause problems.

WINDOW_UPDATE FRAME
The server also sent a WINDOW_UPDATE frame:

```
[  0.107] recv WINDOW_UPDATE frame <length=4, flags=0x00, stream_id=0>
          (window_size_increment=10420225)
```

The WINDOW_UPDATE frame (0x8) is used for flow control, such as to limit the amount of data that can be sent to avoid overwhelming the receiver. Under HTTP/1, only one request can be in flight at a time. If the client started getting overwhelmed with data, it stopped processing TCP packets; then TCP flow control (similar to HTTP/2 flow control) kicked in and slowed the sending of data until the receiver was ready to handle more. In HTTP/2, there are multiple streams on the same connection, so you can't depend on TCP flow control and must implement your own per-stream slow-down method.

The initial window size of data that can be sent is set in the SETTINGS frame, and the WINDOW_UPDATE frame is used to increment this amount. The WINDOW_UPDATE frame is, therefore, a simple frame without any flags and with one value (and a reserved bit), as shown in table 4.3.

Table 4.3 WINDOW_UPDATE frame format

Field	Length	Description
Reserved Bit	1 bit	Not used
Window Size Increment	31 bits	The number of octets that can be sent before the next WINDOW_UPDATE frame must be received

The WINDOW_UPDATE frame defines no flags and applies to the stream given, or, if set for stream 0, applies to the entire HTTP/2 connection. Senders, therefore, must track at both stream level and total level.

HTTP/2 flow control applies only to DATA frames. All other frame types (or at least those defined so far) can continue to send even when the flow-control window has been used up. This feature prevents important control messages (such as the WINDOW_UPDATE message itself) from being blocked by large DATA frames. Also, the DATA frame should be the only frame of any size.

I examine the HTTP/2 flow-control mechanism in chapter 7.

PRIORITY FRAME

The next frames are several PRIORITY frames (0x2):

```
[  0.107] send PRIORITY frame <length=5, flags=0x00, stream_id=3>
            (dep_stream_id=0, weight=201, exclusive=0)
[  0.107] send PRIORITY frame <length=5, flags=0x00, stream_id=5>
            (dep_stream_id=0, weight=101, exclusive=0)
[  0.107] send PRIORITY frame <length=5, flags=0x00, stream_id=7>
            (dep_stream_id=0, weight=1, exclusive=0)
[  0.107] send PRIORITY frame <length=5, flags=0x00, stream_id=9>
            (dep_stream_id=7, weight=1, exclusive=0)
[  0.107] send PRIORITY frame <length=5, flags=0x00, stream_id=11>
            (dep_stream_id=3, weight=1, exclusive=0)
```

This code creates several streams with various priorities for nghttp to use. In fact, nghttp doesn't use streams 3–11 directly; it hangs other streams from the ones it sets up at the beginning, using dep_stream_id. This use of the precreated priority streams allows requests to be prioritized appropriately without the need to explicitly set up the priorities for each subsequent new stream. Not all HTTP/2 clients predefine streams, and nghttp based its implementation on the Firefox model,[22] so don't be concerned if you're using another tool and don't see these PRIORITY frames.

---

[22] https://nghttp2.org/documentation/nghttp.1.html#dependency-based-priority

Stream priorities under HTTP/2 can get complicated, so I hold off looking at them until chapter 7. For now, be aware that some requests (such as the initial HTML, critical CSS, and critical JavaScript) can be prioritized over less important requests (such as images or noncritical asynchronous JavaScript). The frame format is shown in table 4.4, but this format won't make a lot of sense to you until you get to chapter 7.

Table 4.4 `PRIORITY` frame format

Field	Length	Description
`E` (Exclusive)	1 bit	Indicates whether the stream is exclusive (set only if the `Priority` flag is set for this frame)
`Stream Dependency`	31 bits	An indicator of which stream this header depends on (set only if the `Priority` flag is set for this frame)
`Weight`	8 bits	The weighting of this stream (set only if the `Priority` flag is set for this frame)

The `PRIORITY` frame (`0x2`) is fixed-length and doesn't define any flags.

HEADERS FRAME

Finally, after all this setup, you get to the meat of the protocol and can make an HTTP/2 request. An HTTP/2 request is sent in a `HEADERS` frame (`0x1`):

```
[  0.107] send HEADERS frame <length=43, flags=0x25, stream_id=13>
          ; END_STREAM | END_HEADERS | PRIORITY
          (padlen=0, dep_stream_id=11, weight=16, exclusive=0)
          ; Open new stream
          :method: GET
          :path: /
          :scheme: https
          :authority: www.facebook.com
          accept: */*
          accept-encoding: gzip, deflate
          user-agent: nghttp2/1.28.0
```

If you ignore the first few lines of the HTTP/2 frame header, the rest should look somewhat similar to HTTP/1 requests. As you may recall from chapter 1, an HTTP/1 request is made up of a combination of the first line and the mandatory host header (along with any other HTTP headers):

```
GET / HTTP/1.1↵
Host: www.facebook.com↵
```

In HTTP/2, instead of having a specific request frame type or a different first line in the `HEADERS` frame, *everything* is sent as a header, and new *pseudoheaders* (which start with a colon) have been created to define the various parts of the HTTP request line:

```
:method: GET
:path: /
:scheme: https
:authority: www.facebook.com
```

Note that the `:authority` pseudoheader has replaced the HTTP/1.1 `Host` header. The HTTP/2 pseudoheaders are strictly defined,[23] and unlike standard HTTP headers, they can't be added to without changing HTTP/2, so you can't create a new pseudoheader like this:

```
:barry: value
```

You must stick to normal HTTP headers, without the initial colon, for any app-specific headers:

```
barry: value
```

You can create pseudoheaders with new specifications, however, which has already happened once at the time of this writing: the `:protocol` pseudoheader was added in the *Bootstrapping WebSockets with HTTP/2* RFC.[24] The use of new pseudoheaders will likely require a new `SETTINGS` parameter to indicate support by client and server.

These pseudoheaders can also be shown in client tools like Chrome's developer tools (figure 4.11), so they also indicate an HTTP/2 request (though other browsers, such as Firefox, don't show pseudoheaders at this writing).

HTTP/2 pseudoheaders
in Chrome developer
tools Network tab

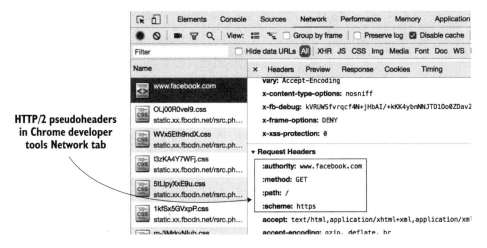

Figure 4.11   HTTP/2 pseudoheaders in Chrome developer tools

Also note that HTTP/2 enforces lowercase HTTP header names. HTTP/1 was officially case-insensitive for header names, though some implementations didn't strictly honor this specification. HTTP header values can contain different cases, but the header names themselves can't. HTTP/2 also is stricter about badly formatted HTTP

---

[23] https://tools.ietf.org/html/rfc7540#section-8.1.2
[24] https://tools.ietf.org/html/rfc8441#section-3

headers. Leading spaces, double colons, and newlines can cause problems in HTTP/2, even though most HTTP/1 implementations would process them. This example is one strong use case for examining HTTP/2 messages at frame level, as you're doing here. These errors are usually highlighted at this low level, whereas clients return more cryptic error messages (such as ERR_SPDY_PROTOCOL_ERROR in Chrome) to the user when they find invalid HTTP headers, preventing your site from working. The HEADERS frame format is shown in table 4.5.

Table 4.5 HEADERS **frame format**

Field	Length	Description
Pad Length	8 bits (optional)	An optional field indicating the length of the Padding field (set only if the Padded flag is set for this frame)
E (Exclusive)	1 bit	Indicates whether the stream is exclusive (set only if the Priority flag is set for this frame)
Stream Dependency	31 bits	Indicates the stream on which this header depends (set only if the Priority flag is set for this frame)
Weight	8 bits	The weighting of this stream (set only if the Priority flag is set for this frame)
Header Block Fragment	Length of the frame minus the other fields in this table	The request headers (including pseudoheaders)
Padding	Indicated by the Pad Length field (optional)	Set to 0 for each padded byte (set only if the Padded flag is set for this frame)

I discuss the E, Stream Dependency, and Weight fields in chapter 7. The Pad Length and Padding fields are added for security reasons to optionally allow the true length of the message to be hidden. The Header Block Fragment field is where all the headers (including pseudoheaders) are sent. This field isn't clear-text, as the nghttp output may suggest. I look into the HPACK header compression format in chapter 8, so don't worry about it now, especially because tools such as nghttp automatically decompress HTTP headers for you.

The HEADERS frame defines four flags that can be set in the common frame header:

- END_STREAM (0x1) is set if no other frames follow this HEADERS frame (such as a DATA frame for a POST request). Somewhat counterintuitively, CONTINUATION frames (discussed later in this chapter) are exempt from this restriction; they're considered to be continuations of the HEADERS frame rather than additional frames and are controlled by the END_HEADERS flag.
- END_HEADERS (0x4) indicates that all the HTTP headers are contained in this frame and aren't followed by a CONTINUATION frame with additional headers.

- PADDED (0x8) is set when padding is used. This flag means that the first 8 bits of the DATA frame indicate how much padding has been added to the end of the HEADERS frame.
- PRIORITY (0x20) indicates that the E, Stream Dependency, and Weight fields are set in this frame.

If an HTTP header is larger than a single frame, a CONTINUATION frame is used (immediately after the HEADERS frame it's continuing), rather than an additional HEADERS frame. This process may seem to be overly complex compared with HTTP bodies, which use as many DATA frames as required. But the other fields discussed in table 4.5 can be used only once, and setting them differently in subsequent HEADERS frames for the same request would cause issues. The requirement to have CONTINUATION frames immediately follow HEADERS frames rather than allow interleaving also limits the multiplexed nature of HTTP/2, and alternatives were considered.[25] The reality is that CONTINUATION frames are rarely used and that most requests will fit in a single HEADERS frame.

Looking at the output with this knowledge, you can understand the first part of the message a little better now:

```
[  0.107] send HEADERS frame <length=43, flags=0x25, stream_id=13>
          ; END_STREAM | END_HEADERS | PRIORITY
          (padlen=0, dep_stream_id=11, weight=16, exclusive=0)
          ; Open new stream
          :method: GET
          :path: /
          :scheme: https
          :authority: www.facebook.com
          accept: */*
          accept-encoding: gzip, deflate
          user-agent: nghttp2/1.28.0
```

Each new request is given a unique stream ID incremented from the last-used stream ID (11 in this case, from the last of the PRIORITY frames that nghttp created, so this frame is created with stream ID 13, as even headers are reserved for the server). Various flags are set that combine to make the hexadecimal value 0x25 and that nghttp2 helpfully displays on the line below. The END_STREAM (0x1) and END_HEADERS (0x4) flags are set to indicate that this frame contains the complete request and that there's no DATA frame (as there might be for a POST request). The PRIORITY flag (0x20) is set to indicate that prioritization is used in this frame. Adding these hexadecimal values together (0x1 + 0x4 + 0x20), you get the 0x25 shown in the frame header. This stream is dependent on stream ID 11, so it's given the appropriate priority and a weighting of 16 within that priority. Again, don't worry too much about this topic now; I explain prioritization in chapter 7. nghttp notes that this stream is new (Open new stream) and then lists the various HTTP pseudoheaders and HTTP request headers.

---

[25] https://github.com/http2/http2-spec/wiki/ContinuationProposals

HTTP responses are also sent with a HEADERS frame on the same stream, as you see in this example:

```
[  0.257] recv (stream_id=13) :status: 200
[  0.257] recv (stream_id=13) x-xss-protection: 0
[  0.257] recv (stream_id=13) pragma: no-cache
[  0.257] recv (stream_id=13) cache-control: private, no-cache, no-store,
must-revalidate
[  0.257] recv (stream_id=13) x-frame-options: DENY
[  0.257] recv (stream_id=13) strict-transport-security: max-age=15552000;
preload
[  0.257] recv (stream_id=13) x-content-type-options: nosniff
[  0.257] recv (stream_id=13) expires: Sat, 01 Jan 2000 00:00:00 GMT
[  0.257] recv (stream_id=13) set-cookie: fr=0m7urZrTka6WQuSGa..BaQ4Ay.61.A
AA.0.0.BaQ42y.12345678; expires=Tue, 27-Mar-2018 12:10:26 GMT; Max-Age=7776
000; path=/; domain=.facebook.com; secu
re; httponly
[  0.257] recv (stream_id=13) set-cookie: sb=so11234567890TZ7e-i5S2To; expi
res=Fri, 27-Dec-2019 12:10:26 GMT; Max-Age=63072000; path=/; domain=.facebo
ok.com; secure; httponly
[  0.257] recv (stream_id=13) vary: Accept-Encoding
[  0.257] recv (stream_id=13) content-encoding: gzip
[  0.257] recv (stream_id=13) content-type: text/html; charset=UTF-8
[  0.257] recv (stream_id=13) x-fb-debug: yrE7eqv05dkxF8R1+1234567890nVI+AP
DyG7HCW6t7NCEtGkIIRqJadLwj87Hmhk6z/N3O212zTPFXkT2GnSw==
[  0.257] recv (stream_id=13) date: Wed, 27 Dec 2017 12:10:26 GMT
[  0.257] recv HEADERS frame <length=517, flags=0x04, stream_id=13>
         ; END_HEADERS
         (padlen=0)
         ; First response header
```

Here, you first see the status pseudoheader (:status: 200), which, unlike in HTTP/1.1, gives only the three-digit HTTP code (200), not the text representation of that status code (such as 200 OK). This pseudo-header is followed by various HTTP headers, though again, this isn't how they're sent on the wire, as you'll see when we look at HPACK in chapter 8. Then nghttp lists the HEADERS frame details. Confusingly (at least to me), nghttp gives frame details after the frame payload rather than before it, as I would have preferred.[26] These details include the END_HEADERS flag (0x04), signaling that the entire HTTP response header fits into this single frame.

Trailing headers

HTTP/1.1 introduced the concept of trailing headers, which can be sent after the body. These headers allow for metadata that can't be calculated up front. For streaming data, for example, a checksum or digital signature of the content could be calculated and included as a trailing HTTP header.

---

[26] https://github.com/nghttp2/nghttp2/issues/1163

Trailing headers *(continued)*

In reality, trailing headers are poorly supported and rarely used. But HTTP/2 decided to continue supporting them, so a HEADERS frame (or a HEADERS frame followed by one or more CONTINUATION frames) appears before and optionally after all the DATA frames for that stream.

DATA FRAME

After the HEADERS frame is the DATA frame (0x0), which is used to send message bodies. In HTTP/1, the body of the message is sent in the response after the HTTP headers, after a double line break (signaling the end of the HTTP headers). In HTTP/2, data is a separate message type. You can send headers followed by some of the body, part of a different stream, more of the body, and so on. By separating HTTP/2 responses into one or more frames, you can have multiplexed streams over the same connection.

HTTP/2 DATA frames are simple, containing whatever data is needed: UTF-8 encoded, gzipped, HTML code, bytes that make up a JPEG picture, or whatever. The main frame header includes the length, so length isn't required in the DATA frame format itself. Like the HEADERS frame, the DATA frame allows the use of padding to obscure the size of the message for security reasons, so a Pad Length field can be used at the beginning to state the length. The DATA frame format, therefore, is simple, as shown in table 4.6.

Table 4.6   DATA frame format

Field	Length	Description
Pad Length	8 bits (optional)	An optional field indicating the length of the Padding field (include only if the PADDED flag is set)
Data	Length of the frame minus any Padding fields	The data
Padding	Indicated by the Pad Length field (optional)	Set to 0 for each padded byte (include only if the PADDED flag is set)

The DATA frame defines two flags that can be set in the common frame header:

- END_STREAM (0x1) is set if this frame is the last in the stream.
- PADDED (0x8) is set when padding is used. It means that the first 8 bits of the DATA frame is used to indicate how much padding has been added to the end of the frame.

In the example, I stripped out most of the content for space reasons, but the ...etc. lines normally would be filled with the appropriate data:

```
<!DOCTYPE html>
<html lang="en" id="facebook" class="no_js">
<head><meta charset="utf-8" />
...etc.
[   0.243]  recv DATA frame <length=1122, flags=0x00, stream_id=13>
...etc.
[   0.243]  recv DATA frame <length=2589, flags=0x00, stream_id=13>
...etc.
[   0.264]  recv DATA frame <length=13707, flags=0x00, stream_id=13>
...etc.
[   0.267]  send WINDOW_UPDATE frame <length=4, flags=0x00, stream_id=0>
            (window_size_increment=33706)
[   0.267]  send WINDOW_UPDATE frame <length=4, flags=0x00, stream_id=13>
            (window_size_increment=33706)
...etc.
[416.688]  recv DATA frame <length=8920, flags=0x00, stream_id=13>
```

Here, you see HTML code being sent in various DATA frames (nghttp helpfully un-gzips the data for you), and as the client processes these frames, it sends back WINDOW_UPDATE frames, allowing the server to keep sending more data. It's interesting that Facebook chooses to send relatively small DATA frames initially (1,122 octets, 2,589 octets, and so on), despite the fact that the client is willing to handle much larger frames (up to 65,535 octets). I'm not sure whether this choice is intentional (to get as much of the data to the client as quickly as possible), due to an initially small TCP congestion window, or for some other reason.

As HTTP/2 DATA frames can by default be split into parts, there's no need for chunked encoding (discussed in section 4.1.1). The HTTP/2 spec even goes as far as to say "The chunked transfer encoding . . . MUST NOT be used in HTTP/2."

GOAWAY FRAME

The GOAWAY frame (0x7) is the next message:

```
[417.226]  send GOAWAY frame <length=8, flags=0x00, stream_id=0>
            (last_stream_id=0, error_code=NO_ERROR(0x00), opaque_data(0)=[])
```

This somewhat-rude-sounding frame type is used to shut down the connection, either because there are no more messages to send or because a serious error occurred. The GOAWAY frame format is shown in table 4.7.

Table 4.7 GOAWAY frame format

Field	Length	Description
Reserved Bit	1 bit	Not used
Last-Stream-ID	31 bits	The last incoming stream ID processed, to allow the client to know whether a recently initiated stream was missed

Table 4.7 GOAWAY frame format *(continued)*

Field	Length	Description
Error Code	32 bits	The error code, in case the GOAWAY frame was sent due to an error: • NO_ERROR (0x0) • PROTOCOL_ERROR (0x1) • INTERNAL_ERROR (0x2) • FLOW_CONTROL_ERROR (0x3) • SETTINGS_TIMEOUT (0x4) • STREAM_CLOSED (0x5) • FRAME_SIZE_ERROR (0x6) • REFUSED_STREAM (0x7) • CANCEL (0x8) • COMPRESSION_ERROR (0x9) • CONNECT_ERROR (0xa) • ENHANCE_YOUR_CALM (0xb) • INADEQUATE_SECURITY (0xc) • HTTP_1_1_REQUIRED (0xd)
Additional Debug Data	Remainder of the frame length (optional)	Undefined, implementation-specific format

The GOAWAY frame doesn't define any flags.

Looking at the final message in the previous nghttp output, you see an example of a GOAWAY frame:

```
[417.226] send GOAWAY frame <length=8, flags=0x00, stream_id=0>
          (last_stream_id=0, error_code=NO_ERROR(0x00), opaque_data(0)=[])
```

The nghttp client sent the GOAWAY frame rather than receiving it from the server. In this example, nghttp got the homepage HTML and didn't request all the dependent resources (CSS, JavaScript, and so on) that a normal browser would request. When the response is processed and the client isn't waiting on any more data, it sends this frame to shut down the HTTP/2 connection. Web browsers will likely leave the connection open in case a subsequent request is made, but nghttp was finished after getting this one response, so decided to close the connection before quitting. A browser may do the same thing to any open connections when you quit it.

The frame was sent with the minimum 8-octet length (1 bit + 31 bits + 32 bits); no flags were set; and the frame was sent on stream 0. The last stream ID received from the server was 0, so there were no server-initiated streams. There were no error codes (NO_ERROR [0x00]) and no additional debug data. In summary, this example is a standard way to close the connection cleanly when it's no longer needed.

4.3.4 *Other frames*

The nghttp Facebook example covered many of the HTTP/2 frame types, but a few more types weren't used in this simple flow. Also, HTTP/2 has been written to allow expansion of frame types. Three new frame types have been added—ALTSVC, ORIGIN, and CACHE_DIGEST—and are discussed at the end of this section. At this writing, only the first two have been formally standardized, but the last one and perhaps more will be standardized by the time this book is published. Each new HTTP/2 frame type, HTTP/2 setting, and HTTP/2 error code must be registered with the Internet Assigned Numbers Authority (IANA).[27]

CONTINUATION FRAME

The CONTINUATION frame (0x9) is used for large HTTP headers and immediately follows a HEADERS frame or a PUSH_PROMISE frame. Because the entire HTTP header is needed before a request can be processed, and to keep the HPACK dictionary in check (see chapter 8), the CONTINUATION frame must immediately follow the HEADERS frame that it's continuing. As I mentioned when discussing the HEADERS frame, this requirement limits the multiplexed nature of HTTP/2, and there has been much argument about whether the CONTINUATION frame is needed or whether larger HEADERS frames should be allowed. For now, the frame stays, though it isn't expected to be used much.

The CONTINUATION frame is simpler than the HEADER or PUSH_PROMISE frame that it continues. It contains extra header data. The frame format is shown in table 4.8.

Table 4.8 CONTINUATION **frame format**

Field	Length	Description
Header Block Fragment	Length of the frame minus this field	The data

The CONTINUATION frame defines only one flag, which can be set in the common frame header. END_HEADERS (0x4), when set, indicates that all the HTTP headers are finished in this frame and aren't followed by another CONTINUATION frame with additional headers.

The CONTINUATION frame doesn't use the END_STREAM flag to indicate that there's no body, as this frame is driven off the original HEADERS frame.

PING FRAME

The PING frame (0x6) is used to measure a round trip from the sender and can also be used to keep an otherwise-unused connection alive. When it receives this frame, the receiver should immediately respond with a similar PING frame. Both PING frames should be sent only on the control stream (stream ID 0). The PING frame format is shown in table 4.9.

---

[27] https://www.iana.org/assignments/http2-parameters/http2-parameters.xhtml

Table 4.9 PING frame format

Field	Length	Description
Opaque Data	64 bits (8 octets)	Data to be sent in the returning PING request

The PING frame defines one flag that can be set in the common frame header. ACK (0x1) should not be set in the initial PING frame, but it should be set on the returning PING frame.

PUSH_PROMISE FRAME

The PUSH_PROMISE frame (0x5) is used by the server to tell the client that the server is going to push an asset that the client didn't explicitly ask for. The PUSH_PROMISE frame needs to provide the client information about the asset that's about to be pushed, so it includes all the HTTP headers that normally would be included in a HEADERS frame request (and similarly can be followed by a CONTINUATION frame for push requests with headers larger than can fit in a single frame). The PUSH_PROMISE frame format is shown in table 4.10.

Table 4.10 PUSH_PROMISE frame format

Field	Length	Description
Pad Length	8 bits (optional)	An optional field indicating the length of the Padding field
Reserved Bit	1 bit	Not used
Promised Stream ID	31 bits	Indicates the stream on which this push promise will be sent
Header Block Fragment	Length of the frame minus the other fields in this table	The HTTP headers of the pushed resource
Padding	Indicated by Pad Length field (optional)	Set to 0 for each padded byte

The PUSH_PROMISE frame defines two flags that can be set in the common frame header:

- END_HEADERS (0x4) indicates that all the HTTP headers are contained in this frame and aren't followed by a CONTINUATION frame with additional headers.
- PADDED (0x8) is set when padding is used. It means that the first 8 bits of the DATA frame are used to indicate how much padding has been added to the end of the PUSH_PROMISE frame.

I discuss HTTP/2 server push in chapter 5.

RST_STREAM FRAME

The final frame defined in the original HTTP/2 specification is the RST_STREAM frame (0x3), which is used to immediately cancel (or reset) a stream. This cancelation could be due to an error or because the request is no longer required. Perhaps the client has navigated away, canceled the loading, or doesn't need a server-pushed resource.

HTTP/1.1 doesn't offer this functionality. If you start to download a large resource on a page, unless you kill the connection, you're stuck downloading the resource even if you navigate away from the page. You have no way to cancel a request in flight. This feature is yet another way in which HTTP/2 improves on HTTP/1.1. The RST_STREAM frame format is shown in table 4.11.

Table 4.11 RST_STREAM frame format

Field	Length	Description
Error Code	32 bits	The error code, to explain why the stream is being terminated: ■ NO_ERROR (0x0) ■ PROTOCOL_ERROR (0x1) ■ INTERNAL_ERROR (0x2) ■ FLOW_CONTROL_ERROR (0x3) ■ SETTINGS_TIMEOUT (0x4) ■ STREAM_CLOSED (0x5) ■ FRAME_SIZE_ERROR (0x6) ■ REFUSED_STREAM (0x7) ■ CANCEL (0x8) ■ COMPRESSION_ERROR (0x9) ■ CONNECT_ERROR (0xa) ■ ENHANCE_YOUR_CALM (0xb) ■ INADEQUATE_SECURITY (0xc) ■ HTTP_1_1_REQUIRED (0xd)

The RST_STREAM frame doesn't define any flags.

The spec gives little guidance on what these error codes mean, and even when it does, it's sometimes less than clear. It states the following, for example, to show that one of two error codes can be used to cancel pushed responses:

> *If the client determines, for any reason, that it does not wish to receive the pushed response from the server or if the server takes too long to begin sending the promised response, the client can send a RST_STREAM frame, using either the CANCEL or REFUSED_STREAM code and referencing the pushed stream's identifier.*

Ultimately, it's up to implementers to decide which error codes to use and when. Implementations may not always agree.

ALTSVC FRAME

The ALTSVC frame (0xa) was the first frame to be added to HTTP/2 since the HTTP/2 specification was approved. It's detailed in a separate specification[28] and allows a server

---

[28] https://tools.ietf.org/html/rfc7838

to advertise alternative services that are available to fetch this resource, as discussed in section 4.2.4. This frame may be used to upgrade (such as to an h2c connection from h2) or to direct traffic to another version. See table 4.12.

Table 4.12   `ALTSVC` **frame format**

Field	Length	Description
Origin-Len	16 bits	The length of the `Origin` field
Origin	Indicated by `Origin-Len` field (optional)	The alternative URL
Alt-Svc-Field-Value	Length of the frame minus the other fields in this table	The alternative service type

The `ALTSVC` frame doesn't define any flags.

ORIGIN FRAME

The `ORIGIN` frame (`0xc`) is a new frame, standardized in March 2018,[29] that allows the server to indicate which origins (such as domain name) this server will respond to. This frame is useful for a client to decide whether to coalesce connections to this HTTP/2 connection. The `ORIGIN` frame format is shown in table 4.13.

Table 4.13   `ORIGIN` **frame format**

Field	Length	Description
Origin-Len	16 bits	The length of the `Origin` field
Origin	Indicated by `Origin-Len` field (optional)	The alternative URL

Multiple `Origin-Len`/`Origin` pairs can be included up to the length of the frame. The `ORIGIN` frame doesn't define any flags.

I return to the `ORIGIN` frame when discussing connection coalescing in chapter 6.

CACHE_DIGEST FRAME

The `CACHE_DIGEST` frame (`0xd`) is a new frame proposal.[30] This frame allows the client to indicate which assets it has cached. It indicates that the server shouldn't push any of these resources, for example, because the client already has them. The `CACHE_DIGEST` frame format at this writing (and subject to change) is shown in table 4.14.

---

[29] https://tools.ietf.org/html/rfc8336
[30] https://tools.ietf.org/html/draft-ietf-httpbis-cache-digest

Table 4.14 `CACHE_DIGEST` **frame format**

Field	Length	Description
Origin-Len	16 bits	The length of the `Origin` field
Origin	Indicated by `Origin-Len` field (optional)	The origin this digest refers to
Digest-Value	Length of the frame minus the other fields in this table (optional)	The `Cache-Digest` (discussed in chapter 5)

The `CACHE_DIGEST` frame defines the following flags:

- `RESET` (0x1) allows the client to tell the server to reset any currently held `CACHE_DIGEST` information.
- `COMPLETE` (0x2) indicates that the included cache digests are the complete representation of the cache rather than a subset of the cache.

I return to the `CACHE_DIGEST` frame when discussing HTTP/2 server push in chapter 5.

Summary

- HTTP/2 is a binary protocol with a specific, detailed format and structure for its messages.
- For this reason, the client and server must agree to use HTTP/2 before sending any HTTP messages.
- For web browsers, this agreement is made mostly in the HTTPS connection negotiation, using a new extension called ALPN.
- In HTTP/2, requests and responses are sent and received in HTTP/2 frames.
- An HTTP/2 GET request, for example, usually is sent as a HEADERS frame, and the response usually is received as a HEADERS frame followed by DATA frames.
- Most web developers and web server administrators don't need to concern themselves with HTTP/2 frames, though tools are available for viewing them.
- Several HTTP/2 frames exist, and new frames can be added.

5

Implementing HTTP/2 push

This chapter covers

- What is HTTP/2 push?
- The various ways to request an HTTP/2 push
- How HTTP/2 push works from the server and client sides
- What to push and what not to push
- Troubleshooting HTTP/2 push
- Some of the risks of HTTP/2 push

5.1   What is HTTP/2 server push?

HTTP/2 server push (hereafter known as *HTTP/2 push*) allows servers to send back extra resources that weren't requested by the client. Before the introduction of HTTP/2, HTTP was a simple request-and-response protocol; a browser requested a resource, and the server responded with that resource. If the page needed extra resources to be displayed (such as CSS, JavaScript, fonts, images, and so on), the browser had to download the initial page, see that extra resources were referenced, and then request them. For images, making these extra requests may not have been too problematic; images don't often hold up initial paint time, and the page would start rendering with an empty space where the image should be. Some resources, however, are critical to page rendering (such as CSS and JavaScript), and the browser won't even attempt to render the page until these resources are downloaded. This process adds at least one extra round trip, so it slows web browsing. HTTP/2 multiplexing allows all the resources to be requested in parallel on the same connection, so it's better than HTTP/1, as there should be less queuing. But without HTTP/2 push, the browser would have to make those extra requests after downloading the initial page. Therefore, most web-page requests take at least two round trips in the best-case scenario, and maybe twice as long to display as you'd like them to take. Figure 5.1 shows a CSS file and a JavaScript file being downloaded at the same time in the second set of requests.

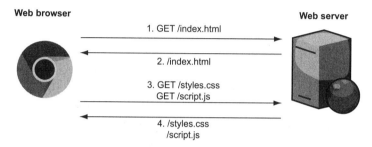

Figure 5.1   Critical resources require an extra request round trip.

Figure 5.2 shows that it takes approximately two round-trip requests to do the initial paint. Note that the styles.css and script.js resources arrive at slightly different times rather than at the same time due to networking or processing constraints; they're not run in parallel.

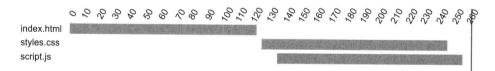

Figure 5.2   Critical resource round-trip lag as a waterfall diagram

This round-trip delay led to performance optimizations such as inlining style sheets directly onto the HTML page with `<style>` tags and doing something similar in JavaScript with `<script>` tags. By inlining the critical resources, browsers could start the first render as soon as the original page was downloaded and parsed rather than wait for additional critical resources.

Inlining resources has several down sides, though. For CSS, only the critical styling (the styling needed for the initial paint) is typically included; the full stylesheet is loaded later to minimize the amount of code inlined and avoid making the page too big. It's complicated to pull out the critical styles needed from the CSS resources and embed them in the HTML file, though tools do exist to help with this task. Besides being complicated, this process is wasteful; the critical CSS is duplicated on every page of the website rather than being stored in one CSS file that can be cached and reused on other pages. Worse, critical CSS that's inlined usually is still included in the main CSS file that's loaded later; it's not only duplicated across pages, but also duplicated within each page! Other disadvantages include the requirement to use JavaScript to load any noncritical CSS files, because using only the standard `<link rel="stylesheet" type="text/css" href="…">` would cause the rendering to be paused until the files are loaded, as there's no `async` attribute for CSS `link` tags. Additionally, if you want to change any of this critical CSS (such as with a site redesign), you need to change every page rather than update one common CSS file. All in all, inlining gives good performance benefits for the first visit, but it's a bit of a hack. It would be better to solve this problem in some other way, which is what HTTP/2 push aims to do.

HTTP/2 push breaks the "one request = one response" paradigm that HTTP has always worked under. It allows the server to respond to one request with many responses. "Can I get this page, please?" can be answered "Certainly, and here are some extra resources you'll want to load that page." Figure 5.3 shows only one round trip to get the page and the critical resources needed to start rendering that page.

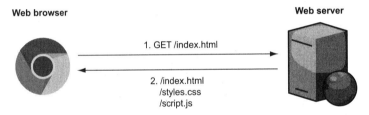

Figure 5.3   Using HTTP/2 push can remove the round-trip delay for critical resources.

This process can also be depicted as a waterfall diagram, as shown in figure 5.4. Again, the three resources don't arrive back at the same time, as shown by the short gaps between them, but the time required is slightly more than one round trip rather than two round trips.

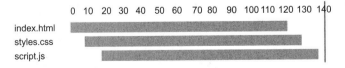

Figure 5.4   Waterfall diagram of using HTTP/2 push to receive all requests in the same round trip

The time saving can also be illustrated by request-and-response diagrams of the type I introduced in chapter 2. Figure 5.5 shows the significant time saved by sending back all critical resources with the initial page.

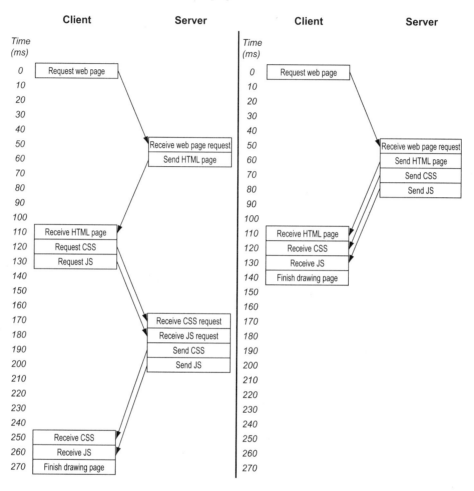

Figure 5.5 Request flow for a basic web page without HTTP/2 push (left) and with HTTP/2 push (right)

HTTP/2 push can improve load times if it's used correctly, but it can also hinder load times if you *overpush* resources that the client won't use or already has in its cache. You'll waste bandwidth that you could better use downloading a resource that you *do* need. HTTP/2 push should be used with caution and some thought, as I discuss in this chapter.

> **Is HTTP/2 push a replacement for WebSockets or SSE?**
>
> One crucial point to note is that pushed resources are still sent only in response to an initial request. It's impossible to push resources with HTTP/2 based purely on the server deciding that the client may want or need a resource. Technologies such as WebSockets and server-sent events (SSE) do allow a two-way flow, but HTTP/2 isn't truly bidirectional; everything is still initiated from a client-side request. Pushed resources are extra responses made in response to an initial request. When that initial request is finished, the stream is closed, and no other resources can be pushed unless another client request is made. Therefore, HTTP/2 push isn't a replacement for WebSockets or SSE as it's currently specified, though perhaps it could be if it were expanded further (see section 5.9).

5.2   How to push

How to push depends on your web server, because not every server supports HTTP/2 push at this writing. Some web servers can push with HTTP link headers or with configuration. Others (such as IIS) require writing code, so they can push only from dynamically generated pages rather than static HTML files. Consult your web-server documentation to see whether your server supports HTTP/2 push and how to use it. For the remainder of this chapter, I mostly use Apache, nginx, and NodeJS in examples. The concepts apply to most HTTP/2 web servers even if the implementation details vary slightly. If your web server doesn't support HTTP/2 push, you can still wrap a content delivery network around your server (see chapter 3) and use that CDN to provide push capability.

5.2.1   Using HTTP link headers to push

Many web servers (such as Apache, nginx, and H2O) and some CDNs (such as Cloudflare and Fastly) use *HTTP link headers* to notify the web server to push. If the web server sees these HTTP headers, it pushes the resources referenced in the header. In Apache, you can use config like this to add such a link header:

```
Header add Link "</assets/css/common.css>;as=style;rel=preload"
```

If you're using nginx, the syntax is similar:

```
add_header Link "</assets/css/common.css>;as=style;rel=preload"
```

Push link headers are often wrapped in conditional statements to apply the push only for certain paths or file types. In Apache, for example, to push the CSS stylesheet with index.html files rather than all resources, use syntax like the following:

```
<FilesMatch "index.html">
    Header add Link "</assets/css/common.css>;as=style;rel=preload"
</FilesMatch>
```

Other web servers have similar ways of adding HTTP headers, though not all web servers use the HTTP link header method to push resources. For those that do, when the request is sent back to the client, the web server reads these headers, requests that resource, and sends it as well. The `rel=preload` attribute needs to be set to indicate to the web server that this resource is to be pushed, but the `as=style` part (which indicates the type of resource) may be optional. This `as` attribute can be used to decide on prioritization, for example, though other web servers may not require it: Apache uses the Content type rather than the as attribute for prioritization.

Preload HTTP headers and HTTP/2 push

The preload link header predates HTTP/2 and was originally meant to be a client hint (discussed in chapter 6). This header would allow browsers to fetch these resources immediately, without waiting to download, read, and parse the whole page before deciding whether an asset needs to be downloaded. Preload headers allow the website owner to say, "This resource will definitely be needed, so I suggest that you request it as soon as you can if you don't already have it in your cache."

The preload link header has been repurposed by many HTTP/2 implementations to implement server push to take this hint one step further and send the resource proactively. If you want to use the original *preload* purpose but not push the resource, you usually can use the `nopush` attribute:

```
Header add Link "</assets/css/common.css>;as=style;rel=preload;nopush"
```

Currently, you have no standard way to do the reverse (saying that the link header should be pushed but not treated as a preload header), though the H2O web server (and the CDN Fastly, which uses this web server[a]) has added the `x-http2-push-only` attribute to handle this case:

```
link: </assets/jquery.js>;as=script;rel=preload;x-http2-push-only
```

Preload can also be set in the HTML itself in the HEAD tag, with code like this:

```
<link rel="preload" href="/assets/css/common.css" as="style">
```

Only the HTTP header version usually works for HTTP/2 push, however. The HTML version is ignored for HTTP/2 push purposes because it would be more complicated and time-consuming for servers to parse HTML to extract these headers than it is to read the HTTP headers. Web browsers need to parse the HTML anyway, so they accept either method for preload hints.

For client hints, the as attribute must be specified, but for HTTP/2 push, this may not be the case. To avoid confusion, I recommend always setting this attribute. The complete set of as attributes is listed on the w3.org website[b] and includes `script`, `style`, `font`, `image`, and `fetch`. Note that some of these attributes (particularly fonts) require the `crossorigin` attribute as well.[c]

Preload HTTP headers and HTTP/2 push (*continued*)

Some people find the reuse of preload headers for HTTP/2 push to be confusing. They say that it wasn't a good idea to reuse existing functionality for a new purpose[d] and suggest changing this feature. Despite this concern, use seems to be growing. One added benefit of using the preload header for both client hints and server push is that client/server combinations that don't support HTTP/2 push can still use the header to preload the resource with high priority, so you may still get some performance gain. I return to preload directives in section 5.8 to discuss the differing use cases for them and HTTP/2 push. I wanted to give a little information here for those readers who recognize the overlap with client hints.

[a] https://www.fastly.com/blog/optimizing-http2-server-push-fastly
[b] https://www.w3.org/TR/preload/#as-attribute
[c] https://drafts.csswg.org/css-fonts/#font-fetching-requirements
[d] https://github.com/w3c/preload/issues/99

While testing in Apache, you should turn off `PushDiary`, which attempts to prevent pushing the same resource twice on the same connection (more on this in section 5.4.4):

```
H2PushDiarySize 0
```

An explicit refresh request in the browser (F5) causes Apache to ignore `PushDiary`, but it's easier to turn `PushDiary` off while testing; otherwise, you may see inconsistent results. Other servers may have similar push tracking that needs to be turned off. You can also push multiple headers by using two link headers:

```
Header add Link "</assets/css/commoncss>;rel=preload;as=style"
Header add Link "</assets/js/common.js>;rel=preload;as=script"
```

or by combining the headers into one comma-separated header:

```
Header add Link "</assets/css/common.css>;rel=preload;as=style,
</assets/js/common.js>;rel=preload;as=script"
```

In chapter 1, I stated that these two methods are syntactically identical in the HTTP protocol, so either can be used.

5.2.2   *Viewing HTTP/2 pushes*

Pushed resources are indicated in the Initiator column of Chrome developer tools, as shown in figure 5.6.

Here you can see that the second resource (common.css) was pushed by the server. You also see that the resource starts downloading right away, with no green `Waiting` (`TTFB`) in the waterfall diagram for this request, as you see for the subsequent requests.

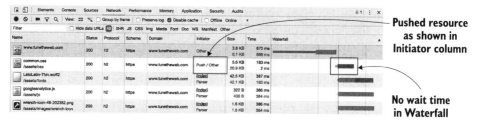

Figure 5.6   HTTP/2 pushed resource on the Network tab of Chrome's developer tools

Figure 5.7 shows the same page load without push (where the common.css request has moved from the second to the third requested resource and wasn't pushed).

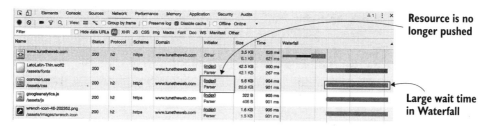

Figure 5.7   Same page load as in figure 5.6 without HTTP/2 push

The waterfall diagrams generated by webpagetest.org don't indicate pushed resources in any distinct way. But clicking the resource shows SERVER PUSHED in the details section, as shown in figure 5.8.

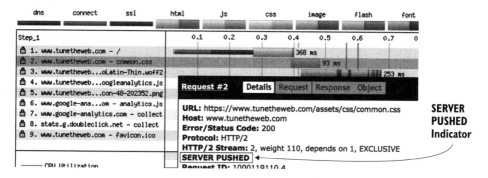

Figure 5.8   A pushed resource in WebPagetest

You can also use nghttp to make the web request so that you can see the frames discussed in chapter 4. Use the following command (changing the URL appropriately):

```
$ nghttp -anv https://www.tunetheweb.com/performance/
```

This command requests the resource and any assets that the page needs (-a flag), doesn't show the data downloaded onscreen (-n flag), and turns on verbose output to show the HTTP/2 frames (-v flag).

After connecting and getting the connection set up with the SETTINGS and PRIORITY frames, nghttp2 makes the request for the page by using the HEADERS frame:

```
[  0.013] send HEADERS frame <length=53, flags=0x25, stream_id=13>
          ; END_STREAM | END_HEADERS | PRIORITY
          (padlen=0, dep_stream_id=11, weight=16, exclusive=0)
          ; Open new stream
          :method: GET
          :path: /performance/
          :scheme: https
          :authority: www.tunetheweb.com
          accept: */*
          accept-encoding: gzip, deflate
          user-agent: nghttp2/1.28.0
```

Before you receive the page back, you see that it receives a PUSH_PROMISE frame for the pushed resource, as follows. Remember that nghttp shows the frame contents of received frames first and the frame details next:

```
[  0.017] recv (stream_id=13) :scheme: https
[  0.017] recv (stream_id=13) :authority: www.tunetheweb.com
[  0.017] recv (stream_id=13) :path: /assets/css/common.css
[  0.017] recv (stream_id=13) :method: GET
[  0.017] recv (stream_id=13) accept: */*
[  0.017] recv (stream_id=13) accept-encoding: gzip, deflate
[  0.017] recv (stream_id=13) user-agent: nghttp2/1.28.0
[  0.017] recv (stream_id=13) host: www.tunetheweb.com
[  0.017] recv PUSH_PROMISE frame <length=73, flags=0x04, stream_id=13>
          ; END_HEADERS
          (padlen=0, promised_stream_id=2)
```

The PUSH_PROMISE frame is similar to the HEADERS frame sent by the browser to get the original resource, but it has two important differences:

- The frame is sent by the server to the browser rather than the other way around. It's a heads-up from the server, telling the client, "I'm about to send you this resource as though you requested it like this."

- It includes promised_stream_id, which is the stream ID for the pushed resource, as shown on the last line, stating that the pushed resource will be sent on stream ID 2. Server-initiated streams (which at the moment are used only for push streams) are even-numbered.

After this, the server returns the originally requested resource on the request stream (13) by using a HEADERS frame followed by DATA frames. Then it sends the pushed resource on the promised stream (2), again using a HEADERS frame followed by DATA frames:

```
[  0.017]  recv (stream_id=13) :status: 200
[  0.017]  recv (stream_id=13) date: Sun, 04 Feb 2018 12:28:07 GMT
[  0.017]  recv (stream_id=13) server: Apache
[  0.017]  recv (stream_id=13) last-modified: Thu, 18 Jan 2018 21:52:14 GMT
[  0.017]  recv (stream_id=13) accept-ranges: bytes
[  0.017]  recv (stream_id=13) cache-control: max-age=10800, public
[  0.017]  recv (stream_id=13) expires: Sun, 04 Feb 2018 15:28:07 GMT
[  0.017]  recv (stream_id=13) vary: Accept-Encoding,User-Agent
[  0.017]  recv (stream_id=13) content-encoding: gzip
[  0.017]  recv (stream_id=13) link: </assets/css/common.css>;rel=preload
[  0.017]  recv (stream_id=13) content-length: 6755
[  0.017]  recv (stream_id=13) content-type: text/html; charset=utf-8
[  0.017]  recv (stream_id=13) push-policy: default
[  0.017]  recv HEADERS frame <length=2035, flags=0x04, stream_id=13>
           ; END_HEADERS
           (padlen=0)
           ; First response header
[  0.017]  recv DATA frame <length=1291, flags=0x00, stream_id=13>
[  0.017]  recv DATA frame <length=1291, flags=0x00, stream_id=13>
[  0.018]  recv DATA frame <length=1291, flags=0x00, stream_id=13>
[  0.018]  recv DATA frame <length=1291, flags=0x00, stream_id=13>
[  0.018]  recv DATA frame <length=1291, flags=0x00, stream_id=13>
[  0.018]  recv DATA frame <length=300, flags=0x01, stream_id=13>
           ; END_STREAM
[  0.018]  recv (stream_id=2) :status: 200
[  0.018]  recv (stream_id=2) date: Sun, 04 Feb 2018 12:28:07 GMT
[  0.018]  recv (stream_id=2) server: Apache
[  0.018]  recv (stream_id=2) last-modified: Sun, 07 Jan 2018 14:57:44 GMT
[  0.018]  recv (stream_id=2) accept-ranges: bytes
[  0.018]  recv (stream_id=2) cache-control: max-age=10800, public
[  0.018]  recv (stream_id=2) expires: Sun, 04 Feb 2018 15:28:07 GMT
[  0.018]  recv (stream_id=2) vary: Accept-Encoding,User-Agent
[  0.018]  recv (stream_id=2) content-encoding: gzip
[  0.018]  recv (stream_id=2) content-length: 5723
[  0.018]  recv (stream_id=2) content-type: text/css; charset=utf-8
[  0.018]  recv HEADERS frame <length=63, flags=0x04, stream_id=2>
           ; END_HEADERS
           (padlen=0)
           ; First push response header
[  0.018]  recv DATA frame <length=1291, flags=0x00, stream_id=2>
[  0.018]  recv DATA frame <length=1291, flags=0x00, stream_id=2>
[  0.018]  recv DATA frame <length=1291, flags=0x00, stream_id=2>
[  0.018]  recv DATA frame <length=1291, flags=0x00, stream_id=2>
[  0.018]  recv DATA frame <length=559, flags=0x01, stream_id=2>
           ; END_STREAM
```

5.2.3 *Pushing from downstream systems by using link headers*

If you're using HTTP link headers to indicate resources to be pushed, these headers don't need to be set in the web-server configuration. As discussed in chapter 3, it's common to have a web server such as Apache in front of downstream application code (perhaps an application server such as Tomcat, NodeJS, or some PHP handler) for performance and security reasons. If these application servers are proxied through a web server that supports HTTP/2 push by using HTTP link headers (as Apache and nginx

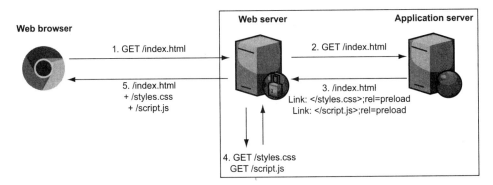

Figure 5.9 HTTP/2 pushing link headers from downstream application servers

do), as long as you have the ability to set HTTP response headers, the application server can ask the web server to push resources, as shown in figure 5.9.

Using link HTTP headers allows the application to tell the web server what to push, so all logic can be in one place without having changing web-server configuration and application code each time. This process works even if those backend connections are HTTP/1 connections. You don't need HTTP/2 on the backend server even if you want to push from there—which, given the complications that this process may involve (discussed in chapter 3), is a real blessing! Figure 5.10 shows how this flow looks in a request-and-response diagram.

To see an example of this flow, create a simple node service by using HTTP/1.1, as shown in listing the following listing.

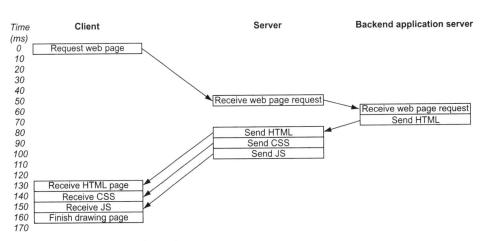

Figure 5.10 Using link headers to push resources from a backend application server

Listing 5.1 HTTP/1.1 node service with HTTP link header

```
var http = require('http')
const port = 3000

const requestHandler = (request, response) => {
  console.log(request.url)
  response.setHeader('Link','</assets/css/common.css>;rel=preload');
  response.writeHead(200, {"Content-Type": "text/html"});
  response.write('<!DOCTYPE html>\n')
  response.write('<html>\n')
  response.write('<head>\n')
  response.write('<link rel="stylesheet" type="text/css"
href="/assets/css/common.css">\n')
  response.write('</head>\n')
  response.write('<body>\n')
  response.write('<h1>Test</h1>\n')
  response.write('</body>\n')
  response.write('</html>\n')
  response.end();
}

var server = http.createServer(requestHandler)
server.listen(port)
console.log('Server is listening on ' + port)
```

Put this code in a file called app.js and then run it with the following command:

```
node app.js
```

You should see a line like this:

```
Server is listening on 3000
```

This code listens on port 3000 and returns a simple hardcoded web page that references a stylesheet in the HEAD tag and includes that stylesheet as a link header. You can use curl to check this result in another window:

```
$ curl -v http://localhost:3000
* Rebuilt URL to: http://localhost:3000/
*   Trying ::1...
* TCP_NODELAY set
* Connected to localhost (::1) port 3000 (#0)
> GET / HTTP/1.1
> Host: localhost:3000
> User-Agent: curl/7.56.1
> Accept: */*
>
< HTTP/1.1 200 OK
< Link: </assets/css/common.css>;rel=preload;as=style
< Content-Type: text/html
< Date: Sun, 04 Feb 2018 15:46:12 GMT
< Connection: keep-alive
```

```
< Transfer-Encoding: chunked
<
<!DOCTYPE html>
<html>
<head>
<link rel="stylesheet" type="text/css" media="all"
    href="/assets/css/common.css">
</head>
<body>
<h1>Test</h1>
</body>
</html>
* Connection #0 to host localhost left intact
```

To allow this node server to be called via Apache, add the following line to the Apache configuration. You'll need to have mod_proxy and mod_proxy_http enabled in Apache:

```
ProxyPass /testnodeservice/ http://localhost:3000/
```

Then the code calls this service through Apache, listening over HTTPS on port 443. This code allows you to call this service over HTTP/2 in a browser even though the Node application isn't set up for HTTP/2 or HTTPS; Apache takes care of that process for you. You see that Apache has pushed the stylesheet, as shown in figure 5.11.

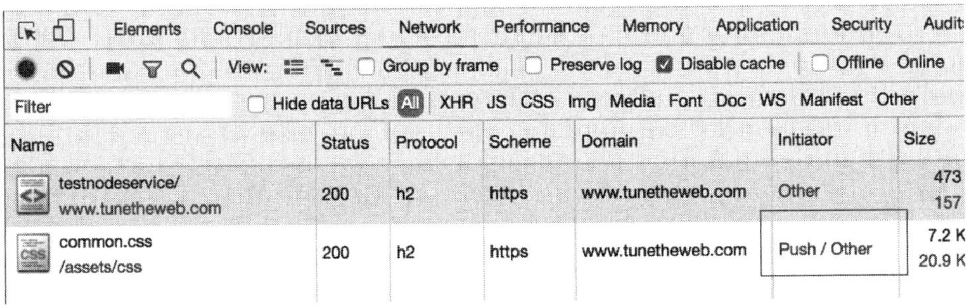

Figure 5.11   Resources referenced in a link header can allow pushes from downstream systems.

In this example, the pushed resource (common.css) is served by Apache. The linked resource can be served by Apache itself, by the downstream application (NodeJS, in this case), or by another downstream system. As long as Apache is able to make a request for the resource, it can push any such resource.

A web server can't push a resource for another domain. If you load a page from example.com, which loads images from google.com, for example, you can't push that image; only google.com can push it. See section 5.5.1 for more discussion of this topic.

The preceding example, in which the stylesheet is always pushed, is simple, but you can create more complex examples in any downstream server language that you're proxying through a web server (or a CDN) that uses HTTP link headers. The application can make decisions about what to push and when, based on what it knows about the request or that user session, but still offload the actual pushing to the web server.

5.2.4 *Pushing earlier*

Setting HTTP link headers in your web-server configuration isn't the only way to push resources. How to do this depends on your web server, because the process is implementation-specific. Apache, for example, uses the `H2PushResource` directive:

```
H2PushResource add /assets/css/common.css
```

nginx offers similar syntax:

```
http2_push /assets/css/common.css;
```

> **Unused push resources don't appear in Chrome developer tools**
>
> Pushed resources are shown only on the Network tab of Chrome developer tools if they're used by the page. For preload hints, the preloader counts as a use, so all resources pushed with the HTTP link header method appear (provided that the `as` attribute is included). If you use another method to push, however, and the page doesn't use this resource, the resources will be pushed in the background but won't show up in Chrome developer tools.
>
> If you're having trouble seeing your push resource in Chrome developer tools, check whether the web page actually needs the pushed resource. If the page doesn't need the push resource, it's wasteful to push it.

The advantage of direct pushing, over the HTTP link headers method, is that the server doesn't have to wait for the resource to be returned to inspect the linked headers and then push the resource. Instead, the dependent resources can be pushed while the original request is processed by the server. This may not matter much for simple, static resources that a web server serves itself straight from disk and therefore generates quickly, but it can have a considerable impact on resources that are slower to generate.[1] Figure 5.12 shows a request-and-response diagram similar to figure 5.5 earlier in this chapter, but this time, the web page takes 100 ms to generate, perhaps because it requires a database lookup or some other dynamic processing.

This figure shows a large gap in which nothing is being sent or received across the HTTP/2 connection, which is wasteful and reminiscent of some of the head-of-line blocking issues that HTTP/2 tries to solve. The CSS and JavaScript may be quicker to generate, as they could be static and fetched by the web server from local disk (or even cached in the web server). That time could be used to push some resources so that the dependent resource is already there by the time the page itself arrives, as shown in figure 5.13.

---

[1] https://icing.github.io/mod_h2/earlier.html

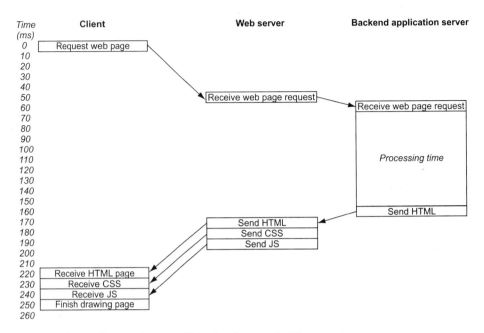

Figure 5.12   Loading a web page with backend processing time

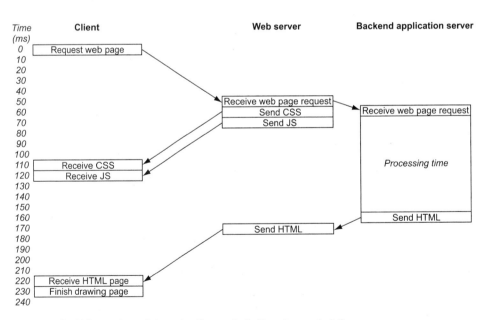

Figure 5.13   Using early push to make the most of otherwise-wasted time

To demonstrate, change the simple NodeJS service to simulate a delay, as shown in the following listing. Note that the async/await code requires NodeJS 7.10 or later.

Listing 5.2 Node service with HTTP link header and 10 ms delay

```
var http = require('http')
const port = 3000

async function requestHandler (request, response) {

  console.log(request.url)

  //Start getting the response ready
  response.setHeader('Link','</assets/css/common.css>;rel=preload ')

  //Pause here for 10 seconds to simulate a slow resource
  await sleep(10000)

  //And now return the resource
  response.writeHead(200, {"Content-Type": "text/html"})
  response.write('<!DOCTYPE html>\n')
  response.write('<html>\n')
  response.write('<head>\n')
  response.write('<link rel="stylesheet" type="text/css"
media="all" href="/assets/css/common.css">\n')
  response.write('</head>\n')
  response.write('<body>\n')
  response.write('<h1>Test</h1>\n')
  response.write('</body>\n')
  response.write('</html>\n')
  response.end();
}

function sleep(ms){
    return new Promise(resolve=>{
        setTimeout(resolve,ms)
    })
}

var server = http.createServer(requestHandler)
server.listen(port)
console.log('Server is listening on ' + port)
```

If you repeat the nghttp call with this code and pipe it into grep to show only the recv frame lines, you see a 10-second delay after setting up the connection until the PUSH_PROMISE frame is sent (corresponding to the 10-second sleep in the preceding code):

```
$ nghttp -anv https://www.tunetheweb.com/testnodeservice/ | grep "recv.*frame"
[  0.209] recv SETTINGS frame <length=6, flags=0x00, stream_id=0>
[  0.209] recv WINDOW_UPDATE frame <length=4, flags=0x00, stream_id=0>
[  0.213] recv SETTINGS frame <length=0, flags=0x01, stream_id=0>
[ 10.225] recv PUSH_PROMISE frame <length=73, flags=0x04, stream_id=13>
[ 10.225] recv HEADERS frame <length=647, flags=0x04, stream_id=13>
[ 10.225] recv DATA frame <length=139, flags=0x01, stream_id=13>
[ 10.226] recv HEADERS frame <length=108, flags=0x04, stream_id=2>
[ 10.226] recv DATA frame <length=1291, flags=0x00, stream_id=2>
```

```
[ 10.226] recv DATA frame <length=1291, flags=0x00, stream_id=2>
[ 10.226] recv DATA frame <length=1291, flags=0x00, stream_id=2>
[ 10.226] recv DATA frame <length=1291, flags=0x00, stream_id=2>
[ 10.226] recv DATA frame <length=559, flags=0x01, stream_id=2>
```

If you change the Apache config to push by `H2PushResource` instead of waiting for the link headers, the push happens immediately, before the 10-second delay, because the pushed resources are no longer being held up by the main resource:

```
$ nghttp -anv https://www.tunetheweb.com/testnodeservice/ | grep "recv.*frame"
[  0.248] recv SETTINGS frame <length=6, flags=0x00, stream_id=0>
[  0.248] recv WINDOW_UPDATE frame <length=4, flags=0x00, stream_id=0>
[  0.253] recv SETTINGS frame <length=0, flags=0x01, stream_id=0>
[  0.253] recv PUSH_PROMISE frame <length=73, flags=0x04, stream_id=13>
[  0.253] recv HEADERS frame <length=675, flags=0x04, stream_id=2>
[  0.253] recv DATA frame <length=1291, flags=0x00, stream_id=2>
[  0.253] recv DATA frame <length=1291, flags=0x00, stream_id=2>
[  0.253] recv DATA frame <length=1291, flags=0x00, stream_id=2>
[  0.253] recv DATA frame <length=1291, flags=0x00, stream_id=2>
[  0.253] recv DATA frame <length=559, flags=0x01, stream_id=2>
[ 10.262] recv HEADERS frame <length=60, flags=0x04, stream_id=13>
[ 10.262] recv DATA frame <length=139, flags=0x01, stream_id=13>
```

This improvement is useful. Although most resources ideally don't have a 10-second delay (exaggerated for effect here), the earlier you can push, the more efficiently you can use the available bandwidth without having to contend with the main request when it's ready to be sent later.

The downside of using the web server's early push commands, such as `H2Push-Resource`, is that you're no longer able to have the application initiate these pushes, and the application may well be in the best position to decide whether to push. To address this situation, a new HTTP status code—`103 Early Hints`[2]—allows earlier indication of a resource's requirements through *preload HTTP link headers*. Like all status codes in the `100` range, it's informational and can be ignored, but it allows an early response with only the headers to be sent (including the link headers needed for HTTP/2 push), followed by a standard `200` response code. In the HTTP/1.1 world, this code looks like responses following each other:

```
HTTP/1.1 103 Early Hints
Link: </assets/css/common.css>;rel=preload;as=style

HTTP/1.1 200 OK
Content-Type: text/html
Link: </assets/css/common.css>;rel=preload;as=style

<!DOCTYPE html>
<html>
...etc.
```

---

[2]   https://tools.ietf.org/html/rfc8297

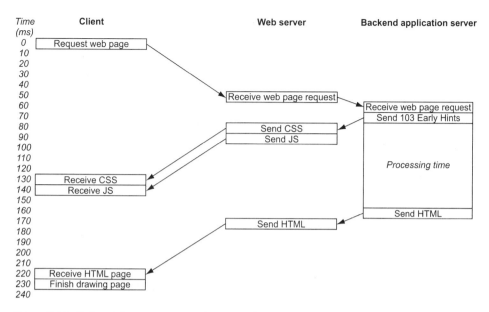

Figure 5.14   Using status `103 Early Hints` to tell the web server to push resources earlier

Figure 5.14 shows the request-and-response diagram.

Here, the backend server has sent an early `103` response, saying that the CSS and JavaScript are needed by the page. The web server uses HTTP/2 push to push those two static resources while it's waiting for the page itself to be generated. Later, when the page is generated and forwarded, the client can use these pushed resources immediately. You can render the page as soon as the web page arrives, but without splitting the logic between the backend server and the web server (and also without using the inlining hack).

This process may be slower than having the web server configured to know which resources to push. In figure 5.14, the push could start at the 60 ms mark, if configured in the web server instead of via the link header, though it doesn't start until 80 ms, but the advantage of having the backend server control the push makes that short delay worthwhile in many scenarios.

Under nghttp, such a scenario would look like this:

```
$ nghttp -anv https://www.tunetheweb.com/testnodeservice/ | grep
    "recv.*frame"
[  0.307] recv SETTINGS frame <length=6, flags=0x00, stream_id=0>
[  0.307] recv WINDOW_UPDATE frame <length=4, flags=0x00, stream_id=0>
[  0.307] recv SETTINGS frame <length=0, flags=0x01, stream_id=0>
[  0.308] recv HEADERS frame <length=60, flags=0x04, stream_id=13>
[  0.308] recv PUSH_PROMISE frame <length=73, flags=0x04, stream_id=13>
[  0.309] recv HEADERS frame <length=675, flags=0x04, stream_id=2>
[  0.309] recv DATA frame <length=1291, flags=0x00, stream_id=2>
[  0.310] recv DATA frame <length=1291, flags=0x00, stream_id=2>
```

```
[  0.310] recv DATA frame <length=1291, flags=0x00, stream_id=2>
[  0.310] recv DATA frame <length=1291, flags=0x00, stream_id=2>
[  0.310] recv DATA frame <length=559, flags=0x01, stream_id=2>
[ 10.317] recv HEADERS frame <length=60, flags=0x04, stream_id=13>
[ 10.317] recv DATA frame <length=1291, flags=0x01, stream_id=13>
[ 10.317] recv DATA frame <length=1291, flags=0x00, stream_id=13>
[ 10.318] recv DATA frame <length=1291, flags=0x00, stream_id=13>
[ 10.318] recv DATA frame <length=1291, flags=0x00, stream_id=13>
[ 10.318] recv DATA frame <length=1291, flags=0x00, stream_id=13>
[ 10.318] recv DATA frame <length=300, flags=0x01, stream_id=13>
```

After the initial setup, you see the following:

- The 103 response is received first as a HEADERS frame on stream 13 at the 0.308-second mark.

- A PUSH_PROMISE frame (also on stream 13) warns the client that a push is coming.

- The resource is pushed in a HEADERS frame and several DATA frames, all sent on stream 2 at the 0.309- and 0.310-second marks.

- When the real response has been processed after that artificial 10-second delay, it's sent back as a HEADERS frame, followed by one or more DATA frames at 10.317 seconds.

At this writing, support for 103 Early Hints (which is new) is limited. Node, for example, doesn't support it natively,[3] though you can add this support by using a third-party library[4] or writing raw HTTP to the stream, which is what that third-party library does. Apache supports processing 103 responses and will process any link headers in them to push resources, but it deliberately doesn't forward 103 responses to the browser, because some browsers don't support those responses and get confused. Forwarding can be enabled with the H2EarlyHints[5] directive.

Support is limited also because it involves sending multiple responses to one request. Although this behavior is valid HTTP for responses in the 100 range, it's unusual compared with other HTTP responses because it's an extra response in addition to the final response. Not every HTTP implementation handles this extra response well and may incorrectly expect only one response back to an HTTP request. The other status codes in the 100 range (such as 100 Continue, 101 Switching Protocols, and 102 Processing) are used only for specific scenarios, such as switching to WebSockets. Many tools and libraries allow you to set different status codes, even ones that weren't known when those tools were created, but few can process two requests properly for manually set response codes as required by 103 response codes. When support inevitably comes along, this response code will prove to be useful, and I expect its use to grow quickly.

---

[3] The status code has been added but not the option to use it: https://github.com/nodejs/node/pull/16644.

[4] https://www.npmjs.com/package/early-hints

[5] https://httpd.apache.org/docs/2.4/mod/mod_http2.html#h2earlyhints

5.2.5 *Pushing in other ways*

Web servers aren't the only ways to enable push; some backend application servers also allow developers to push programmatically. The following listing shows how to create a simple NodeJS server with push. This listing requires the `http2` module, which requires NodeJS v9 or later.

Listing 5.3 Node service with server push

```
'use strict'

const fs = require('fs')
const http2 = require('http2')

const PORT=8443

//Create a HTTP/2 server with HTTPS certificate and key
const server = http2.createSecureServer({
  cert: fs.readFileSync('server.crt'),
  key: fs.readFileSync('server.key')
})

//Handle any incoming streams
server.on('stream', (stream, headers) => {

  //Check if the incoming stream supports push at the connection level
  if (stream.session.remoteSettings.enablePush) {

    //If it supports push, push the CSS file
    console.log('Push enabled. Pushing CSS file')

    //Open the File for reading
    const cssFile = fs.openSync('/www/htdocs/assets/css/common.css', 'r')

    //Get some stats on the file for the HTTP response headers
    const cssStat = fs.fstatSync(cssFile)
    const cssRespHeaders = {
       'content-length': cssStat.size,
       'last-modified': cssStat.mtime.toUTCString(),
       'content-type': 'text/css'
    }

    //Send a Push Promise stream for the file
    stream.pushStream({ ':path': '/assets/css/common.css' },
    (err, pushStream, headers) => {
      //Push the file in the newly created pushStream
      pushStream.respondWithFD(cssFile, cssRespHeaders)
    })
  } else {
    //If push is disabled, log that
    console.log('Push disabled.')
  }
```

```
  //Respond to the original request
  stream.respond({
    'content-type': 'text/html',
    ':status': 200
  })
  stream.write('<DOCTYPE html><html><head>')
  stream.write('<link rel="stylesheet" type="text/css" media="all"
ref="/assets/css/common.css">')
  stream.write('</head><body><h1>Test</h1></body></html>')
})

//Start the server listening for requests on the given port
server.listen(PORT)
console.log(`Server listening on ${PORT}`)

})
```

This code allows NodeJS to push assets to your browser. This simple example supports HTTP/2 only over HTTPS. For a real server, you probably should enable HTTP/1.1 and nonencrypted HTTP access as well (which shows why using a web server in front of an application server such as Node is usually easier). Other programming languages (such as ASP.NET and Java) have similar ways of pushing resources.

Pushing all the way through?

As I mentioned earlier, it's common to have a load balancer or web server as the entry point to the system (often called the edge server) and then proxy requests to a back-end application server or service. In fact, I recommend this setup, because web servers typically are more performant and secure than dynamic application servers. When it comes to HTTP/2 push, you may think that it's preferable to speak HTTP/2 all the way through your infrastructure so that you can, for example, push resources from the application infrastructure through your web server to the browser. This process, however, often leads to additional complications when an intermediary is involved. What if the application server and the edge server support push, but the client doesn't, or vice versa? How do you handle tracking of pushed resources across three (or more) players?

The HTTP/2 specification states[a]

> An intermediary can receive pushes from the server and choose not to forward them on to the client. In other words, how to make use of the pushed information is up to that intermediary. Equally, the intermediary might choose to make additional pushes to the client, without any action taken by the server.

The reality is that it's much easier to let the edge server handle push and to use HTTP link headers (with or without 103 Early Hints) to do that. Sometimes, the application server is telling the web server to push a resource that it must then fetch from the application server, which may seem to be a bit of a roundabout process, but it's simpler and allows application servers to push resources that they don't control (such as static files and media that are stored at the web server layer).

At this writing, I'm not aware of any web servers that allow HTTP/2 push all the way through. The Apache HTTP/2 proxy module (`mod_proxy_http2`) is one of the few implementations of backend HTTP/2 connections that exist at this writing; it explicitly turns off push for backend connections, using the `SETTINGS` frame to prevent complications.[b]

Looking back to the HTTP/2 infrastructure setup options discussed in chapter 3, the lack of backend HTTP/2 support on web and proxy servers is yet another reason why supporting HTTP/2 all through the infrastructure may not be necessary or even beneficial—at least until HTTP/2 support is ubiquitous and there's no reason *not* to support it.

---

[a] https://httpwg.org/specs/rfc7540.html#PushResources
[b] https://github.com/icing/mod_h2/issues/154

5.3   How HTTP/2 push works in the browser

Regardless of how you push a resource at the server side, the browser handles this process differently from what you might expect. Instead of being pushed straight to a web page, a resource is pushed to a cache. The web page is processed as it is normally. When the page sees the resource that it needs, it checks the cache, finds it there, and loads it from the cache rather than requesting it from the server.

The details are browser-specific and not detailed in the HTTP/2 specification, but most browsers seem to have implemented HTTP/2 push with a special *HTTP/2 push cache*, which is different from the normal *HTTP cache* that most web developers are familiar with. The best documentation at this writing is a blog post by Jake Archibald[6] (of the Google Chrome team) about experimenting with HTTP/2 push to see how each browser treated it. This post details how HTTP/2 should work in theory and how it works in practice, often in unexpected ways. Bugs have been raised because of his work, some fixed at this writing and some not yet fixed.

HTTP/2 push is a new concept, and some work must be done to iron out all the implementation issues on the browser side (and likely on the server side too). I'll do my best to highlight some of the major bugs, but new ones are likely to be introduced.

5.3.1   Seeing how the push cache works

Pushed resources are held in a separate bit of memory (the HTTP/2 push cache) waiting for the browser to request them, at which point they're loaded into the page; if the caching headers are set, they're also saved in the browser's HTTP cache as usual for later reuse. One notable exception is that Chromium-based browsers (Chrome and Opera) don't cache resources for untrusted certificates (such as self-signed certificates, which use a red padlock). The cache still isn't used even if the certificate error is clicked

---

[6] https://jakearchibald.com/2017/h2-push-tougher-than-i-thought/

through.[7] To use HTTP/2 push, you must have a full green padlock by using a real certificate or accepting your self-signed certificate in the browser's trust store; otherwise,
pushed resources will be ignored.[8]

   The *push cache* isn't the first place where the browser looks for a resource.
Although the process is browser-specific, experiments show that if a resource is available in the usual *HTTP cache*, the browser won't use the pushed resource. Even if the
pushed resource is newer than the cached resource, the browser still prefers to use
its older cached content as long as it considers the cached resource to be usable
(based on the *cache-control headers*). Service workers are also checked before the push
cache for websites that use them. You can easily waste resources pushing a resource
that won't be used. Figure 5.15 shows what happens when a resource is loaded and
which caches are checked for each resource needed by the page in the Chrome
browser.

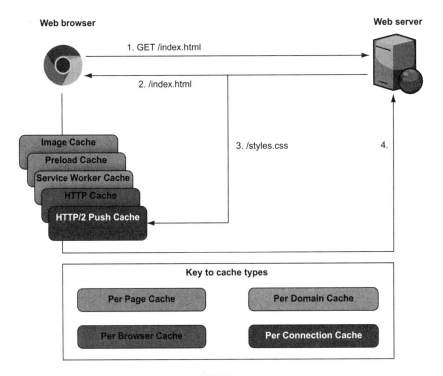

Figure 5.15   Browser interaction with HTTP/2 push

---

[7]   https://bugs.chromium.org/p/chromium/issues/detail?id=103875#c8

[8]   https://bugs.chromium.org/p/chromium/issues/detail?id=824988

When a page is requested (1) and returned (2), any pushed resources are put in the HTTP/2 push cache (3), and the caches are checked in order before a request is made to the web server (4). Following is a brief explanation of each cache:

- The *image cache* is a short-lived, in-memory cache for that page that prevents the browser from fetching an image twice if it's referenced twice on the page, for example. When the user browses away from the page, the cache is destroyed.

- The *preload cache* is another short-lived, in-memory cache used to hold pre-loaded resources (see chapter 6). Again, this cache is page-specific. Don't pre-load something for another page, because it won't be used.

- *Service workers* are fairly new background applications that run independently of a web page and act as go-betweens for the web page and the website. They allow a website to act more like a native application even if you lose your network connection, for example. They have their own caches linked to the domain.

- The *HTTP cache* is the main cache that most developers know about and is a disk-based persistent cache shared across the browser, with a limited size to be used for all the domains.

- The *HTTP/2 push cache* is a short-lived, in-memory cache that is bound to the connection and is checked last.

When the server pushes styles.css, it's pushed into the HTTP/2 push cache. When the web browser decides that it needs styles.css, it doesn't know (or care) that the server has pushed that resource, and it checks all the caches in order before making the network request to the origin. If a valid styles.css exists in the main HTTP cache, the browser picks it up from that cache, even if a newer copy is in the HTTP/2 push cache. Using the chrome://net-export tool discussed in section 4.3.1, you see a summary of unclaimed push resources for all current active pages, as shown in figure 5.16.

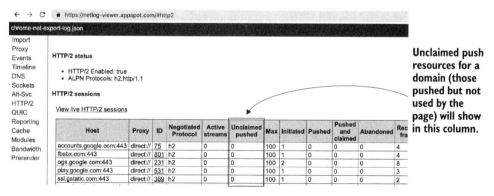

Figure 5.16   Unclaimed push resource tracking in Chrome

The fact that the HTTP/2 push cache is bound to the connection also means if the connection isn't used, the pushed resource isn't used. This process is different from the HTTP cache that most developers are used to working with and leads to some interesting considerations. For a start, if the connection is lost, so are the push cache and any pushed resources that haven't been used (so you've wasted resources in pushing them). If another connection is used, pushed resources may not be used. With HTTP/2, there should be a single connection, so you may not think that this situation is much of a problem, but the case may differ among browsers, which may decide to implement features differently. Earlier, I touched on noncredentialed requests, which most browsers handle with a separate connection. The Web Hypertext Application Technology Working Group (WHATWG), however, is discussing making a change to allow the same connection to be used for both credentialed and noncredentialed requests.[9] One consequence is that you can't push cross-origin fonts (those loaded from another domain, including a sharded domain), because they must be uncredentialed requests. Also, separate tabs or browser processes may start separate connections depending on the browser: Chrome and Firefox share connections across tabs; Edge doesn't; Safari seems to open multiple connections even within the same tab.[10] As the HTTP/2 push cache is at connection level rather than page level, it's possible to push assets for a future page navigation, but the short-lived nature of this cache, coupled with the fact that the connection may be dropped, makes this idea a bad one.

Finally, when the asset is "claimed" from the connection's push cache, it's removed and can't be loaded from the push cache again, although, if the HTTP `cache-control` headers are set, it can be used from the browser's HTTP cache. The push cache also differs from the HTTP cache in that uncacheable resources (those set with `no-cache` and `no-store` HTTP `cache-control` headers) can be pushed and read from the push cache. It's not a cache in the traditional sense, but a holding area for requests. Yoav Weiss, a web performance architect, calls it the "unclaimed push streams container,"[11] but admits that this term is less catchy than push cache.

5.3.2 Refusing pushes with RST_STREAM

A client can refuse a pushed resource by sending an `RST_STREAM` frame on the push stream with a `CANCEL` or `REFUSED_STREAM` code. This frame could be used because the browser already has the item being pushed or for some other reason (such as the user's browsing away from a page while it's still loading, so the browser no longer needs the item).

This process may sound like a good way of preventing overpushing resources that the browser doesn't need. The problem is that it takes time to send this `RST_STREAM` frame back to the server, and in the meantime, the server continues to send `HEADERS` and `DATA` frames, which the browser will throw away. An `RST_STREAM` frame is a control signal and isn't as aggressive as dropping the connection, which can't be done in HTTP/2 without interrupting the other streams on that connection. The entire

---

resource may have been sent before the RST_STREAM frame is received and actioned by the server to stop sending the resource.

An RST_STREAM frame is useful only if the browser realizes that it doesn't need the resource being pushed. If a browser already has a resource in its HTTP cache, there's an obvious scenario to use an RST_STREAM frame to stop the push. But what if a huge image is pushed but never referenced on the page? A page may have been updated to not use that image anymore, but the push instruction may not have been updated. The browser won't know that the image isn't needed and will happily receive the entire resource, but never use it. Depending on browser tools, you may not even know that you're sending this image needlessly, as it may not appear on the network tab of developer tools.

All in all, the RST_STREAM frame is a useful way to stop a stream, and especially a pushed resource stream, but you shouldn't depend on it as a way of controlling incorrectly pushed resources. Overpushing resources is a waste of resources, but even if your server can handle it, remember that bandwidth isn't free. Mobile connections in particular usually cap bandwidth, so you're costing your visitors more if you send unnecessary resources, not to mention that the wasted bandwidth is bandwidth that could be better used to send resources that the page *does* need.

5.4 How to push conditionally

One big risk of using HTTP/2 push is pushing resources needlessly. Some risks are due to the implementation issues discussed earlier in this chapter (if the connection isn't reused, for example), but mostly, the problem is pushing resources that the browser already has.

If you decide that it's a good idea to push your stylesheet, for example, you may improve the page load time for the first request. But if you continue to push the stylesheet with every page request as the visitor browses around your site, you're needlessly pushing a resource that the user already has (assuming that you're using good cache-control headers to ensure that the resource is cached).

As the RST_STREAM frame is inefficient in stopping pushed assets without wasting resources, what other methods can you use to ensure that you don't push a resource that the client won't use?

5.4.1 Tracking pushes on the server side

A server could keep track of what assets it has pushed on a certain client connection. The technique would be up to the server, but could be based on the connection or perhaps a session ID. Each time you push a resource, for example, the server flags that this connection/session shouldn't push that resource again even if asked to. This process is what Apache uses and why you have to turn off the H2PushDiarySize setting while testing. This feature could be implemented in the web application rather than in the web server software to give the web developer more control.

The downside is that the server is making an educated guess about whether it should push. If the browser cache has been cleared, for example, the resource won't be available, but the server still won't push. Also, busy servers may have resource constraints on tracking pushed resources, and load-balanced servers may not have the complete picture about what has been pushed if the same server doesn't always serve a client.

Ultimately, the process is complicated, and this crude attempt to add state to the stateless HTTP protocol probably isn't the best method. HTTP/2 adds the concept of state to other parts of the protocol (HPACK header compression and the stream states, as discussed in chapters 7 and 8), so perhaps this problem could—and should—be resolved at protocol level for a better implementation. I discuss one such proposal (cache digests) in section 5.4.4, but first, I look at other methods that can be used now.

5.4.2 Using HTTP conditional requests

If a client sends an `if-modified-since` or `etag` HTTP header, this page is already on the browser's cache but has expired. If you normally push a CSS asset, you could choose not to push it when you see such headers in the request, as the stylesheet is likely to be cached, too (perhaps even longer than the page that references it, as is often the case). This process is simpler than tracking this server side but has many of the same downsides, such as the fact that the server is making an educated guess about what's on the client side and the scenario of navigating to another page that uses a stylesheet that's already cached.

5.4.3 Using cookie-based pushes

The next option is to record the fact that the asset has been pushed on the client side. Cookies could be natural vehicles for this purpose, and `LocalStorage` or `Session-Storage` could also be used.

The idea is that when you push a resource, you set a cookie that's valid for that session (short-cached resources) or for the same time as the pushed resource (long-cached resources). As each page request comes in, you check for the presence of the cookie. If the cookie isn't present, the resource likely isn't in the browser cache, so push it and set the cookie. If the cookie is present, don't push the resource. This functionality can be implemented in any client application or even in server config. Here's an example in Apache:

```
#Check if there's a cookie saying the css has already been loaded
#If so, set an environment variable for use later
SetEnvIf Cookie "cssloaded=1" cssIsloaded

#If no cookie, and it's an html file, then push the css file
#and set a session-level cookie so next time it won't be pushed:
<FilesMatch "index.html">
    Header add Link "</assets/css/common.css>;as=style;rel=preload"
      env=!cssIsloaded
    Header add Set-Cookie "cssloaded=1; Path=/; Secure; HttpOnly"
      env=!cssIsloaded
</FilesMatch>
```

Similar logic could be implemented in any server-side language.

This method is a further improvement on the preceding two strategies. Nothing needs to be tracked server-side, so the logic is less complicated, and you're tracking a bit more based on the browser status. Cookies aren't the same as the HTTP cache, however. Although you can set the expiration time the same, cookies can be reset independently (turned off in the browser or running in incognito mode, for example), although the same could be said of any server-side tracking methodology.

At this writing, cookies are probably the best ways of tracking whether an asset has been pushed and is likely to be in the cache, but they still have issues.

5.4.4 Using cache digests

Cache digests are a proposal[12] to allow a browser to inform the server what's in its cache. When the connection is made, the browser sends a new CACHE_DIGEST frame, which lists all the resources currently held in the HTTP cache for that domain (or other domains over which this connection is authoritative; see chapter 6). The server gets the contents of the cache as the URL along with the etag header value to get some sort of versioning of the URL. This method is much better than using the previous roundabout methods of guessing the contents of the cache, because the browser has definitively told the server what's in its cache. The server can remember the contents of the client's cache for the connection and even update it as it sends more resources. The CACHE_DIGEST frame should be sent once near the beginning of the connection (preferably after the first request is made).

The contents of the cache can be large, so rather than sending full URLs and etags, the proposal is for the client to encode them in a cuckoo filter–based digest. I'm not going into detail on cuckoo filters,[13] but suffice it to say that these filters are efficient ways of sending cache contents, with a low risk of clashes (such as incorrectly implying that a resource is in the cache when it's not, or vice versa).

At this writing, cache digests aren't an approved standard and aren't generated by any browser. Interestingly, some servers (such as Apache, http2server, and H2O) have added support for the current draft standard (which came out of the H2O implementation). Because browsers currently aren't sending a CACHE_DIGEST frame to initialize any server-side cache, these implementations are used only to track requests pushed by the server. These servers keep track of resources that they've sent, so they shouldn't push resources twice (even if instructed to). This feature is useful but would be much more useful if the state could also be initialized with the browser cache state, which requires the CACHE_DIGEST frame. As I mentioned at the start of this section, you turned this Apache feature off earlier with the following config while you were testing HTTP/2 push:

```
H2PushDiarySize 0
```

---

[12] https://tools.ietf.org/html/draft-ietf-httpbis-cache-digest
[13] https://www.cs.cmu.edu/~dga/papers/cuckoo-conext2014.pdf

This line sets the maximum push diary size to 0, saying that you don't have a push diary, and therefore allow resources to be pushed even if they're already sent. Without setting this size to 0, if you test a page multiple times, you see that resources are sometimes pushed and sometimes not, which can be confusing when you're testing HTTP/2 push. When you finish testing, remove this config and use the default H2PushDiarySize (256 entries per connection) or set it appropriately. Other servers may have a similar implementation to Apache, so check your server documentation.

It's possible to use an implementation of cache digests on the browser side now if you're using service workers in your web application, because service workers allow you to intercept and change your HTTP requests. Some implementations exist for this purpose.[14] As the CACHE_DIGEST frame isn't approved or implemented in any browsers or servers, it can't be used; instead, these implementations usually send the cache digest in an HTTP header or cookie. Your server may use this cookie or HTTP header to initialize the cache digest. Your web application needs to send this header manually (using service workers), and then use it to initialize the server side. Although testing this feature may be interesting, it would be better if this was standardized and sent by the browser. However, in January 2019, the HTTP Working Group stated they will not continue work on standardizing cache digests at this time.[15]

The last point of concern about cache digests is security. The browser cache may contain sensitive information such as what URLs were visited previously, or may allow fingerprinting of users without the use of cookies and the like. The server is likely to have access to some of this data anyway (the requests must be made to the server at some point), but security is still a concern. The current draft suggests that browsers not send cache digests in privacy mode or when cookies aren't used or cleared. The security and privacy concerns are another reason the cache digest standardization has been stopped at this time.

5.5   *What to push*

By now, you should have a good understanding of HTTP/2 push and how it works on both the server and client sides. But you need to give careful thought to what assets you push.

5.5.1   *What can you push?*

The specification dictates some ground rules for HTTP/2 push:[16]

- Clients can disable push by setting the SETTINGS_ENABLE_PUSH option to 0 in the SETTINGS frame. Thereafter, servers must not use PUSH_PROMISE frames.
- Pushed requests must be cacheable methods (GET, HEAD, and some POST requests).
- Pushed requests must be safe (usually GET or HEAD).

---

[14] https://www.npmjs.com/package/cache-digest-immutable
[15] https://lists.w3.org/Archives/Public/ietf-http-wg/2019JanMar/0033.html
[16] https://httpwg.org/specs/rfc7540.html#PushResources

- Pushed requests must not include a request body (though they usually include a response body).
- Pushed requests must be sent only to domains over which the server is authoritative.
- A client can't push; only the server can push.
- Resources can be pushed only in response to a current request. It's not possible for a server to initiate a push if no request is in process.

In reality, because of these rules, only GET requests are pushed. The preceding rules are about what you *can* push, but a lot more thought is needed about what you *should* push.

The authoritative restriction limits you to pushing only resources that the web server serves (directly or indirectly). If the website uses Bootstrap loaded from get-bootstrap.com (or if it uses jQuery hosted on jquery.com or a similar site), that can't be pushed by your server. If you want to proxy those requests through your server, you can, but you'd need to update all references to expect the request from your server, and at that point, why not host the page locally and remove the complication of proxying it?

An interesting proposal called Signed HTTP Exchanges[17] (formally called Web Packaging) would allow you to serve signed resources from your domain as though they came directly from the original domain, allowing you to effectively push other domain's resources. The proposal is still being defined, however, and isn't available in any browsers or servers as of this writing, but it's certainly something to watch for.

5.5.2 What should you push?

A key question that website owners who want to use HTTP/2 push must answer is what assets to push—and, perhaps more important, what *not* to push. HTTP/2 push is intended to be a performance optimization, but it can become a performance drag if you push too much and waste vital bandwidth pushing assets that the client won't use, instead of using the available resources to download assets that the page will use.

Ideally, you should push only critical assets that the page needs. Pushing resources that won't be used is a waste of resources. Resources that won't be used include assets that aren't used (such as unreferenced assets), assets that the client can't use (such as image formats that aren't supported by that client), and assets that may not be used depending on the client (such as images that are displayed only for certain screen sizes). I stated earlier that only critical resources should be pushed. Although it may be tempting to push everything that the page needs, you may be slowing the delivery of critical resources, depending on how the pushed resources are prioritized in comparison with the other client-initiated requests.

---

[17] https://tools.ietf.org/html/draft-yasskin-http-origin-signed-responses

Also, you need to consider whether the client already has an asset in one of its caches (see section 5.3). You should push only if there's a high likelihood that the pushed asset isn't already cached.

You should use HTTP/2 push to make the most of idle network time. Therefore, pushing all the assets that the page needs is unlikely to improve performance, because you're overriding any loading prioritization that the browser may make. The Chrome team wrote an in-depth paper on what to push,[18] in which one of the main recommendations was pushing the minimum needed "to fill idle network time, and no more." Other research[19] indicates that similar conservative strategies should be used with push. For this reason, early pushes and the `103` status code are important improvements over basic push strategies.

In short, it's better to *underpush* than to *overpush*. The worst that can happen if a resource isn't pushed is that it will need to be requested anyway, and the page may not improve as much as it could under optimum conditions. On the flip side, the worst that can happen with overpushing is sending needless assets, thereby wasting resources on the client, network, and server, and making the page load slower. But *HTTP/2 push, even with overpushing,* shouldn't break the page. The page won't be as performant as it could be and may waste resources (which isn't without cost), but the page itself will load—eventually.

5.5.3   *Automating push*

You also need to devise a strategy on what to push. Does a website owner or developer have to decide what to push (perhaps per page), and then configure this decision in the server? Or should the process be more automated? Jetty[20] is a Java servlet engine that chooses the second option and tries to automate pushes.[21] It watches requests and subsequent requests with a `Referer` header of that request. Then it uses what it sees to build up suggested push resources for similar future requests from other clients. This engine certainly removes a lot of the complexity of deciding what to push, but then you're dependent on whether you agree with that implementation and whether it's a good match for your website. Deciding what to push is complex, and automating push for every site is equally complex. Jetty's implementation is an interesting one, and coupled with some form of cache digests to prevent overpushing, it may be sufficient. Alternatively, website owners may want more direct control, because they should know their website and visitors better and should be able to come up with a better idea of what to push.

---

[18] https://docs.google.com/document/d/1K0NykTXBbbbTlv60t5MyJvXjqKGsCVNYHyLEXIxYMv0/ also available at https://goo.gl/89RLGQ

[19] https://calendar.perfplanet.com/2016/http2-push-the-details/

[20] https://www.eclipse.org/jetty/

[21] https://www.eclipse.org/jetty/documentation/current/http2-configuring-push.html

5.6   *Troubleshooting HTTP/2 push*

HTTP/2 push is easiest to see in the Initiator column of the Network tab of Chrome Developer tools (or in similar Chromium-based browsers such as Opera). But what if you don't see the pushed resource in this column? Here are some common reasons:

- *Are you using HTTP/2?* If not, push won't work. Add the Protocol column to make sure you're using HTTP/2. See chapter 3 for troubleshooting tips for when HTTP/2 isn't being used, even though you expect it to be.

- *Does your server support HTTP/2 push?* Some servers and CDNs don't support HTTP/2 push at this writing. Unfortunately, the client states whether it supports push in the SETTINGS frame, not the server, so it's not possible to see whether the server supports it by looking at the SETTINGS frame with nghttp or Chrome's net-export page.

- *Is your server behind other infrastructure?* If your server is behind a load balancer or other infrastructure that terminates the HTTP/2 connection, it may not support HTTP/2 push, even if your server does. Even if it does support HTTP/2 push, it may not be passing on the pushed resources, which need to be pushed by this edge infrastructure.

  If you have Apache in front of a backend application server (such as Node or Jetty), Apache won't allow the backend server to push resources itself, and it must use the HTTP link header to make Apache push resources.

- *Is the asset being pushed by the server?* You can use nghttp to examine the actual frames to investigate whether the PUSH_PROMISE frame and the asset itself are being sent to see whether the problem is a browser issue.

- *Are the assets needed by the page?* If the page doesn't need the assets, the browser won't use them, and Chrome won't even show them on the Network tab. You can use the chrome net-export tool to see a summary of unclaimed push resources for all current active pages, as shown in figure 5.16 and discussed in section 5.3.1.

  If you're pushing by using the HTTP link header with rel=preload and an as attribute, however, Chrome thinks that the assets are needed by the page (by virtue of a preload hint) and shows them on the Network tab. This situation can be both useful and confusing.

  One way to debug is to remove the as attribute (such as as=style) from the link header. Chrome won't use the assets as a preload hint, but your web server should still push them (because the as attribute isn't mandatory for push, depending on the implementation). If the resources don't appear on the Network tab but do when it has the as attribute, you know that you're pushing a resource that the page doesn't need.

- *Are you using the correct way to push for your server?* How you push depends on the server. A lot of servers use HTTP link headers, but not all of them do, so you can't presume that they'll use this method to push. Check your server documentation or online guides for details on how to push on your server.

- *Has the server explicitly decided not to push the resource?* If you've implemented cache-aware pushing (see section 5.4) or some other method to push only in certain circumstances, that implementation may explain why the push isn't happening. If refreshing the page or restarting the browser (or even the server) causes assets to appear as being pushed some of the time, check when the push resource is set to send. For Apache, you can set `H2PushDiarySize` to 0 to turn off the push diary feature, which tries to prevent pushing resources that the server thinks the client already has. This feature can be useful for debugging when you want the server to push the same resource multiple times.

- *Does the pushed asset exist?* It's easy to make a typo when you're specifying a resource to push, and if a resource doesn't exist, it can't be pushed! Pushing a resource that doesn't exist results in a `404` (Not Found) status code in your web server logs. Similarly, this `404` status code appears in the returned frame if you're using nghttp. If you're using the HTTP link header with `rel=preload` and an as attribute, it appears on the Network tab as a `404` or as a canceled[22] request.

- *Are you pushing on a different connection from the one that the browser expects?* As discussed in section 5.2.1, HTTP/2 push is linked to the connection. If you're pushing on one connection, but the browser expects the resource to be sent on another connection, the browser won't use the pushed resource. Fonts are the most obvious problems, because they must be loaded on uncredentialed connections, but several browser issues and quirks can cause a different connection to be used. The connection view in WebPagetest probably is the best way to see this situation.

- *Are you using a self-signed or otherwise-untrusted certificate?* Chrome ignores push requests for untrusted HTTPS certificates (including self-signed dummy certificates created for localhost).[23] You must add the certificate to your computer's trust store to enable the green padlock for push resources to be used. Chrome also insists that the certificate have a valid Subject Alternative Name (SAN). Many tutorials on creating self-signed certificates include only the older Subject field, so even after they're added to the trust store, these certificates aren't recognized; they must be replaced by certificates with both a Subject and a SAN for push to work.

---

[22] https://bugs.chromium.org/p/chromium/issues/detail?id=811077
[23] https://bugs.chromium.org/p/chromium/issues/detail?id=824988

5.7 The performance impact of HTTP/2 push

The impact of HTTP/2 push varies from website to website and depends on round-trip time—the time it takes to serve resources—and on how optimized the website is. At present, few sites use HTTP/2 push, so meaningful information about its performance impact is thin on the ground.

The key to using HTTP/2 push effectively is to use gaps in bandwidth when the connection isn't being used. For pages that take a long time to generate server-side, the gains can be large. For static pages, the gains are less obvious. Although a potential one-round-trip savings exists, because of bandwidth and processing limitations, the pushed resources will likely queue behind the higher-priority main resources anyway, reducing the gains in the request lag (half a round trip). Figure 5.17 shows this effect. The two waterfalls look identical for the first four resources, so there are few gains from using push.

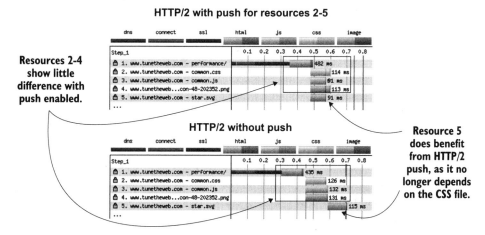

Figure 5.17   HTTP/2 pushed resources don't arrive at the same time as the requested resource.

The fifth `star.svg` resource does benefit from being pushed; it no longer needs to wait for the stylesheet to be downloaded to discover that it's necessary. (Later in this chapter I discuss preload, which provides a similar benefit). In this example, push doesn't seem to solve its original use case, removing the need for inlining resources, but it can still offer dramatic benefits if used right.

At the 102nd IETF meeting in Montreal in July 2018, Akamai[24] and the Chrome teams[25] presented their observations on the effects of HTTP/2 push. Akamai showed some statistical improvements when it preemptively pushed resources that were deemed critical. Chrome also showed small improvements, but experimented with

---

[24] https://github.com/httpwg/wg-materials/blob/gh-pages/ietf102/akamai-server-push.pdf
[25] https://github.com/httpwg/wg-materials/blob/gh-pages/ietf102/chrome_push.pdf

disabling push and measuring the difference. These slightly different methodologies raise some questions. Are Akamai customers more representative of the Web in general, as Chrome looks only at sites that have already enabled push (which are few and probably operated by HTTP/2 advocates)? Is Akamai deciding the correct assets to push, and is its decision better or worse than that of sites that decided what to push themselves, as they would in the Chrome experiment?

Two big problems were highlighted, particularly by the Chrome team: few sites were using HTTP/2 push (0.04% of HTTP/2 sessions, according to Chrome), and the potential of push to make performance worse is a real concern. The Chrome team even questioned whether anyone would notice if push were switched off. The low use in itself is telling, and I've shown in this chapter that push is complicated, so many people are questioning its usefulness and suggesting alternatives.

5.8   *Push versus preload*

HTTP/2 push has a lot of subtle nuances even if it works as it's supposed to (which isn't always the case). There are clear risks in using HTTP/2 push, such as wasting bandwidth and slowing your website instead of speeding it up. As I mentioned earlier, the risks aren't that site owners will break their pages, but that they will waste resources that are perhaps better used elsewhere. One of the main problems is that the server isn't aware of what's in the browser's HTTP cache, and perhaps cache digests may solve that problem, if they become standardized. Until that happens, some people are asking whether HTTP/2 push is ready for mainstream use or whether we should be satisfied with *preload*.

Preload[26] is a way to indicate to the browser that a resource is needed for a page, rather than waiting for the browser to discover this fact. As mentioned in section 5.1.1, you can preload by using the HTTP link header (perhaps with the nopush attribute to prevent pushing):

```
Link: "</assets/css/common.css>;rel=preload;as=style;nopush"
```

In HTML

```
<link rel="preload" href="/assets/css/common.css" as="style">
```

Regardless of which method is used, the browser should take this line as a sign to fetch a resource with a high priority. As I mentioned earlier, a big difference with HTTP/2 push is that the as attribute is more important for a preload resource; excluding it can lead to the preload hint's being ignored or a resource's being downloaded twice.

Preload isn't as fast as HTTP/2 push in pushing a resource before being asked for it, but it's a browser-initiated request, which has several advantages:

---

[26] https://w3c.github.io/preload/

- The browser is aware of what is in its cache(s) and uses that knowledge appropriately to decide whether to make the request. Unlike HTTP/2 push, a preload hint won't cause new downloads of resources that the client already has. If the browser already has the resource, it ignores the preload hint. Because many HTTP/2 servers use HTTP link headers to push resources, however, you should add a nopush attribute if you don't want to push a resource.
- You have fewer push-cache worries and complications when you use preload hints, which should be downloaded and pulled into the HTTP cache. If a preloaded resource isn't used, you're still wasting time downloading it, but that rule applies whether you're using preload or HTTP/2 push.
- You can also use preload to load resources from other domains, whereas you can use HTTP/2 push only for resources on your own domain.
- Chrome developer tools shows all preloaded requests whether they're used or not, but it shows only used pushed requests (although a workaround is sending a preload HTTP link header for each pushed resource).

These advantages may be sufficient for now, and some people are recommending sticking with the less-risky preload method for now. Analysis by Hooman Beheshti of Fastly showed that only 0.02% of sites were using HTTP/2 push in February 2018[27] (almost three years after HTTP/2 was formally approved), which is similar to the Chrome team's analysis, covered in section 5.7. Some people are hesitant to use this technology—and with good reason, especially if preload resource hints offer most of the same benefits with considerably fewer risks.

Using preload with the new 103 HTTP status code brings the performance gap between preload and HTTP/2 push closer still, as resources that take a while to load can send a 103 response earlier, with the preload HTTP link headers, and tell the browser to start requesting them. The resources may already be there by the time they're needed, depending on the page and how long it takes to generate. In section 5.2.4 earlier in this chapter, I discuss how 103 responses coupled with HTTP/2 push allow you to use the processing time, when the network would otherwise be idle, to proactively push resources. To save you from going back, I'll repeat that earlier diagram in figure 5.18.

The figure shows that the backend application server can use a 103 Early Hints response to tell the web server to push the resources while processing is happening to generate the web page requested. In this case, as the 103 response is used only to tell the web server to push some responses, it can be swallowed by the web server, because it's of no real benefit to send it on to the client (and, as discussed earlier, some browsers don't handle the 103 response well).

If this push option isn't something you want to implement, for all the reasons discussed in this chapter, a less-risky option may be not using HTTP/2 push and instead sending the 103 response back to the browser (when browser support arrives). Then

---

[27] https://www.youtube.com/watch?v=wR1gF5Lhcq0

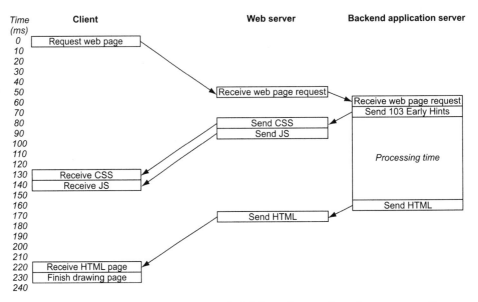

Figure 5.18   Using status `103 Early Hints` **to tell the web server to push resources earlier**

the browser can use the preload HTTP link headers to preload the resources, as shown in figure 5.19.

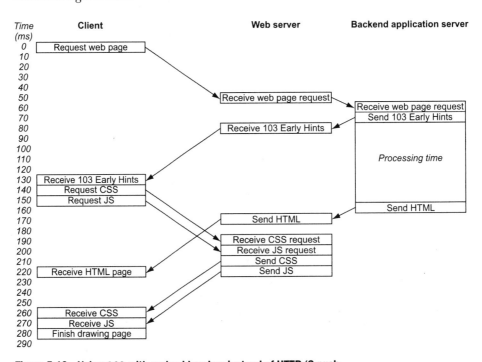

Figure 5.19   Using `103` **with preload headers instead of HTTP/2 push**

This process isn't as fast as pushing, because the browser still needs to request these resources, but it's faster than waiting for the browser to realize that the web page needs these resources. In this example, there's also some overlap of the requesting of the additional responses and the sending of the main page, which makes this flow a bit more complicated, but this flow probably represents real life. The advantage of this process over push, however, is there are fewer concerns about wasting bandwidth. If the browser already has the resources, it won't request them. Depending on the timing, the preloaded resources may be fully received before the page that needs them, which would make the process as fast as using HTTP/2 push. Even when it's not quite as fast, as in figure 5.19, preload may prove to be a safer middle ground until developers figure out better ways to use HTTP/2 push safely and without wasting resources.

At this writing, no browser supports `103 Early Hints` processing (though Chrome[28] and Firefox[29] are working on it), and not all browsers support preload link headers.[30] Perhaps by the time the `103 Early Hints` header is better supported, the overpushing concern will also have been solved by cache digests or similar techniques; then developers will have two options.

5.9   *Other use cases for HTTP/2 push*

At present, HTTP/2 push is for a specific use case: pushing critical resources early to speed page loading without requiring inlining of resources. From the beginning, however, some people have been asking whether this use case could be extended.[31] The use cases being discussed include the following:

- *Could HTTP/2 push replace WebSockets or SSE if the requirement to use push only in response to specific requests were relaxed?* Those technologies allow two-way communication between client and server (such as to update a web page when new information is available on the server). Or is it sufficient to use HTTP/2 in conjunction with WebSockets or SSE?[32] Currently, as mentioned at the beginning of the chapter, HTTP/2 push isn't a good replacement, but with some changes to make communication truly two-way, there's potential here (though the overheads of HTTP may mean this solution isn't desirable compared with the raw format of, say, WebSockets). On a related note, the BBC Research and Development department looked at using HTTP/2 push as a broadcast method in an interesting paper.[33]
- *Could HTTP/2 push be used to update browser caches when resources change?* At the moment, caching and cache-busting[34] techniques are complicated. But if HTTP/2

---

[28] https://crbug.com/671310
[29] https://bugzilla.mozilla.org/show_bug.cgi?id=1407355
[30] https://caniuse.com/#feat=link-rel-preload
[31] https://www.igvita.com/2013/06/12/innovating-with-http-2.0-server-push/
[32] https://www.infoq.com/articles/websocket-and-http2-coexist
[33] https://www.bbc.co.uk/rd/publications/whitepaper336
[34] https://css-tricks.com/strategies-for-cache-busting-css/

push allowed you to push resources directly into the *HTTP cache* (which it currently doesn't), new opportunities would be available to handle changes on websites.

- *Could it be used to improve progressive JPEGs?* Progressive JPEGs, which start showing a fuzzy image that gets clearer as more of the file downloads, would benefit from being able to download many images in parallel. This could get more interesting with HTTP/2 push if you could change the priority after the initial views are sent.[35] That way, the server could send an initial view with high priority and then back off to send the remainder of the image with low priority. Shimmercat is one web server that uses this technique, which is discussed in chapter 7.

- *Could it be used for APIs?* At least one API developer has suggested that HTTP/2 push could be used to push additional information but still maintain separation of resources, which could lead to lots of interesting use cases, perhaps not limited by browsers' push caches. The protocol allows for push to be used in reply to any request. But in many ways, browsers are limiting the use of push by not allowing pushed resources to be used or even notifying the page unless the page subsequently requests the resources. A non-browser-based HTTP/2 client could remove such limitations.

- *Would adding a notification lead to other use cases?* Adding an HTTP/2 push notification event or API to browsers could lead to other interesting use cases. A news or social media website, for example, could poll its server with a short "Are there any updates?" request. If updates occur (such as breaking news), any required resources could be pushed as standard HTTP resources (HTML, JSON-based data, images, and so on); then an event could be sent to the web app to inform the client to fetch and display those resources when they arrive. This technique could allow instant loading of those web pages. The advantages of this technique over WebSockets or SSE are all the advantages of HTTP (such as caching, file formats, and simplicity).

In summary, there could be better use cases for HTTP/2 push than improving first paint time. I think that HTTP/2 push has been underused for its original use case—for good reasons discussed in this chapter—but it has a lot of potential, perhaps for some of the ideas mentioned in this chapter and perhaps for other ideas.[36] The Internet Engineering Task Force (IETF) has started an informational RFC that tracks HTTP/2 server push use cases.[37]

Alternatively, are we restricting ourselves too much in trying to maintain the old concept of HTTP being a request-and-response protocol? WebSockets and SSE show a need and appetite for a two-way protocol delivered over HTTP, and perhaps we

---

[35] https://calendar.perfplanet.com/2016/even-faster-images-using-http2-and-progressive-jpegs/

[36] https://groups.google.com/a/chromium.org/forum/#!msg/net-dev/yfkW4mkWIPU/5RckmfktJgAJ; also available at https://goo.gl/gTJrwC

[37] https://tools.ietf.org/html/draft-bishop-httpbis-push-cases

should allow it in the protocol. At least one proposal has been written to this effect,[38] and the binary framing layer introduced with HTTP/2 lends itself to these sorts of implementations. I return to this topic in chapter 10.

HTTP/2 push is new, and site owners should approach it with caution. It's an interesting feature, and experimentation will show whether the performance boosts that HTTP/2 push promises materialize or whether HTTP/2 push makes everything overly complex for little extra gain.

I hope that this chapter shows that although HTTP/2 push has great potential, you may not want to rush into it without careful thought. In fact, you may not want to consider it until more best practices and cache-aware techniques are well defined.

Summary

- HTTP/2 push is a new concept in HTTP/2 that allows multiple responses to be sent back to a single HTTP request.
- HTTP/2 push was proposed as an alternative to inlining critical resources.
- Many servers and CDNs implement HTTP/2 push by using HTTP link headers.
- The new 103 Early Hints status code can be used to provide link headers earlier.
- HTTP/2 push is implemented in the browser in ways that may not be obvious.
- Overpushing resources is easy and can have a detrimental effect on website performance.
- The performance benefit of HTTP/2 push may not be great, and the risks are high.
- It may be better to use preload hints, perhaps with 103 Early Hints, rather than push.
- HTTP/2 push may have other use cases, though some would require changes in the protocol.

---

[38] https://tools.ietf.org/html/draft-benfield-http2-p2p

Optimizing for HTTP/2

This chapter covers

- What HTTP/2 changes for web developers
- Whether HTTP/1.1 web performance techniques are antipatterns under HTTP/2
- Other performance techniques and whether they're still relevant under HTTP/2
- How to optimize for HTTP/1 and HTTP/2
- Connection coalescing

You've gained a good understanding of HTTP/2: what it aims to solve and how it works, and some of the new features and opportunities it brings. I still have some more advanced topics to cover in the third part of this book, but you've enough information to look at what HTTP/2 means for your websites and how you can optimize for it. How should you change your development practices? Can you drop some performance techniques? What new techniques can you use? What do you do for those users who can't use HTTP/2? This chapter aims to answer those questions.

6.1 What HTTP/2 means for web developers

You've seen that HTTP/2 fundamentally changes how HTTP messages are sent to servers, and should bring performance benefits as a result. But do developers need to change their development languages and practices? Should you use particular Java-Script frameworks to take advantages of HTTP/2? On the whole, the answer to these questions is that no changes are required, though some may be beneficial.

HTTP/2 is designed to be backward-compatible. If your server supports HTTP/2, you should be able to switch it on, and, in most cases, see an immediate performance benefit without changing a single line of code. Some new features (such as *HTTP/2 push*) require changes to use them, and performance enhancement improvements are possible with a deeper understanding of HTTP/2 that this chapter aims to provide, but HTTP/2 shouldn't require you to make those changes after you switch over. The changes are, for the most part, optional extras that further improve performance.

Switching on HTTP/2 may not be as simple as you'd like, however (covered in chapter 3 and the appendix). You may need to upgrade your infrastructure or even consider new infrastructure, such as having a reverse proxy or content delivery network in front of your web server. This decision may lead to other decisions and opportunities that you may be able to capitalize on at the same time as the upgrade or in the future. These topics are somewhat separate, though. In this chapter, I aim to explain what HTTP/2 means for web developers, assuming that they have access to it.

> ### How to make HTTP/2 calls from the browser
>
> One of the best things about HTTP/2 is that after you've supported it on the server side, you don't need to make any changes at the client end; the browser takes care of this task for you. You don't need to upgrade your version of JQuery, use a different AJAX syntax, or switch from Angular to React (or vice versa). From a web developer's perspective, every frontend HTTP request and response works exactly as it did before—except (ideally) faster because no queuing occurs. These libraries and tools let the browser handle the low-level details of making the network call, so only the browser needs to know about HTTP/2.
>
> At the moment, frontend developers can't specify whether HTTP/1.1 or HTTP/2 should be used any more than they can specify whether to use HTTP/1.1 or HTTP/1.0 (or even HTTP/0.9). This situation may change in the future, because being able to provide the priority of a call in either HTML or AJAX,[a, b, c] for example, or to register a callback for an HTTP/2 push,[d] would be incredibly useful.
>
> ---
> [a] https://bugzilla.mozilla.org/show_bug.cgi?id=559092
> [b] https://bugs.chromium.org/p/chromium/issues/detail?id=41501
> [c] https://github.com/WICG/priority-hints
> [d] https://github.com/whatwg/fetch/issues/65

6.2   *Are some HTTP/1.1 optimizations now antipatterns?*

HTTP/2 was designed to address some of the fundamental performance problems in HTTP/1.1. These performance problems made requesting separate resources under HTTP/1.1 expensive, which led to various techniques for increasing the number of HTTP connections or minimizing the number of resources requested. Increasing the number of HTTP connections required browsers to open multiple connections and even host resources on multiple domains (sharding). Reducing the number of requests meant using concatenation to merge multiple CSS and JavaScript files into one big file or creating image sprites of all the little images used by a website (such as social media icons or other small icons), which could be extracted again with the clever use of CSS. Both types of optimizations involved transferring the same data (or at least similar data) with fewer HTTP requests.

These workarounds addressed some of the inefficiencies of HTTP/1.1 but introduced new problems, as described in chapter 2. HTTP/2 attempts to fix many of these issues at a protocol level. Requests are now almost free at a protocol layer due to the binary framing layer; therefore, are the workarounds no longer needed? In fact, there has been much talk about these HTTP/1.1 performance techniques becoming antipatterns under HTTP/2. Well, not so fast; I said *almost* free and *only* at a protocol layer.

6.2.1   *HTTP/2 requests still have a cost*

When a web page references a resource, many things are going on, some of which are improved by HTTP/2 and some of which aren't. Figure 6.1 details some of the many decisions and processes a browser needs to make when a web page asks to include a resource.

At a high level, the browser needs to check whether a valid copy exists in the various caches (discussed in chapter 5), and if, not make an HTTP request for it. Making an HTTP request may involve using an existing connection or starting a new connection, depending on which domain is used and the type of request. After the resource has been downloaded, the client needs to look at the caching headers to decide whether to save the resource to the cache for potential reuse. Even after all these steps, the browser must process the resource (parse the CSS or JavaScript, process the JPEG image, and so on).

A lot is going on even before you get to the actual specifics of HTTP sending and receiving the requests, never mind what to do with it when you have the resource. All these processes take time—often, tiny amounts of time. But if you remove the typical six-connection limit of HTTP/1.1 and have hundreds of resources, you start to see some new, interesting problems.

In 2016, as HTTP/2 use was ramping up, the Chrome developers noticed significant delays when using HTTP/2 for large numbers of resources.[1] Some sites froze for

---

[1]   https://bugs.chromium.org/p/chromium/issues/detail?id=655585

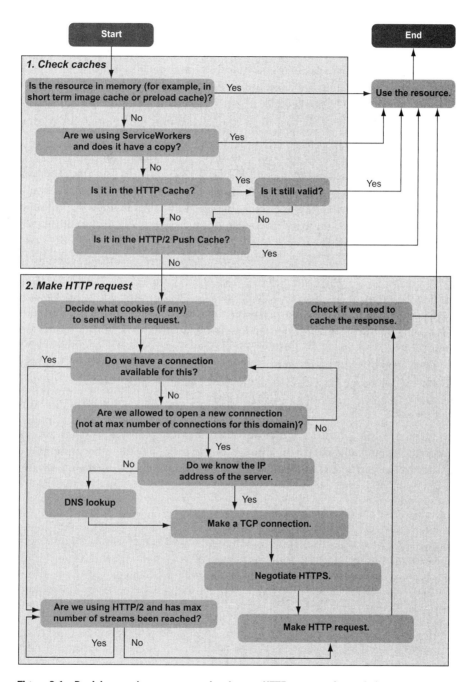

Figure 6.1   Decisions and processes made when an HTTP resource is needed

400 to 500 ms when not a single request was sent, for example. This problem had nothing to do with the HTTP/2 protocol per se. You'll see in chapter 7 that stream prioritization should allow these concurrent requests to be prioritized appropriately at a protocol level. The problem was purely a bottleneck in getting the resources sent. During this time, the browser was busy completing all the tasks mentioned in the preceding section. HTTP/2 may allow many resources to be in flight together without the performance penalty of waiting for a free connection, but that ability moves the bottleneck elsewhere.

To prevent this delay, the Chrome team had to limit the number of resources that could be queued even under HTTP/2, back to the six-connections limit of HTTP/1, until the team could optimized the code. This limitation was enforced only on nonessential resources, so in theory, HTTP/2 was no worse than HTTP/1.1 and shouldn't have mattered to websites. But an interesting scenario arose: JavaScript resources with the `async` or `defer` attribute (normally added for performance reasons to prevent blocking on these resources) were throttled, whereas JavaScript resources without these attributes were not. Websites that used performance best practices (such as making JavaScript nonblocking) were being artificially limited and loading more slowly than websites that didn't follow these best practices. Websites using `async` or `defer` ended up loading exactly like HTTP/1.1 requests, as shown in figure 6.2.

Whether this situation mattered that much is up for debate; the JavaScript was marked with `async` or `defer` and therefore wasn't critical to load. But it surprised some website owners who saw this HTTP/1-like behavior when they had implemented HTTP/2.[2]

This throttling has been removed from later versions of Chrome but does show that care is needed when you remove bottlenecks like the six-connections limit in browsers, because the bottlenecks may be masking other performance issues.

---

[2] https://stackoverflow.com/questions/45384243/google-chrome-does-not-do-multiplexing-with-http2/45775288#45775288

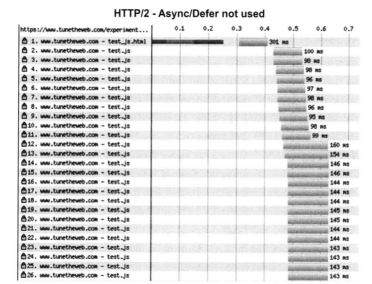

Figure 6.2   Nonrender blocking JavaScript being artificially slowed in Chrome

6.2.2   *HTTP/2 isn't limitless*

The other point to note is that HTTP/2 hasn't entirely removed the limit. You saw in chapter 5 that although `SETTINGS_MAX_CONCURRENT_STREAMS` defaults to unlimited, many implementations add limits, as shown in tables 6.1 and 6.2.

Table 6.1   Concurrent stream limits on popular HTTP/2 server-side implementations

Software	Type	Default concurrent streams
Apache HTTPD (v2.4.35)	Web server	100[a]
nginx (v1.14.0)	Web server	128[b]
H2O (2.3.0)	Web server	100[c]
IIS (v10)	Web server	100
Jetty (9.4.12)	Web and Java servlet container	128[d]
Apache Tomcat (9.0)	Web and Java servlet container	200[e]
Node (10.11.0)	JavaScript runtime environment	100[f]
Akamai	CDN	100
Amazon CloudFront and S3	CDN	128
Cloudflare	CDN	128
MaxCDN	CDN	128

[a]   https://httpd.apache.org/docs/2.4/mod/mod_http2.html#h2maxsessionstreams
[b]   http://nginx.org/en/docs/http/ngx_http_v2_module.html#http2_max_concurrent_streams
[c]   https://h2o.examp1e.net/configure/http2_directives.html#http2-max-concurrent-requests-per-connection
[d]   https://www.eclipse.org/jetty/documentation/9.4.x/http2-configuring.html
[e]   https://tomcat.apache.org/tomcat-9.0-doc/config/http2.html
[f]   https://nodejs.org/api/http2.html

Table 6.2   Concurrent stream limits on popular HTTP/2 web browsers

Software	Default concurrent streams
Chrome (v69)	1000
Firefox (v62)	Not set (uses HTTP/2 default of unlimited)
Safari (v12)	1000
Opera (v56)	1000
Edge (v17)	1024
Internet Explorer 11	1024

Some of these settings were taken from documentation and others from experimentation. For the CDNs, I used Wireshark to intercept requests to the home page or other page hosted on that CDN and looked at the SETTINGS *frame* as described in chapter 4 (section 4.3.3). For the browsers, I set up an nghttp server with verbose logging and examined the SETTINGS frames that the various browsers sent on establishing the HTTP/2 connection.

What is immediately apparent is that server-side settings are a lot lower than web browser limits. In fact, Firefox doesn't set a limit and uses the default unlimited value, which makes sense, as, ultimately, the browser has control of what requests are sent, so it can add limits outside the protocol (as Chrome did initially in the preceding section). Additionally, the browser is likely to be servicing a much smaller number of requests than a server, which may be responding to multiple users at the same time. Given the performance issues that Chrome experienced when requesting many resources, however, it may be better if browser makers limit the default number of connections a bit further until HTTP/2 gets fully settled in. Sites with more than 200 resources are rare but may become common when HTTP/2 is fully embedded and if websites stop concatenating and spriting resources. If you have a website that needs 500 resources, and you think that under HTTP/2 you don't need to concatenate these resources, it's likely that only 100 to 128 resources will be fetched initially and the rest will be queued as under HTTP/1.1. This behavior is exactly as described in chapter 2 (section 2.6.1) when the 100-stream server limit was reached. There are examples in which sites have tried to remove concatenation and run into these new limits.[3]

6.2.3 Compression is more efficient for larger resources

All web resources should be compressed before being sent over the network. For some formats (such as JPEG and PNG for images and WOFF and WOFF2 for fonts), compression is built into the format, and the web server shouldn't attempt it on top of this compression. For primarily text-based formats such as HTML, CSS, and JavaScript, compression such as gzip (or the newer brotli format[4]) is used, often on the fly by the web server.

The one thing that nearly all these compressed formats have in common is that they can compress larger files more efficiently than smaller files. How each compression algorithm works is covered in section 7.3.4, but suffice it to say that most of these algorithms work by finding duplicated series of data and replacing them with references to a single version of that data. With larger files, more duplicates can be found, and the compression ratio can be larger. The net effect is that it's always better to compress one large file of 100 KB than to compress 10 files of 10 KB separately, even though the total uncompressed data is exactly the same. By no longer bundling assets (as you did under HTTP/1.1), you may lose some compression benefits and end up sending *more* data across the wire under HTTP/2, even if the uncompressed amount is identical.

Exactly how much of a difference this situation makes depends on your files. To examine some real-world examples, download some popular jQuery files:

```
curl -OL https://code.jquery.com/jquery-3.3.1.min.js
curl -OL https://code.jquery.com/mobile/1.4.5/jquery.mobile-1.4.5.min.js
curl -OL https://code.jquery.com/ui/1.12.1/jquery-ui.min.js
```

---

[3] http://engineering.khanacademy.org/posts/js-packaging-http2.htm#http-2-0-has-service-issucs
[4] https://tools.ietf.org/html/rfc7932

Then combine these files by using the Linux cat command:

```
cat jquery-3.3.1.min.js jquery.mobile-1.4.5.min.js jquery-ui.min.js >
jquery_combined.js
```

If you list the files, you should see the file sizes total up:

```
-rw-r--r--  1 barry  p    86927 19 May 19:31 jquery-3.3.1.min.js
-rw-r--r--  1 barry  p   253668 19 May 19:31 jquery-ui.min.js
-rw-r--r--  1 barry  p   200143 19 May 19:31 jquery.mobile-1.4.5.min.js
-rw-r--r--  1 barry  p   540738 19 May 19:31 jquery_combined.js
```

86,927 + 200,143 + 253,668 = 540,738 KB—the size of the combined file, as expected.

Then compress all the files by using gzip with the standard settings:

```
gzip jquery*
```

Now look at the new file sizes:

```
-rw-r--r--  1 barry  p    30371 19 May 19:31 jquery-3.3.1.min.js.gz
-rw-r--r--  1 barry  p    68058 19 May 19:31 jquery-ui.min.js.gz
-rw-r--r--  1 barry  p    55649 19 May 19:31 jquery.mobile-1.4.5.min.js.gz
-rw-r--r--  1 barry  p   152652 19 May 19:31 jquery_combined.js.gz
```

Doing the same addition (30,371 KB + 68,058 KB + 55,649 KB) yields 154,078 KB, but the combined file compresses to 152,652 KB. It's only 1% smaller, but there's a difference, and with nonminified files (which I discuss in section 6.3.1), the differences may be larger.

On the flip side, no longer bundling files may allow developers to be more targeted about what they include on a page. Some developers, for example, may have included one large concatenated JavaScript file with every page on the site. Some pages required some parts of this JavaScript, and other pages required other parts, but because HTTP/1.1 was inefficient with multiple files, it usually was more efficient to send one large file with every page rather than create custom bundles for each page. With HTTP/2, multiple downloads are less an issue, so each page can be changed to include only the JavaScript it requires, which reduces the amount of data to be transferred for each page.

Does the reduction in data transferred offset the loss in compression ratios? The answer depends on your site, how far you take unbundling, and how much unnecessary data you were sending before that you don't need to send now. Some example case studies[5] have shown a small increase in data transferred on the wire even when removing unnecessary code, though the sheer amount of JavaScript being delivered in these cases is perhaps a bigger concern. Even with slightly larger resources, the performance improvements due to processing less data on some pages may more than

---

[5] http://engineering.khanacademy.org/posts/js-packaging-http2.htm#bundling-improves-compression

offset the performance loss from sending more raw bytes when using unbundling. To conclude, HTTP/2 may not require as much bundling as HTTP/1.1 did, but consider any loss in compression ratios before unbundling.

6.2.4 *Bandwidth limitations and resource contention*

HTTP/1.1 created a natural throttling on the HTTP/1.1 requests that could be in flight at any time. Web browsers, therefore, worked hard on prioritizing the most important resources to be sent first. Yes, web developers tried to work around this situation by concatenating and *sharding*, but these solutions were limited. Now that the limits have been dramatically increased (if not removed), you can more easily get into a situation in which some requests starve others of bandwidth.

In the example site in chapter 2, downloading 360 images over HTTP/2 resulted in 100 images being downloaded in parallel, as opposed to the six-resource limit under separate HTTP/1.1 connections. Because the 100 downloads happened at the same time, each resource took longer to download under HTTP/2, as shown in figure 6.3.

Overall, the images downloaded much faster over HTTP/2, but it may be preferable to have some resources completely downloaded first (as happens naturally under HTTP/1.1), rather than downloading a little of every image (as happens naturally under HTTP/2, unless an explicit prioritization is used to prevent this behavior).

99design, a web design website, saw similar issues when it first switched to HTTP/2.[6] All the resources that the web page needed were now able to download in parallel, including some large, high-quality images (as you might expect from a design website). But some images at the top of the page loaded slower under HTTP/2, as offscreen images were downloading at the same time and using the bandwidth. Under HTTP/1.1, the browser had to prioritize the onscreen images to be downloaded first, and the six-connection limit ensured that those images weren't delayed by many lower-priority offscreen images.

Both these cases can be improved by prioritizing the requests appropriately. I've touched on prioritization under HTTP/2 briefly so far, but cover it in depth in chapter 7. Prioritization is largely out of the site owner's hands (which is why I left it for a later chapter), but it may prove to be a key differentiator for the performance of both browsers and servers. If a browser can suggest an appropriate priority (such as downloading images in the viewport with a higher priority than images farther down the page), and if the server can respond to those suggestions, prioritization can lead to more-performant pages. Alternatively, images can be downloaded completely in the order requested, which is what Chrome does currently (see chapter 7).

Therefore, this issue was more an early-implementation issue than a problem with the HTTP/2 protocol itself. Given that developers have 20 years of experience with HTTP/1, however, it's highly unlikely to be the last such issue during the move to an HTTP/2 world.

---

[6] https://99designs.com/tech-blog/blog/2016/07/14/real-world-http-2-400gb-of-images-per-day/

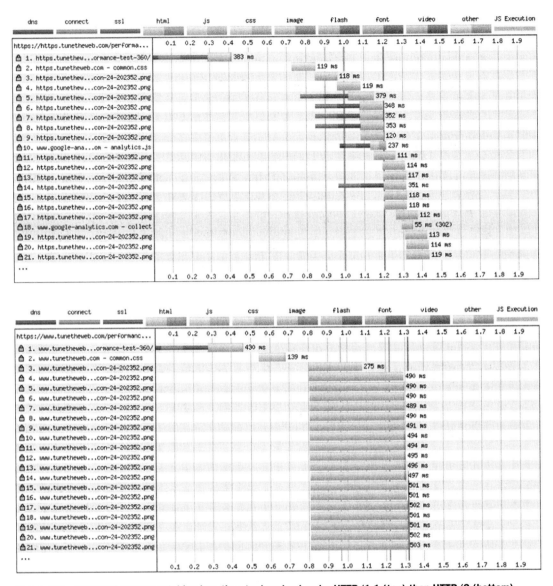

Figure 6.3   Individual resources taking less time to download under HTTP/1.1 (top) than HTTP/2 (bottom)

6.2.5   Sharding

Sharding was used to break the six-connection limit that browsers typically imposed on domains. By hosting media on subdomains or separate domains, websites could have more downloads in parallel. In my opinion, the impact of sharding may have been overstated except for a large number of resources, in which case *concatenation* or *spriting* may have been a better solution. Studies have shown that many extra connections are often used for only one or two resources, so the time required to set up those connections may outweigh any performance gain in using them efficiently. As always, websites should measure the impact of techniques such as sharding rather than blindly putting them in place under the assumption that they'll always improve performance.

In the HTTP/2 world, sharding doesn't make as much sense, and the effort to set up and manage separate infrastructure produces limited gains. Also, some parts of HTTP/2 (such as *HTTP/2 push* and HPACK header compression) work better over a single connection, so sharding would cause worse performance. Therefore, I expect sharding to be used less as HTTP/2 becomes more prevalent. As you'll see in section 6.4.4, HTTP/2 has a method to reverse sharding, allowing the best of both worlds. In some specific scenarios, sharding may still be valuable over lossy connections (see chapter 9), but in general, it should no longer be needed except in those specific scenarios. Even in those cases, it may be better for browsers to decide to open multiple connections when required rather than leave it up to sites to set sharding for all connections whether they're lossy or not.

6.2.6   *Inlining*

Inlining of critical CSS, or scripts, has always been a bit of a hack to me[7]—a powerful hack, but a hack nonetheless. Putting CSS code in the head of pages improves the first page load, but then that code either duplicates the content when the real CSS is loaded or doesn't allow caching for subsequent page loads on the same site. Also, inlining only the critical CSS can be complicated, as can be overriding the default way CSS stylesheets are loaded to prevent them from render blocking.

HTTP/2 push was supposed to eliminate the need for inlining, but as chapter 5 showed, this technology has proved complicated to use efficiently, so it hasn't taken off as much as expected. I expect inlining to remain a common performance benefit for a while, for those websites that are willing to use it and want to squeeze every last ounce out of the first page load.

6.2.7   *Conclusion*

One of the main aims of HTTP/2 was to counter the problem of costly requests in HTTP/1.1. HTTP/2 has made considerable improvements, but HTTP requests still have costs. Often, this problem is due to issues outside the protocol (such as the cost of multiple requests to browsers), but others are due at least in part to the way that HTTP/2 works. Too many simultaneous requests, for example, can cause a slowdown for some metrics (such as first paint) if critical requests are starved of resources.

You must also consider the fact that HTTP/2 implementations aren't yet mature; some suboptimal implementations will undoubtedly improve over time. Bugs may be found, or the new protocol may be used inefficiently (such as not prioritizing requests appropriately). I strongly advise you to keep your HTTP/2 software (server and browsers) up-to-date during this early phase.

---

[7]   https://www.tunetheweb.com/blog/inlining-css-is-not-for-me/

To repeat an earlier point, after 20 years, developers have a deep understanding of HTTP/1 and mature technology stacks, but HTTP/2 is still in its infancy. The technology doesn't appear to have many show-stopping issues, but there are many instances of unexpected bottlenecks and inefficiencies where HTTP/2 perhaps isn't as efficient as it could be.

HTTP/2 also dramatically increases the parallel download limits (from the previous six connections), but doesn't remove them. My recommendation is that you keep each domain's requests to fewer than 100 resources for now. Don't remove concatenation if doing so will result in hundreds of files, but use the increased limitations to bundle more appropriately.

The performance optimizations that became prevalent under HTTP/1.1 are required less, but it's premature to remove them while developers are getting used to this new protocol and what it means. Instead, scale them back to an appropriate level (using less concatenation rather than no concatenation, for example). Developers should perhaps group their code into groups of assets that are likely to be used together rather than concatenating files into one large file, as they may have done in the past. Reducing the use of HTTP/1.1 techniques rather than eradicating them seems to be the general consensus that researchers and website owners are reaching.[8] When HTTP/2 first came out, there was a lot of talk that many HTTP/1.1 performance techniques were now antipatterns, but this isn't strictly true.

The key takeaway is to not assume that HTTP/2 is a silver bullet. Most sites will see improvements, but a minority may suffer. Explaining any expected behavior requires careful measuring and understanding of the protocol.

6.3   Web performance techniques still relevant under HTTP/2

HTTP/2 improves some of the inefficiencies of earlier versions of the HTTP protocol, as discussed in this chapter, which makes some of the performance techniques somewhat less relevant under HTTP/2. HTTP protocol optimizations aren't the only techniques you can use to improve performance of websites, but by the nature of the web, which involves client and server interactions often over some distance, a large part of web performance is optimizing network level use. It's worthwhile to review other related performance best practices that affect data transfer and to explain why they're still relevant under HTTP/2, as well as to point out any new opportunities under HTTP/2.

6.3.1   Minimizing the amount of data transferred

No matter what improvements HTTP/2 provides for handling requests and responses, it's always better to send less data. HTTP/2 doesn't magically make internet connections bigger; it allows them to be more efficient. Websites appear to load faster, but

---

[8] https://uhdspace.uhasselt.be/dspace/bitstream/1942/23909/1/h2bestpractices_RobinMarx_WEBIST2017.pdf

they generally load the same amount of data (perhaps even slightly more if compression isn't as efficient, as discussed in section 6.2.3). Therefore, it still pays to reduce the amount of data you send as much as possible. All the techniques you use to achieve this reduction are equally relevant under HTTP/2.

USING APPROPRIATE FILE FORMATS AND SIZES

Media-rich web pages may be interesting, but media takes time to download and display. According to the HTTP Archive, nearly 80% of a web page's size is due to images and video[9] (see figure 6.4), so it's still important to send the appropriate media format and size.

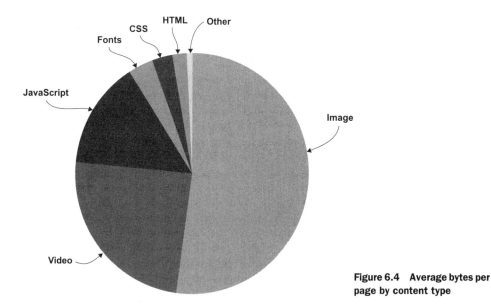

Figure 6.4   Average bytes per page by content type

Video and audio are a bit specialized, so we won't cover them here, but we will discuss images a bit.[10] Typically, you use JPEG (aka JPG) format for photographs and PNG for other graphics. WebP was pushed by Google but doesn't seem to have caught on, even though it has been out for several years.[11] SVG is growing in use but still has some way to go. Nearly all websites use JPEG and PNG formats,[12] and for good reason; these formats are universally supported and provide a good balance between size and quality.

JPEG is a lossy format; you'll lose some of the image quality, but can set the level of compression versus quality. It's easy to reduce image quality and produce much smaller images without any apparent dip in perceptible quality to the naked eye. Images can

---

[9]   https://httparchive.org/reports/page-weight

[10]   https://developer.mozilla.org/en-US/docs/Web/HTML/Supported_media_formats

[11]   https://caniuse.com/#feat=webp

[12]   https://w3techs.com/technologies/overview/image_format/all

also contain a considerable amount of metadata (when the photograph was taken, what camera took it, what ISO setting was used, and so on). Most of this metadata is irrelevant to those who browse your web page and should be stripped out, but take care about images that you don't own in case the licensing terms restrict alterations. Various tools and image editing software can change the quality and metadata to reduce file size, but for ease of use, I recommend tinypng.com,[13] which compresses JPEGs and PNGs quickly and without a fuss. It's also available at tinyjpg.com; both sites use the same tool and can handle both formats. Figure 6.5 shows how most images can be dramatically reduced in size.

Figure 6.5   Dragging and dropping files in tinypng can dramatically reduce file size.

In addition to looking at the quality level, you should look at size. Sending a 5120 × 2880-pixel image to display it at 100-pixel width wastes both the download time and the browser's processing time. Large print-quality, print-size images should never be placed on web pages. If you need these types of images to be available, add them as separate download links.

Sending appropriately sized images also often means using different images for mobile and desktop sites, and possibly also for the various screen sizes in between. Although visitors who are lucky enough to be visiting your site on a large screen may appreciate high-quality images, those who are using mobile devices will likely curse your slow website if the same images are sent to them. Figure 6.6 shows that desktop and mobile site sizes are converging, perhaps because more sites are moving to a

---

[13] https://tinypng.com/

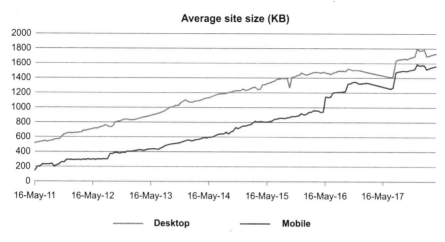

Figure 6.6   Site sizes of mobile and desktop are converging.

responsive design, with a single website for both, but fail to use techniques on that single website to deliver different image sizes to the two different platforms.

In summary, HTTP/2 doesn't change the file formats that can be sent and doesn't change the data that's transferred to or used at the client end. Continue to use the most appropriate file format and optimize your media before putting it on your website.

COMPRESSING TEXT DATA

Although media compression is often handled by the image format, the fundamental technologies of the web—HTML, CSS, and JavaScript—are text-based and you should look to reduce the size of these resources as much as possible too. Under HTTP/1.1, you compressed HTTP bodies by using gzip or similar tools to reduce the amount of data sent, and you should continue to do so under HTTP/2. HTTP/2 doesn't change what data is sent on the whole, only *how* it's sent. Compressing text response bodies, therefore, is still as relevant under HTTP/2 as it was under HTTP/1.1. Text compresses incredibly well, and you can easily achieve compression up to 90%. Table 6.3 shows the compression ratios of common JavaScript and CSS libraries.[14]

Table 6.3   Compression ratios of common libraries using gzip

Library	Size	Compressed size	Compression ratio
jquery-1.11.0.js	276 KB	82 KB	70%
angular-1.2.15.js	729 KB	182 KB	75%
bootstrap-3.1.1.css	118 KB	18 KB	85%
foundation-5.css	186 KB	22 KB	88%

[14] https://developers.google.com/web/fundamentals/performance/optimizing-content-efficiency/optimize-encoding-and-transfer?hl=en#text-compression-with-gzip

The only downsides to compressing data before it's sent are the time and compute power required to compress on the server side and decompress on the browser side, but this power is almost negligible on modern hardware. The network benefits of sending fewer bytes are almost always far higher than the time and compute cost of compression.

Gzip remains the most popular compression technology,[15] though compression algorithms such as Brotli[16] are becoming more prevalent. Brotli offers better compression (depending on the settings[17]), and, therefore, even bigger savings. These tools should be used in addition to gzip for browsers that don't support brotli yet.[18] HTTP/2 handles different content encodings in the same way as HTTP/1.1, so changing to HTTP/2 makes no difference as to whether to compress your response bodies (please do!) or what format to use. The only slight relevance is that some newer formats such as brotli require HTTPS, and potentially later versions of your web server. If you migrated to HTTPS and HTTP/2 at the same time or had to upgrade your web-server software for HTTP/2, you may now have the option to use these new formats, though perhaps it's best to get through your HTTP/2 migration before adding these formats to the mix.

The best thing about compression is that except for a little setup on the server, it's seamless. When they're set up, web servers compress resources on the fly, web browsers decompress resources automatically, and most website owners can forget about compression after it's enabled. Some web servers allow you to serve precompressed content to reduce load on the web server. This technique requires some extra effort each time you want to add new content (to precompress it before you upload it), but that effort doesn't change under HTTP/2.

Regardless of what version of HTTP you use, you should continue to compress your HTTP bodies. The content encoding will be communicated to the browser in the `content-encoding` HTTP header as it was under HTTP/1.1.

> ### Compressing HTTP headers
> While I'm on the subject of compression, one thing that does change under HTTP/2, and that I haven't discussed in much detail yet, is header compression. HTTP/1 allowed compression only of request-and-response *bodies*, whereas HTTP/2 also compresses HTTP *headers* by using a format known as HPACK. This format is another way that HTTP/2 reduces the performance overhead of multiple requests. Without HPACK, sending the same content over two requests would lead to sending twice the header data that needs to be sent. This improvement is especially important as the use of HTTP headers continues to grow, because for many small requests, headers can make up a proportionally large part of both request and response.

---

[15] https://w3techs.com/technologies/details/ce-compression/all/all
[16] https://opensource.googleblog.com/2015/09/introducing-brotli-new-compression.html
[17] https://blogs.akamai.com/2016/02/understanding-brotlis-potential.html
[18] https://caniuse.com/#feat=brotli

Because header compression is handled by the underlying browser and there's little for website owners and developers to do, I don't cover this topic further right now, but I explain how this process works in chapter 8.

MINIFYING CODE

Another data-reduction method is minifying code, whether that code is HTML, CSS, or JavaScript. This method involves stripping out whitespace and comments, and often rewriting code to reduce the sizes of local variable names and remove unnecessary delimiters. Like compression, this method doesn't change under HTTP/2, so if you minimized before, you probably should continue to do so after moving to HTTP/2.

But HTTP/2 potentially allows code to be deployed without much (or at least without *as* much) concatenation, so a build step may no longer be required. You may want to use this opportunity to bring your deployed code more in line with your source code now that there no longer needs to be such a difference. In such a case, you may no longer want to minify. Not minifying may add a slight performance cost, but in my opinion, minification on top of compression adds only a little extra cost, because compression already strips out repeated strings (such as whitespace) reasonably well. On the negative side, it's more difficult to read minimized code if you're trying to debug problems in production. Unfortunately not all bugs are easily reproducible in development environments! You can add source maps that allow you to "unminimize" your production code somewhat, but that process can be complicated.[19]

Consider a real-world example of code to see the space benefits of minification: the popular Bootstrap v4.0.0 library. This library provides both minified and original versions of its CSS and JavaScript code, so compare these versions, starting with the Bootstrap CSS. In Chrome, open developer tools, make sure that the Size column appears, and load the Bootstrap CSS file from https://stackpath.bootstrapcdn.com/bootstrap/4.1.3/css/bootstrap.min.css, as shown in figure 6.7.

If the Size column doesn't show both numbers, click the Use Large Request Rows button. In this example, the Size column shows both the compressed size (21.0 KB) and the uncompressed value (138 KB). Technically these numbers aren't comparable, however: the top value is the transferred size, so it includes the HTTP headers (request and response), whereas the bottom value is only the raw body size returned. I measured the headers separately, and they're about 0.5 KB uncompressed. So ignore these differences, because they have a negligible effect. It's also possible to download and gzip the files separately (as in section 6.2.3) to get a more accurate value, but that technique introduces questions about what gzip settings the command line and the web server are using.

---

[19] https://www.html5rocks.com/en/tutorials/developertools/sourcemaps/

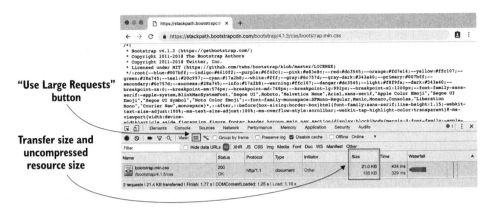

"Use Large Requests" button

Transfer size and uncompressed resource size

Figure 6.7   Viewing the compressed and uncompressed size of a request

Repeating this process for the unminified version and then putting them together produces the values in table 6.4.

Table 6.4   Effect of gzip and minification on Bootstrap CSS (v4.1.3)

Compression type	Bootstrap.css	Bootstrap.min.css
Original file	170 KB	138 KB (81% of original size)
gzip	22.8 KB (13% of original size)	21.0 KB (12% of original size)

As you can see, the unminified version shrinks to 13% of the size, whereas the minified version is 12% of the size. Minifying and gzipping are better, but you're talking about a difference of only 1%, or 1.8 KB. Yes, every byte counts, and for a provider like Bootstrap, it makes sense to provide a minified version of the library. But for your own code, the saving often isn't huge.

The saving depends on the individual code. Although there doesn't appear to be a huge benefit for the Bootstrap CSS file, you see a larger benefit when you look at the Bootstrap JavaScript file (table 6.5).

Table 6.5   Effect of gzip and minification on Bootstrap JavaScript (v4.1.3)

Compression type	Bootstrap.js	Bootstrap.min.js
Original file	121 KB	49.8 KB (41% of original size)
gzip	20.9 KB (17% of original size)	14.2 KB (12% of original size)

Here, you see a bigger compression gain (17% gzipped only, 12% gzipped and minified), which leads to a bigger saving of 5%, or 6.7 KB. Most people comment their JavaScript code more than they do their CSS code, and JavaScript often uses more whitespace than CSS does and includes more variable names, so this result isn't unexpected. In fact, you can see that minifying alone, without gzipping, reduces the JavaScript file to 41% of the size, whereas the CSS is still 81% of the original size. Incidentally, both minified-only file sizes are much larger than the gzipped-only version, which backs up my point that gzip (or similar compression) is the main optimization to use; minification gives you a little extra improvement if you want to use it too.

For larger sites and website owners who have the necessary expertise, however, minification is likely to be worth the effort. Table 6.6 expands on table 6.5, showing compression sizes for some common web development libraries. You see a noticeable difference in the minified version of some of these libraries, jQuery and Angular in particular.

Table 6.6 **Compression ratios of common libraries**

Library	Size	Compressed size	Compression ratio
jquery-3.3.1.js	265 KB	78.9 KB	30%
jquery-3.3.1.min.js	84.9 KB	30.0 KB	35%
angular-1.7.2.js	960 KB	297 KB	31%
angular-1.7.2.min.js	168 KB	56.6 KB	34%
bootstrap-4.1.3.css	121 KB	20.9 KB	17%
bootstrap-4.1.3.min.css	49.8 KB	14.2 KB	29%
foundation-6.4.3.css	158 KB	18.8 KB	12%
foundation-6.4.3.min.css	118 KB	14.7 KB	12%

The other reason to minimize code is obfuscation. Trying to use obfuscation to hide any logic is of limited use, however, as unminifying code is trivial. Nevertheless, stripping out comments may prevent any embarrassing thoughts of internal developers leaking out into the real world (such as "Must get around to fixing this awful code at some point"). Finally, minimized code can in theory perform marginally better, as there's less for the browser to parse, though the first step of any parse effectively minimizes the code, so there may not be large benefits.

To sum up, HTTP/2 should have no direct effect on your decision to minify your code. But if moving to HTTP/2 changes your development practices (such as concatenating less), you may want to revisit the benefits of minification to see whether they still apply. Minification is more complex than having the web server compress files, and the improvements of minification on top of compression are considerably less.

6.3.2   *Using caching to prevent resending data*

An often-repeated quote about web performance (though no one seems to remember who said it first[20]) is: "The fastest HTTP request is the one not made." HTTP/2 seeks to improve the performance of an HTTP request, but it will never be faster than not making the request at all by caching as much as possible. If visitors need that resource again, they can pick it up from the HTTP cache, which is always quicker than making the full network request, no matter whether the protocol is HTTP/1, HTTP/2, or some future version.

Caching as much as possible was an excellent performance tip for HTTP/1, and it remains one in HTTP/2. The same `cache-control` and `expires` HTTP headers exist in HTTP/2 and should still be used—though some people argue, not unreasonably, that the `expires` header is no longer needed, because all common clients understand HTTP/1.1, and HTTP/1.0 is rarely used in real life, especially by applications that need to be aware of caching.[21]

Caching can be complicated. How you maximize caching without causing stale content to be shown after you update it is a tricky topic that requires a good bit of thought and cache-busting techniques.[22] Caching common assets (stylesheets, Java-Script, logos, and so on) can be one of the biggest differences between a snappy, responsive website and one that's slow and painful to use. Because caching is such an important topic, it's worth understanding HTTP caching and the 304 (Not Modified) response code, which I mentioned briefly in chapter 1.

When an HTTP response is received, it can include a `cache-control` HTTP header (or the older `expires` HTTP header), which indicates how long the resource should be considered valid for. Consider a real-world example. If you load Wikipedia from a fresh browser, you should see the header in figure 6.8.

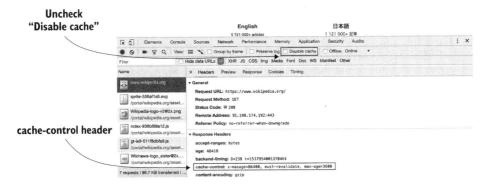

Figure 6.8   Wikipedia cache-control header

---

[20] The most likely candidate, Steve Souders, denies that it was him, despite the quote's often being attributed to him: https://www.stevesouders.com/blog/2012/03/22/cache-them-if-you-can/.

[21] https://www.fastly.com/blog/headers-we-dont-want

[22] https://css-tricks.com/strategies-for-cache-busting-css/

This figure shows that the Wikipedia home page can be cached for 3,600 seconds (max-age=3600), or 1 hour, after which it must be revalidated before use (must-revalidate). The figure also specifies that other intermediary caches, such as proxies, can cache the page for 86,400 seconds, or 1 day (s-maxage=86400). But these intermediaries often use other techniques to keep up-to-date (a topic that's beyond the scope of this book), so you can ignore that setting.

Make sure that the Disable Cache check box shown in the figure isn't checked. Then browse back and then forward a page, and you should see something similar to figure 6.9.

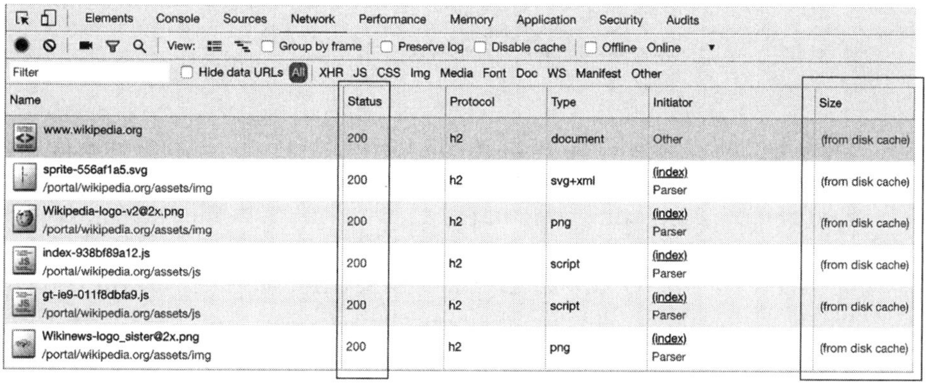

Name	Status	Protocol	Type	Initiator	Size
www.wikipedia.org	200	h2	document	Other	(from disk cache)
sprite-556af1a5.svg /portal/wikipedia.org/assets/img	200	h2	svg+xml	(index) Parser	(from disk cache)
Wikipedia-logo-v2@2x.png /portal/wikipedia.org/assets/img	200	h2	png	(index) Parser	(from disk cache)
index-938bf89a12.js /portal/wikipedia.org/assets/js	200	h2	script	(index) Parser	(from disk cache)
gt-ie9-011f8dbfa9.js /portal/wikipedia.org/assets/js	200	h2	script	(index) Parser	(from disk cache)
Wikinews-logo_sister@2x.png /portal/wikipedia.org/assets/img	200	h2	png	(index) Parser	(from disk cache)

Figure 6.9   Wikipedia loaded from the disk cache

As expected, the website has been loaded from the disk cache, as shown in the Size column. If you see this (from memory cache) rather than (from disk cache), it's likely that you came from another Wikipedia page rather than from a different site, so these resources are in the more recent memory cache, but the principle is the same. The old cached response is shown in figure 6.9, including the 200 status code (slightly dimmed to show that it's a cached response, which may be difficult to see in the figure).

To make things more interesting, wait an hour for the cache to expire and then try the experiment again. To save that time, reload the page (which has the same effect). You should see something similar to figure 6.10.

Here, you see a 304 response code instead of the usual 200. Incidentally, if you reloaded the same window, you also see that Chrome used the in-memory image cache for the images rather than the usual disk-based HTTP cache, per the discussion of figure 6.9. That 304 response appears because the browser made a conditional GET request, as shown in figure 6.11.

The browser found the home page in the cache, saw that it was out-of-date, and sent a request for the page—but it said "Send me the page if it's newer than the one I already got based on the last modified date (if-modified-since) or the eTag value (if-none-match) that you sent with the page last time." The eTag value allows more

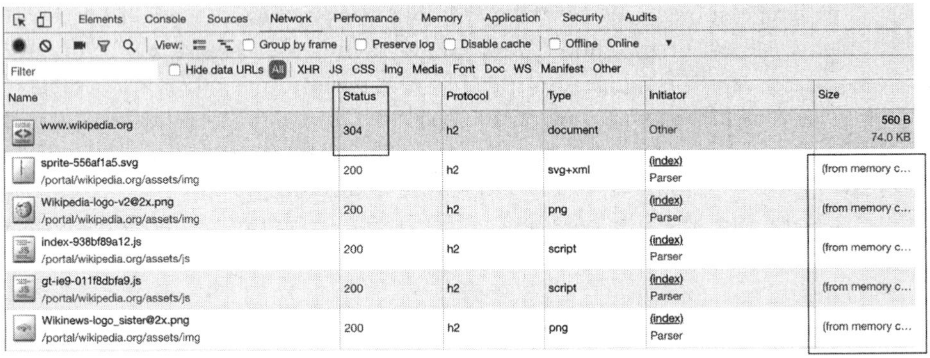

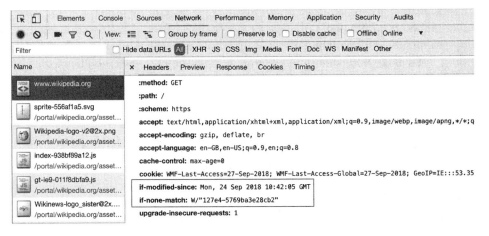

Figure 6.10 Wikipedia reloading from a stale cache

than the date to be used to indicate freshness. This value is implementation-specific, but could be a hash of the contents, for example. If both values are given (as in figure 6.11), the `eTag` value given in the `if-none-match` header takes precedence. The server checks, sees the page hasn't changed, and sends a `304` response to say that the copy the web browser has is still good. A `304` response has no HTTP body, so it's quicker to download than the full resource.

`304` responses are still slow; they require a network call all the way to the server and back. Network trips are cheaper (but not free!) under HTTP/2. Under HTTP/1, however, because an HTTP request was relatively expensive, sending a `304` response was almost as costly as sending the full `200` response, so `304` responses may not have been used as much as they could have been. Many websites don't cache their HTML pages at all, for example. Each time you go to the home page, the browser downloads the page again and then uses the cache only for the resources it

Figure 6.11 Conditional `GET` request

needs. Not caching the web page can make browsing the website feel slower. If you're on a home page, and you click another page and then want to go back to the home page, the reload should be instantaneous, but there's often a small delay while the browser reloads the home page. Adding a `cache control` directive to the web page, even a short-lived one, can make the site feel more responsive (it loads from cache immediately during that cache time) and also can save bandwidth (by using `304` responses even after cache expiry).

It's important to realize that `304` responses still carry a cost, however, so I'm not suggesting that you use them as replacements for caching—but perhaps as replacements for some resources that you haven't cached until now. When I took the screenshots for the preceding figures, I struggled to find a website that cached the web page itself, as Wikipedia does. Some news and social media websites depend on the page to be up-to-date, but there are other, better ways to load content into the page than to serve pregenerated HTML that shouldn't be cached, such as with JavaScript AJAX requests. I argue that websites should cache the pages for a short period, at least when using HTTP/2, because a `304` response costs considerably less than a `200` response.

A lot of advice on HTTP caching suggests using long-lived cache times so that future visits benefit from the cache, but this technique can be less important than using caching for browsing the site within that session so the website feels responsive when users navigate it. Using caching for in-session browsing improvements works equally well with short-lived cache timings, and shorter-lived caches may make complex cache-busting techniques less necessary. Similarly, using caching on the server side to prevent the edge server from querying a backend server can lead to dramatic improvements, even with a short cache time.[23]

One of the other downsides of a short cache time is that the resources may be cleared from the cache because the browser assumes that they're invalid. The best option is a "Cache this for a long time but revalidate it after a shorter time" option, but such an option doesn't exist. Mark Nottingham, who co-chairs the HTTP Working Group,[24] suggested a `Stale-While-Revalidate` option[25] that allows this scenario, but no browser has taken up that suggestion yet.

To conclude, HTTP/2 doesn't change caching options directly, but the reduced cost of network requests may lead to a reevaluation of caching strategies. Also, it has been suggested that HTTP/2 push could be changed to allow caches to be updated (see chapter 5), but this change currently isn't possible.

---

[23] https://www.nginx.com/blog/benefits-of-microcaching-nginx/
[24] https://httpwg.org/
[25] https://www.mnot.net/blog/2014/06/01/chrome_and_stale-while-revalidate

6.3.3   Service workers can further reduce load on the network

Service workers[26] are relatively new features available in all modern browsers except Internet Explorer 11.[27] They provide a way of launching a JavaScript proxy that sits between the web page and the network, as shown in figure 6.12.

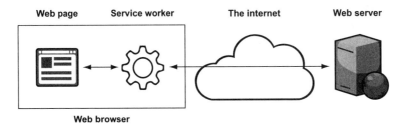

Figure 6.12   Service workers

Service workers can see, answer, or change HTTP requests. They can be used to provide similar experiences to native mobile apps, particularly when offline. Even if the web page itself is cached, a page reload attempts to connect to the website to check whether the cached version is still valid, and the reload will fail if no network connection exists. The same experience usually doesn't happen in a mobile app, which doesn't allow you to refresh offline. When a service worker is used on a website, the service worker can interrupt the requests, and, when offline, return a previously cached version of the resource. This method allows the cached site to load even offline, as mobile apps do.

Service workers create all sorts of interesting opportunities for optimizing the HTTP side of web development. You could use short caching periods but not purge items from the service worker cache even after expiry. This technique would allow you to use 304 responses more often without the danger of long-term caching. As the use of service workers doesn't change under HTTP/2, and as service workers are a topic for a full book in their own right, I don't cover service workers any further. But I expect the use of service workers to increase considerably over the next few years, as service workers provide powerful options to handle HTTP requests.

6.3.4   Don't send what you don't need

Continuing the theme of not making unnecessary HTTP requests, another performance improvement is to make sure you send only the data that's actually needed. Although this point may seem to be obvious, there are lots of reasons why you might send data that isn't actually used.

The techniques mentioned in section 6.2—concatenating files and using image sprites—often result in sending more data than may be strictly necessary to reduce the

---

[26] https://developers.google.com/web/fundamentals/primers/service-workers/
[27] https://caniuse.com/#feat=serviceworkers

number of HTTP requests. As this reduction in requests is less necessary under HTTP/2, you may want to revisit those techniques from a data perspective. You may be comfortable continuing to use them if you've integrated them into a build process for website releases and therefore see no pressing need to remove them, but you should also consider whether you're sending more data than necessary as a result of these techniques.

There are other ways resources that aren't needed could be loaded. You may be including images that are hidden in mobile view but still downloaded, for example. HTTP/2 makes no changes to prevent you from sending resources that won't be used. In fact, it adds a new way to do this (*HTTP/2 push*) that needs extra care, as discussed in chapter 5.

HTTP/2 may make it seem quicker to download resources, but it does nothing to improve the amount of data downloaded (HTTP header compression aside). Sites should continue to ensure that only necessary data is downloaded.

6.3.5   HTTP resource hints

I introduced the preload resource hint in chapter 5. This hint is part of a suite of resource hints[28] that can be used to further optimize HTTP use, and these options are as relevant under HTTP/2 as they were under HTTP/1. Each hint is implemented as a `link` HTTP header or as a `<link>` element in HTML. HTTP resource hints have been around for a while, but recently gained traction and support. They provide additional ways to complement HTTP/2.

DNS-Prefetch

You saw this hint being used by Amazon in chapter 2. This piece of code is included in the HEAD section of the home page:

```
<link rel='dns-prefetch' href='//m.media-amazon.com'>
```

As the name implies, this hint causes the DNS lookup to happen well before the connection is needed, saving this time (see line 17 of figure 6.13).

Figure 6.13   DNS prefetch in use

This hint may save only a small bit of time, but it requires only a small bit of code to implement! Support is strong, with all major browsers supporting it for some time.[29] DNS lookups do have a time to live (TTL), so websites shouldn't look up a domain too early (such as one that is used only for the next navigation), because the lookup may

---

[28] https://w3c.github.io/resource-hints/
[29] https://caniuse.com/#feat=link-rel-dns-prefetch

need to be repeated if the TTL expires. But a 300-second TTL or higher is common, and ideally, your pages don't take more than 5 minutes to load, so it should be safe to use for resources on the current page. This hint is useful only for late-discovered resources, however. There's no point in doing a `dns-prefetch` before referencing the resource, as that reference will do the DNS lookup anyway. This technique is most useful for a connection needed by a dependent resource that isn't apparent from parsing the HTML alone. Most websites load content from any other domains, so there are good gains to be had by using this header.

PRECONNECT

Preconnect takes the concept one step further. Instead of doing only the DNS lookup, it continues to make the connection, which can save the costly TCP and HTTPS setup costs associated with making new connections. Browser support is strong,[30] with most modern browsers supporting it. Don't preconnect too early; the TCP slow-start algorithm will kick in after a period of no use, or, worse, the connection will be dropped (see chapter 9).

Like DNS-prefetch, preconnect is useful when critical resources are needed from other domains.

PREFETCH

Prefetch fetches resources that have a low priority. Unlike *preload* (discussed next), which attempts to make the current page load quicker, prefetch is normally used for future navigations; because it's fetched with such a low priority, it won't be used until the current page finishes loading. The resources that it downloads are stored in the cache, ready for use later. It's supported by most modern browsers[31] except Safari (at this writing). I don't see use of prefetch changing due to HTTP/2.

PRELOAD

Preload tells the browser to load a resource for this page with high priority. It's the next local step from preconnect, but unlike prefetch, it's intended for resources on this page. Web browsers are pretty good at scanning ahead in HTML and loading all the necessary resources, but preload allows resources that aren't directly included on the page (such as fonts referenced in CSS files) to be fetched ahead of time. Support took some time, but preload is now supported by many modern browsers.[32]

Preload gains some relevance for HTTP/2 push (discussed in chapter 5), but more because it was hijacked for that purpose than as an intended use case. Given the complications of HTTP/2 push, the preload resource hint (without HTTP/2 push) may prove to be an easier option. Many people recommend using preload instead of HTTP/2 push at present, in which case be sure to use the `nopush` attribute when using the link header (there is no need to use this with the HTML version, since web servers do not use that as an indication to push that resource).

---

[30] https://caniuse.com/#feat=link-rel-preconnect
[31] https://caniuse.com/#feat=link-rel-prefetch
[32] https://caniuse.com/#feat=link-rel-preload

Preload may become even more useful when the `103 Early Hints` HTTP response code (discussed in chapter 5) becomes more widespread, as it can contain HTTP preload link headers (even under HTTP/1.1).

PRERENDER

Prerender is the most expensive resource hint. It allows full pages to be downloaded and prerendered (including any resources the page needs). The idea is that if the next page navigation can reliably be estimated, that page can be loaded instantly. Support is limited to Chrome and IE 11 at this writing,[33] though Chrome is looking to deprecate it and may not support it much longer.[34] The risks of overusing prerender are considerable, wasting both bandwidth and processing time for the client. I don't see the use of prerender changing due to HTTP/2 and don't expect it to be a priority for other browsers to implement.

6.3.6   *Reduce last-mile latency*

HTTP/2 aims to reduce the impact of latency by ensuring that the single TCP connection can be used for other HTTP requests while a request is in flight. HTTP/2 hasn't solved the latency problem, however, and every effort should still be made to reduce latency. Web servers are usually connected to the rest of the internet with high-speed, high-bandwidth, always-on infrastructure, but users browsing the web often connect over much less reliable connections, including broadband and mobile networks. The last mile refers to this final hop to the end user and is often where latency particularly affects the connection.

The easiest way to solve this problem is to be located as close as possible to the browser, which for global websites usually involves having a network of local servers near your user base. This network can be a privately managed network or (increasingly common) a CDN. Most CDNs support HTTP/2.[35] Given the complications of upgrading your web server to support it and higher HTTPS requirements for it, a CDN in front of your web server is an easy option for moving to HTTP/2 (as mentioned in chapter 3) and also improving latency.

6.3.7   *Optimize HTTPS*

The world is moving to HTTPS. New features such as HTTP/2 require HTTPS for both technical and ideological reasons, as the people who run the key components of the internet (browser vendors, the HTTP Working Group, and so on) believe that the world should be encrypted. Whereas HTTPS was initially used only by certain websites or on certain web pages within those sites, websites are moving toward using HTTPS for *all* pages.

---

[33] https://caniuse.com/#feat=link-rel-prerender
[34] https://groups.google.com/a/chromium.org/forum/#!topic/blink-dev/0nSxuuv9bBw
[35] http://cdncomparison.com/

The growth of HTTPS has taken a considerable step up in the past few years, with the launch of free certificate providers such as Let's Encrypt[36] and push from browser vendors such as Chrome[37] and Mozilla Firefox,[38] as shown in figure 6.14.[39] HTTP/2 only provides more reason to move to it.

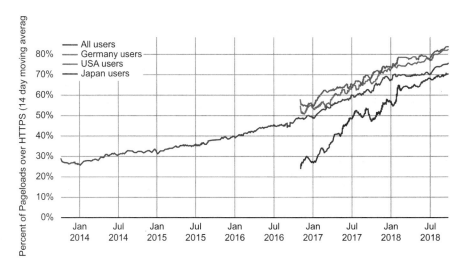

Figure 6.14   HTTPS growth in past few years, as tracked by Let's Encrypt (based on Firefox telemetry statistics)

HTTPS adds extra delays to web page loads to establish the HTTPS session. Thereafter, delays are minimal, as the compute needed to encrypt and decrypt the traffic is negligible even for mobile devices, but the initial connection time is affected. You can use preconnect (discussed in section 6.3.5) to try to connect in advance to reduce the effect for any dependent domains, but this technique doesn't help the initial connection.

It's important to ensure that your HTTPS setup is optimized to reduce the time needed to make this HTTPS connection and provide a strong level of security (for your visitors and to prevent any browser warnings). Optimizing HTTPS setup is important for all sites that use HTTPS (and, hence, all sites that use HTTP/2), because it implies that you're using HTTPS because of the browser requirements. Following are recommendations to ensure optimal HTTPS use (with HTTP/1 or HTTP/2):

---

[36] https://letsencrypt.org/
[37] https://blog.chromium.org/2018/02/a-secure-web-is-here-to-stay.html
[38] https://blog.mozilla.org/security/2017/01/20/communicating-the-dangers-of-non-secure-http/
[39] https://letsencrypt.org/stats/#percent-pageloads

- *Ensure that you load only HTTPS resources to avoid mixed-content warnings.* Consider using `upgrade-insecure-requests`[40] in a content security policy to enforce this practice, because it has strong browser support.[41]

- *Ensure that your HTTPS certificate is renewed on time.* An expired certification prevents access to your site. The renewal process used to be manual, but automatic solutions are becoming more common, driven by Let's Encrypt. Let's Encrypt allows only 90-day certificates, practically mandating automation, because changing short-lived certificates manually is more work than automating the process.

- *Review your HTTPS setup regularly.* HTTPS protocols, ciphers, and configuration change frequently, with new options being added and older options becoming less secure as compute power increases. The online SSLLabs Server Test tool[42] provides a comprehensive test of HTTPS setup, as well as known HTTPS vulnerabilities and best practices. An A grade ensures that you have no issues, and scanning regularly (at least quarterly) to maintain that grade should ensure that you get no surprises.

- *Implement Transport Layer Security (TLS) session resumption.*[43] The TLS handshake takes considerable time and effort, so minimizing it is critical. One of the best ways is to allow TLS *session resumption* so that the full handshake need not be undertaken for each new connection. Under HTTP/2, fewer connections should be used, but there can be performance gains for later or additional connections (such as credentialed and noncredentialed connections). TLS session resumption introduces some security concerns,[44] because the HTTPS connection can be weaker on a subsequent reconnection (though TLSv1.3 solves most of these problems), but most websites still want to enable TLS resumption for the considerable performance gains.

- *Don't go overboard with security.* Security is important, but it's always a balance with performance. If you allow only the latest TLS protocol and ciphers with the strongest settings, you create a slow website that many people can't access. At this writing, a 2048 RSA key, TLSv1.2, and TLS_ECDHE_RSA_WITH_AES_128_GCM_SHA256 cipher are sufficient and well supported. This situation will change as time progresses, but the key is to choose the right level of security. You can also use the Mozilla Configuration Generator[45] to generate the appropriate configuration for common web servers and the SSLLabs tool to scan other sites to see what settings they use and how you compare. I often scan the ssllabs.com site on itself, assuming that SSLLabs knows best how to configure it.

---

[40] https://www.w3.org/TR/upgrade-insecure-requests/
[41] https://caniuse.com/#feat=upgradeinsecurerequests
[42] https://www.ssllabs.com/ssltest/
[43] https://calendar.perfplanet.com/2014/speeding-up-https-with-session-resumption/
[44] https://timtaubert.de/blog/2014/11/the-sad-state-of-server-side-tls-session-resumption-implementations/
[45] https://mozilla.github.io/server-side-tls/ssl-config-generator/

- *Consider whether you're best placed to handle HTTPS setup.* HTTPS is complicated. Outsourcing this function to experts or using cloud providers or a CDN can be easier than managing it yourself and can ensure that your users see strong HTTPS setup at all times. When you literally hand over the keys to your HTTPS setup, however, you need to ensure that you trust the other party; otherwise, you're defeating the point of having security!
- *Enable TLSv1.3 when it becomes available.* This protocol was standardized in August 2018,[46] but may not be available to many readers initially. It contains many performance (and security) improvements over previous versions.[47]

HTTPS is here to stay. Many sites are already on HTTPS, and the previously mentioned points apply to them anyway. HTTP/2 requiring HTTPS gives other sites yet another reason to move to HTTPS. HTTPS takes some managing, however, and it's up to website owners to decide how best to do that. The points mentioned here should be seriously considered by everyone who runs a website nowadays, on HTTP/2 or not.

6.3.8   *Non-HTTP-related web performance techniques*

In this section, I concentrate on tips and techniques related to transporting resources over HTTP. Many other web performance improvements are unrelated to how data is downloaded. Nonperformant JavaScript in particular can easily slow a website to a crawl. Loading lots of advertising networks and trackers can use resources that your website may need. And low-spec servers may struggle to cope with the volume of requests that a website receives. These topics are well beyond the topic of this book, but it's incorrect to think that as long as you optimize your use of HTTP by using some of the tips and techniques here, you'll never have any performance problems.

HTTP-related performance techniques are important, and any web performance resources (books, blogs, or talks) concentrate on them heavily, but they aren't the end-all and be-all of web performance. So make sure that you're not spending too much time optimizing HTTP usage if you can realize bigger gains in looking at other areas of the website or web application.

6.4   *Optimizing for both HTTP/1.1 and HTTP/2*

HTTP/2 should be available to most of your visitors, given the strong browser support for it.[48] Some users, however, don't use HTTP/2 due to using older browsers or older devices on which the browser may not be easy to update (such as mobile phones). Or perhaps proxies (including antivirus software) downgrade connections between browser and server. If you're using any of the HTTP/2-specific techniques in this chapter (such as concatenating less), what happens to those users? The good thing is that your website should still work for them even if you begin optimizing for HTTP/2.

---

[46] https://tools.ietf.org/html/rfc8446
[47] https://blog.cloudflare.com/rfc-8446-aka-tls-1-3/
[48] https://caniuse.com/#feat=http2

At worst, the site may be slower if you remove HTTP/1 optimizations, but it shouldn't break. For the foreseeable future, however, until HTTP/1 use on your website becomes a lot smaller, you may want to optimize for both HTTP/1 and HTTP/2.

6.4.1 Measuring HTTP/2 traffic

The first thing you should do is measure the amount of traffic that uses each protocol. At this point, I assume that you've already upgraded to HTTP/2 but not yet changed your site, so you still have your HTTP/1.1 optimizations. If the vast majority of your traffic is already on HTTP/2, it may make little sense to worry about the HTTP/1 traffic. The website will still work, but it will be a bit slower than ideal.

The easiest way to measure HTTP/2 traffic is to log it in your web server logs. In Apache, you can add this data in the `LogFormat` directive, usually set in the main httpd.conf file (or apache2.conf on some distributions) by adding a `%H` to the Log-Format:

```
LogFormat "%h %l %u %t %{ms}T %H \"%r\" %>s %b \"%{Referer}i\"
"%{User-Agent}i\" %{SSL_PROTOCOL}x %{SSL_CIPHER}x
%{Content-Encoding}o %{H2_PUSHED}e" combined
CustomLog /usr/local/apache2/log/ssl_access_log combined
```

The following appears in the access logs:

```
78.17.12.1234 - - [11/Mar/2018:22:04:47 +0000] 3 HTTP/2.0 "GET / HTTP/2.0"
200 1847 "-" "Mozilla/5.0 (Macintosh; Intel Mac OS X 10_13_3)
    AppleWebKit/537.36 (KHTML, like Gecko) Chrome/64.0.3282.186
    Safari/537.36" TLSv1.2 ECDHE-RSA-AES128-GCM-SHA256 br
```

Here, you see that the protocol (`HTTP/2.0`) is logged before the request (`GET / HTTP/2.0`). As Apache prints the request in HTTP/1-style format in the logs, the protocol can be obtained in the request line (`%r`), but it's probably easier to list it separately in the log file using `%H` so that you can parse it more easily.

nginx allows a similar method of logging the protocol, using the `$server_protocol` environment variable:

```
log_format my_log_format '$remote_addr - $remote_user [$time_local] '
                '$server_protocol "$request" $status $body_bytes_sent '
                '"$http_referer" "$http_user_agent"';
access_log /usr/local/nginx/nginx-access.log my_log_format;
```

Consult your web server documentation if you're using another web server.

Importance of your edge server

If you're using a load balancer in front of several web servers, you may need to measure the protocol measured at the load balancer, depending on what type of load balancer you have.

> **Importance of your edge server** *(continued)*
>
> An HTTP load balancer (also called a Layer 7 load balancer, following the OSI model mentioned in chapter 1) terminates the HTTP connection at the load balancer and sets up another HTTP connection from the load balancer to the actual web server. Therefore, if you're measuring this protocol at the web server, the web server logs show the protocol used for that load balancer–web server connection, but this protocol may not be the same as the main client–load balancer connection, which you're probably more interested in. In this case, you should measure the protocol use at the load balancer rather than at the web server.
>
> A TCP load balancer (also known as a Layer 4 load balancer) works at a TCP level and forwards the payload of the TCP packets (the HTTP messages) to downstream web servers. Therefore, the HTTP messages are the original messages, and the protocol can be measured at the web-server level.
>
> The so-called edge server is the entry point for the user of the protocol you're interested in (HTTP, in this case), so when you're trying to measure your traffic, it's important to know your infrastructure and the appropriate place to measure.

When you're logging the protocols used, you can analyze the logs to see the percentage of traffic using each protocol. If you're on a Linux- or UNIX-based system, you can use a combination of grep, sort, and uniq to do so easily:

```
$ grep -oh 'HTTP\/[0-9]\.[0-9]*' ssl_access_log | sort | uniq -c
    196 HTTP/1.0
   1182 HTTP/1.1
   5977 HTTP/2.0
```

Here, you see that you're still getting a small amount of HTTP/1.0 traffic (which tends to be bots rather than real traffic). Of the rest, 16% is HTTP/1.1, and 81% is HTTP/2.

6.4.2   *Detecting HTTP/2 support on the server side*

Assuming that HTTP/1 visitors are still a sizable proportion of your web traffic, you may want to detect whether the current connection is over HTTP/1.1 or HTTP/2 and deliver a different response for each type. HTTP/1 users could have fully concatenated resources and even load assets from *sharded* domains, whereas HTTP/2 users could get fewer concatenated resources and load everything from the main domain.

Being able to handle the two protocols differently requires knowing what protocol the incoming connection is using. As when measuring protocol use, you need to measure the protocol being used at your edge server (see the above sidebar, "Importance of your edge server"), which depends on that edge server's capabilities. It may be important to send this information downstream.

Most web servers set various environment variables, which can be used to make decisions and change configuration. CGI and PHP scripts can access the SERVER_PROTOCOL environment variable, which should be set to HTTP/1.1 or HTTP/2.0 as appropriate.

Some web servers set additional variables. An Apache server, for example, sets up environment variables[49] that can be used as shown in table 6.7.

Table 6.7   Apache HTTP/2 environment variables

Variable name	Value type	Description
HTTP2	Flag	HTTP/2 is being used.
H2PUSH	Flag	HTTP/2 server push is enabled for this connection and also supported by the client.
H2_PUSH	Flag	This name is an alternative name for H2PUSH.
H2_PUSHED	String	This variable is empty or PUSHED for a request being pushed by the server.
H2_PUSHED_ON	Number	This variable identifies the HTTP/2 stream number that triggered the push of this request.
H2_STREAM_ID	Number	This variable is the HTTP/2 stream number of this request.
H2_STREAM_TAG	String	This variable is the unique stream identifier of the HTTP/2 process, consisting of the connection ID and the stream ID separated by a hyphen.

These environment variables are available to Apache config as well as CGI and PHP scripts. They can also be used in LogFormat directives, so it's worth adding a %{H2_PUSHED}e part to the custom log format, as I did earlier, to track pushed resources in log files.

The nginx web server has a $http2 variable[50] that's set to h2 when HTTP/2.0 is used over HTTPS (as all browser connections will be) or h2c when unencrypted HTTP/2 connections are used. At this writing, nginx doesn't provide any more environment variables, such as whether push is enabled.

Many people also use Apache and nginx as a reverse proxy and proxy requests to a downstream application (such as Node or a Java-based application server such as Tomcat). In Apache, you use the ProxyPass directive:

```
ProxyPass /webapplication/ http://localhost:3000/
```

In this scenario, because these systems are downstream, they won't have access to the Apache environment variables. It's possible, however, to set extra HTTP headers to inform the downstream system using the RequestHeader directive:

```
#Set up a HTTP_VERSION variable as Apache doesn't have a variable for this
#(SERVER_PROTOCOL and Request_Protocol aren't full environment variables)
SetEnvIf Request_Protocol "(.*)" HTTP_VERSION=$1
```

---

[49] https://httpd.apache.org/docs/2.4/mod/mod_http2.html#envvars
[50] http://nginx.org/en/docs/http/ngx_http_v2_module.html#variables

```
#Then use this variable to set a HTTP Header for downstream systems to see
RequestHeader set protocol "%{HTTP_VERSION}e"
#Add some other, pre-defined HTTP2 variables
RequestHeader set http2 %{HTTP2}e
RequestHeader set h2push %{H2PUSH}e
ProxyPass /webapplication/ http://localhost:3000/
```

The downstream application can read these HTTP headers as it would any other
HTTP headers.

Similar syntax for nginx is

```
location /webapplication/ {
    proxy_set_header protocol $server_protocol;
    proxy_set_header http2 $http2;
    proxy_pass http://localhost:3000;
}
```

Using node as an example, you can return to your simple server from chapter 5 and
add two extra lines to log the HTTP/2 support, as shown in the following listing.

Listing 6.1   Node with HTTP header checks

```
'use strict'

var http = require('http')
const port = 3000

const requestHandler = (request, response) => {
  const { headers } = request;
  console.log('HTTP Version: ' + headers['protocol'])
  console.log('HTTP2 Support: ' + headers['http2'])
  console.log('HTTP2 Push Support: ' + headers['h2push'])
  response.setHeader('Link','</assets/css/common.css>;rel=preload')
  response.writeHead(200, {"Content-Type": "text/html"})
  response.write('<!DOCTYPE html>\n')
  response.write('<html>\n')
  response.write('<head>\n')
  response.write('<link rel="stylesheet" type="text/css"
href="/assets/css/common.css">\n')
  response.write('</head>\n')
  response.write('<body>\n')
  response.write('<h1>Test</h1>\n')
  response.write('</body>\n')
  response.write('</html>\n')
  response.end();
}

var server = http.createServer(requestHandler)
server.listen(port)
console.log('Server is listening on ' + port)
```

Visiting /webapplication/ from a browser, through a correctly configured Apache server, prints the following in the node logs:

```
HTTP Version: HTTP/2.0
HTTP2 Support: on
HTTP2 Push Support:on
```

HTTP/1 browsers print:

```
HTTP Version: HTTP/1.1
HTTP2 Support: (null)
HTTP2 Push Support: (null)
```

nginx prints something slightly different:

```
HTTP Version: HTTP/2.0
HTTP2 Support: h2
HTTP2 Push Support: undefined
```

An HTTP/1.1 request via nginx looks like this:

```
HTTP Version:HTTP/1.1
HTTP2 Support:undefined
HTTP2 Push Support:undefined
```

An alternative method is to pass details as query parameters rather than HTTP headers. But I find HTTP headers to be cleaner and easier to add for both GET and POST requests. Regardless, you can see that it's possible to know what protocol is used and have your application react differently depending on the protocol.

6.4.3 *Detecting HTTP/2 support on the client side*

Client-side applications may also want to know whether you're using HTTP/1 or HTTP/2. At present, there's no standard way to get this information, although the Resource Timing Level 2 API includes a nextHopProtocol[51] attribute that provides it.

Measuring what the client thinks is available is tricky, though, because of intermediate proxies. It could be that a web browser is limited to HTTP/1.1, but a proxy connects via HTTP/2 to the server (though in reality, the reverse is likely to be the case, where browsers support HTTP/2 but are held back to HTTP/1.1 due to a proxy). For this reason, I think that it's always better to detect the protocol used on the server side and then send the results back to the client. You could send the results back in several ways, including an HTTP header or a JavaScript variable. The only caveat is to consider how caching of the resource that indicates this information may affect future connections. If you start on an HTTP/2 connection and cache the resource that the client side uses to indicate the connection, and then the client switches to an HTTP/1 connection, you may be optimizing incorrectly.

---

[51] https://www.w3.org/TR/resource-timing-2/#dom-performanceresourcetiming-nexthopprotocol

6.4.4 *Connection coalescing*

The HTTP/2 specification allows the same HTTP/2 connection to be reused for multiple domains if they're *authoritative* for each domain[52]—that is, if the domain resolves to the same IP address and the HTTPS certificate covers both domains. The intention is to maximize the single connection and allow automatic unsharding of domains that are hosted on the same server (also known as *connection coalescing*).

Suppose that your site at www.example.com uses the images.example.com domain to host images. If both of these domains are hosted on the same server and are simply separate virtual hosts on that server, under HTTP/2, they can be served by the same connection if you set the appropriate `:authority` *pseudo-header*. This scenario may happen if you created these *sharded* domains purely due to HTTP/1 inefficiencies and don't use a separate server for them, as shown in figure 6.15.

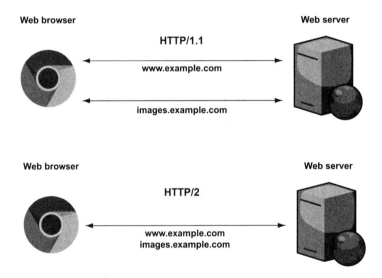

Figure 6.15   Connection coalescing under HTTP/2

At a higher level (such as in a browser's developer tools), the HTTP requests look exactly the same as they would sharded; only at connection level can the client decide to coalesce. Websites can continue to have sharded domains that HTTP/1.1 connections will use automatically, and HTTP/2 connections will coalesce automatically, acting as though they're unsharded domains and everything is served from the one connection. This situation sounds ideal, requiring no extra effort to continue to support the HTTP/1 user, or to optimize for HTTP/2 users. The reality, as always, is a little trickier.

---

[52] https://httpwg.org/specs/rfc7540.html#reuse

For a start, this process works only if you're hosting these domains on the same server. If the servers are separate, they need to have separate connections. The other caveat is that the browser needs to have implemented connection reuse, and not all browsers have done so.[53] The specification says that a connection *can* be reused, not that it *has* to be. Safari and Edge don't coalesce at this writing, whereas Chrome and Firefox do.

Also, this feature can result in problems, depending on how the browser implements it. With multiple IP address for domains (some of which may be shared with other domains), a browser may think that it can reuse (or coalesce) a connection when it can't. Suppose that you have the IP addresses shown in table 6.8.

Table 6.8   Connection coalescing example

Domain	IP addresses
`www.example.com`	1.2.3.4 1.2.3.5
`images.example.com`	1.2.3.4 1.2.3.6

In this case, any connection on IP address 1.2.3.4 can serve both www.example.com and images.example.com requests under HTTP/2 if the client wants to do so, but the connection on the other IP addresses (1.2.3.5 and 1.2.3.6) can't. Firefox has implemented aggressive connection coalescing and will attempt to use any connection for both domains, no matter which of the three IP addresses is used for that actual connection, if it knows about this overlap. This situation results in errors, as the BBC noticed when it migrated to HTTP/2 initially.[54]

The new HTTP status code `421` has been created to allow the server to politely tell the browser that it used the wrong connection and to take another look at where it should be sending these requests. Support of this status code is still limited, however, as the BBC discovered. As an alternative solution, the `ORIGIN` frame[55] allows a server to inform the client which domains it's *authoritative* for rather than have the client guess. The frame is new at this writing, but a few servers already support it,[56, 57] and others have open requests to track it.[58, 59] On the browser side, Firefox[60] already supports the frame, and other browsers are expected to follow now that the frame has

---

[53] https://daniel.haxx.se/blog/2016/08/18/http2-connection-coalescing/

[54] https://medium.com/bbc-design-engineering/http-2-is-easy-just-turn-it-on-34baad2d1fb1

[55] https://tools.ietf.org/html/rfc8336

[56] https://github.com/nghttp2/nghttp2/pull/901

[57] https://github.com/h2o/h2o/pull/1199

[58] https://github.com/icing/mod_h2/issues/96

[59] https://trac.nginx.org/nginx/ticket/1530

[60] https://bugzilla.mozilla.org/show_bug.cgi?id=1337791

been approved as a proposed standard.[61] This frame will likely be sent at the beginning of the connection (ideally, as the HTTP/2 SETTINGS frame has been sent), which should also prevent bad requests from being sent. On a related note, Secondary Certificate Authentication in HTTP/2[62] is another proposal that would allow connection coalescing even when different certificates are used but the IP address is the same.

In short, connection coalescing is complicated, so I advise against depending on it. Instead, look at whether *sharding* is required and whether it's giving you performance benefits. If sharding is something that you want to keep, it may be better to host it on separate servers to prevent coalescing complications.

6.4.5   *How long to optimize for HTTP/1.1 users*

The final consideration in optimizing for both sets of users is how long to continue to do it. Optimizing takes extra effort, so consider whether you want to perform that extra work, and, if so, for how long. Alternatives are available, including not undoing HTTP/1.1 workarounds for the moment, as they should be no worse under HTTP/2 but are no longer as necessary. Alternatively, if a large proportion of your visitors is already on HTTP/2, it may be better to optimize for the majority at the expense of the minority, and let those on HTTP/1.1 connections suffer slower loads than strictly necessary. Each website owner should make this decision based on his or her base and the expected effects of any changes. Because browser support of HTTP/2 is strong, users who can't use HTTP/2 fall into a few categories:

- Those who have older versions of software (and are likely to be missing features anyway, depending how diligent you are about supporting older versions)
- Those behind corporate proxies (likely on faster connections)
- Those behind antivirus proxies (likely to be desktop users, mostly on broadband)
- Those using obscure browsers (which may have other issues with rendering your site)
- Bots and crawlers (which you may have less interest in keeping happy)

Ultimately, it's worth looking at which of your visitors are still on HTTP/1 and then deciding whether the effort of optimizing for both protocols is worthwhile. For large sites, the answer probably is yes, but for smaller operations, the work may not be worthwhile. The fact that the site will still work (albeit more slowly) if you no longer optimize for HTTP/1 makes this option worth considering. In a similar way, graceful degradation is used in website design to deliver a working but unoptimized site for browsers that don't support the features required for the optimal experience.

---

[61] https://tools.ietf.org/html/rfc8336
[62] https://tools.ietf.org/html/draft-ietf-httpbis-http2-secondary-certs

Summary

- HTTP/2 was designed to address HTTP/1.1 performance inefficiencies.
- The hope was that HTTP/1.1 performance optimizations, which require effort and have drawbacks, would no longer be required. This hope has been only partially realized. Although you should have less need to use these techniques, it may be premature to remove them.
- Other web performance techniques remain mostly relevant under HTTP/2, but it may be worthwhile revisiting them for your site when moving to HTTP/2.
- It's possible to optimize for both HTTP/1.1 connections and HTTP/2.
- Connection coalescing allows a browser to unshard domains automatically, but the process is complicated.

Part 3

Advanced HTTP/2

The first part of this book introduced HTTP/2. The second part looked at the details of HTTP/2 and how it should be used. Chapter 4 introduced the basics of HTTP/2 and how it works; chapter 5 was devoted to HTTP/2 push, which is a new concept to HTTP; and chapter 6 looked at how HTTP/2 should and shouldn't change development practices.

In this part, I delve a little deeper, covering some advanced topics that few people truly understand. Chapter 7 finishes the parts of the specification that weren't covered previously, and chapter 8 looks at the separate HPACK HTTP header compression specification. These two chapters will help you transform your solid foundation to expert-level understanding of the HTTP/2 protocol. You'll be able to tackle any HTTP/2 problem and perhaps even help contribute to the evolving protocol going forward!

Advanced HTTP/2 concepts

This chapter covers the remaining parts of the HTTP/2 protocol, roughly in the order in which they appear in the specification.[1] Many of these parts aren't under the direct control of web developers and may even be out of the control of server administrators (unless they're writing an HTTP/2 server themselves), so these topics are definitely more advanced. Knowledge of them, however, will give you deep understanding of how the protocol works and help with debugging, if you're looking to implement your own HTTP/2 server. Additionally, in the future, more control may be made available to developers or at least web server administrators. Chapter 8 looks at the HPACK protocol, which is a separate specification from HTTP/2.

---

[1] https://httpwg.org/specs/rfc7540.html

7.1   *Stream states*

An HTTP/2 stream is created for a single download and then discarded. This is one reason why HTTP/2 streams aren't exact analogs for HTTP/1.1 connections, even though this is probably the easiest way of explaining them when first teaching HTTP/2. Many diagrams draw parallels between HTTP/2 streams and HTTP/1 connections (like the ones I used in chapter 2 and repeat in figure 7.1), but this convention isn't strictly true, because streams aren't reused.

After a stream finishes delivering its resource, the stream is closed. When a new resource is requested, a new stream is started. Streams are a virtual concept and are

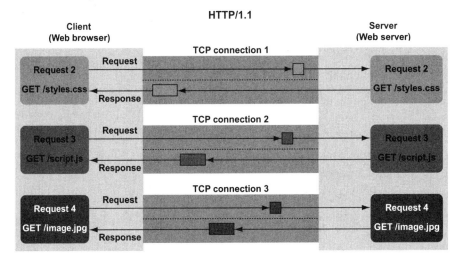

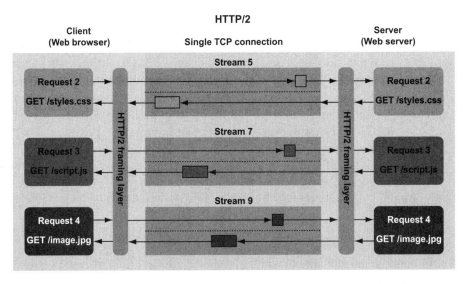

Figure 7.1   HTTP/1.1 connections and HTTP/2 streams can be represented as similar even though they're different.

nothing more than a number each frame is tagged with, known as the *stream identifier*. The cost of closing a stream or opening a new one, therefore, is considerably lower than the cost of opening an HTTP/1.1 connection (which involves a TCP three-way handshake and an optional HTTPS protocol negotiation before a request is sent). In fact, HTTP/2 connections are even more costly than HTTP/1 connections, as they additionally require the HTTP/2 "magic" preface message and at least one SETTINGS frame to be sent before a single request can be made. HTTP/2 streams are much cheaper.

HTTP/2 streams go through a lifecycle of states. A HEADERS frame sent from a client starts an HTTP request (such as a GET request), the request is answered by the server, and then the stream is closed. This process goes through the following states:

- *Idle*—When the stream is created or referenced. In reality, most streams don't remain in this state long, as it's rare to reference a stream unless you intend to use it, so most idle streams are used immediately and then immediately enter the next phase: open.

- *Open*—When the stream has been used to send the request HEADERS frame, the stream is considered to be open and is available for two-way communication. The stream stays in the state while the client is still sending data. Because most HTTP/2 requests can be sent in a single HEADERS frame, a stream is likely to enter the next phase (half-closed) when that frame has been sent.

- *Half-closed*—When the client has indicated, with the END_STREAM flag, that the request HEADERS frame contains everything it wants out of this request, the stream is considered to be half-closed and should be used only for sending the response back to the client; it shouldn't be used to send any more data from the client (except for control frames such as WINDOW_UPDATE).

- *Closed*—When the server has finished sending and used the END_STREAM flag on the last frame, the stream is considered to be closed and shouldn't be used anymore.

Although this list explains the state transitions for a simple client-initiated HTTP request, the same can happen in a server-initiated request. At present, only *HTTP/2 push* responses are server-initiated (though there's nothing to say that some new frame in the future won't be server-initiated). In this case, a stream starts another stream (the promised stream identifier), and that new promised stream goes through a similar transition of states:

- *Idle*—When the promised stream is first created or referenced by the PUSH_PROMISE frame sent on another stream.

- *Reserved*—When the pushed stream immediately enters the reserved state until the server is ready to push the resource. You know that the stream exists (so it's at least idle); you know that it'll be used for a specific resource (so it's more than idle, hence the reserved state); but you don't know the full details of what that resource is, as in the first example after the HEADERS frame has been received. Because it's for a pushed resource, however, the stream should never be in the open state, as you never expect the client to send data on this stream. It should be reserved and then go into a half-closed state when the HEADERS frame is sent (after the PUSH_PROMISE frame is sent on the original stream). This state, not coincidentally, is the next state.

- *Half-closed*—When the server starts pushing the response, the promised stream enters the half-closed state and should be used only to send the data for that pushed resource.
- *Closed*—When the server has finished sending and used the END_STREAM flag on the last DATA frame, the stream is considered to be *closed* and shouldn't be used anymore.

The full HTTP/2 state diagram is shown in figure 7.2, including the two flows indicated in the preceding list and several other possibilities (such as when the RST_STREAM frame is used to end a connection prematurely).

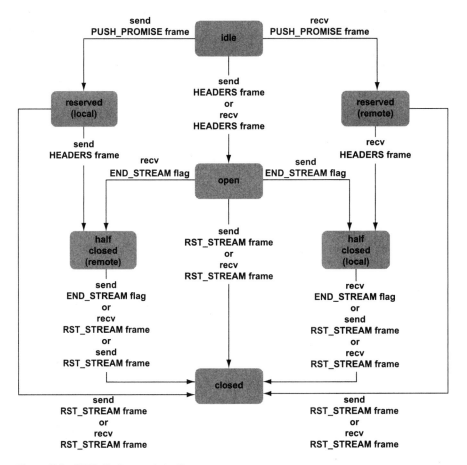

Figure 7.2   HTTP/2 stream state diagram

In each of these flows, the client and server have a slightly different view of the stream status, depending on whether it initiated that state or moved to that state based on a message from the other side. Therefore, some of these states have a local or remote indicator (depending on whether you're the initiator of the stream or the recipient, respectively), and there are send and recv transitions from each state.

Going back to the first example of a GET request, you know that it goes through the following states: idle, open, half-closed, and closed. The half-closed state is ambiguous, however: it's closed to the client (so it can't send data and can only receive data), but it's not half-closed to the server. The client sees the stream as half-closed (local), and the server sees it as half-closed (remote). A request, therefore, doesn't flow down the state diagram in the same way for the client and the server; it flows down either the left or the right of the diagram at the same time, depending on whether you're looking at the client or server view.

Also, the state diagram shows only state transitions. Some frames don't result in a state transition. CONTINUATION frames, for example, are considered to be extensions of the preceding HEADERS frames, so they're considered to be part of HEADERS in the diagram. Similarly, other frames (such as PRIORITY, SETTINGS, PING, and WINDOW_UPDATE) never result in a state transition, so aren't captured in this diagram.

To be perfectly honest, the HTTP/2 state diagram isn't important for most users of HTTP/2 and is more a concern for implementors of low-level HTTP/2 libraries to understand what frames can and can't be sent at each state. The diagram is in the HTTP/2 specification,[2] however, and the various states are referenced a lot in this spec, so understanding it helps. Any attempts at state transitions that aren't allowed by HTTP/2 should result in PROTOCOL_ERROR messages. Again, understanding the state diagram can help you understand why you get such an error (though this error usually is due to a bug in the underlying HTTP/2 implementation and beyond what most web developers can fix themselves).

The HTTP/2 state diagram can be intimidating at first, and unlike some of the concepts I've covered so far, it isn't something you can see in a browser's developer tools or even by using some of the other tools in this book (such as nghttp and Wireshark). It's more an internal status that HTTP/2 implementations need to maintain and track. Given that fact, it can be complicated to understand. Going back to the main use case (requesting an HTTP resource), however, as described before the diagram, usually takes some of the mystery out.

7.2 Flow control

Flow control is an important part of networking protocols. It allows a receiver to stop a sender from sending it data if it isn't yet ready to process, perhaps because it's too busy to process any more incoming data. Flow control is necessary because different clients can consume data at different speeds. A high-speed server may be able to send data

---

[2] https://httpwg.org/specs/rfc7540.html#StreamStates

quickly, but if a lower-speed client (such as a mobile phone) isn't able to keep up, it starts to buffer data in memory, and when that buffer is filled, it starts to drop packets, requiring them to be sent again. As a result, resources are wasted on the server side, the network, and the client side.

Flow control wasn't required in HTTP/1.1 because there was only one message in flight at any time. Therefore, *TCP flow control* could be used at a connection level. If the receiver stops consuming TCP packets, it no longer acknowledges those packets, and the sender stops sending them because its TCP congestion window (CWND) would be used up (see chapter 2).

In HTTP/2, you have a *multiplexed* connection of independent streams, so connection-level flow control is no longer sufficient. Control needs to be at a connection level and at a stream level. It may be that you're happy to receive more data on one stream but not the other. Chapter 4 provides an example of a website with a video that the user has paused. In this case, you may not want the video to continue downloading while it's paused, but you want to allow other streams on the HTTP/2 connection to continue to be used.

Flow control is handled in HTTP/2 in a similar manner to TCP. At the beginning of the connection (using the SETTINGS frame), the flow control window size is decided (or the default 65,535 octets is used, if the size isn't specified). Then each piece of data sent is subtracted from that total, and each bit of data acknowledged (via the WINDOW_UPDATE frame) is added back. There's a connection-level flow control window, which kind of mirrors the TCP flow control window, and one per stream as well. Senders can send only up to the maximum size of the smallest flow control window (connection-level or for that stream), and when the flow control window reaches zero, the sender must stop sending data until it receives acknowledgments, resulting in a nonzero flow control window. If you implement an HTTP/2 client or server and forget to implement WINDOW_UPDATE frames, you'll soon notice that the other side stops talking to you!

Flow control is used for DATA frames (though future HTTP/2 frame types may also fall under flow control). Control frames (and in particular the WINDOW_UPDATE frames needed to control flow control) can still be sent when a client has stopped acknowledging frames.

7.2.1 Example of flow control

For an example of flow control, I'll go back to using the nghttp tool. In this section, we initiate a request to Facebook for the home page and all the required resources and then pipe this into grep to show only the important parts:

```
$ nghttp -anv https://www.facebook.com | grep -E "frame
<|SETTINGS|window_size_increment"
[  0.110] recv SETTINGS frame <length=30, flags=0x00, stream_id=0>
        [SETTINGS_HEADER_TABLE_SIZE(0x01):4096]
        [SETTINGS_MAX_FRAME_SIZE(0x05):16384]
        [SETTINGS_MAX_HEADER_LIST_SIZE(0x06):131072]
```

```
       [SETTINGS_MAX_CONCURRENT_STREAMS(0x03):100]
       [SETTINGS_INITIAL_WINDOW_SIZE(0x04):65536]
[ 0.110] recv WINDOW_UPDATE frame <length=4, flags=0x00, stream_id=0>
       (window_size_increment=10420225)
[ 0.110] send SETTINGS frame <length=12, flags=0x00, stream_id=0>
       [SETTINGS_MAX_CONCURRENT_STREAMS(0x03):100]
       [SETTINGS_INITIAL_WINDOW_SIZE(0x04):65535]
```

Here, you see that the Facebook server has decided to use a flow control window size of 65,536 octets (the SETTINGS_INITAL_WINDOW_SIZE value in the recv SETTINGS frame), and nghttp is using 65,535 octets (the SETTINGS_INITAL_WINDOW_SIZE value in the sender's SETTINGS frame). Incidentally, 65,535 is also the default size, so nghttp didn't need to send it at all. The code also shows that the two sides can have different flow control window sizes (even though they're near enough the same here, differing by only 1 octet).

In the middle of those two SETTINGS frames, you see your first WINDOW_UPDATE frame (highlighted in the code):

```
[ 0.110] recv WINDOW_UPDATE frame <length=4, flags=0x00, stream_id=0>
       (window_size_increment=10420225)
```

This frame states that Facebook is prepared to receive up to 10,420,225 octets, and as the frame was sent on stream 0, this limit is the connection-level limit to be used across all streams, in addition to their stream-level limit. Stream 0 should never be used for DATA frames and doesn't need its own flow control, which is why it can be used for connection-level flow control. These 10,420,225 allowed octets are on top of the 65,535 octets for the initial window size, so Facebook could also have set the initial size to the sum of both (10,485,761), but it's also permissible to implement this way.

Next, nghttp acknowledges the server's settings, followed by a few more frames in which nghttp sets up for prioritizing (incidentally, one of the few instances in which a frame can be created in *idle* state and stay there until used):

```
[ 0.110] send SETTINGS frame <length=0, flags=0x01, stream_id=0>
[ 0.110] send PRIORITY frame <length=5, flags=0x00, stream_id=3>
[ 0.110] send PRIORITY frame <length=5, flags=0x00, stream_id=5>
[ 0.110] send PRIORITY frame <length=5, flags=0x00, stream_id=7>
[ 0.110] send PRIORITY frame <length=5, flags=0x00, stream_id=9>
[ 0.110] send PRIORITY frame <length=5, flags=0x00, stream_id=11>
```

I discuss the PRIORITY frames next, so ignore them for now.

Next, you see that the first request is sent by means of a HEADERS frame on stream 13:

```
[ 0.110] send HEADERS frame <length=43, flags=0x25, stream_id=13>
```

Recall that client-initiated streams must have odd-numbered stream identifiers. Stream 13 is the next free one because 11 was used by the last PRIORITY frame.

Then the server acknowledges the SETTINGS frame, and another WINDOW_UPDATE frame increasing the window size of stream 13 to 10,420,224 octets (oddly, 1 octet smaller than the connection-level size, but nothing says the sizes have to be the same):

```
[  0.134]  recv SETTINGS frame <length=0, flags=0x01, stream_id=0>
[  0.134]  recv WINDOW_UPDATE frame <length=4, flags=0x00, stream_id=13>
           (window_size_increment=10420224)
```

Next, nghttp starts to receive the resource's HEADERS and DATA frames:

```
[  0.348]  recv HEADERS frame <length=293, flags=0x04, stream_id=13>
[  0.349]  recv DATA frame <length=1353, flags=0x00, stream_id=13>
[  0.350]  recv DATA frame <length=2571, flags=0x00, stream_id=13>
[  0.351]  recv DATA frame <length=8144, flags=0x00, stream_id=13>
[  0.374]  recv DATA frame <length=5563, flags=0x00, stream_id=13>
[  0.375]  recv DATA frame <length=2572, flags=0x00, stream_id=13>
[  0.376]  recv DATA frame <length=1491, flags=0x00, stream_id=13>
[  0.377]  recv DATA frame <length=2581, flags=0x00, stream_id=13>
[  0.378]  recv DATA frame <length=4072, flags=0x00, stream_id=13>
[  0.379]  recv DATA frame <length=5572, flags=0x00, stream_id=13>
```

After it has received a few DATA frames, nghttp decides to let the server know that it has consumed that much data. Adding up the DATA frames only (1353 + 2571 + 8144 + 5563 + 2572 + 1491+ 2581 + 4072 + 5572) gives 33,919, so that's what nghttp tells the server that it has consumed at connection level (stream 0) and on stream 13:

```
[  0.379]  send WINDOW_UPDATE frame <length=4, flags=0x00, stream_id=0>
           (window_size_increment=33919)
[  0.379]  send WINDOW_UPDATE frame <length=4, flags=0x00, stream_id=13>
           (window_size_increment=33919)
```

It's important to note that only the length of the DATA frame payload (as given by the length field) is included in the flow control calculation and that the nine-octet frame header is excluded from the flow control.

The connection continues in a similar manner until all the resources are delivered, and the connection is closed by the client sending the ever-so-polite GOAWAY frame:

```
[  0.381]  recv DATA frame <length=2563, flags=0x00, stream_id=13>
[  0.382]  recv DATA frame <length=1491, flags=0x00, stream_id=13>
[  0.384]  recv DATA frame <length=2581, flags=0x00, stream_id=13>
[  0.398]  recv DATA frame <length=4072, flags=0x00, stream_id=13>
[  0.400]  recv DATA frame <length=2332, flags=0x00, stream_id=13>
[  0.402]  recv DATA frame <length=1491, flags=0x00, stream_id=13>
[  0.403]  recv DATA frame <length=1500, flags=0x00, stream_id=13>
[  0.405]  recv DATA frame <length=1500, flags=0x00, stream_id=13>
[  0.406]  recv DATA frame <length=3644, flags=0x00, stream_id=13>
[  0.416]  send HEADERS frame <length=250, flags=0x25, stream_id=15>
[  0.417]  recv DATA frame <length=9635, flags=0x00, stream_id=13>
[  0.417]  recv DATA frame <length=807, flags=0x00, stream_id=13>
[  0.419]  send WINDOW_UPDATE frame <length=4, flags=0x00, stream_id=0>
           (window_size_increment=33107)
```

```
[ 0.419] send WINDOW_UPDATE frame <length=4, flags=0x00, stream_id=13>
         (window_size_increment=33107)
[ 0.420] recv DATA frame <length=16384, flags=0x00, stream_id=13>
[ 0.420] recv DATA frame <length=369, flags=0x00, stream_id=13>
[ 0.424] recv DATA frame <length=16209, flags=0x01, stream_id=13>
[ 0.444] recv WINDOW_UPDATE frame <length=4, flags=0x00, stream_id=15>
         (window_size_increment=10420224)
[ 0.546] recv (stream_id=15) x-frame-options: DENY
[ 0.546] recv HEADERS frame <length=255, flags=0x04, stream_id=15>
[ 0.546] recv DATA frame <length=1293, flags=0x00, stream_id=15>
[ 0.546] recv DATA frame <length=2618, flags=0x00, stream_id=15>
[ 0.547] recv DATA frame <length=3135, flags=0x00, stream_id=15>
[ 0.547] send WINDOW_UPDATE frame <length=4, flags=0x00, stream_id=0>
         (window_size_increment=34255)
[ 0.547] recv DATA frame <length=10, flags=0x01, stream_id=15>
[ 0.547] send GOAWAY frame <length=8, flags=0x00, stream_id=0>
```

Not seeing WINDOW_UPDATE frames?

If you're using an example other than Facebook (perhaps your own site), you may be surprised not to see any WINDOW_UPDATE frames. Maybe the site you're using is too small and can download in its entirety before a single WINDOW_UPDATE frame is sent.

Even in the Facebook example, nghttp sent a WINDOW_UPDATE frame after only 9 frames and 33,919 octets—well before the 65,535 limit that we previously stated that we could handle. If nghttp hadn't sent this WINDOW_UPDATE frame at this point, the server would have happily continued to send data for a bit longer.

Exactly when the WINDOW_UPDATE frame is sent (after each DATA frame is consumed? when you're close to the limit? periodically?) is up to the client. nghttp decides to send them when it has consumed more than half of the flow control window[a] (32,768 octets in this example). This is why it sent it after the 5572 DATA frame above, as before that frame, the total was 28,347 octets (below this limit), and after the frame, the total was 33,919 octets (above this limit).

If we use Twitter as an example, the response sent back to nghttp is smaller than 32 KB (at least for a non-logged-in request), so nghttpd doesn't need to use any WINDOW_UPDATE frames, which wouldn't have made for an interesting example. Readers can experiment on their own sites with nghttp by using the -w and -W flags to use different initial window sizes.[b]

---

[a] Search for the nghttp2_should_send_window_update function in https://github.com/nghttp2/nghttp2/blob/master/lib/nghttp2_helper.c

[b] https://nghttp2.org/documentation/nghttp.1.html#cmdoption-nghttp-w

7.2.2 Setting flow control on the server

Apache allows you to set the flow control window size with the H2WindowSize directive:[3]

```
H2WindowSize 65535
```

Other servers may also allow this directive to be set. NodeJS, for example, allows this directive to be set with the initialWindowSize setting,[4] and the Jetty servlet engine allows it to be set with the jetty.http2.initialStreamRecvWindow setting.[5] Many other servers (such as nginx and IIS) don't give you any control of this directive at the time of this writing. The reality, though, is that you're unlikely to need to change the directive from the default setting unless you want detailed control of your server.

7.3 Stream priorities

Next we look at *stream priorities*. HTTP/2 introduces the concept of prioritization to allow the client to suggest the relative importance of a request. After a browser downloads a page, it requests the resources needed to view this page. Critical, render-blocking resources (think CSS and any blocking JavaScript) are high-priority, and any images or async JavaScript can be requested with a much lower priority. Priorities can be used by the server to decide the order in which it should send frames; more-important frames can be sent first, so they arrive earlier and aren't held up due to any flow control or bandwidth issues.

> **Stream priority: hints or instructions?**
>
> Stream priorities are sent by the requester (such as the client), but it's the sender (such as the server) that ultimately decides what frames to send. Priorities, therefore, are suggestions or hints, and it's entirely within the sender's remit to ignore the priorities and send the data in the order that the sender thinks is most appropriate. The specification makes this fact clear, saying that "expressing priority is . . . only a suggestion."[a]
>
> Are browsers or servers best to decide the priority? Browsers have traditionally taken this role because they had a limited number of HTTP/1.1 connections and had to decide how to use them best, but HTTP/2 flips this situation on its head and says that the server is in charge. That situation may make sense if the website administrator tunes the web server to the specific site that he or she knows best, but without this advanced tuning (which most website owners are unlikely to want to undertake), a web browser is likely to have a much better understanding of priorities than a web server.
>
> I suspect that most web servers use the prioritization hints provided by the clients to decide priority, so ultimately, the clients (such as web browsers) are likely to keep

---

[3] https://httpd.apache.org/docs/2.4/mod/mod_http2.html#h2windowsize
[4] https://nodejs.org/api/http2.html#http2_settings_object
[5] https://github.com/eclipse/jetty.project/blob/master/jetty-documentation/src/main/asciidoc/administration/http2/configuring-http2.adoc

dictating the priority. There may be opportunities to override these settings on the server side (see section 7.3.4), but mostly, I expect the client prioritization requests to be followed.

Some web servers may decide not to bother using prioritization at all, as it can be quite complicated to implement, but I suspect that those that do implement it will see a performance improvement compared with those that don't, so pick your web server (and web browser) wisely!

---

a   https://httpwg.org/specs/rfc7540.html#StreamPriority

HTTP/2 defines two different methods for setting the priority:

- Stream dependency
- Stream weighting

These priorities can be set with requests in a HEADERS frame or can be reprioritized at any time through a separate PRIORITY frame.

7.3.1   Stream dependencies

A stream can be made dependent on another stream, so it should be used to send resources only when the dependent stream doesn't need to use the connection to send anything. Figure 7.3 shows one such example.

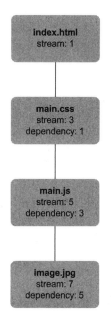

Everything is dependent by default on stream 0 (not shown in figure 7.3), which is the control stream and represents no dependency. In this example, main.css is the first dependency on index.html and should be sent with the highest priority, followed by main.js and finally image.jpg. Usually, index.html is fetched first, followed by the dependencies, so there may be no need to put a dependency on the HTML document file as shown here. But a large index.html may still be downloading as the other requests are made, so it isn't necessarily wrong to make all the requests dependent on it.

This dependency hierarchy doesn't mean that dependent streams block on their parents. If main.css isn't immediately available to the web server and has to be fetched from a backend server, for example, the server can send main.js in the meantime, assuming that it's available. If neither file is available, image.jpg can be sent while the server waits for those files. The aim of stream prioritization is to make the most efficient use of the connection rather than act as a blocking mechanism.

Figure 7.3   Example of an HTTP/2 stream dependency

The server may start to send image.jpg while it fetches main.css and main.js, and when those files are available to send, the server may pause sending image.jpg and send main.css, followed by main.js, before unpausing image.jpg and sending the remainder of that file. Alternatively, the server could have a simpler model and finish sending image.jpg when it has started while the others queue as they become ready. The choice is up to the server.

Streams can also have multiple dependents, as shown in figure 7.4, because each stream can specify the stream it's dependent on.

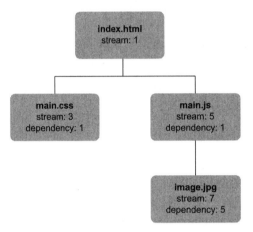

Figure 7.4   Multiple streams can be dependent on the same parent stream.

In this example, both main.css and main.js are dependent on stream 1, and the image is dependent on main.js stream. If the image file is lower-priority than both these critical resources, ideally it would be dependent on both the CSS and JS streams, as shown in figure 7.5, but the concept of multiple dependencies isn't supported.

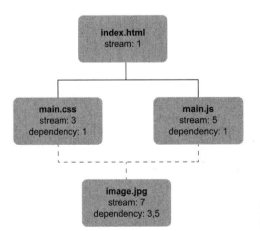

Figure 7.5   Multiple parent dependencies aren't supported in HTTP/2.

If multiple dependencies were supported, the file would be downloaded only when both main.css and main.js don't need the connection, but multiple dependencies aren't supported by the HTTP/2 dependency model (though they can be approximated with the use of weightings).

Stream priorities can be complicated to manage as resources available for the server to send become available. It can be further complicated by adding new requests or finishing in-flight requests. Often, the server must reevaluate dependencies multiple times during the life of a request for optimum performance. Apache discovered early in its HTTP/2 implementation that not doing this reprioritization led to inefficiencies.[6]

Streams can also be added as exclusive dependencies. A stream should get exclusive access to its dependency, and any existing dependencies should be made dependent on this new exclusive stream. Figure 7.6 shows adding critical.css to the mix and making it dependent on stream 0 without (left) and with (right) the exclusive flag set.

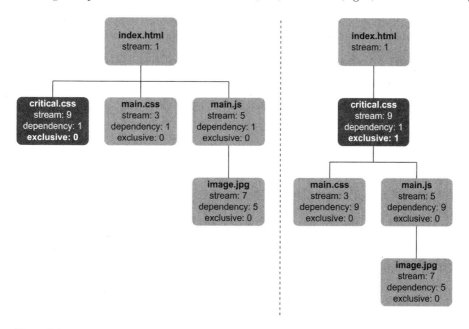

Figure 7.6   Adding a new critical.css dependency with and without the exclusive flag set

As you see, without the exclusive flag, critical.css is at the same dependency level as main.css and main.js, but when the exclusive flag is set to 1, it takes priority and moves everything to be dependent on it, which may well be what's needed in this example, based on the name (critical.css).

---

[6] http://icing.github.io/mod_h2/nimble.html

7.3.2   *Stream weighting*

The other concept that helps define stream priorities is weighting, which is used to prioritize two requests that are dependent on the same parent resource. Stream weightings allow more complicated scenarios than assuming even weighting for resources at the same dependency level. The critical.css scenario, for example, could have been implemented in an (almost) similar manner with the use of weightings, as shown in figure 7.7.

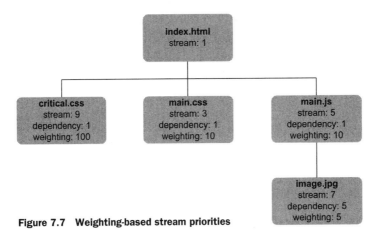

Figure 7.7   Weighting-based stream priorities

Here, critical.css (weighting 100) should get 10 times the resource allocations of main.css (weighting 10) and main.js (weighting 10). Using weightings isn't the same as making them dependent, as with the exclusive flag, but it's close. When critical.css is delivered, main.css and main.js get 50% of the resources, as they're evenly weighted.

The 5 weighting for image.jpg isn't used in the scenario. If main.js finishes sending before main.css (or if main.js can't be sent yet), image.jpg gets 50% of the resources, as it gets main.js's share. Therefore, to prevent that situation and give the CSS and JS files much higher weightings than images, a better dependency graph might be the flatter one shown in figure 7.8.

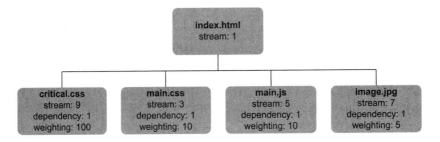

Figure 7.8   Weighting-based dependencies

To make prioritization easier, some clients set up dummy streams with the appropriate priorities in advance, using the PRIORITY frame, and hang requests off them. The concept of allowing dummy PRIORITY frames was added late in the ratification of HTTP/2[7], but provides a lot of flexibility and allows for a lightweight priority model. It allows dependency trees, for example, as shown in figure 7.9.

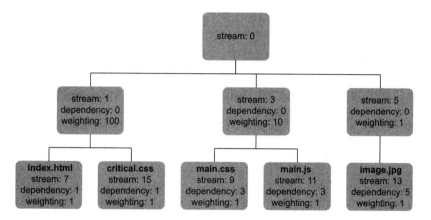

Figure 7.9 Using dummy streams to hang requests from to set dependencies appropriately

These dummy streams are used only for prioritization and never to send requests directly. You see this situation when nghttp sets up streams 3, 5, 7, 9, and 11 at the beginning of a connection for priority reasons:

```
$ nghttp -nva https://www.facebook.com:443
[  0.041] Connected
The negotiated protocol: h2
[  0.093] recv SETTINGS frame <length=30, flags=0x00, stream_id=0>
         (niv=5)
         [SETTINGS_HEADER_TABLE_SIZE(0x01):4096]
         [SETTINGS_MAX_FRAME_SIZE(0x05):16384]
         [SETTINGS_MAX_HEADER_LIST_SIZE(0x06):131072]
         [SETTINGS_MAX_CONCURRENT_STREAMS(0x03):100]
         [SETTINGS_INITIAL_WINDOW_SIZE(0x04):65536]
[  0.093] recv WINDOW_UPDATE frame <length=4, flags=0x00, stream_id=0>
         (window_size_increment=10420225)
[  0.093] send SETTINGS frame <length=12, flags=0x00, stream_id=0>
         (niv=2)
         [SETTINGS_MAX_CONCURRENT_STREAMS(0x03):100]
         [SETTINGS_INITIAL_WINDOW_SIZE(0x04):65535]
[  0.093] send SETTINGS frame <length=0, flags=0x01, stream_id=0>
         ; ACK
         (niv=0)
[  0.093] send PRIORITY frame <length=5, flags=0x00, stream_id=3>
         (dep_stream_id=0, weight=201, exclusive=0)
```

[7] https://lists.w3.org/Archives/Public/ietf-http-wg/2014OctDec/0467.html

```
[  0.093] send PRIORITY frame <length=5, flags=0x00, stream_id=5>
          (dep_stream_id=0, weight=101, exclusive=0)
[  0.093] send PRIORITY frame <length=5, flags=0x00, stream_id=7>
          (dep_stream_id=0, weight=1, exclusive=0)
[  0.093] send PRIORITY frame <length=5, flags=0x00, stream_id=9>
          (dep_stream_id=7, weight=1, exclusive=0)
[  0.093] send PRIORITY frame <length=5, flags=0x00, stream_id=11>
          (dep_stream_id=3, weight=1, exclusive=0)
```

This code leads to the dependency tree shown in figure 7.10, which has a high-priority stream 3 (with a dependent stream 11), a low-priority stream 7 (with a dependent stream 9), and a middling priority stream 5.

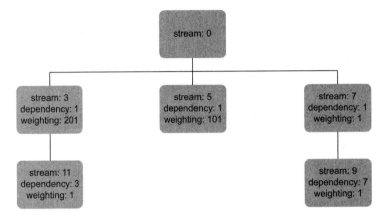

Figure 7.10   nghttp stream priorities

Any requests are made dependent on one of these streams:

```
[  0.093] send HEADERS frame <length=43, flags=0x25, stream_id=13>
          ; END_STREAM | END_HEADERS | PRIORITY
          (padlen=0, dep_stream_id=11, weight=16, exclusive=0)
          ; Open new stream
          :method: GET
          :path: /
          :scheme: https
          :authority: www.facebook.com
          accept: */*
          accept-encoding: gzip, deflate
          user-agent: nghttp2/1.31.0
```

This setup is based on the original Firefox dependency tree. Critical CSS and Java-Script are made dependent on stream 3, noncritical JavaScript is made dependent on stream 5, and everything else is made dependent on stream 11. Note that streams 7 and 9 aren't used at this writing.[8] By always being able to hang resources from the same streams, you can create a reasonably efficient dependency model easily.

---

[8]   https://nghttp2.org/documentation/nghttp.1.html#dependency-based-priority

7.3.3   *Why does prioritization need to be so complicated?*

Why do you need stream dependencies *and* weighting? This question was debated a fair bit when HTTP/2 was standardized, and SPDY, on which HTTP/2 is based, initially had only weight-based prioritization. The truth is that prioritization *is* complicated, and allowing both dependencies and weightings, or a mixture of the two, allows the greatest flexibility for prioritization. The added capability to create streams purely for prioritization purposes leads to more implementation options.

There's no requirement to support stream prioritization, however, and many implementations on both the client and server side choose not to, as I discuss in the next section. As I stated in section 6.2.4, the ability to handle HTTP/2 stream prioritization efficiently could become another key differentiator between browser and server implementations, though the technicalities may be lost on most web users and developers.

Real world usage of HTTP/2 prioritization since HTTP/2 was standardized, and the fact that no implementation has yet found a perfect prioritization scheme, as we will discuss next, have led to more calls to simplify this.[9] Whether this leads to any changes in HTTP/2 or is considered for future versions (HTTP/3) remains to be seen.

7.3.4   *Prioritization in web servers and browsers*

HTTP/2 prioritization is a potentially powerful option that allows the single HTTP/2 connection to be used efficiently. This option has the advantage over six separate HTTP/1.1 connections when there's no concept of relative prioritization other than not using one of the connections. Prioritization is complicated, however, and support is limited at this time. Although many implementations on both the server and client sides support prioritization, few give the website owner much control.

SETTING PRIORITIES FOR WEB SERVERS

Server support for prioritization is a mixed bag at this writing. Some servers support it with configuration options, some support it without configuration options, and some don't support it. Table 7.1 summarizes prioritization support in popular HTTP/2 web servers.

Table 7.1   Priority support in popular HTTP/2 web servers

Server (and version)	HTTP/2 prioritization support
Apache HTTPD (v2.4.35)	Prioritization is supported, but only the Push priority can be explicitly configured.[a]
IIS (v10.0)	Prioritization isn't supported.[b]
nginx (v1.14)	Prioritization is supported,[c] but no configuration options are available.[d]

---

[9]   https://lists.w3.org/Archives/Public/ietf-http-wg/2019JanMar/0073.html

Table 7.1   Priority support in popular HTTP/2 web servers *(continued)*

Server (and version)	HTTP/2 prioritization support
Node (v10)	Prioritization is supported and can be set explicitly.[e]
nghttpd (1.34)	Prioritization is fully supported.[f]

[a]   https://httpd.apache.org/docs/2.4/mod/mod_http2.html#h2pushpriority
[b]   https://forums.iis.net/t/1233780.aspx
[c]   https://www.nginx.com/blog/http2-module-nginx/#prioritization
[d]   http://nginx.org/en/docs/http/ngx_http_v2_module.html
[e]   https://nodejs.org/api/http2.html#http2_http2stream_priority_options
[f]   https://nghttp2.org/blog/2014/04/27/how-dependency-based-prioritization-works/

Most of the other web servers make little reference to HTTP/2 prioritization, suggesting that it's perhaps not supported and certainly isn't configurable if it is. Among servers that do support it, the prevailing thought seems to be to allow the client to specify the priority in requests rather than to allow server-side prioritization configuration.

Shimmercat is a fairly new web server that takes an interesting approach, allowing image requests to be sent with an initial high prioritization and then dialed back to lower priority. This approach allows the first few bytes to be sent, which allows the browser to know the size of the image and other metadata needed to lay out the page as early as possible and dial down the priority for the remainder of the image file.

Perhaps more web servers will allow this type of innovation or more control. But for now, most servers use the client-suggested priorities or don't support them.

SETTING PRIORITIES FOR WEB BROWSERS

Web browser support is also a bit hit-and-miss. Finding documentation on this topic is tricky, but it's possible to see stream prioritization and infer what it's doing. To do so, you can set up Wireshark as discussed in chapter 4, but this technique allows you to intercept only browsers that export the HTTPS key settings (such as Chrome, Opera, and Firefox on the desktop). A better way is to run the nghttpd server in verbose mode and look at the incoming messages. You can also pipe the output into `grep` to filter only the important messages. Windows users without a Linux terminal can do the equivalent with `findstr` or `select-string` if they're using PowerShell:

```
nghttpd -v 443 server.key server.crt | grep -E "PRIORITY|path|weight"
```

Then create a dummy index.html file in the same folder, with a load of references to various media types, to get a flavor of how each media type is sent by each browser:

```
<html>
<head>
<title>This is a test</title>
<link rel="stylesheet" type="text/css" media="all" href="head_styles.css">
<script src="head_script.js"></script>
</head>
<body>
```

```
<h1>This is a test</h1>
<img src="image.jpg" />
<script src="body_script.js" /></script>
</body>
</html>
```

It isn't important for the referenced stylesheets, JavaScript, or image files to exist for this simple test. The test is slightly easier if these items don't exist, in fact, as you see only 404 HEADERS frame responses rather than HEADERS frame and DATA frame responses, which only add noise.

Next, you connect to the server (such as https://localhost) and look at the frames sent. Firefox (v62) sends the frames similarly to the nghttp client, which is unsurprising, because nghttp is based on the Firefox implementation:

```
[id=1] [  3.010] recv PRIORITY frame <length=5, flags=0x00, stream_id=3>
            (dep_stream_id=0, weight=201, exclusive=0)
[id=1] [  3.010] recv PRIORITY frame <length=5, flags=0x00, stream_id=5>
            (dep_stream_id=0, weight=101, exclusive=0)
[id=1] [  3.010] recv PRIORITY frame <length=5, flags=0x00, stream_id=7>
            (dep_stream_id=0, weight=1, exclusive=0)
[id=1] [  3.010] recv PRIORITY frame <length=5, flags=0x00, stream_id=9>
            (dep_stream_id=7, weight=1, exclusive=0)
[id=1] [  3.010] recv PRIORITY frame <length=5, flags=0x00, stream_id=11>
            (dep_stream_id=3, weight=1, exclusive=0)
[id=1] [  3.010] recv PRIORITY frame <length=5, flags=0x00, stream_id=13>
            (dep_stream_id=0, weight=241, exclusive=0)
[id=1] [  3.010] recv (stream_id=15) :path: /
            ; END_STREAM | END_HEADERS | PRIORITY
            (padlen=0, dep_stream_id=13, weight=42, exclusive=0)
[id=1] [  3.033] recv (stream_id=17) :path: /head_styles.css
            ; END_STREAM | END_HEADERS | PRIORITY
            (padlen=0, dep_stream_id=3, weight=22, exclusive=0)
[id=1] [  3.034] recv (stream_id=19) :path: /head_script.js
            ; END_STREAM | END_HEADERS | PRIORITY
            (padlen=0, dep_stream_id=3, weight=22, exclusive=0)
[id=1] [  3.035] recv (stream_id=21) :path: /image.jpg
            ; END_STREAM | END_HEADERS | PRIORITY
            (padlen=0, dep_stream_id=11, weight=12, exclusive=0)
[id=1] [  3.035] recv (stream_id=23) :path: /body_script.js
            ; END_STREAM | END_HEADERS | PRIORITY
            (padlen=0, dep_stream_id=5, weight=22, exclusive=0)
```

The output shows that Firefox has added an extra stream 13 with a weight of 241 (a super-urgent stream?) used for the original request, making it higher-priority than any CSS request.

Chrome (v69) uses no up-front PRIORITY frames, like nghttp or Firefox, but it sets a priority on requests when they're sent and adds dependencies on previous streams. It also likes exclusive dependencies, creating a tall dependency graph:

```
[id=3] [112.082] recv (stream_id=1) :path: /
            ; END_STREAM | END_HEADERS | PRIORITY
            (padlen=0, dep_stream_id=0, weight=256, exclusive=1)
```

```
[id=3]  [112.101] recv (stream_id=3) :path: /head_styles.css
             ; END_STREAM | END_HEADERS | PRIORITY
             (padlen=0, dep_stream_id=0, weight=256, exclusive=1)
[id=3]  [112.101] recv (stream_id=5) :path: /head_script.js
             ; END_STREAM | END_HEADERS | PRIORITY
             (padlen=0, dep_stream_id=3, weight=220, exclusive=1)
[id=3]  [112.101] recv (stream_id=7) :path: /image.jpg
             ; END_STREAM | END_HEADERS | PRIORITY
             (padlen=0, dep_stream_id=5, weight=147, exclusive=1)
[id=3]  [112.107] recv (stream_id=9) :path: /body_script.js
             ; END_STREAM | END_HEADERS | PRIORITY
             (padlen=0, dep_stream_id=0, weight=183, exclusive=1)
```

The benefit of such use of the exclusive bit is still in debate.[10] The Chromium team's main argument seems to be that most requests are unusable until the full resource is received (HTML and progressive JPEGs being the primary exceptions), so it often doesn't make sense to dilute the connection by sending multiple resources at the same time.

Opera (v59) does the same thing as Chrome (being another Chromium-based browser), but Safari (v12.0) seems to do weighting based on prioritization and doesn't use stream dependencies (the opposite of Chrome!):

```
[id=9]  [213.347] recv (stream_id=1) :path: /
             ; END_STREAM | END_HEADERS | PRIORITY
             (padlen=0, dep_stream_id=0, weight=255, exclusive=0)
[id=9]  [213.705] recv (stream_id=3) :path: /head_styles.css
             ; END_STREAM | END_HEADERS | PRIORITY
             (padlen=0, dep_stream_id=0, weight=24, exclusive=0)
[id=9]  [213.705] recv (stream_id=5) :path: /head_script.js
             ; END_STREAM | END_HEADERS | PRIORITY
             (padlen=0, dep_stream_id=0, weight=24, exclusive=0)
[id=9]  [213.706] recv (stream_id=7) :path: /image.jpg
             ; END_STREAM | END_HEADERS | PRIORITY
             (padlen=0, dep_stream_id=0, weight=8, exclusive=0)
[id=9]  [213.706] recv (stream_id=9) :path: /body_script.js
             ; END_STREAM | END_HEADERS | PRIORITY
             (padlen=0, dep_stream_id=0, weight=24, exclusive=0)
```

Edge (v41) has the poorest implementation, choosing not to use stream priorities at this writing, so every resource gets the default priority weighting of 16:

```
[id=4]  [ 64.393] recv (stream_id=1) :path: /
[id=4]  [ 64.616] recv (stream_id=3) :path: /head_styles.css
[id=4]  [ 64.641] recv (stream_id=5) :path: /head_script.js
[id=4]  [ 64.642] recv (stream_id=7) :path: /image.jpg
[id=4]  [ 64.642] recv (stream_id=9) :path: /body_script.js
```

As you can see, a large variance exists among the browsers, which leads to different performance at the same site. Some researchers have performed much more extensive

---

[10] https://bugs.chromium.org/p/chromium/issues/detail?id=651538

testing of the differences among browsers.[11] There are likely to be more research studies and improvements in this area to come. HTTP/2 provides the tools for specific prioritization, but I've yet to find the best ways to use them.

7.4 HTTP/2 conformance testing

Now that you understand all the finer details of HTTP/2, you can compare the various implementations on both the client and server sides.

7.4.1 Server conformance testing

H2spec[12] is an HTTP/2 conformance tester that sends various messages to an HTTP/2 server and checks whether it follows the specification accurately. Download the version for your computer type,[13] and point it at an HTTP/2 server:

```
h2spec -t -S -h localhost -p 443
```

> **NOTE** if you're using an untrusted certificate (such as a self-signed certificate for localhost), you may need to pass in the -k option to ignore certificate errors:
>
> ```
> h2spec -t -S -h -k localhost -p 443
> ```

This code should run several tests against your server and show you whether each test passes or fails:

```
$ ./h2spec -t -S -h localhost -p 443
Generic tests for HTTP/2 server
  1. Starting HTTP/2
    ✓ 1: Sends a client connection preface

  2. Streams and Multiplexing
    ✓ 1: Sends a PRIORITY frame on idle stream
    ✓ 2: Sends a WINDOW_UPDATE frame on half-closed (remote) stream
    ✓ 3: Sends a PRIORITY frame on half-closed (remote) stream
    ✓ 4: Sends a RST_STREAM frame on half-closed (remote) stream
    ✓ 5: Sends a PRIORITY frame on closed stream

  3. Frame Definitions
    3.1. DATA
      ✓ 1: Sends a DATA frame
      ✓ 2: Sends multiple DATA frames
      ✓ 3: Sends a DATA frame with padding

    3.2. HEADERS
      ✓ 1: Sends a HEADERS frame
      ✓ 2: Sends a HEADERS frame with padding
      ✓ 3: Sends a HEADERS frame with priority
  ...etc
```

---

[11] https://speakerdeck.com/summerwind/2-prioritization and https://www.researchgate.net/publication/324514529_HTTP2_Prioritization_and_its_Impact_on_Web_Performance
[12] https://github.com/summerwind/h2spec
[13] https://github.com/summerwind/h2spec/releases

I've run the tool against some popular web servers, and the results are shown in table 7.2.

Table 7.2   HTTP/2 specification conformance for popular web servers

Server (and version)	Tests passed
Apache (v2.4.33)	146/146 (100%)
nghttpd (v1.13.0)	145/146 (99%)
Apache Traffic Server (v7.1.3)	140/146 (96%)
CaddyServer (v0.10.14)	137/146 (94%)
HAProxy (v1.8.8)	136/146 (93%)
IIS (v10)	119/146 (82%)
AWS ELB	115/146 (79%)
nginx (v1.13.9)	112/146 (77%)

I made similar tests on the home pages of some of common content delivery networks, under the assumption that the home pages run on the CDN infrastructure, which admittedly may not be a valid assumption. Table 7.3 shows the results.

Table 7.3   HTTP/2 specification conformance for popular CDNs

CDN (and site tested)	Tests passed
Fastly (www.fastly.com)	137/146 (94%)
Google (www.google.com)	135/146 (92%)
Cloudflare (www.cloudflare.com)	113/146 (77%)
MaxCDN (www.maxcdn.com)	113/146 (77%); note that test 6.3.2 hung
Akamai (www.akamai.com)	107/146 (73%)

Kudos to Apache for achieving the only perfect score. But does it matter that some implementations don't match the specification as they should? Arguably not, because they often fail when trying to process incorrect messages that shouldn't be sent in the first place. Many popular servers/CDNs handle HTTP/2 traffic successfully and without problems despite not getting 100% conformance.

If you look at nginx's results as one example, you see the following as one of the tests the server is failing:

```
4.2. Frame Size
   ✓ 1: Sends a DATA frame with 2^14 octets in length
   ✗ 2: Sends a large size DATA frame that exceeds the
SETTINGS_MAX_FRAME_SIZE
      -> The endpoint MUST send an error code of FRAME_SIZE_ERROR.
```

```
Expected: GOAWAY Frame (Error Code: FRAME_SIZE_ERROR)
          RST_STREAM Frame (Error Code: FRAME_SIZE_ERROR)
          Connection closed
  Actual: WINDOW_UPDATE Frame (length:4, flags:0x00, stream_id:1)
```

nginx doesn't handle a large DATA frame as it should, but at the same time, no client should be sending such a frame. Moving on to the next errors, you see some state errors:

```
5. Streams and Multiplexing
  5.1. Stream States
   ✗ 1: idle: Sends a DATA frame
      -> The endpoint MUST treat this as a connection error of type
   PROTOCOL_ERROR.
          Expected: GOAWAY Frame (Error Code: PROTOCOL_ERROR)
                    Connection closed
            Actual: Timeout
   ✗ 2: idle: Sends a RST_STREAM frame
      -> The endpoint MUST treat this as a connection error of type
   PROTOCOL_ERROR.
          Expected: GOAWAY Frame (Error Code: PROTOCOL_ERROR)
                    Connection closed
```

Again, nginx isn't correctly handling frames sent incorrectly when the stream is in an idle state, but again, these frames shouldn't be sent by the client. Most of the other errors follow suit.

If you're writing an HTTP/2 server, the h2 spec tool is useful for checking whether your server is implementing the specification correctly, but the reality is that many major web servers get away with less-than-perfect implementations. The web has always been a forgiving place on the technology side, and (unlike many programming languages) slight errors are often overlooked. Still, these errors can lead to more unexpected errors later, so it's interesting to know how your server behaves. When I published the preceding statistics on Twitter,[14] several server implementations took note and sought to improve their compliance.

7.4.2   *Client conformance testing*

A client equivalent of the tool (such as for testing browsers) does exist,[15] though built versions aren't supplied, so this tool must be compiled from source. I leave this task to the reader as an exercise.

Summary

- HTTP/2 has several advanced concepts that are rarely discussed, because many people concentrate on the higher-level concepts.
- Most of the low-level details in this chapter aren't under the control of server administrators or website developers.

---

[14] https://twitter.com/tunetheweb/status/988196156697169920

[15] https://github.com/summerwind/h2spec/pull/74

- HTTP/2 has stream states and a state diagram that shows valid transitions between states.
- HTTP/2 allows fine-grained flow control at stream level rather than leaving it to TCP to manage at connection level (as HTTP/1.1 does).
- HTTP/2 introduces stream priorities, which allow a client to suggest the priority for the server to use in returning the requests.
- The HTTP/2 stream priority system is based on dependencies and weights, either of which (or both) can be used.
- Different browsers and servers use stream prioritization differently.
- Many HTTP/2 implementations don't conform precisely to the specification.

HPACK header
compression

This chapter covers

- Background on data compression
- Why HTTP/2 needed its own compression technique for HTTP headers
- The HPACK compression format
- Decompressing HPACK encoded headers
- HPACK in client and server implementations

The next topic is header compression. HTTP/1 has always allowed HTTP bodies to be compressed, but only since HTTP/2 has it been possible to compress the HTTP headers too.

8.1 Why is header compression needed?

It's true that, in general, HTTP headers are relatively small in comparison with HTTP bodies, but they're still chatty and repetitive. A typical HTTP/2 GET request from Chrome looks like this:

```
:authority: www.example.com
:method: GET
:path: /url
```

```
:scheme: https
accept: text/html,application/xhtml+xml,application/xml;q=0.9,
        image/webp,image/apng,*/*;q=0.8
accept-encoding: gzip, deflate, br
accept-language: en-GB,en-US;q=0.9,en;q=0.8
upgrade-insecure-requests: 1
user-agent: Mozilla/5.0 (Macintosh; Intel Mac OS X 10_13_4) AppleWebKit/537
.36 (KHTML, like Gecko) Chrome/66.0.3359.139 Safari/537.36
```

Only the parts that are highlighted in bold are liable to change for the next request
sent to this server: the method of the request (GET) and the path (/url). Of the 403
characters in this code, only 7 won't be repeated next time. In fact, even the method
is probably set to GET for the large majority of web page requests, though web services might use the other methods. Therefore, only the :path or URL is liable to
change, so 399 characters of every Chrome request are duplicated each time—a
huge amount of waste.

The problem is exacerbated because some of these headers are long, such as the
accept and user-agent headers shown in the preceding code, and cookie headers
can get even longer. Following is the request header to Twitter (with the cookie values
obfuscated):

```
:authority: twitter.com
:method: GET
:path: /
:scheme: https
accept: text/html,application/xhtml+xml,application/xml;q=0.9,
image/webp,image/apng,*/*;q=0.8
accept-encoding: gzip, deflate, br
accept-language: en-GB,en-US;q=0.9,en;q=0.8
cookie: _ga=GA1.2.123432087.1234567890; eu_cn=1; dnt=1; kdt=rmnAfbecvko4123
4oRYSzztq7n12345abcdABCD12; remember_checked_on=1; personalization_id="v1_k
0123451/EKaVeysDnuhKg=="; guest_id=v1%3A152383314680123456; ads_prefs="HBES
AAA="; twid="u=3374717733"; auth_token=12791876dfc0e57eae12345897b7940f55ac
7dfd; tfw_exp=1; csrf_same_site_set=1; csrf_same_site=1; lang=en; _twitter_
sess=BAh7CSIKZ12345678zonQWN0aW9uQ29udHJvbGxcjo6Rmxhc2g60kZsYXNo%250ASGFza
HsABjoKQHVzZWR7ADoPY3JlYXRlZF9hdGwrCPdpPx12345HaWQiJWY4%250AZGUwOGM3ZjRiYzJ
mYjRiAbCdEfGwNjIyZTk1Ogxjc3JmX21kIiVkYjg3%2501234kZTVkMDdlMTAxMGI2YTgyZDFhN
TA0MmZiNQ%253D%253D--fd52ba1537f8fb9bf35dbd6080a6cd413edc6cd2; ct0=713653a0
6266b507960945523226bcc4; _gid=GA1.2.1893258168.1525002762; external_refere
r=1234567890w%3D|0|S381234567896Dak8Eqj76tqsc12345Lq4vYdCl5zxIvK6Q123vRkA%3
D%3D; app_shell_visited=1
referer: https://twitter.com/
upgrade-insecure-requests: 1
user-agent: Mozilla/5.0 (Macintosh; Intel Mac OS X 10_13_4) AppleWebKit/537
.36 (KHTML, like Gecko) Chrome/66.0.3359.139 Safari/537.36
```

This code is now 1,278 characters, and again, it's likely that only the :path pseudoheader will change with the next request, so 1,277 characters are pretty much wasted
for each request. Responses are no better. Figure 8.1 shows the response for Twitter.

**Large
content-security-policy
HTTP Header**

Figure 8.1   Twitter response header

This response is a frankly ridiculous 5,804 characters, made up mostly of a detailed (and large) `content-security-policy` header, a security feature that allows the website to tell the browser what type of content it's allowed to load on this site.[1]

Computer scientists abhor repetition, and all this repetition is one of the reasons why HTTP header compression was a key part of HTTP/2 and why it was built into its predecessor (SPDY) from the beginning. Compressing and decompressing data takes time and processing power, but relatively small amounts of that time compared with the time required to send network requests, so compressing data before sending it on a network is almost always worthwhile. Also, HTTPS requires encryption, which is more computationally expensive than compression. It's better to compress first and then encrypt the smaller amount of data.

8.2   *How compression works*

To understand the rest of this section on HTTP compression, you need a little background on data compression. This topic is fairly high-level, and I deliberately avoid the complex mathematics, but this section should give you enough detail to understand how and why HTTP/2 implements header compression the way it does.

Some compression is *lossy compression*; some of the detail can be discarded because it's not needed. This type of compression is typically used for media: music files, images, and videos can be compressed heavily without losing the overall meaning of the data. If you compress too much, you lose detail, so that an image can no longer be zoomed in, for example. Lossy compression is a careful balance between reducing size and maintaining quality.

HTTP headers are important data, even if they're repeated a lot, so lossy compression isn't an option, even though it usually delivers better compression. *Lossless compression* works by removing repetitive data that's easily added back later when the data needs to be uncompressed. You have three ways to do this:

---

[1] https://developer.mozilla.org/en-US/docs/Web/HTTP/CSP

- Lookup tables
- More-efficient encoding techniques
- Lookback compression

I describe each of these methods in the following sections.

8.2.1 Lookup tables

The first method involves taking long, repeated bits of data and replacing them with references. Uncompressing involves replacing the references with the original text from the lookup table. This process can be dynamic but works particularly well for data that's structured the same way. Look at a simple GET request:

```
:authority: www.example.com
:method: GET
:path: /url
:scheme: https
```

This request is 64 characters. If you had a lookup table like this

```
$1=:authority:
$2=:method:
$3=:path:
$4=:scheme:
```

you could encode this text like this:

```
$1 www.example.com
$2 GET
$3 /url
$4 https
```

This request is 39 characters—a 40% improvement! The lookup table, however, may need to be included in the compressed version, depending on whether it's a standard lookup table known by the format or a dynamic one generated by the specific text. If the table is included, the overall size may be the same size or larger than the original text, which would defeat the point. Lookup tables benefit you only if the values are repeated often.

In this simple example, the lookups are commonly used HTTP header names, so a preagreed static lookup table could be used for them and would not need to be sent each time. This table could be supplemented by a dynamic lookup table for extra values to use on top of that preagreed list. The domain www.example.com, for example, is likely to be reused in subsequent requests, so it could be added to a dynamic list for subsequent referencing.

8.2.2 More-efficient encoding techniques

Several techniques fall into this category, but they all recognize the fact that the data being compressed could be represented in a smaller size if a more specific way is used to represent the data.

Pixel-based images, for example, can be based on a 1-bit pixel range (black and white). If you have a picture that has only red and yellow, you could use an 8-bit color palette and use only two of those colors. Alternatively, you could use a 1-bit palette, but state at the beginning that 0 is yellow and 1 is red. Similarly, for text you can use ASCII (7 bits), UTF-8 (8 bits for the ASCII characters, 16 bits for commonly used Western characters, 24 bits for most other common characters, and up to 32 bits for other characters), or UTF-16 (16 bits for most characters and up to 32 bits for other characters). If you're writing in English, UTF-8 makes the most sense, but if you're writing in non-Western languages, UTF-16 may make more sense, as UTF-8 often uses 24 bits for these languages, compared with the 16 bits in UTF-16. Picking the appropriate format can result in more efficient encoding.

For even more savings, look at variable-length encoding. Most encoding techniques involve fixed-size encoding. ASCII, for example, uses 7-bit characters, as shown in table 8.1.

Table 8.1   A subset of the ASCII codes

Binary	Character
01000001	A
01000010	B
01000011	C
01000100	D
01000101	E
01000110	F
01000111	G
And so on	

This arrangement is nice and simple but not too efficient, because each letter takes up the same space regardless of how often it's used. In English, E is the most common letter, followed by T and A, down to the least common letters (X, J, Q, and Z, respectively). Why should you treat them all as equal, given that they won't be used equally?

Rather than using 7 bits for all ASCII characters, it would be more efficient for English text to use variable-length characters. This technique would use binary values sized less than 7 bits for commonly used characters and binary values sized larger than 7 bits for less frequently used letters. Unicode (UTF-8 and UTF-16) uses this method to some extent via distinct blocks of characters (1–4 octets), depending on how commonly used the characters are. The main complication is recognizing the boundaries between characters (because they're not all 7 bits long anymore in this format).

Huffman coding takes variable-length encoding to a more extreme level. It works by assigning a unique code to each value based on the frequency with which it's used, and it ensures that no code is the prefix of another code. How the unique codes are calculated is beyond the scope of this book, but it might lead to a table like table 8.2 (based on the Huffman codes based on the English-language letter-frequency distribution).

Table 8.2 A subset of the ASCII codes with Huffman coding

Binary	Huffman coding	Character
01000001	1111	A
01000010	101000	B
01000011	01010	C
01000100	11011	D
01000101	100	E
01000110	01011	F
01000111	00001	G

In Huffman encoding, no code is fully represented as the start of another code. The code 0101 isn't used to represent a letter, as that code could be confused as being that letter, the beginning of C, or the beginning of F. By choosing the coding strings carefully, it's possible to reliably decode the data. As long as you start at the beginning of the text, you can decode it by reading along until you match a letter; then you start the next letter and continue until the whole text is unencoded.

Using these codes as examples, if you wanted to encode the word *face*, you could use regular ASCII (4 x 7 bits = 28 bits) or Huffman coding (5 + 4 + 5 + 3 = 17 bits). Huffman encoding is smaller even in this simple example. With a longer piece of text, the gains would be considerable.

Huffman code compression is an extension of the lookup tables. Like the more regular lookup tables discussed earlier in this chapter, Huffman tables can be defined in advance based on the known structure to which the data is likely to be similar (such as English-language text); they can be generated dynamically based on the data being encrypted; or they can be a combination of both.

8.2.3 *Lookback compression*

Lookback compression involves referencing repeated text in terms of the current placing. This type of compression is demonstrated particularly well in HTML text:

```
<html>
<body>
<h1>This is a title</h1>
<p>This is some text</p>
</body>
</html>
```

This text could be compressed as follows:

```
<html>
<body>
<h1>This is a title</(-20,3)
<p>(-24,6)some text</(-19,2)
</(-58,4)
</(-73,4)
```

Each repeated bit of text is replaced by a reference stating how far back the decompressor can find the repeated text and how much of it to take. The reference (-20,3) says to go back 20 characters and take the next three characters, which is what should replace this reference. As you can see, this process works well for HTML text, in which closing tags repeat opening tags (although as there are few tags in this example, a lookup table might be better for HTML). You can also use this type of compression for HTTP headers, such as the accept header:

```
accept: text/html,application/xhtml+xml,application/xml;q=0.9,
        image/webp,image/apng,*/*;q=0.8
```

As you can see, html is repeated twice in this header—as are application, xml, and image—so it could be encoded with lookback functions. A computer doesn't care about looking back for whole words only; I'm only doing this to make the explanation clearer. ml is used in html and xml, for example, so maybe it's better to use it.

8.3 *HTTP body compression*

HTTP body compression generally is used for text data. Media is typically precompressed depending on the particular format and is often excluded from compression. JPEG, for example, is a specific compression format for images that shouldn't then be further compressed by the web server; the image won't compress more (and may even end up being larger) and therefore wastes processing. Text works well for all of the preceding compression techniques. The techniques used by web servers and browsers (deflate, gzip, and brotli) are fairly similar; they're variants on the Deflate-based algorithm and use a combination of techniques to achieve good compression rates. When making a request, the browser informs the server what compression algorithms it supports by using the accept-encoding HTTP header:

```
accept-encoding: gzip, deflate, br
```

The server picks one of these algorithms and compresses the header, and in the response, it informs the browser which algorithm it used to compress the resource:

```
content-encoding: gzip
```

This technology allows new compression algorithms to be introduced (such as brotli), and these algorithms will be used only when both client and server support them.

Deflate-based compression has one major flaw: it has proved to be insecure. The problem is that you can use the length to guess the contents, particularly if you can influence some of those contents. Although HTTP bodies can contain some sensitive data (such as if your name or account number is displayed on the page), most security concerns are about HTTP headers, as they contain cookies and other tokens used to supply authentication. Suppose that you have the following request:

```
:authority: www.example.com
:method: GET
:path: /secretpage
:scheme: https
cookie: token=secret
```

If you could get hold of that token value (`secret`), you'd be able to impersonate this user. You can't do that, of course, because the message is encrypted—and ideally, the cookie is marked as `HttpOnly`,[2] so it can't be seen by any JavaScript, even if you could inject it into the page.

If you could get access to the page, however, you could send out the following requests with slightly different URLs and measure the length of the message sent:

```
https://www.example.com/secretpage?testtoken=a
https://www.example.com/secretpage?testtoken=b
https://www.example.com/secretpage?testtoken=c
…etc.
```

Because Deflate-based compression techniques work by recognizing and replacing repeat patterns, you may notice eventually that one test (`testtoken=s`) is shorter than the other tests because it repeats the first part of the real cookie (`token=secret`). Now you know the first letter of the token! You can repeat this process until you get the full token:

```
https://www.example.com/secretpage?testtoken=sa
https://www.example.com/secretpage?testtoken=sb
https://www.example.com/secretpage?testtoken=sc
https://www.example.com/secretpage?testtoken=sd
https://www.example.com/secretpage?testtoken=se - this is shorter!
https://www.example.com/secretpage?testtoken=sea
https://www.example.com/secretpage?testtoken=seb
https://www.example.com/secretpage?testtoken=sec - this is shorter!
https://www.example.com/secretpage?testtoken=seca
https://www.example.com/secretpage?testtoken=secb
https://www.example.com/secretpage?testtoken=secc
…etc.
```

---

[2] https://www.owasp.org/index.php/HttpOnly

This process may sound long, but it's easy to script and is a real practical attack known as CRIME (Compression Ratio Info-leak Made Easy).[3] This attack was demonstrated against SPDY, which used gzip for HTTP header compression.

8.4   *HPACK header compression for HTTP/2*

Due to the insecurities demonstrated with CRIME, HTTP/2 needed to use a different compression method that wasn't susceptible to such attacks. The HTTP Working Group created a new specification called HPACK (not an acronym) that was based on lookup tables and Huffman encoding but (crucially) not lookback-based compression.

HPACK[4] is a separate specification from HTTP/2. At one point, there were discussions about merging the two specifications, but in the end, the working group decided to keep them separate. The HTTP/2 specification is light on details about HPACK, deferring most details to the separate HPACK specification,[5] but it does state that header compression is part of HTTP/2 and that it's stateful (more on why in section 8.4.2).

One interesting fact about HPACK is that unlike many HTTP specifications, it's not flexible or designed to be extended. In fact, the HPACK specification explicitly says:[6]

> *The HPACK format is intentionally simple and inflexible. Both characteristics reduce the risk of interoperability or security issues due to implementation error. No extensibility mechanisms are defined; changes to the format are only possible by defining a complete replacement.*

Although I'm not sure that I agree with calling HPACK simple, I agree that it's unusually rigid for an internet specification, which (as the quote explains) was done for security reasons. Eventually, a new version of HPACK will undoubtedly be introduced (possibly QPACK as part of QUIC; see chapter 9). How this version will be implemented will need to be defined (likely a new setting on connection establishment), but for now, HPACK is fairly rigidly defined.

---

[3] https://blog.qualys.com/ssllabs/2012/09/14/crime-information-leakage-attack-against-ssltls
[4] https://httpwg.org/specs/rfc7541.html
[5] https://httpwg.org/specs/rfc7540.html#HeaderBlock
[6] https://httpwg.org/specs/rfc7541.html#rfc.section.1

8.4.1 HPACK static table

HPACK has a static table of 61 common HTTP header names (and in some cases values), part of which is shown in table 8.3. For the full table, see the HPACK specification.[7]

Table 8.3   Part of the HPACK static table

Index	Header name	Header value
1	:authority	
2	:method	GET
3	:method	POST
4	:path	/
5	:path	/index.html
6	:scheme	http
7	:scheme	https
8	:status	200
9	:status	204
10	:status	206
11	:status	304
12	:status	400
13	:status	404
14	:status	500
15	accept-charset	
16	accept-encoding	gzip, deflate
17	accept-language	
18	accept-ranges	
19	Accept	
...	...	...
60	Via	
61	www-authenticate	

This table is used for both requests and responses, and allows an HTTP message to efficiently compress commonly used names, as well as some commonly used name and value pairs. As a result, the header

```
:method: GET
```

---

[7]   https://httpwg.org/specs/rfc7541.html#static.table.definition

can be compressed as a reference to index 2.

As another example, the header

```
:method: DELETE
```

doesn't exist in the table but can be compressed with a reference to index 2 for the header name and the encoded value of DELETE. That is, even the name/value pair table entries (such as :method: GET) can be used to provide the name part only (such as :method). The reverse isn't true, however; there's no facility to look up a value associated with another header. A header1: GET header for example, couldn't use the GET value from index 2.

It would be equally correct to encode this :method: DELETE header to index 3 and the encoded value of DELETE instead of index 2. Both methods refer to the :method header name, so both are valid. I return to this topic in section 8.6.

8.4.2 HPACK dynamic table

In addition to the static table, HPACK has a connection-level dynamic table starting at position 62 (after the static table) up to the maximum table size defined by the SETTINGS_HEADER_TABLE_SIZE value in the SETTINGS frame. The default is 4,096 octets if not explicitly defined. When the maximum table size is reached, the oldest entry is evicted. To make this process easier, each entry is incremented when the table is written to. If a request contains the two custom headers

```
Header1: Value1
Header2: Value2
```

Header1 would be given table entry 62 initially. When Header2 was seen, Header1 would be moved to table entry 63, and Header2 would be added as table entry 62. That is, the table entry position for a header isn't static; it increments continually as new headers are added to the table in both this request and future requests. For this reason, HEADER and CONTINUATION frames must be received in order to maintain the integrity of the dynamic table. TCP guarantees this order, so in HTTP/2 the dynamic table is unique to each TCP connection.

This process is complicated and best illustrated with a real example, which I provide in section 8.5. First, you need to understand a bit more about how these headers are referenced in static and dynamic tables.

8.4.3 HPACK header types

Headers can be set to add to the dynamic table or not. There are four types of HPACK headers, described in the following sections.

Literal header field representation

Literal header field representation (which starts with 1) is a straight lookup from the table (either static or dynamic), so it's used when both the header name and value already exist in the table. This header consists of a table index value padded out to 7 bits minimum. Figure 8.2 shows the format.

0	1	2	3	4	5	6	7
1	Index (7+)						

Figure 8.2   Literal header field representation format

For larger numbers that need 7 bits or more, some additional logic exists.[8] I don't cover that logic here, but suffice it to say that it involves filling all these 7 bits with 1 and using additional octet(s) to specify the larger index value.

To encode :method: GET, for example, use index 2 (binary 10, or 000 0010 when padded out with leading zeros). When you add the leading 1 for literal header field compression, you end up with 1000 0010, or 82 in hexadecimal, as you can see if you use Wireshark to look at traffic (figure 8.3). Section 8.5 explains how to view these frames in Wireshark, so take these screenshots as examples.

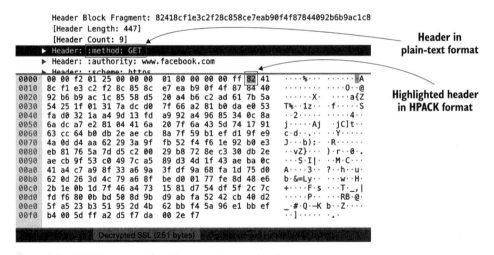

Figure 8.3   HPACK compression of :method: GET header

LITERAL HEADER FIELD WITH INCREMENTAL INDEXING

The *literal header field with incremental indexing* type (which starts with 01) is used when the header value isn't available in the table but should be added to the dynamic table for use later.

This type contains the header name (which may be an index reference to the header name already in the table or an actual header name not already in the table) and the header value.

---

[8]   https://httpwg.org/specs/rfc7541.html#integer.representation

If an indexed header name is used (the header name already exists in the table), the bits following `01` (padded to a minimum 6 bits) define the index value, followed by the header value itself, as shown in figure 8.4.

0	1	2	3	4	5	6	7
0	1	Index (6+)					
H	Value Length (7+)						
Value String (Length octets)							

Figure 8.4   Literal header field with incremental indexing format 1

The header value string can be Huffman-encoded or not (depending on whether this process would make it shorter), and the 1-bit H value is set to `1` if Huffman encoding is used or `0` if it's the ASCII value. Ideally, the shortest encoding should be used, so some headers may be Huffman-encoded and others may be straight ASCII text.

Figure 8.5 shows a real-world example. The `:authority:` header is index 1, so it should be encoded as `01000001`, or `41` in hexadecimal, followed by the Huffman-encoded value (which I discuss in section 8.4.4).

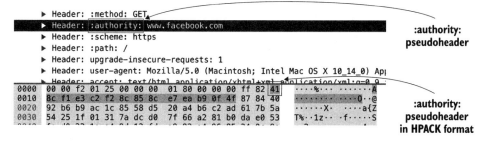

Figure 8.5   HPACK encoding of `:authority:` pseudoheader with new value

Otherwise, for a new header name that isn't in the lookup table, the 6 bits after the initial `01` are set to `0`, and then the header name and value are given as length/value pairs, as shown in figure 8.6.

0	1	2	3	4	5	6	7
0	1	0					
H	Name length (7+)						
Name string (length octets)							
H	Value length (7+)						
Value string (length octets)							

Figure 8.6   Literal header field with incremental indexing format 2

The first 8 bits, therefore, are `01000000` or `40`. Figure 8.7 shows a real-world example that starts with `40`.

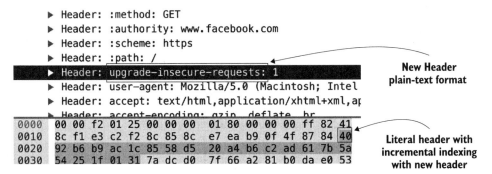

Figure 8.7   A new HPACK header to be indexed

LITERAL HEADER FIELD WITHOUT INDEXING

The *literal header field without indexing* type (which starts with `0000`) is used for items that are likely to change in each request, which would make adding to the dynamic table wasteful (such as the `path`). This header type contains the header name (which may be an index reference to the field name in the table or an actual field name), but the header name and value aren't saved as entries in the dynamic table. The two formats (depending whether the header name is referenced with a table index or given in full) are shown in figures 8.8 and 8.9.

0	1	2	3	4	5	6	7
0	0	0	0	Index (4+)			
H	Value length (7+)						
Value string (length octets)							

Figure 8.8   Literal header field without indexing format 1

0	1	2	3	4	5	6	7
0	0	0	0	0			
H	Name length (7+)						
Name string (length octets)							
H	Value length (7+)						
Value string (length octets)							

Figure 8.9   Literal header field without indexing format 2

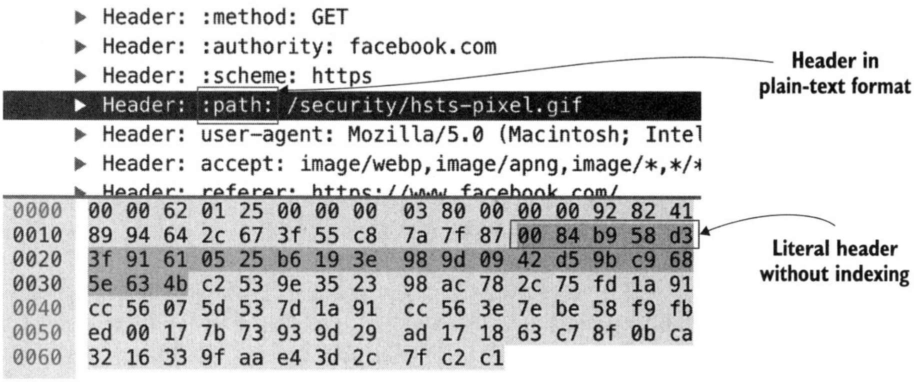

▶ Header: :method: GET
▶ Header: :authority: facebook.com
▶ Header: :scheme: https   **Header in**
                                                    plain-text format
▶ Header: :path: /security/hsts-pixel.gif
▶ Header: user-agent: Mozilla/5.0 (Macintosh; Intel
▶ Header: accept: image/webp,image/apng,image/*,*/*
▶ Header: referer: https://www.facebook.com/

```
0000  00 00 62 01 25 00 00 00  03 80 00 00 00 92 82 41
0010  89 94 64 2c 67 3f 55 c8  7a 7f 87 00 84 b9 58 d3     Literal header
0020  3f 91 61 05 25 b6 19 3e  98 9d 09 42 d5 9b c9 68     without indexing
0030  5e 63 4b c2 53 9e 35 23  98 ac 78 2c 75 fd 1a 91
0040  cc 56 07 5d 53 7d 1a 91  cc 56 3e 7e be 58 f9 fb
0050  ed 00 17 7b 73 93 9d 29  ad 17 18 63 c7 8f 0b ca
0060  32 16 33 9f aa e4 3d 2c  7f c2 c1
```

Figure 8.10 HPACK without indexing header example

Figure 8.10 shows an example. As the encoded header starts with `00` in hex (or `0000 0000` in binary), you know that this header is the second type and isn't referencing the header name (`:path`) from the table.

The `:path` name is Huffman-encoded into `84 b9 58 d3 3f`, and the header value (`/security/hsts-pixel.gif`) is Huffman-encoded into `91 61 05`...etc., as I discuss in section 8.4.4, giving the total compressed header as `00 84 b9 58 d3 3f 91 61 05` and so on.

This coding seems to be a little odd and wasteful, because the `:path` header already exists in the table (at positions 4 and 5). The header could have been encoded with format 1 and would have been 5 octets shorter:

- Format 1 (index 5): **05** `91 61 05` and so on
- Format 2 (no index): **00 84 b9 58 d3 3f** `91 61 05` and so on

If you try the same thing with Firefox, it uses index 5, but Chrome seems to prefer to send the header name for unknown reasons. This example shows you that clients may not encode in the way you always expect!

LITERAL HEADER FIELD NEVER INDEXED

The *literal header field never indexed* type (which starts with `0001`) is similar to the preceding value except that the value must not be added to a dynamic table in any subsequent reencodings (such as when a server is acting as a proxy between two HTTP/2 implementations). This header type is used for sensitive information (such as username, password, or both) that you don't like to see implemented in a shared HTTP header index. The header is an instruction on how to handle reencodings as well as the existing encoding if the header is transmitted on.

Should cookies be stored in an HPACK table?

Cookies are sensitive data and seem to be exactly what this last type was designed for. The downside is the reduced compression for cookies on subsequent requests. Cookies can be large and repeated, so ideally, they *should* be compressed.

Unlike with partial lookback compression, with HPACK the whole cookie needs to be guessed before the effect can be seen (perhaps the request size is smaller). Some implementations (such as Firefox and nghttp)[a] use only the Never Index type with small cookies (less than 20 bytes), the theory being that larger cookies are harder to guess, making the compression gains worthwhile. For larger cookies, these implementations index the value so that it can be referenced with subsequent requests. Chrome seems to use the Index type regardless of the length of the cookie, so it doesn't appear to use this Never Index compression type.

---

[a] https://github.com/nghttp2/nghttp2/blob/master/lib/nghttp2_hd.c

If the sender chooses to use this type, the settings are similar to those of the preceding "without indexing" formats (figures 8.11 and 8.12), depending on whether the header is referenced with an index to the current table or given in full.

0	1	2	3	4	5	6	7
0	0	0	1	Index (4+)			
H	Value length (7+)						
Value string (length octets)							

Figure 8.11 Literal header field without indexing format 1

0	1	2	3	4	5	6	7
0	0	0	1	0			
H	Name length (7+)						
Name string (length octets)							
H	Value length (7+)						
Value string (length octets)							

Figure 8.12 Literal header field without indexing format 2

8.4.4 Huffman encoding table

Huffman encoding depends on defining a table of codes to use for each character in the text. For HPACK, this table is defined in the specification, so both client and server know the values to use to encode and decode header names and values. Table 8.4 shows part of the HPACK Huffman codes. For the full table, see the HPACK specification.[9]

Table 8.4   Part of the HPACK Huffman encoding values

Symbol	ASCII code	Huffman code (binary)	Length (bits)
' '	(32)	|010100	[6]
'!'	(33)	|11111110|00	[10]
'"'	(34)	|11111110|01	[10]
'#'	(35)	|11111111|1010	[12]
'$'	(36)	|11111111|11001	[13]
...	...	...	...
'0'	(48)	|00000	[5]
'1'	(49)	|00001	[5]
...	...	...	...
'A'	(65)	|100001	[6]
'B'	(66)	|1011101	[7]
'C'	(67)	|1011110	[7]
'D'	(68)	|1011111	[7]
'E'	(69)	|1100000	[7]
...	...	...	...
'L'	(76)	|1100111	[7]
...	...	...	...
'T'	(84)	|1101111	[7]
...	...	...	...

To return to a previous example, look at the header

```
:method: DELETE
```

---

[9] https://httpwg.org/specs/rfc7541.html#huffman.code

This header can be compressed with a reference to index 2 and the encoded value DELETE:

Letter	D	E	L	E	T	E
Huffman code	1011111	1100000	1100111	1100000	1101111	1100000

When grouped up to octets, the header would be 1011 1111 1000 0011 0011 1110 0000 1101 1111 1000 00, with the last octet padded out with ones to 0011. This header translates to bf 83 3e 0d f8 3f in hex, which needs to be preceded by the Huffman flag and the length. The length is 6 octets in this case, which is 110 in binary or 000 0110 when padded out to 7 bits. Adding the Huffman encoding bit as 1 at the beginning of the length octet (1000 0110 or 86), you end up with the fully encoded header as 86 bf 83 3e 0d f8 3f.

8.4.5 *Huffman encoding script*

HPACK Huffman encoding and decoding can easily be automated. The following listing shows one such implementation in Perl. Note that only part of the Huffman table is shown for space reasons. The full listing is available at the book's GitHub page.[10]

Listing 8.1   A simple HPACK Huffman encoder

```perl
#!/usr/bin/perl

use strict;
use warnings;

#Read in the string to convert from the command line.
my ($input_string) = @ARGV;

if (not defined $input_string) {
  die "Need input string\n";
}

#Set up and populate a hash variable with all the Huffman lookup values.
#Note that only printable values are used in this simple example.
my %hpack_huffman_table;

$hpack_huffman_table{' '} = '010100';
$hpack_huffman_table{'!'} = '1111111000';
$hpack_huffman_table{'\"'} = '1111111001';
$hpack_huffman_table{'#'} = '111111111010';
...etc.
$hpack_huffman_table{'}'} = '11111111111101';
$hpack_huffman_table{'~'} = '1111111111101';
```

---

[10] https://github.com/bazzadp/http2-in-action

```
#Set up a binary string variable
my $binary_string="";

#Split the input string by character
my @input_array = split(//, $input_string);

#For each inoput character, look up the string in the Huffman hash table
#And add it to the binary_string variable.
foreach (@input_array) {
  $binary_string = $binary_string . $hpack_huffman_table{$_};
}

#Pad out the binary string to ensure that it's divisble by 8
while (length($binary_string) % 8 != 0) {
        $binary_string = $binary_string . "1";
};

#Calculate the length by dividing by 8.
my $string_length = length($binary_string)/8;

#This simple implementation doesn't handle large strings
#(left as an exercise for the reader).
if ($string_length > 127) {
        die "Error string length > 127 which isn't handled by this
    program\n";
}

#Set the most significant bit (128) to indicate that Huffman encoding is used
#and include the length
#(again, this simple version naively assumes 7 bits for the length).
printf("Huffman Encoding Flag + Length: %x\n",128+$string_length);

#Iterate though each 4-bit value and convert to hexidecimal
printf("Huffman Encoding Value       : ");
for(my $count=0;$count<length($binary_string);$count = $count + 4) {
        printf("%x",oct("0b" . substr($binary_string,$count,4)));
}
printf ("\n");
```

This code encodes strings into hexadecimal HPACK Huffman-encoded strings. Following is an example:

```
$ ./hpack_huffman_encoding.pl DELETE
Huffman Encoding Flag + Length: 86
Huffman Encoding Value       : bf833e0df83f
```

You could use a similar script to decode HPACK Huffman-encoded strings. This script could be enhanced to take in a list of headers and handle a dynamic table state. I leave both of these tasks as exercises for you to complete in your language of choice.

Although Huffman encoding is complicated for people to handle, it's easy to implement in code and efficient for computers to encode and decode. As a result, it's unlikely that you'll want to encode or decode manually, as I've done in this chapter.

8.4.6   *Why Huffman encoding isn't always optimal*

For some values, Huffman encoding may lead to larger values than if plain ASCII had been used. If you decide to encode `delete` by using ASCII, for example, you can jump straight to hex (because each ASCII code is 1 octet long):

Letter	D	E	L	E	T	E
ASCII hex code	44	45	4C	45	54	45

You can see that the ASCII coding version is also of length 6, and with the Huffman encoding flag set to 0, you precede the header with 06 and get 06 44 45 4C 45 54 45 as the fully encoded header.

In this case, there's no difference between using Huffman encoding and not using it—both are 7 octets long. Even though all the Huffman codes used in this particular example are 7 bits (compared with 8-bit ASCII codes), padding is needed to round up to complete octets, so the codes ended up being the same size. For some other headers, ASCII encoding may be smaller, as would be the case if some infrequent characters from the Huffman table (longer than 8 bits) were used in the header. For this reason, the HPACK specification allows Huffman encoding to be used or not as the client sees fit, and the encoding can change with each header. Whichever encoding can express the value in the fewest octets should be used.

In general, however, Huffman encoding is often more efficient than ASCII. This efficiency is due in part to the fact that ASCII requires only 7 bits, but the full 8-bit octet is used, so 1 bit is wasted for every ASCII encoded value. Huffman encoding allows the use of variable-length encodings, so in theory, bits aren't wasted. In this variable-length encoding, however, less frequently used characters use more than 8 bits, so those values may be more efficiently encoded in ASCII. These values should by definition be rare (assuming that the HPACK Huffman encoding table reflects real-life use). Finally, looking up from the static or dynamic tables is always going to be more efficient than encoding in either Huffman or ASCII format.

8.5   *Real-world examples of HPACK compression*

I presented a lot of theory in the preceding sections. In this section, I show you some real examples to help you understand all this theory. Most HTTP/2-aware tools take care of HPACK for you and don't expose all the extra hard work it has to do for you on this front, so head back to Wireshark to see the raw data being sent on the wire (and the decoded version of that data). I cover Wireshark in chapter 4, so refer to that chapter to get it working.

Assuming that you have HTTP/2 traffic sniffing working, start looking at the HTTP/2 headers. Figure 8.13 shows one example of a request to Facebook with the first HEADERS frame (the second line in the window) selected.

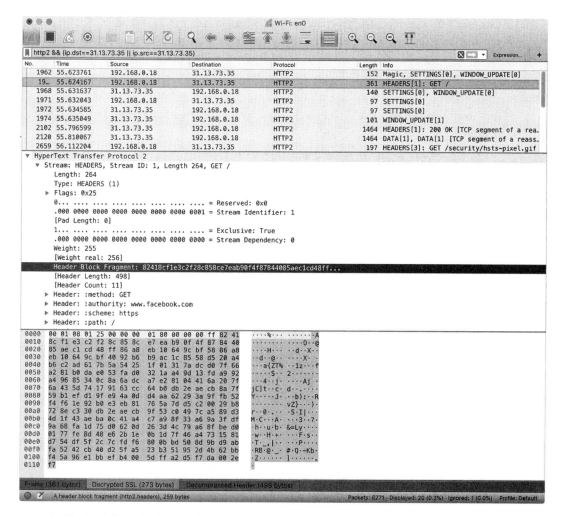

Figure 8.13 HTTP/2 header frame in Wireshark

At the bottom of the figure, you see that the Wireshark frame (a generic term for the packet and not to be confused with an HTTP/2 frame) is 361 bytes. When that frame is decrypted, it becomes 273 bytes, and when it's decompressed, it becomes 498 bytes. Header compression even for this first frame is great, with a 45% saving (273/498 = 55%), though some of that saving is used up again when the data is encrypted.

When you strip out the HTTP/2 frame details (such as the header type, the flags, the weight, and so on), you get the encoded header in hexadecimal format:

```
82 41 8c f1 e3 and so on
```

Decode this header with your newfound knowledge. Because you're dealing with variable-length Huffman encoding, looking at a header as octets isn't useful, so convert it to binary:

```
82418cf1e3... = 1000 0010 0100 0001 1000 1100 1111 0001 1110 0011...
```

At this point, you can start to read the header. You know that there are four types of headers:

- *Literal header field representation* (starts with 1)
- *Literal header field with incremental indexing* (starts with 01)
- *Literal header field without indexing* (starts with 0000)
- *Literal header field never indexed* (starts with 0001)

This header block starts with 1, so it's the first type. The next 7 bits give the table index, which is 2, which equates to :method: GET—your first uncompressed header! This header was stored in 1 octet (82) as opposed to the 12 octets needed to encode each of those 12 characters in ASCII—a huge saving. So the first 8 bits are decoded:

~~1000 0010~~ 0100 0001 1000 1100 1111 0001 1110 0011...

The next part starts with 01, so you know that it's a literal header field with incremental indexing. Because it's not followed by 6 zeros, you know that the index name is referenced by those 6 bytes. Figure 8.14 repeats the incremental format with the binary values filled in.

Bits								Actual values
0	1	2	3	4	5	6	7	
0	1	Index (6+)						0100 0001
H	Value length (7+)							1000 1100
Value string (length octets)								1111 0001...and so on

Figure 8.14 Literal header field with incremental indexing format 1

Now decode the first octets of the next header (0100 0001).

After you strip off 01, the index number is 00 0001 or 1, which is the :authority header in the table. The first 16 bits are decoded:

~~1000 0010 0100 0001~~ 1000 1100 1111 0001 1110 0011 1100...

Now you need to find the value for that :authority header. The first character of the next octet is 1, so you know that the upcoming value is a Huffman-encoded value and that the length is the remainder of that octet, or 000 1100 = 8 + 4 = 12 octets:

```
1000 1100   Huffman encoded-string with length of 12.
```

The first 24 bits are decoded:

~~1000 0010 0100 0001 1000 1100~~ 1111 0001 1110 0011 1100…

When you look at the next 12 octets, you see the following:

```
1111 0001 1110 0011 1100 0010 1111 0010 1000 1100 1000 0101
1000 1100 1110 0111 1110 1010 1011 1001 0000 1111 0100 1111
```

Each bit is read until a unique Huffman value is found. I'll do the Huffman table look-ups to save you time (easy to program but much more difficult to do manually):

- 1111000 is uniquely identified as w.
- 1111000 is uniquely identified as w.
- 1111000 is uniquely identified as w.
- 010111 is uniquely identified as ..
  and so on
- 00100 is uniquely identified as c.
- 00111 is uniquely identified as o.
- 101001 is uniquely identified as m.
- 111 is padding to fill out the last octet.

The full value is www.facebook.com, and when it's coupled with the header name (:authority), you get the full header:

```
:authority: www.facebook.com
```

This header is added to the dynamic table with index 62. The static index ends at 61 indexed values, so 62 is the next free value.

Continuing through the rest of the HEADERS frame in a similar way, you end up with the dynamic table shown in table 8.5.

Table 8.5 Dynamic header after first HEADERS frame is received

Index	Header	Value
62	accept-language	en-GB,en-US;q=0.9,en;q=0.8
63	accept-encoding	gzip, deflate, br
64	Accept	text/html,application/xhtml+xml, application/xml;q=0.9,image/webp, image/apng,*/*;q=0.8
65	user-agent	Mozilla/5.0 (Macintosh; Intel Mac OS X 10_14_0) AppleWebKit/537.36 (KHTML, like Gecko) Chrome/69.0.3497.100 Safari/537.36

Table 8.5 Dynamic header after first `HEADERS` frame is received (continued)

Index	Header	Value
66	`upgrade-insecure-requests`	`1`
67	`cache-control`	`no-cache`
68	`Pragma`	`no-cache`
69	`:authority`	`www.facebook.com`

As you can see, the `:authority:` index header has been pushed all the way down to index 69. The ordering of the headers, therefore, is important and may not match the headers shown in developer tools: Chrome orders the headers alphabetically in developer tools but doesn't send them alphabetically, for example. Note also that not all headers were added. The `:scheme: https` and `:path: /` pseudoheaders, for example, were already in the static table (at index 7 and 4, respectively), so they weren't added to the dynamic table.

The first request likely involves filling up the dynamic table, as these values won't be in the table, so you won't get optimum compression. Subsequent requests can use these values and get much better compression, as shown in figure 8.15.

I'll skip the next received `HEADERS` frame and instead go to the next sent `HEADERS` frame. You can see the direction in which each request is traveling based on the source and destination IP addresses. Sent and received headers are handled separately but in an identical fashion. Here, I concentrate on the client sending side; everything applies equally on the server sending side, but with a separately managed dynamic header table.

For the second sent request, you start with `82`, which is the same as before, and you know that it's uncompressed/unencoded to `:method: GET`, so I won't repeat myself here. The second header is more interesting. `41` is the `:authority` header, identical to the previous request, which is followed by the Huffman-encoded authority (`facebook.com`). What's interesting is that this domain is different from the first request (`facebook.com` as opposed to `www.facebook.com`), so the previously stored dynamic value can't be reused, and instead the value must be sent. This example also shows connection coalescing in action, because a separate HTTP/2 connection wasn't needed for this request even though the domain is different. See chapter 6 for more information on connection coalescing.

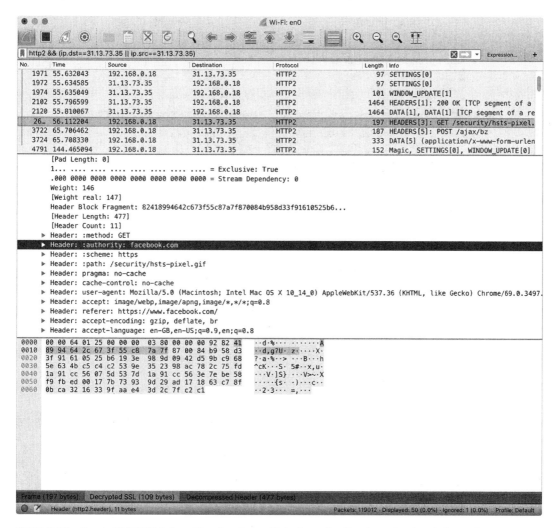

Figure 8.15 Reusing HTTP/2 indexed headers is an efficient way to allow large headers to be sent.

The next few headers are interesting, and I demonstrate them with the user-agent header, as shown in figure 8.16.

As you can see, the first request requires the full long user-agent header,[11] using 94 octets to send it. In the second request, the user-agent header hasn't changed, so it can be sent in two octets (c2) for a massive saving! This saving is even bigger compared with the 131 octets that would be needed for a plain-text HTTP/1.1 ASCII header.

---

[11] Check out https://webaim.org/blog/user-agent-string-history/ if you're curious about why this header is so long.

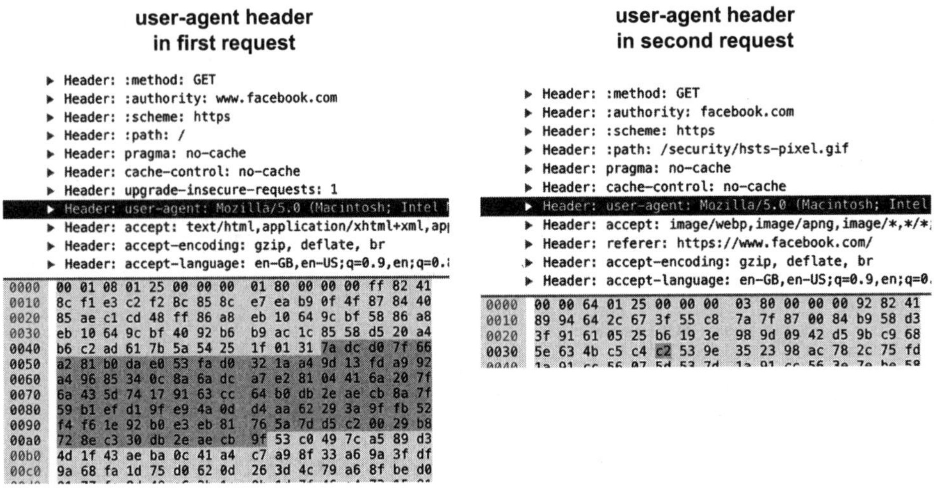

user-agent header in first request	user-agent header in second request

user-agent header in first request

- Header: :method: GET
- Header: :authority: www.facebook.com
- Header: :scheme: https
- Header: :path: /
- Header: pragma: no-cache
- Header: cache-control: no-cache
- Header: upgrade-insecure-requests: 1
- Header: user-agent: Mozilla/5.0 (Macintosh; Intel
- Header: accept: text/html,application/xhtml+xml,ap|
- Header: accept-encoding: gzip, deflate, br
- Header: accept-language: en-GB,en-US;q=0.9,en;q=0.;

```
0000  00 01 08 01 25 00 00 00  01 80 00 00 00 ff 82 41
0010  8c f1 e3 c2 f2 8c 85 8c  e7 ea b9 0f 4f 87 84 40
0020  85 ae c1 cd 48 ff 86 a8  eb 10 64 9c bf 58 86 a8
0030  eb 10 64 9c bf 40 92 b6  b9 ac 1c 85 58 d5 20 a4
0040  b6 c2 ad 61 7b 5a 54 25  1f 01 31 7a dc d0 7f 66
0050  a2 81 b0 da e0 53 fa d0  32 1a a4 9d 13 fd a9 92
0060  a4 96 85 34 0c 8a 6a dc  a7 e2 81 04 41 6a 20 7f
0070  6a 43 5d 74 17 91 63 cc  64 b0 db 2e ae cb 8a 7f
0080  59 b1 ef d1 9f e9 4a 0d  d4 aa 62 29 3a 9f fb 52
0090  f4 f6 1e 92 b0 e3 eb 81  76 5a 7d d5 c2 00 29 b8
00a0  72 8e c3 30 db 2e ae cb  9f 53 c0 49 7c a5 89 d3
00b0  4d 1f 43 ae ba 0c 41 a4  c7 a9 8f 33 a6 9a 3f df
00c0  9a 68 fa 1d 75 d0 62 0d  26 3d 4c 79 a6 8f be d0
```

user-agent header in second request

- Header: :method: GET
- Header: :authority: facebook.com
- Header: :scheme: https
- Header: :path: /security/hsts-pixel.gif
- Header: pragma: no-cache
- Header: cache-control: no-cache
- Header: user-agent: Mozilla/5.0 (Macintosh; Intel
- Header: accept: image/webp,image/apng,image/*,*/*;
- Header: referer: https://www.facebook.com/
- Header: accept-encoding: gzip, deflate, br
- Header: accept-language: en-GB,en-US;q=0.9,en;q=0.

```
0000  00 00 64 01 25 00 00 00  03 80 00 00 00 92 82 41
0010  89 94 64 2c 67 3f 55 c8  7a 7f 87 00 84 b9 58 d3
0020  3f 91 61 05 25 b6 19 3e  98 9d 09 42 d5 9b c9 68
0030  5e 63 4b c5 c4 c2 53 9e  35 23 98 ac 78 2c 75 fd
```

Figure 8.16   User agent header in first and second requests

To see how c2 translates to the `user-agent` header, first you need to realize that a new header (`:authority: facebook.com`) was added and that it would have been stored in the dynamic table, shifting everything up as shown in table 8.6.

Table 8.6   Dynamic header after first `HEADERS` frame is received

Index	Header	Value
62	`:authority`	`facebook.com`
63	`accept-language`	`en-GB,en-US;q=0.9,en;q=0.8`
64	`accept-encoding`	`gzip, deflate, br`
65	`Accept`	`text/html,application/xhtml+xml,` `application/xml;q=0.9,image/webp,` `image/apng,*/*;q=0.8`
66	`user-agent`	`Mozilla/5.0 (Macintosh; Intel Mac OS X` `10_14_0) AppleWebKit/537.36 (KHTML, like` `Gecko) Chrome/69.0.3497.100 Safari/537.36`
67	`upgrade-insecure-requests`	`1`
68	`cache-control`	`no-cache`
69	`Pragma`	`no-cache`
70	`:authority`	`www.facebook.com`

Then you can unpack the `user-agent` header:

```
c5 = 1100 0010
```

The first `1` is a literal lookup of the header name and value, and the `100 0010` translates to 66, which (as you see in table 8.6) is the previously stored `user-agent` header.

This makes sense only if both the sender and receiver keep their dynamic HPACK table in sync, however, which you can do only if you preserve the ordering of the HEADERS frames—which, thanks to TCP's guaranteed delivery, is the case. This process may seem to be complex, especially if you're doing it manually, but it can be automated easily by computer. Using tools such as Wireshark is much less painful and error-prone, but now you know how to decode manually, should manual decoding be required.

The gains from this easily automated complexity are impressive. In figure 8.15, you may have noticed that the decrypted SSL size was 109 bytes, compared with 273 bytes from the first request in figure 8.13. Even for this simple site, by loading three resources over this connection (the rest are loaded from a sharded domain) without any large cookies or complex headers, you achieve savings of 68% of the bytes you'd send in HEADERS frames, as shown in table 8.7.

Table 8.7 HPACK header savings

Request	Decrypted SSL	Decompressed header	Saving
1	273	498	45%
2	109	477	77%
3	99	547	82%
Total	481	1522	68%

As the first request is the least compressed, average gains increase the more the connection is used.

8.6 HPACK in client and server implementations

Before I close this chapter, consider a few more important points. First, there are several duplicated headers in the static and dynamic tables, some of which are shown in table 8.8.

Table 8.8 Examples of duplicate headers in HPACK static and dynamic tables

Index	Header name	Header value
1	`:authority`	
2	`:method`	`GET`
3	`:method`	`POST`
4	`:path`	`/`
5	`:path`	`/index.html`

Table 8.8   Examples of duplicate headers in HPACK static and dynamic tables *(continued)*

Index	Header name	Header value
...	...	...
19	accept	
...	...	...
64	accept	text/html,application/xhtml+xml,application/xml; q=0.9,image/webp, image/apng,*/*;q=0.8

I mentioned earlier in this chapter that a :method of DELETE could be referenced with index 2 or 3, followed by the value DELETE, as both index 2 and 3 refer to the :method header. Similarly, the :path has two entries in the table for common :path values, and after the first request is received in the example, so does accept. The HPACK specification doesn't give any guidance as to which index should be used in cases like this one. Senders can decide to use the first instance, the last instance, or one in the middle (if one exists), or they can choose not to refer to a previously defined header name index number and add another one (as Chrome did with the :path header name).

As another example of how browsers can handle encoding differently, Chrome and Firefox use slightly different methods for multiple headers within the same request.[12] If you send two cookie headers, for example, after the first header is encoded, you have two references to the cookie header name in the table: the original reference in the static table and another reference in the dynamic table for the value you encoded. To encode the second cookie header, Chrome uses the static table reference at index 32, and Firefox uses the cookie header it added to the dynamic table (at an index position greater than 62).

To be clear, all these methods are valid. As long as the reference ultimately resolves to the correct header name, the sender is free to use whichever index lookup it likes. All the examples I've given so far are for duplicate header names, with different values. But the specification explicitly states that entire name/value pairs can be duplicated exactly if the client so desires. The client can send the same header and value that are already in the table, with instructions to index them instead of referencing them from previously indexed values:[13]

> *The dynamic table can contain duplicate entries (entries with the same name and same value). Therefore, duplicate entries MUST NOT be treated as an error by a decoder.*

This process would lead to less compression for that header the first time the duplicate header was used, but technically, it's allowed.

---

[12] https://stackoverflow.com/questions/49437846/weird-http-2-hpack-encoding-in-firefox
[13] https://httpwg.org/specs/rfc7541.html#dynamic.table

Finally, it's not required that the dynamic table be used by the sender. The nginx web server uses only the static table, for example,[14] presumably because it's easier to implement and manage. A patch is available that implements full HPACK encoding.[15] This patch improves compression by 40% to 95%, according to the authors of the patch, but it isn't included in the base nginx code at this writing.[16]

8.7 *The value of HPACK*

HPACK can be complicated and intimidating at first sight (the RFC for it is nearly the size of the whole HTTP/2 specification itself), but I've squeezed it into a single chapter. I hope that this chapter has taken some of the mystery out of HPACK and will make the RFC itself less intimidating to tackle, should you need to. Most HTTP/2 users and web developers can ignore the intricate details and accept that HTTP/2 headers are compressed in an efficient manner, leading to considerable space savings, especially on the request side, where headers are the majority of the data. Cloudflare, one of the largest CDNs, saw a 53% reduction in request data when HPACK was enabled[17]. On the response side, although HTTP headers can be large, they're typically dwarfed by the HTTP bodies, so savings seem to be less significant. (Cloudflare saw only 1.4% savings on average.) But most consumer network connections have limited upload bandwidth compared with download, and requesting resources is the first stage, so the request side is arguably where the gains are more important anyway.

Summary

- There are different methods of compressing data.
- HTTP headers contain sensitive data such as cookies, so they can't use the same compression technique as HTTP bodies, because they can leak data through various attacks.
- HPACK is a compression format specifically written for HTTP header compression in HTTP/2.
- HPACK format has a specific binary format that uses a predefined static table of common header names (and in some cases values) and a dynamic table created during the session.
- Values that aren't table references can be transmitted in ASCII or Huffman-encoded format.
- Huffman-encoded format typically results in smaller values.
- There are multiple ways to send HTTP headers in HPACK, and browsers may encode HTTP headers differently.

---

[14] https://trac.nginx.org/nginx/changeset/12cadc4669a7/nginx and
[15] https://github.com/cloudflare/sslconfig/blob/master/patches/nginx_1.13.1_http2_hpack.patch
[16] https://twitter.com/igrigorik/status/1029827634815856640
[17] https://blog.cloudflare.com/hpack-the-silent-killer-feature-of-http-2/

Part 4

The future of HTTP

By now, you should have in-depth knowledge of the HTTP/2 protocol and be in a position to fully understand the specification. In this final part, I look at the future of HTTP. HTTP/2 is here and now, being used by an increasing number of websites, but those who help define internet protocols aren't sitting on their laurels. In some ways, HTTP/2 is old news, and people are already looking at the next advancement of the protocol.

Chapter 9 looks at QUIC. QUIC is a new protocol that aims to continue the work started with HTTP/2 and address problems lower in the TCP layer. It's due for standardization imminently (and may already be standardized by the time this book is published), but I suspect that it may take a bit longer to be in widespread use. QUIC uses many of the concepts of HTTP/2, so readers who have made it this far should be in a strong position to start learning this protocol and perhaps help with its adoption.

Back up the protocol layer, in chapter 10, I also look at HTTP and where (and how) it might evolve. HTTP has been robust and extensible, and HTTP/2 continues this concept, so there are numerous options for taking the protocol further.

TCP, QUIC, and HTTP/3

This chapter covers

- TCP inefficiencies
- TCP optimizations
- An introduction to QUIC
- Differences between QUIC and HTTP/2

HTTP/2's aim was to improve the inefficiencies inherent in the HTTP protocol, mainly by allowing a single, multiplexed connection. Under HTTP/1.1, the connection was vastly underused, because it could be used for only one resource at a time. If there were any delays in answering a request (such as because the server was busy generating that resource), the connection was blocked and not being used. HTTP/2 allows the connection to be used for multiple resources, so other resources can still use the connection in this scenario.

In addition to preventing wasted connections, HTTP/2 provides improved performance, because HTTP connections are inefficient in themselves. There's a cost to creating an HTTP connection; otherwise, there'd be no real benefit in multiplexing. The costs aren't due to HTTP itself, but to the two underlying technologies used to create this connection: TCP and TLS used to provide HTTPS.

In this chapter, I investigate these inefficiencies and show that although HTTP/2 is better at handling most of these inefficiencies, in certain scenarios, HTTP/2 can be slower than HTTP/1.1 because of these inefficiencies. Then I discuss QUIC, which makes several improvements.

9.1   *TCP inefficiencies and HTTP*

HTTP depends on a network connection that guarantees that data is delivered reliably and in order. Until recently, that guaranteed connection was achieved by using TCP (Transmission Control Protocol). TCP allows a connection between two endpoints (typically, browser and web server) and takes care of passing the messages, ensuring that they arrive, dealing with any retransmissions if the messages don't arrive, and ensuring that the messages are ordered correctly before being passed to any application layer (HTTP). HTTP doesn't need to implement any of these complications; instead, it assumes that these criteria have been met. The protocol was built on that assumption.

TCP enforces this guaranteed integrity by assigning a sequence number to each TCP packet and then rearranging the packets on arrival (if they're received out of order) or rerequesting any missing sequence number packets (if a packet is detected to be missing). TCP works on a CWND basis (which also formed the basis of how HTTP/2 flow control works; see chapter 7), whereby the maximum amount of data that can be sent is decided on (the CWND size), and sent messages decrease this window and acknowledged packets increase it again. The window starts small but grows over time, as the capacity of the network proves to be able to handle the increased load. The window can also shrink if it appears that the client can't keep up. This process works reasonably well, and TCP/IP has been the backbone of the internet because of it. The fundamental way that TCP works, however, also leads to five main problems with the protocol, at least where HTTP is concerned:

- There's a setup delay. Sequence numbers that are to be used by sender and receiver must be agreed on at the start of the connection.
- The *TCP slow start* algorithm restricts the performance of TCP, as it's cautious about how much data it sends to avoid retransmissions as much as possible.
- Underuse of the connection causes TCP to throttle back. TCP scales the CWND back down if the connection isn't fully used, as it can't be sure that the network parameters haven't changed since the last optimal CWND was established.
- Lost packets cause TCP to throttle back. TCP assumes that all packet loss is due to congestion, which may not always be the case.
- Packets may be queued. Packets received out of order may be held back to ensure that order is guaranteed.

These problems haven't changed under HTTP/2, and some of them are reasons why using a single TCP connection is better under HTTP/2. The last two issues, however, can cause HTTP/2 to be slower than HTTP/1.1 under certain lossy conditions.

9.1.1 Setup delay in creating an HTTP connection

I discussed the TCP three-way handshake in chapter 2. That handshake, coupled with HTTPS setup that's increasingly required by HTTP (and by all browsers for HTTP/2 connections), result in a significant delay before the first HTTP message is sent, as shown in figure 9.1.

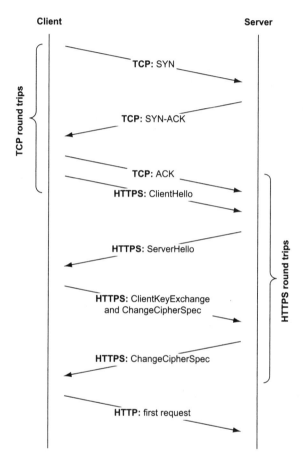

Figure 9.1 TCP and HTTPS setup traffic required for an HTTPS connection

Depending on the size of the HTTPS handshake messages, it takes at least three round trips to set up a connection to a server (1.5 for TCP, 2 for HTTPS, with an overlap of 0.5) before you can send your first request. This diagram doesn't include any DNS lookup, which is likely to add another delay.

These connection setup steps cause noticeable delays in real life, especially under HTTP/1.1, but also under HTTP/2. Figure 9.2 shows the waterfall diagram for Amazon from chapter 2, with all the connection delays highlighted.

Under HTTP/2, it's considerably better to use a single connection, but an initial delay still occurs for each connection. Also, any separate domains that can't be *coalesced*

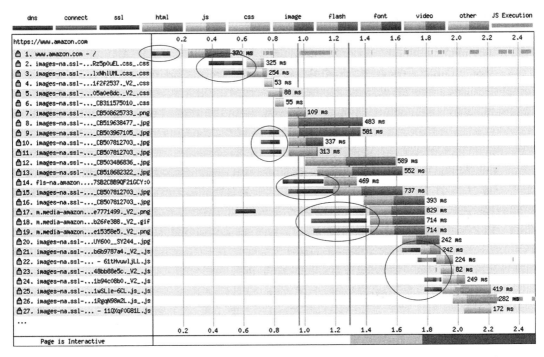

Figure 9.2   Connection setup delays for Amazon under HTTP/1.1

(see chapter 6) are subject to these delays. Amazon has upgraded to HTTP/2 since figure 9.2, but I still see connection delays for the initial connection and for any subsequent connection that can't use the same HTTP/2 connection (because it doesn't resolve to the same server or because it's authenticated versus unauthenticated), as shown in figure 9.3.

HTTP/2 massively reduces the number of connections and therefore dramatically reduces the 15 or so connection delays shown in figure 9.3, but it would be better to resolve these three remaining delays, too.

9.1.2   *Congestion control inefficiencies in TCP*

Even after the connection is made, TCP inefficiencies can cause other performance problems, primarily due to the guaranteed nature of TCP: all TCP packets are guaranteed to arrive in order. This seemingly simple statement requires several considerations to be built into the protocol, in particular *congestion control.*

Congestion control aims to prevent *network collapse,* when the network spends more time retransmitting dropped packets than sending new packets. This concept was close to becoming reality in the mid-1980s, when the internet started to take off.[1]

---

[1]   https://tools.ietf.org/html/rfc2914#section-3.1

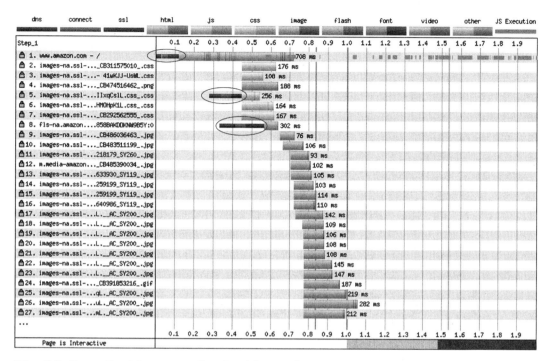

Figure 9.3 Connection delays are greatly reduced, but remain under HTTP/2.

To prevent these problems, TCP was enhanced in the late 1980s with various *congestion control* features that continue to be tweaked and changed to this day. These congestion control algorithms and concepts introduced stability but also inefficiencies, especially for HTTP.

TCP SLOW START

The *TCP slow start* mechanism finds the optimal throughput of TCP over the network without swamping, and potentially endangering, the network. TCP is a cautious algorithm that starts at a low rate and builds up to full capacity, during which time it carefully monitors the connection and capacity that it thinks it can handle.

The amount of data that a TCP connection can send is based on the congestion window size. This congestion window starts conservatively, with 10 segments of 1460 bytes maximum segment size (MSS), or about 14 KB, for modern PCs and servers (a relatively new change,[2] because many servers are still on the four-segment size used previously). During slow start, the congestion window doubles in size with each round trip, as shown in table 9.1.

---

[2] https://tools.ietf.org/html/rfc6928

Table 9.1   Typical TCP slow start growth

Round trip	MSS	CWND size (segments)	CWND size (KB)
1	1460	10	14
2	1460	20	28
3	1460	40	57
4	1460	80	114
5	1460	160	228

This doubling in size produces exponential growth, and after several round trips reaches the full capacity that the receiver said it's willing to accept (see the first part of figure 9.4).

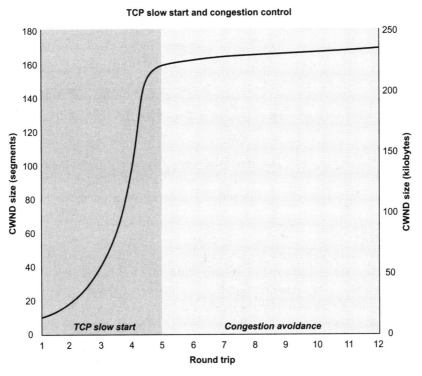

Figure 9.4   TCP slow start ramps up to optimum capacity.

The capping limit is also often much lower than shown in figure 9.4, and 65 KB is common, as that was an initial limit under TCP (see the discussion of window scaling in section 9.1.4). After maximum capacity is reached, assuming that no packet loss occurred, the TCP congestion control enters the congestion avoidance phase and continues to increase, but at a much slower linear rate (as opposed to the exponential

Is TCP slow start that slow?

Due to the exponential nature of TCP slow start, it's not slow by most definitions. In fact, the congestion avoidance phase of TCP is a much slower rate of growth. Slow start refers to the initially small size, which is why it's called slow start rather than slow growth.

It's certainly slower than starting at the maximum that the server can send and scaling down. Every TCP connection goes through this growth, so the protocol is slow initially—deliberately, intentionally slow, but slow nonetheless.

rate during slow start), until it starts to see dropped packets and is assumed to hit capacity, as shown in the second part of figure 9.4.

Unfortunately for HTTP, the initial stage is where you're likely to want full capacity. In a Facebook session, for example, the home page alone is 125 KB, which isn't reached until the fourth round trip at least. After the initial download of the web page and all its assets, there's often less need to download data, which often happens when TCP reaches its optimal capacity.

Squeezing as much as possible into the first 14 KB

One web performance tip that's often touted is to fit all your critical resources into the first 14 KB of your HTML. The theory is that the first 14 KB will be downloaded in the first 10 TCP packets, preventing any TCP acknowledgment delays. Any critical inlined CSS, for example, should be included in the initial 14 KB (assuming that the browser is happy to start processing partial HTML pages, as many browsers do).

This situation changes under an HTTPS connection and in particular under an HTTP/2 connection, in which some of these initial 10 TCP packets would be used by the following (at least):

- Two HTTPS responses (`Server Hello` and `Change Spec`)
- Two HTTP/2 `SETTINGS` frames (the server sending one and acknowledging the client's `SETTINGS` frame)
- One `HEADERS` frame responding to the first request

That connection leaves 5 packets, or about 7 KB, in the best-case scenario. In reality, any of those messages could be larger than one TCP packet, using more than five packets. Also, after you add any `WINDOW_UPDATE` or `PUSH_PROMISE` frames, this figure might be smaller still.

Luckily, however, the client acknowledges those TCP packets as they're sent, which increases the CWND size. In some ways, the initial delays due to HTTPS may mean that the CWND size is already larger by the time you use HTTP, though this fact is offset by the initial setup cost of HTTPS itself.

The main point of putting your critical resources high up in your HTML still stands, but in my opinion, there's no need to get hung up on 14 KB under HTTPS or HTTP/2.

I state in chapter 2 that HTTP/2, with its single connection, has an advantage over HTTP/1.1, but this statement may not be 100% accurate when you get into the details. On one hand, HTTP/1.1 gets to download more initially due to the multiple connections (usually six per domain, more if sharding is used), so it effectively gets multiple initial CWNDs compared with HTTP/2 (assuming that all connections are opened at the same time), as shown in table 9.2.

Table 9.2   Typical TCP slow start growth with six connections

Round trip	MSS	CWND size (segments)	CWND size (KB)	CWND size for six connections (KB)
1	1460	10	14	85
2	1460	20	28	171
3	1460	40	57	342
4	1460	80	114	684
5	1460	160	228	1368

On the other hand, if only one connection is used initially (as is often the case in downloading an HTML web page), any additional new connections under HTTP/1.1 start with the slower, lower limit than the single HTTP/2 connection, which has likely already reached full capacity. TCP slow start affects both versions of the protocol to some extent.

IDLE CONNECTIONS DEGRADE PERFORMANCE

The TCP slow start algorithm causes delays at the start of a connection, as well as when the connection is idle. TCP is cautious, and after a period of idleness, the network conditions may have changed, so TCP throttles back its CWND size and restarts the slow start mechanism to find the optimum CWND size again.

Unfortunately, web browsing is by its very nature made up of bursts of traffic (as you navigate to a new page) followed by periods of idleness (as you read the web page). Then the cycle is repeated, so resetting back to the start during idle periods can have a large effect on web browsing.

In the Amazon HTTP/1.1 example, the page is loaded from the main Amazon domain, but most of the assets used are from subdomains, leading to large periods of inactivity on the initial connection to the main domain, as highlighted in figure 9.5.

Although this inactivity is particularly bad for the first connection highlighted (as it'll likely be used again on any subsequent page navigation), you can see in figure 9.5 that lots of other connections are underused. These gaps show inefficient usage of this connection, as highlighted in chapter 2, but from a TCP point of view, it's worse than you may realize, as TCP throttles back the connection during these periods of inactivity. When those connections need to be used again (such as on page navigation), the process almost starts from the beginning again, although at least the TCP

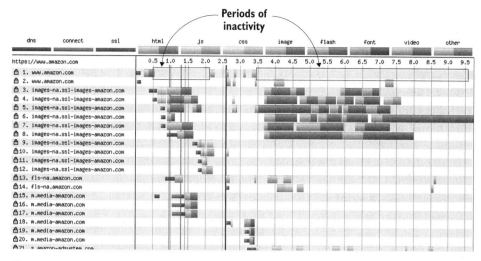

Figure 9.5 Connection use by Amazon under HTTP/1

handshake and HTTPS handshake don't need to be repeated if the connection is kept open.

HTTP/2, with its use of a single connection per domain, fares much better in this situation. Each resource helps keep the single TCP connection active, so it's less likely to be idle. This situation is particularly relevant if any connection regularly communicates back to the server through XHR polling, server-sent events, or similar technology. Such activity keeps the connection warmed up and ready for the next page navigation.

PACKET LOSS DEGRADES TCP PERFORMANCE

In addition to taking a while to get up to capacity at the beginning and when the connection has been idle for some time, TCP handles packet loss as an extreme event. It assumes that this event is due to capacity constraints and reacts sharply, halving the CWND and thereby halving the capacity (depending on the TCP congestion algorithm in use).[3] Then TCP uses the congestion avoidance algorithm to build up capacity and continues in a congestion avoidance phase (again depending on the TCP algorithm), as illustrated in figure 9.6.

This halving of the CWND causes particular problems. Packet loss can occur for many reasons, and network congestion is only one of them. Mobile networks, for example, can be less reliable than wired connections and can lose packets at random, regardless of how much capacity the network has. Therefore, it can be wrong to assume that packet loss is purely due to congestion, and so should result in a dramatic reduction in capacity.

---

[3] https://ieeexplore.ieee.org/document/7796870

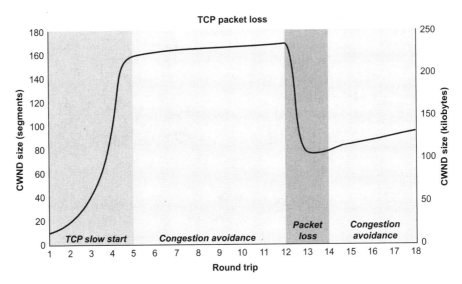

Figure 9.6   TCP CWND size is affected by packet loss.

Newer TCP congestion control algorithms treat these network drops less extremely than the preceding example: they may drop the CWND by less than half, grow faster after packet loss (similar to slow start), or use alternatives to packet loss to decide capacity (such as treating average round-trip time as a better indicator than packet loss). But at a high level, the concepts are roughly similar. Packet loss results in slow-down of the network.

This problem is particularly severe for HTTP/2 with a single connection. A single packet lost in an HTTP/2 world causes all resources being downloaded to suffer. Compare this protocol with HTTP/1.1, which potentially has six independent connections. A single packet loss will slow one of those connections, but the other five will continue at full capacity.

A second packet loss, before the connection has recovered, could have even more dire consequences under HTTP/2, which halves down again to 25% capacity (again assuming the use of basic TCP congestion control). Under HTTP/1.1, this second packet loss could happen on the connection that already experienced the problem (also reducing capacity to 25%) or on a separate connection (reducing it to 50%), but the other TCP connections are unaffected. Table 9.3 shows the results of six resources being downloaded over HTTP/2 and under the two HTTP/1.1 scenarios.

As you see in table 9.3, the average capacity under HTTP/2 is down to 25% for this example, because the whole connection (over which all six resources are being down-loaded) is affected, whereas the effect on six independent connections is a reduction to between 83% and 88%, depending on which connections were affected.

Table 9.3 Results of second packet loss on HTTP/2 versus HTTP/1.1 connections

Resource	HTTP/2	HTTP/1.1: same connection	HTTP/1.1: different connection
Resource 1	25%	25%	50%
Resource 2	25%	100%	50%
Resource 3	25%	100%	100%
Resource 4	25%	100%	100%
Resource 5	25%	100%	100%
Resource 6	25%	100%	100%
Average	25%	88%	83%

If this connection is particularly bad, or if there's a genuine capacity bottleneck, both HTTP/1.1 and HTTP/2 will suffer. The effect is always greater under HTTP/2, however; its single connection always bears the full brunt of any packet loss.

PACKET LOSS CAUSES ITEMS TO QUEUE

HTTP/2 multiplexing allows several streams of requests to be in flight in parallel on the same TCP connection. Doing the same thing under HTTP/1.1 requires multiple TCP connections. An HTTP/2-specific problem arises when you have packet loss as well as reduction in capacity. Suppose that you have three assets in flight, and they're downloading, as shown in figure 9.7.

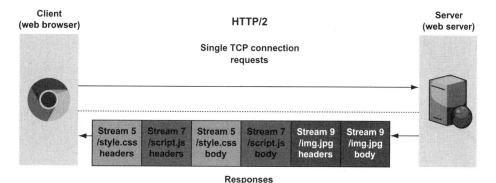

Figure 9.7 Several responses in flight

Now assume that a TCP packet from the first response—the style.css headers response being sent on stream 5—goes missing for some reason. In this case, the client won't acknowledge that packet, and after a while, the server resends it. This retransmission is added to the end of the queue, as shown in figure 9.8. Note that the figure blurs the lines between HTTP/2 frames and TCP packets somewhat for simplicity's sake.

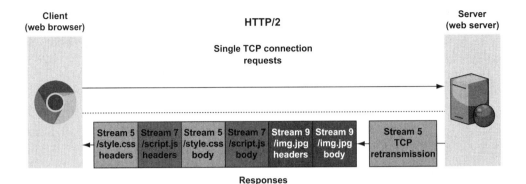

Figure 9.8   TCP retransmission of part of an HTTP/2 frame

If no other packet losses occur, streams 7 and 9 will be received in their entirety before the retransmission arrives. Those responses must be queued, however, because TCP guarantees the order, so script.js and image.jpg can't be used despite being downloaded in full. Under HTTP/1.1, this process would be carried out under three independent TCP connections, as shown in figure 9.9.

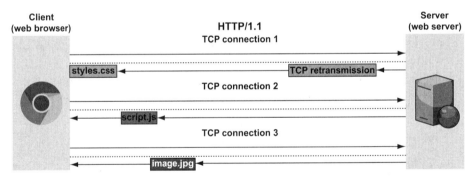

Figure 9.9   TCP retransmissions under HTTP/1.1 affect only the connection that needs the retransmission.

The browser, therefore, can process script.js and image.jpg as soon as they arrive; only style.css is delayed. In this example, the browser may wait until style.css is available, depending on whether it considers this resource to be a critical resource (as CSS often is). The point remains that HTTP/2 is adding a constraint here that isn't present under HTTP/1.1 with multiple connections. Worse, if the connection is unable to queue up all out-of-sequence packets due to limited TCP buffer size, it may drop some packets, requiring them to be retransmitted as well!

HTTP/2 has solved the head-of-line (HOL) blocking issue at HTTP level, because with multiplexing, a single delayed response doesn't prevent the HTTP connection from being used for other resources. HOL blocking is still present at TCP level, however.

A single dropped packet from one stream effectively blocks all the other streams, even though they may not need to be held up.

9.1.3 Effect of TCP inefficiencies on HTTP/2

I've shown that TCP inefficiencies can cause problems for HTTP, but what is the real effect, and is it any different under HTTP/1 and HTTP/2?

I indicated earlier that HTTP/2 generally outperforms HTTP/1.1. Also, Google's experiments with SPDY demonstrated a considerable speed gain in both laboratory experiments and the real world.

The effect of performance loss isn't to be underestimated, however. Hooman Beheshti of Fastly did some experiments[4] with the WebPagetest tool and showed that HTTP/2 performs consistently worse than HTTP/1.1 when a consistent 2% packet loss occurs. Granted, a consistent 2% packet loss indicates a very poor network; most networks lose an occasional packet rather than experience this consistent level of loss. But the experiments show that HTTP/2 may not be the silver bullet for all scenarios. More in-depth studies[5] similarly showed the impact of packet loss and even went so far as to recommend using limited sharding under HTTP/2, which seems to be counterintuitive.

I was able to repeat Beheshti's findings on some popular sites but not on others. If you want to repeat the tests, go to https://www.webpagetest.org/. On the Test Settings tab, choose a custom setting and set your packet loss, as shown in figure 9.10.

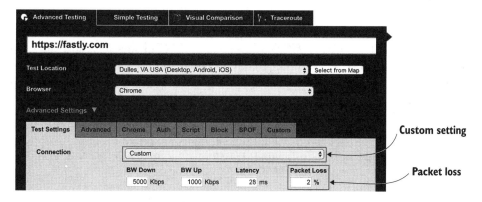

Figure 9.10 Testing packet loss in WebPagetest

---

[4] https://www.youtube.com/watch?v=CkFEoZwWbGQ and https://www.youtube.com/watch?v=wR1gF5Lhcq0
[5] https://arxiv.org/abs/1707.05836

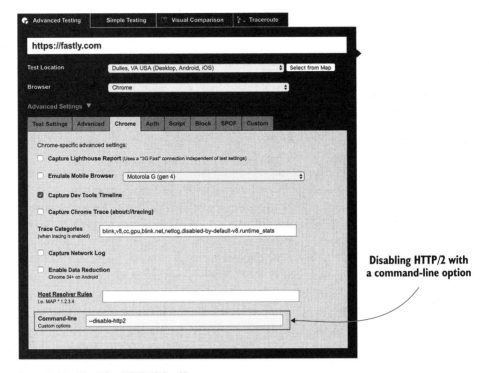

Figure 9.11   Disabling HTTP/2 for Chrome

To test HTTP/2 versus HTTP/1.1, you can use Chrome and add the `--disable-http2` command-line option, as shown in figure 9.11.

For Firefox, you must use a slightly different method. Enter the following on the Script tab, replacing the final `navigate` line with the site you want to test against:

```
firefoxPref  network.http.spdy.enabled         false
firefoxPref  network.http.spdy.enabled.http2   false
firefoxPref  network.http.spdy.enabled.v3-1    false
navigate     https://www.fastly.com/
```

Be aware that you must use tabs, not spaces, between the parts of these settings, as shown in figure 9.12.

To prevent any bias or to keep individual results from skewing overall results, run the tests multiple times, under different network conditions and in different locations. Figure 9.13 shows the results of one test of ebay.com.

As you see in figure 9.13, HTTP/2 (top) is nearly half a second slower. Repeating the same test with zero packet loss shows that HTTP/2 is faster, as expected.

It's also possible to export the raw data by clicking Raw Page Data on the right side of the page, as shown in figure 9.14.

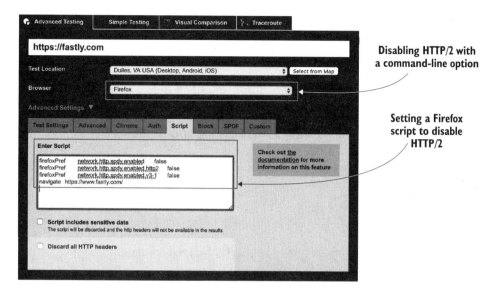

Figure 9.12 Disabling HTTP/2 on Firefox in WebPagetest

HTTP/2 with 2% packet loss

Performance results (median run)

	Load Time	First Byte	Start Render	Speed Index	First Interactive (beta)	Document Complete			Fully Loaded			
						Time	Requests	Bytes In	Time	Requests	Bytes In	Cost
First View (Run 7)	3.101s	0.299s	0.800s	3.386s	> 5.485s	3.101s	38	843 KB	7.310s	135	2,265 KB	$$$$$

HTTP/1.1 with 2% packet loss

Performance results (median run)

	Load Time	First Byte	Start Render	Speed Index	First Interactive (beta)	Document Complete			Fully Loaded			
						Time	Requests	Bytes In	Time	Requests	Bytes In	Cost
First View (Run 4)	2.672s	0.374s	1.000s	4.790s	6.537s	2.672s	38	826 KB	11.998s	137	2,487 KB	$$$$$

Figure 9.13 Loading Ebay's home page with 2% packet loss over HTTP/2 and HTTP/1.1

HOME   TEST RESULT   TEST HISTORY   FORUMS   DOCUMENTATION   ABOUT

Web Page Performance Test for
https://www.ebay.com/

From: Dulles, VA - Chrome - custom
30/09/2018, 16:19:20

Need help improving?

First Byte Time	Keep-alive Enabled	Compress Transfer	Compress Images	Cache static content	Effective use of CDN
A	A	A	A	A	✓

Summary   Details   Performance Review   Content Breakdown   Domains   Processing Breakdown   Screen Shot   Image Analysis   Request Map

Tester: VM2-05-192.168.11.103
First View only
Test runs: 9
Connectivity: 5000/1000 Kbps, 28ms Latency, 2% Packet Loss
Re-run the test

Raw page data - Raw object data
Export HTTP Archive (.har)
View Test Log

Use the Raw Page Data link to export run data

Performance Results (Median Run)

	Load Time	First Byte	Start Render	Speed Index	First Interactive (beta)	Document Complete			Fully Loaded			
						Time	Requests	Bytes In	Time	Requests	Bytes In	Cost
First View (Run 7)	3.101s	0.299s	0.800s	3.386s	> 5.485s	3.101s	38	843 KB	7.310s	135	2,265 KB	$$$$$

Figure 9.14 Exporting WebPagetest raw data to a CSV file

This feature can be handy when you're making multiple runs and want to plot them in a graph. Also, you can click Test History and select both images to see a quick comparison of the effect, as shown in figure 9.15.

	Date/Time	From	Label	Url
✓	**09/30/18 16:19:19**	Dulles, VA - **Chrome - custom** (video)		https://www.ebay.com/
✓	**09/30/18 16:18:57**	Dulles, VA - **Chrome - custom** (video)		https://www.ebay.com/

Figure 9.15   Choosing two results to compare

This feature gives you access to a wealth of views and data, including size by timeline and thumbnails, as shown in figure 9.16.

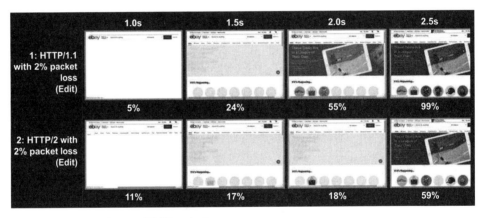

Figure 9.16   Comparing two WebPagetest runs

WebPagetest is a fantastic tool for running performance comparisons like this one. You can also host your own private instance, which is well worth looking into if you plan to perform a lot of checks or want to test development servers that aren't available to the web version.

Should you hold off on migrating to HTTP/2 due to TCP inefficiencies?

Given the fact that HTTP/2 performance can be worse under severe packet loss, should you hold off on moving to HTTP/2? Delaying probably would be overkill. Remember that HTTP/2 is faster than HTTP/1.1 under most scenarios. Should you hold up benefiting users because on some (ideally rare) occasions, it performs worse than HTTP/1.1?

This chapter discusses some real problems with HTTP and TCP, but not the likelihood that those problems will occur. The best measure is real-life metrics, rather than artificial scenarios like those in this chapter. As I stated earlier, a real-life network that experiences continual 2% packet loss is likely to be a poor network. Unfortunately, measuring packet loss in real life is more difficult; statistics are less readily available. Some scientific studies based on more realistic packet loss scenarios,[a] however, have shown that, as expected, in general HTTP/2 outperforms HTTP/1.1.

HTTP/2 implementations are still relatively new and will improve over time. The same is true of websites, which may optimize better for HTTP/2. Finally, TCP itself is still improving and can be optimized (see section 9.1.4). Some people have suggested using multiple TCP connections for HTTP/2 to work around some of these issues, but this workaround negates the reasons for moving to a single connection under HTTP/2. HTTP/2 mostly performs better *because* it uses a single connection.

In a specific scenario in which most of your users have poor network connections that can't be improved, it may be prudent to remain on HTTP/1.1 or to shard HTTP/2 connections that won't be coalesced. Ultimately, the best advice (as always) is to measure and test any changes.

---

[a] https://www.semanticscholar.org/paper/HTTP%2F2-Performance-in-Cellular-Networks-Goel-Steiner/63fa6b3310a7c4d799d5b0b5bf37f0620dd3fc5d?tab=abstract

9.1.4 Optimizing TCP

You've seen that TCP can greatly affect the performance of HTTP. In many ways, the inefficiencies in the HTTP protocol have been engineered out with HTTP/2, but performance bottlenecks that existed elsewhere are now more apparent. HTTP HOL blocking is no longer a problem in HTTP/2, thanks to *multiplexing*, but TCP HOL blocking has become a problem, especially in lossy environments.

The only two solutions to these problems are to improve TCP or to move away from it. The following sections look at the first solution; section 9.2 looks at the second. TCP has had several improvements over the years, some of which may already be in use in some environments.

UPGRADING YOUR OPERATING SYSTEM

The biggest effect is to upgrade your operating system. Although TCP is old, dating back to 1974, improvements and innovations are still being made as new research is completed and as computer use changes. Unfortunately, TCP usually is controlled by the low-level operating system, and you have less opportunity to change it outside the operating system. Therefore, the best way to ensure that you have optimum TCP usage is to ensure that you're running the latest version of your operating system.

In this section, I concentrate on Linux as an example, but these settings apply equally to other operating systems, including Windows and macOS, even if the settings aren't in the same place or as easy to change. Where appropriate, I provide the

Linux version in which a change was introduced. Table 9.4 shows the Linux kernel version included in some of the most popular Linux distributions.

Table 9.4   Linux kernel versions for popular distributions

Distribution	Linux kernel version
RHEL/Centos 6	2.6.32
RHEL/Centos 7	3.10.0
Ubuntu/Debian 14.04	3.13
Ubuntu/Debian 16.04	4.4
Ubuntu/Debian 18.04	4.15
Debian 8 Jessie	3.16
Debian 9 Stretch	4.9

Finding and changing TCP connection settings

Most TCP settings in Linux are available to view in the following directory:

```
/proc/sys/net/ipv4/
```

Despite the directory name, most of these settings apply to IPv6 TCP connections too. You can view the values with `cat`:

```
$ cat /proc/sys/net/ipv4/tcp_slow_start_after_idle
1
```

You can set the values with the `sysctl` command:

```
sysctl -w net.ipv4.tcp_slow_start_after_idle=0
```

Take care when changing any of these settings, however, because TCP is such a critical part of the system. I advise most readers not to change the settings. I suggest instead that readers use this knowledge to make sure that these settings are appropriate and use them as an argument for a whole operating-system upgrade, which should set the values to the best practice values at the time of the kernel release.

INCREASING THE INITIAL CWND SIZE

TCP slow start requires a round trip to increase the CWND size, which started at a size of 1 TCP packet but increased over the years to 2 and then 4; by Linux kernel 2.6.39, the setting increased from 4 to 10 by default. This setting is usually hard-coded into the kernel code, so it's not advisable to change it except by upgrading the operating system.

ALLOWING WINDOW SCALING

Traditionally, TCP allows a maximum CWND window size of 65,535 bytes, but later versions allow a scaling factor to be applied to this value, in theory allowing CWND sizes of up to 1 GB. This setting was made the default in Linux kernel 2.6.8, so it should be on for most readers, but to make sure, you can check it this way:

```
$ cat /proc/sys/net/ipv4/tcp_window_scaling
1
```

USING SELECTIVE ACKNOWLEDGMENT

Selective Acknowledgment (SACK) allows TCP to acknowledge receipt of packets out of order to avoid resending them if another packet is dropped. If packets 1–10 are sent, but packet 4 is dropped, you can acknowledge 1–3 and 5–10. That way, only packet 4 must be resent. Without this feature, packets 4–10 would need to be resent in this example. Confirm that this feature is set to 1 (on) with this command:

```
$ cat /proc/sys/net/ipv4/tcp_sack
1
```

DISABLING SLOW START RESTART

This setting still defaults to potentially the wrong value, at least for web servers, so you may want to consider changing it. A TCP connection throttles back after an idle period, under the assumption that network conditions may have changed, so previous assumptions may be incorrect. By default, however, a web server is somewhat intermittent, with bursts of traffic as users browse the site, pause to read the web page, and potentially browse to other pages, so enabling this setting may not be optimum for web servers.

The setting usually is enabled by default:

```
$ cat /proc/sys/net/ipv4/tcp_slow_start_after_idle
1
```

To disable it, use the following command:

```
sysctl -w net.ipv4.tcp_slow_start_after_idle=0
```

As I stated earlier, you shouldn't change your system TCP settings lightly. But depending on what your server is used for (such as a dedicated web server), changing this setting may be worth considering.

USING TCP FAST OPEN

TCP fast open allows an initial packet of traffic to be sent with the initial SYN part of the TCP three-way handshake. This method prevents some of the setup delay associated with TCP (see section 9.1.1). For security reasons, this packet can be sent only on TCP reconnections rather than on initial connections, and both client and server support are required. TCP fast open effectively allows HTTP (or HTTPS) messages to be sent earlier in the handshake, as shown in figure 9.17.

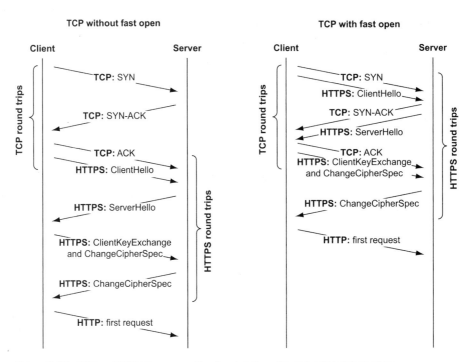

Figure 9.17   TCP and HTTPS reconnection handshake with and without fast open

You can check Linux support of this feature as follows:

```
$ cat /proc/sys/net/ipv4/tcp_fastopen
0
```

The setting usually is disabled (set to 0). Table 9.5 lists some options for this setting.

Table 9.5   TCP fast open settings

Value	Meaning
0	Disabled
1	Enabled for outgoing connections
2	Enabled for incoming connections
3	Enabled for both outgoing and incoming connections

You can change this setting with the following command:

```
echo "3" > /proc/sys/net/ipv4/tcp_fastopen
```

Support for this feature was added in Linux 3.7 and enabled by default in version 3.13, though IPv6 support wasn't added until Linux 3.16.

In addition to setting this setting at the operating-system level, you must configure your server software to use it. On the web-server side, nginx allows this setting[6] but requires compile options and configuration, so it's not enabled by default. Windows IIS[7] supports it, but Apache makes no mention of it in the documentation, so presumably it doesn't support it. Other, less-common servers may not support this feature. On the client side, the setting can be enabled in Edge,[8] and Chrome on Android, but at this writing, it isn't supported in Chrome for Windows or macOS[9] and is switched off in Firefox.[10]

The gains from TCP Fast Open are truly impressive. Google has stated[11] that "based on traffic analysis and network emulation, we show that TCP Fast Open would decrease HTTP transaction network latency by 15% and whole-page load time over 10% on average, and in some cases up to 40%." Support of this relatively new addition to TCP (the RFC was published in 2014)[12] has been slow, however. Given these complexities, TCP Fast Open probably is one to watch for in the future rather than change now.

USING CONGESTION CONTROL ALGORITHMS, PRR, AND BBR

TCP has various congestion control algorithms that control how TCP reacts when packet loss is experienced. Most TCP implementations use the *CUBIC* algorithm[13] (the default since Linux kernel 2.6.19). This algorithm was enhanced by *Proportional Rate Reduction (PRR)*[14] congestion avoidance (the default since 3.2), which reduces the halving of the congestion control window on packet loss.[15] A detailed description of the differences is beyond the scope of this book, but suffice it to say that a better algorithm can significantly improve performance. Use this command to see the current algorithm in use:

```
$ cat /proc/sys/net/ipv4/tcp_congestion_control
cubic
```

The available congestion control algorithms are available here:

```
$ cat /proc/sys/net/ipv4/tcp_available_congestion_control
reno cubic
```

---

[6] https://nginx.org/en/docs/http/ngx_http_core_module.html#listen

[7] https://blogs.technet.microsoft.com/networking/2016/07/18/announcing-new-transport-advancements-in-the-anniversary-update-for-windows-10-and-windows-server-2016/

[8] https://www.windowscentral.com/enable-tcp-fast-open-microsoft-edge-faster-page-load-times

[9] https://bugs.chromium.org/p/chromium/issues/detail?id=635080

[10] https://bugzilla.mozilla.org/show_bug.cgi?id=1398201

[11] https://ai.google/research/pubs/pub37517

[12] https://tools.ietf.org/html/rfc7413

[13] https://tools.ietf.org/html/rfc831

[14] https://tools.ietf.org/html/rfc6937

[15] https://ai.google/research/pubs/pub37486

An even newer algorithm, Bottleneck Bandwidth and Round-trip propagation time (BBR), has been shown to improve performance further,[16] particularly for HTTP/2 connections.[17] BBR was created by Google and is available in Linux kernel 4.9; it requires no client-side changes. To enable it in Linux kernels that have it (version 4.9 or later), use the following commands:

```
#Dynamically load the tcp_bbr module if not loaded already
sudo modprobe tcp_bbr
#Add Fair Queue traffic policing which BBR works better with
sudo echo "net.core.default_qdisc=fq" > /etc/sysctl.conf
#Change the TCP congestion algorithm to BBR
sudo echo "net.ipv4.tcp_congestion_control=bbr" > /etc/sysctl.conf
#Reload the settings
sudo sysctl -p
```

Some researchers,[18] however, claim that BBR potentially isn't a nice player on the network, particularly when running alongside other non-BBR traffic, and can take an unfair proportion of network resources.

9.1.5 *The future of TCP and HTTP*

I've shown you some of the complications of TCP—a seemingly simple protocol that's far more complex than most people realize. Like HTTP/1.1, TCP has some built-in inefficiencies that users may only now be starting to experience, as the inefficiencies in higher-level protocols such as HTTP are addressed, and as demands on networks continue to increase.

The protocol is still evolving, albeit quite slowly. Although new options and congestion control algorithms are being created all the time, and browsers are being upgraded to take advantage of these features if available, it takes some time for them to make it into the network stacks of servers. New features usually are tied to the fundamentals of the operating system, so they require a full operating system upgrade. It may be possible to turn on some of these settings manually if you're running a version of the operating system in which the features have been introduced but not been made defaults, but it's often better to upgrade the operating system. This area is a specialized one, and although I touched on a few recent innovations here that are likely to be beneficial for the next few years, it's usually better to allow the maintainers of the operating system, who have the necessary skills and knowledge, to decide what these settings should be.

Also, I didn't touch on all the network pipes and plumbing that usually lie between a user's web browser and the web server. Even if both sides support some of these relatively new TCP features, if anything sitting between them doesn't, there's potential for

---

[16] https://cloudplatform.googleblog.com/2017/07/TCP-BBR-congestion-control-comes-to-GCP-your-Internet-just-got-faster.html

[17] https://blog.cloudflare.com/http-2-prioritization-with-nginx/

[18] https://doc.tm.uka.de/2017-kit-icnp-bbr-authors-copy.pdf

a problem. Much as HTTP proxies downgrade connections to HTTP/1.1 even when both ends support HTTP/2, innovation in this area can be held back by so-called middleboxes. Because TCP is an old algorithm, some of these middleboxes have certain expectations about how TCP is used and don't react well, or don't allow it to be used in new, unexpected ways.

For these reasons and more, some people are questioning whether TCP is the right underlying protocol for HTTP and whether a new protocol is the way to go—a protocol designed from the ground up for the current (and future) needs of HTTP without the baggage of the past or dependency on the operating system. One such protocol is QUIC.

9.2 *QUIC*

QUIC (pronounced *quick*) is a new UDP-based protocol invented at Google (Google again!) that aims to replace TCP and other parts of the traditional HTTP stack to address many of the inefficiencies mentioned in this chapter. HTTP/2 introduced some TCP-like concepts (such as packets and flow control), but QUIC takes these concepts to the next level and replaces TCP.

What does QUIC stand for?

QUIC originally was an acronym for *Quick UDP Internet Connections*, as shown in most of the Google Chromium documentation when the protocol was introduced.[a, b, c] During formalization, the QUIC Working Group decided to drop this acronym,[d] and the QUIC specification explicitly notes, "QUIC is a name, not an acronym."[e]

Many sources still use the acronym, however. A member of the Working Group amusingly stated, "QUIC isn't an acronym. You're expected to shout it ;)."[f]

---

[a] https://www.chromium.org/quic
[b] https://docs.google.com/document/d/1gY9-YNDNAB1eip-RTPbqphgySwSNS-DHLq9D5Bty4FSU/
[c] https://docs.google.com/document/d/1RNHkx_VvKWyWg6Lr8SZ-saqsQx7rFV-ev2jRFUoVD34/
[d] https://github.com/quicwg/base-drafts/pull/1282
[e] https://tools.ietf.org/html/draft-ietf-quic-transport#section-2
[f] https://www.ietf.org/mail-archive/web/quic/current/msg03844.html

---

QUIC was created with the following features in mind:[19]

- Dramatically reduced connection establishment time
- Improved congestion control
- Multiplexing without HOL line blocking
- Forward error correction
- Connection migration

---

[19] https://www.chromium.org/quic

The first three reasons should be obvious from the TCP (and HTTPS) drawbacks discussed in this chapter. The last two reasons are interesting additions that further address these problems.

Forward error correction (FEC) looks to reduce the need for packet retransmission by including part of a QUIC packet in neighboring packets. The idea is that if only a single packet is dropped, it should be possible to reassemble that packet from the successfully delivered packets. The process has been compared with "RAID 5 on the network level."[20] I said earlier that packets can get lost randomly, but not necessarily as a sign of limits of the connection, and FEC aims to correct this problem. QUIC adds redundancy and overhead costs, but given the fact that HTTP requires guaranteed delivery (unlike, say, video stream protocols, in which packets may be dropped without effect), the gains may be worth the small overhead. At this writing, this feature of QUIC is still experimental[21] and won't be in the initial version of QUIC, as it's explicitly called as out of scope in the QUIC-WG charter.[22]

Connection migration aims to reduce connection setup overhead by allowing a connection to move between networks. Under TCP, the connection is linked to the IP address and port on either side. Changing the IP address requires establishing a new TCP connection. This requirement was acceptable when TCP was invented, because IP addresses were viewed as being unlikely to change during the lifetime of a session. Now, with multiple networks (wired, wireless, and mobile), this situation can no longer be taken for granted. QUIC, therefore, allows you to start your session over Wi-Fi at home and then move to a mobile network without having to restart your session. You should even be able to use both your Wi-Fi and mobile networks at the same time for one QUIC connection via a technique known as multipath that allows increased bandwidth. Again, this multipath feature won't be available in the first release, but connection migration should be.

9.2.1   *Performance benefits of QUIC*

In April 2015, Google published a blog post[23] on the performance benefits of QUIC, including the following:

- 75% of connections take advantage of the zero-round-trip connection time.
- Google Search saw a 3% improvement in mean page load time, and reducing page load time by a second on the slowest networks. These figures may not seem like much, but remember that Google Search is a massively optimized site on which any improvement is special.
- YouTube users reported 30% fewer rebuffers when using QUIC.

---

[20] https://ma.ttias.be/googles-quic-protocol-moving-web-tcp-udp/
[21] https://docs.google.com/document/d/1Hg1SaLEl6T4rEU9j-isovCo8VEjjnuCPTcLNJewj7Nk
[22] https://datatracker.ietf.org/wg/quic/about/
[23] https://blog.chromium.org/2015/04/a-quic-update-on-googles-experimental.html

The measurements presumably were compared with HTTP/2 and SPDY. At that time, 50% of Chrome traffic to Google used QUIC; that percentage is likely to have grown considerably since then. Because QUIC was supported only by Chrome and Google until recently (see section 9.2.6), its use is limited. W3Tech, for example, says that slightly more than 1% of sites use QUIC at this writing,[24] though other measures say that this figure translates to 7.8% of traffic volume,[25] of which 98% is Google.

9.2.2   *QUIC and the internet stack*

QUIC replaces more than TCP. Figure 9.18 shows where QUIC fits into the traditional HTTP technology stack.

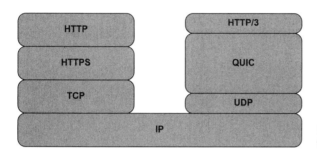

Figure 9.18   **Where QUIC fits into the HTTP technology stack**

As you see in figure 9.18, QUIC replaces most of what TCP traditionally provides (the setup, reliability, and congestion control parts), all of HTTPS (to improve the setup delays), and even part of HTTP/2 (the flow control and header compression parts).

QUIC aims for a one-round-trip connection setup by performing the connection layer (TCP in the traditional world) and encryption layer (TLS in the traditional world) at the same time. To do so, it uses many of the concepts and innovations that have been added to TCP (such as Fast Open) and TLS (such as TLSv1.3).

At a higher level, QUIC doesn't replace HTTP/2, but it takes over some of the Transport layer pieces, leaving a lighter HTTP/2 implementation running on top. As with the move from HTTP/1.1 to HTTP/2, the core syntax of HTTP that most higher-level developers need to care about stays the same under QUIC, and the concepts introduced in HTTP/2 (such as multiplexed streams, header compression, and server push) still exist in much the same way; QUIC takes care of some lower-level details. The move from HTTP/1.1 to HTTP/2 contains bigger changes for developers, but all the concepts remain the same under QUIC, so everything you've read and learned in this book isn't wasted! The protocol is still a multiplexed, stream-based binary protocol, and some of the specifics used to achieve this change at a lower level now fall under QUIC rather than HTTP/2. To reflect the changes from HTTP/2, to differentiate

---

[24] https://w3techs.com/technologies/details/ce-quic/all/all
[25] https://blog.apnic.net/2018/05/15/how-much-of-the-internet-is-using-quic/

it from QUIC itself, and to show that this is the best version of HTTP, it has been agreed HTTP over QUIC will be called HTTP/3 (discussed more in section 10.3 of chapter 10).[26]

9.2.3   *What UDP is and why QUIC is built on it*

QUIC is based on the *User Datagram Protocol (UPD)*, which is a light protocol compared with TCP, but is similarly built on top of Internet Protocol (IP). TCP implements reliability in IP for the network connection, including retransmission, congestion, and flow control. These features normally are good and necessary, but in HTTP/2, they introduce inefficiencies. These features aren't necessarily wanted at the network level under HTTP/2; therefore, they produce an unnecessary TCP HOL blocking issue.

UDP is basic compared with TCP. It has the concept of ports, similar to that of TCP, so several UDP-based services can run on the same computer. It also has an optional checksum so that the integrity of UDP packets can be checked. Except for those two features, there's not much to the protocol. Reliability, ordering, and congestion control don't exist, and if you want them, they have to be built by the application. If a UDP packet is lost, it won't automatically be resent. If a UDP packet arrives out of order, it's still seen by the higher-level application. UDP was originally used for applications that didn't need delivery guarantees (such as video, in which some frames could be dropped without too much loss in service). UDP is also perfect for a multiplexed protocol such as HTTP/2 if that higher-level protocol wants to implement better solutions to these problems than those available in TCP.

WHY NOT IMPROVE TCP?

The most obvious question is why not improve TCP? TCP is still innovating, and the problems could be engineered out by further improvements. The main drawback is the speed of implementation of any such improvements. TCP is such a core protocol that it's nearly always baked into operating systems, and although some changes can be made to configure it or some improvements can be made on the server side, operating-system upgrades are required to benefit from most TCP improvements. The problem isn't that operating systems can't innovate; it's the length of time required for those innovations to be widely deployed. TCP Fast Open is a prime example; it offers huge benefits, but isn't used yet by the vast majority of internet browsers or servers.

This slowness to innovate is exacerbated by the internet infrastructure, which makes certain assumptions about protocols such as TCP and reacts badly when those assumptions are broken. This problem is known as protocol *ossification*, whereby innovation is stifled because of these assumptions. By moving away from TCP, QUIC hopes to have greater freedom and fewer constraints.

---

[26] https://lists.w3.org/Archives/Public/ietf-http-wg/2018OctDec/0065.html

WHY NOT USE **SCTP**?

Instead of building a new transport protocol on top of UDP or waiting for innovations in TCP to become more widespread, QUIC could have used *Stream Control Transmission Protocol (SCTP)*.[27] This protocol shares many characteristics with QUIC, such as stream-based reliable messaging, but it already exists and has been an internet standard since 2007.

Unfortunately, existing as a standard isn't enough to ensure use, and adoption of SCTP is low, primarily because TCP has been good enough until now. Therefore, moving to SCTP is likely to take as long as upgrading TCP. Even after such a move, innovation in the protocol is likely to stall. QUIC aims to improve stream-level congestion control and other issues that affect the internet, such as HTTPS handshake, limited packet loss, and connection migration.

WHY NOT USE **IP** DIRECTLY?

Another option that the QUIC designers could have used was to build on IP, because the requirements of the Transport layer are light. IP is nothing but a source and destination IP address; everything else can be built on top of it.

But using IP directly has the same problems as using SCTP. The protocol would have to be implemented at operating-system level, because few applications get direct access to IP packets. Also, QUIC should be directed at a particular application, so it needs ports, which UDP has. Many clients can open separate HTTP connections over QUIC, such as to run Chrome and Firefox at the same time, and perhaps also an unrelated program that uses HTTP. Without this feature, some QUIC-controlling application would be required to read all QUIC packets and route them to each application as appropriate.

ADVANTAGES OF **UDP**

UDP is a basic protocol that's also implemented in the *kernel*. Anything built on top of it needs to be built in the Application layer, known as the *user space*. Being outside the kernel allows quick innovation by deploying the application on either side. Google uses QUIC in all its services when you use Chrome, so opening developer tools and navigating to a Google site shows you the current version of QUIC in use (version 43, at this writing), as shown in figure 9.19.

In the few short years that QUIC has been around, Google has created 43 versions of it.[28] As it did when deploying SPDY, Google was able to deploy changes to the main client used to browse the web (Chrome) and some of the most popular servers easily and then innovate without users noticing. As of 2017, an estimated 7% of the internet uses QUIC,[29] though this figure is likely to represent mostly Google sites.

---

[27] https://tools.ietf.org/html/rfc4960

[28] The version history is detailed in the source code: https://chromium.googlesource.com/chromium/src/+/master/net/third_party/quic/core/quic_versions.h.

[29] https://ai.google/research/pubs/pub46403

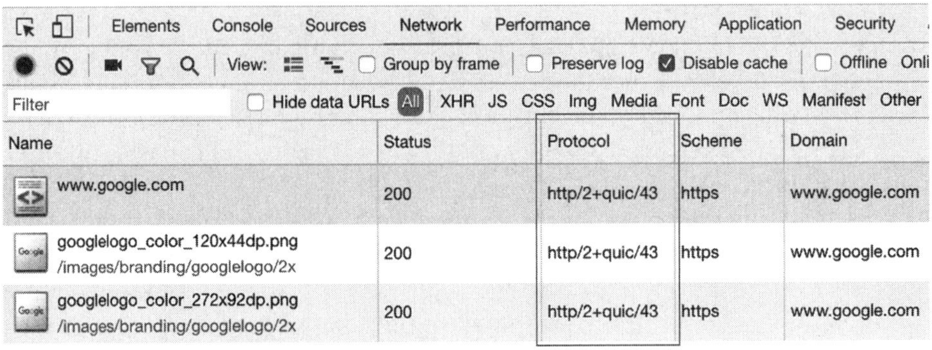

Figure 9.19   Viewing the deployed version of QUIC on www.google.com

Rolling out QUIC so quickly was possible only by using UDP rather than trying to force adoption or changes in existing protocols, which would take time and likely would be blocked by much of the current infrastructure of the internet. Using the light and limited UDP allowed Google to build and innovate the protocol as it saw fit, because it could control both sides of the connection.

UDP isn't without problems. It's a common protocol, but not as common as TCP. DNS works over UDP, for example, because it's a simple protocol that doesn't need the complications or slowness of TCP (though there are moves to allow DNS to work over HTTPS, as discussed in chapter 10). Other applications (such as real-time video streaming and online video games) also use UDP, so it's often supported by network infrastructure. TCP is far more common, however, and UDP is often blocked by firewalls and middleware traffic by default. In this case, Chrome gracefully falls back to HTTP/2 over TCP. This concern was a large one in the beginning, but experiments by Google showed that 93% of UDP traffic made it through, and that percentage has improved over time. Although some infrastructure blocks UDP traffic for HTTP (where port 443 is also used), the vast majority doesn't. UDP is also easy to enable if it becomes common (as it is for Google services, at least).

The other problem with UDP is that user space isn't always as efficient as the highly optimized kernel space. Early measures of QUIC show that servers use up to 3.5 times the CPU of equivalent TLS/TCP-based servers.[30] Although that use has been optimized to be only twice as much, the result still shows that UPD is a more expensive protocol and is likely to remain that way while it lives outside the kernel.

---

[30] https://dl.acm.org/citation.cfm?id=3098842

> ## Will QUIC always use UDP?
>
> In their original FAQ released when it launched QUIC,[a] Google stated, "We are hopeful that QUIC features will migrate into TCP and TLS if they prove effective."
>
> So perhaps UDP will be used for experimentation, and TCP will evolve with it at a slower pace. Will QUIC revert to TCP at some point? That question is difficult to answer, but my opinion is it'll be difficult to give up the freedom to evolve. The internet seems to be in a period of innovation at the transport layer, and it seems unlikely that protocol developers will reach a point where they're happy to stop innovating and settle down to a fixed, difficult-to-upgrade protocol.
>
> Also, QUIC is implementing fundamental changes compared with TCP, and these changes won't be easily adopted into TCP, even if the drive to do so existed.
>
> More likely, HTTP will continue to be available over both TCP (HTTP/2) and UDP (QUIC and HTTP/3), but the TCP implementation will lag UDP in terms of features and performance.
>
> ---
>
> [a] https://docs.google.com/document/d/1lmL9EF6qKrk7gbazY8bldvq3Pno2Xj_l_
>   YShP40GLQE/

9.2.4 Standardizing QUIC

QUIC started as a Google protocol and was announced publicly in June 2013.[31] Google evolved the protocol over the next two years, and in June 2015, the company submitted it to the Internet Engineering Task Force (IETF) as a proposed standard.[32] This submission occurred after Google's last standard (SPDY) was formally adopted as HTTP/2, so the timing was good; many people associated with that standardization were free to work on QUIC. A few months later, the IETF QUIC Working Group was established to work on standardizing the protocol.[33]

THE TWO QUICS: GQUIC AND IQUIC

Like SPDY, QUIC evolved under Google's stewardship while the standardization process worked through it. This evolution has led to two implementations at this writing: gQUIC (for Google QUIC) and iQUIC (for IETF QUIC). Google continues to run its production environment in gQUIC and continues to evolve and improve this protocol as it sees fit, without the need to get formal approval for each change. Like SPDY, gQUIC is expected to die out when iQUIC is formally standardized (expected to happen in early 2019), but for now, gQUIC is the only usable version of the protocol in production environments.

Only Chrome and Chromium-based browsers such as Opera implement QUIC (where it uses gQUIC), and gQUIC undergoes frequent change as the Google team

---

[31] https://blog.chromium.org/2013/06/experimenting-with-quic.html
[32] https://datatracker.ietf.org/doc/draft-tsvwg-quic-protocol/00/
[33] https://datatracker.ietf.org/wg/quic/about/

changes it.[34] On the server side, all the Google services support gQUIC. Other web-server implementations at this writing include Caddy[35] and LiteSpeed,[36] but because they're based on the evolving, nonstandardized gQUIC, they're subject to keeping up with Google changes and may fall behind and stop working with Chrome.[37]

DIFFERENCES BETWEEN gQUIC AND iQUIC

This topic is evolving as each protocol advances, but at this writing, one of the main differences between gQUIC and iQUIC is in the encryption layer. Google used a custom cryptography design, whereas iQUIC is using TLSv1.3.[38] This choice was made only because TLSv1.3 wasn't available when QUIC was invented. Google stated that it will replace its custom cryptography design with TLSv1.3 when it's formally approved,[39] which has now happened, so gQUIC and iQUIC will likely converge. A few other changes exist between the two protocols, which aren't compatible, but at a conceptual level, except for the use of TLSv1.3, they're similar.

THE QUIC STANDARDS

At this writing, there's no one QUIC standard, but six! Like HTTP/2, which is made up of two standards (HTTP/2 and HPACK), QUIC has separate standards for its main parts:

- *QUIC Invariants*[40]—The parts of QUIC, which shouldn't change in future versions
- *QUIC Transport*[41]—The core transport protocol
- *QUIC Recovery*[42]—Loss detection and congestion control
- *QUIC TLS*[43]—How TLS encryption is used in QUIC
- *HTTP/3*[44]—Heavily based on HTTP/2 with some changes
- *QUIC QPACK*[45]—Header compression for HTTP in QUIC

One more experimental document has been proposed: *QUIC Spinbit*[46] would add a single bit to be used for basic monitoring of encrypted QUIC connections. Two additional informational documents on using QUIC are available, for application developers[47] and for managing QUIC on the network.[48]

---

[34] See the Recent Changes by Version section of https://docs.google.com/document/d/1WJvyZflAO2pq77yOLbp9NsGjC1CHetAXV8I0fQe-B_U/.

[35] https://github.com/mholt/caddy/wiki/QUIC

[36] https://blog.litespeedtech.com/2017/07/11/litespeed-announces-quic-support/

[37] https://github.com/mholt/caddy/issues/2194

[38] https://tools.ietf.org/html/rfc8446

[39] https://docs.google.com/document/d/1g5nIXAIkN_Y-7XJW5K45IblHd_L2f5LTaDUDwvZ5L6g

[40] https://tools.ietf.org/html/draft-ietf-quic-invariants

[41] https://tools.ietf.org/html/draft-ietf-quic-transport

[42] https://tools.ietf.org/html/draft-ietf-quic-recovery

[43] https://tools.ietf.org/html/draft-ietf-quic-tls

[44] https://tools.ietf.org/html/draft-ietf-quic-http

[45] https://tools.ietf.org/html/draft-ietf-quic-qpack

[46] https://tools.ietf.org/html/draft-ietf-quic-spin-exp

[47] https://tools.ietf.org/html/draft-ietf-quic-applicability

[48] https://tools.ietf.org/html/draft-ietf-quic-manageability

The IEFT Working Group is working on these documents at this writing. Because the standard is still being worked on, these specifications (and even the number of them) are subject to change.

One important point to note is that QUIC is intended to be a general-purpose protocol; HTTP is only one use of it. Although HTTP currently is the main use case for QUIC and what the working group is concentrating on at present, the protocol is being designed with potential other use cases in mind.

9.2.5 Differences between HTTP/2 and QUIC

QUIC builds on HTTP/2, so many of the core concepts you've learned in this book will stand you in good stead when QUIC becomes a standard and use grows beyond Google servers and browsers. Some key differences exist, however, including the underlying UDP protocol. The following sections discuss other differences.

QUIC AND HTTPS

HTTPS is built into QUIC, and unlike HTTP/2, it doesn't make QUIC available for unencrypted HTTP connections. This choice was made for the same practical and ideological reasons as HTTP/2 being available only over HTTPS for web browsing (see chapter 3).

On the practical side, encrypting the data ensures that parties that are unfamiliar with the protocol won't unwittingly interfere with or make assumptions about the protocol. Although this situation may not seem to be a problem now (no infrastructure should be expecting HTTP traffic over UDP), it has already caused problems for QUIC, with middlebox vendors making assumptions that no longer held true as QUIC evolved.[49] As the protocol evolves, it will become even more important to prevent the ossification experienced under TCP, with assumptions being made by middleboxes inspecting TCP traffic. QUIC aims to encrypt as much as possible. A proposal to allow a single unencrypted bit to allow middleboxes to monitor traffic[50] was met with much consternation,[51] and at this writing, no firm conclusion has been reached (though the proposal is included as a working draft, as mentioned earlier in this chapter).

ESTABLISHING A QUIC CONNECTION

HTTP/2 established several methods to negotiate the HTTP/2 protocol, including ALPN, the `Upgrade` header, prior knowledge, and the Alt-Svc HTTP header or HTTP/2 frame. All these methods assume the use of TCP initially, however. Because QUIC is based on UDP, a web browser connecting to web servers has to start a connection on TCP and upgrade to QUIC.[52] This process introduces a dependency on HTTP over TCP and therefore negates one of the key benefits of QUIC (dramatically reduced connection establishment time). Alternatives include trying both TCP and UDP or accepting

---

[49] https://www.youtube.com/watch?v=BazWPeUGS8M&feature=youtu.be&t=2216

[50] https://datatracker.ietf.org/doc/draft-ietf-quic-spin-exp/

[51] https://news.ycombinator.com/item?id=16695816

[52] https://tools.ietf.org/html/draft-ietf-quic-http-12#section-2.1

the initial performance hit, perhaps remembering next time that the server uses QUIC. Regardless, the ALPN and Alt-Svc identifier h3 will be registered for HTTP/3 (note: this was originally hq for HTTP over QUIC before the HTTP/3 name was agreed upon). This identifier should be used only for the official iQUIC when it becomes standardized; current gQUIC implementations shouldn't use this reserved value.[53]

QPACK

HPACK, which is used for header compression, depends on the guaranteed nature of TCP to ensure that HTTP header frames are received in order, so that the dynamic table can be maintained correctly on both sides, as shown in figure 9.20.

HPACK static table

Index value	Header name	Header value
1	:authority	
2	:method	GET
3	:method	POST
4	:path	/
…	…	…
58	user-agent	
…	…	…
61	www-authenticate	

Request 1

Header	Header value
:method	GET
:authority	www.example.com
:path	/
user-agent	Chrome-69

Compressed request 1

Header	Header value
Indexed 2	
Literal index 24 with indexing	www.example.com
Indexed 4	
Literal index 56 with indexing	Chrome-69

Dynamic table after request 1

Index value	Header name	Header value
62	user-agent	Chrome-62
63	:authority	www.example.com

Request 2

Header	Header value
:method	GET
:authority	www.example.com
:path	/styles.css
user-agent	Chrome-69

Compressed request 2

Header	Header value
Indexed 2	
Indexed 63	
Literal index 4 without indexing	/styles.css
Indexed 62	

Dynamic table after request 2

Index value	Header name	Header value
62	user-agent	Chrome-62
63	:authority	www.example.com

Figure 9.20   HPACK compression example

---

[53] https://github.com/w3c/navigation-timing/issues/71

Request 2 uses header indices defined in request 1 (62 and 63). If part of request 1 is lost, so that the header can't be read in full, the state of the dynamic table can't be known, so request 2 can't be processed until the missing packets are received, as, otherwise, the incorrect references could be used. QUIC aims to remove the need for guaranteed in-order packet delivery at connection level to allow streams to be processed independently, but HPACK still requires this guarantee (at least for header frames), reintroducing HOL blocking, which is the very problem it's trying to solve.

HTTP/3, therefore, needed a variation on HPACK, which was called QPACK (for obvious reasons). This variation is complex and is still being defined at this writing, but it appears to introduce the concept of acknowledged headers. If a sender needs to use an unacknowledged header, it can use it (and risk being blocked on that stream) or can send the header with literals (preventing blocking at the cost of less efficient compression for that header value).

QPACK introduces a few other changes. A bit defines whether the static or dynamic table is used (rather than explicitly counting from 61, as per HPACK). Also, headers can be duplicated more easily and efficiently to allow key headers (such as `:authority` and `user-agent`) to remain near the top of the dynamic table and be transferred in fewer bits.

OTHER DIFFERENCES

There are a few other changes in the frames and streams used by QUIC.[54] Some of the Transport layer protocols' frames are removed from the HTTP/3 layer (such as `PING` and `WINDOW_UPDATE` frames) and moved to the core QUIC-Transport layer, which isn't HTTP-specific (which makes sense as these frames are likely to be used for non-HTTP protocols over QUIC). Also, the `CONTINUATION` frame, which was little used in HTTP/2, has been dropped from HTTP/3. There are also some frame formatting changes, but because the protocol is still evolving at this writing, I won't discuss them here. Conceptually, nearly all of HTTP/2 remains in one format or another, and readers who have made it this far will have a good grounding in QUIC and HTTP/3 when they're formally standardized and become available for client and server implementations.

9.2.6   *QUIC tools*

Because QUIC hasn't yet been standardized, only gQUIC is available in the wild, though many developers are working on iQUIC implementations.[55] Often, the best tool to use to see QUIC is Chrome when it's connected to a Google server. A net-export page similar to HTTP/2 (see section 4.3.1) is available. When you click a QUIC session, you see a screen like figure 9.21.

---

[54] https://github.com/quicwg/wg-materials/blob/master/interim-18-06/HTTP.pdf
[55] https://github.com/quicwg/base-drafts/wiki/Implementations

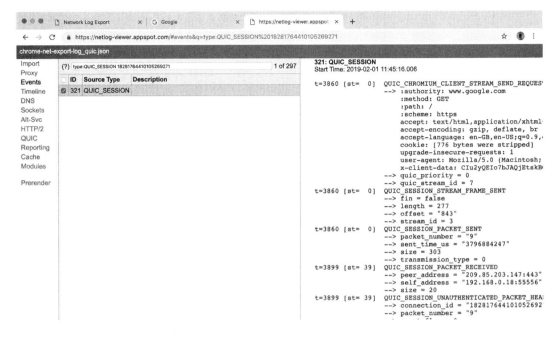

Figure 9.21   Viewing QUIC data from Chrome

Other tools, such as Wireshark, have some support for gQUIC, as shown in figure 9.22.

Because gQUIC isn't standardized and still being changed by Google, it needs to keep up with any changes Google makes. In my experience, you may find malformed packets or encrypted payloads that can't be read by non-Google tools for this reason.

9.2.7   *QUIC implementations*

The story is similar if you want to implement a QUIC server. Caddy had an implementation of gQUIC based on the QUIC implementation in the Go programming language, but that implementation has been turned off as of this writing in the current release version.[56] It's available through compiling Caddy from source code and should make it to the next release. The Go version[57] is usually kept up-to-date, so if you download the latest version, Chrome should be able to speak gQUIC to it. Similarly, LiteSpeed has had a QUIC implementation since June 2017[58] and has kept its implementation up-to-date, but the open source version doesn't support it yet, so it's not a great tool for experimenting with QUIC unless you're already using LiteSpeed. LiteSpeed also open sourced a QUIC client[59] that could be useful. More recently, Aka-

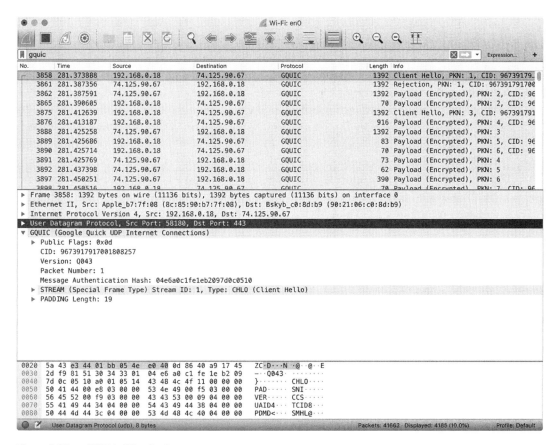

Figure 9.22 gQUIC in Wireshark

mai announced gQUIC support on its content delivery network platform in May 2018,[60] and in June 2018, Google announced gQUIC support for its Google Cloud Platform load balancer,[61] so those who use that platform get gQUIC straight from the horse's mouth, so to speak.

9.2.8   Should you use QUIC?

Unlike SPDY, gQUIC hasn't been taken up by much of the wider community, which seems unlikely to happen now that iQUIC is being standardized. At this point, it's difficult to recommend QUIC except when using the Google cloud platform. For anyone who wants to experiment with QUIC, Go probably is the best option, but it probably shouldn't be used in production for browsers. The browser implementation in Chrome

---

[60] https://community.akamai.com/customers/s/article/FAQ-QUIC-Native-Platform-Support-for-Media-Delivery-Products?language=en_US

[61] https://cloudplatform.googleblog.com/2018/06/Introducing-QUIC-support-for-HTTPS-load-balancing.html

is liable to change quite a bit, and Chrome switches off older versions of gQUIC in browsers quickly after rolling out new versions.

After iQUIC standardizes, I expect more implementations to crop up. There are fewer production implementations at this stage of standardization compared to SPDY. I suspect that the roll-out of QUIC and HTTP/3 will take longer than the roll-out of HTTP/2, as it's a much bigger change and because it uses UDP rather than TCP. QUIC is a protocol to watch in the future, and a few years after standardization, I expect developers to be where they are now with HTTP/2, with use rapidly increasing, eventually becoming the majority player on the web landscape. QUIC adoption for a lot of web traffic may happen quickly, with a few players (such as Google) and CDNs serving the majority of traffic, but the long tail of smaller companies and servers will likely remain on the older TCP and HTTP/2 (or even HTTP/1.1) stack for some time.

Summary

- The current HTTP network stack has several inefficiencies in the TCP and HTTPS layers.
- Because of TCP connection establishment and cautious congestion control, it takes time for a TCP connection to reach maximum capacity, and HTTPS handshaking adds more time.
- Innovations that resolve these inefficiencies exist, but on the TCP side in particular, they're slow to roll out.
- QUIC is a new protocol built on UDP.
- By using UDP, QUIC aims to innovate much faster than TCP can.
- QUIC builds on HTTP/2 and uses many of the same concepts with additional innovations.
- QUIC isn't intended for HTTP only; it may also be used for other protocols in the future.
- HTTP over QUIC will be called HTTP/3.
- QUIC is available in two versions: Google Quic (gQUIC), which is available in a limited fashion but isn't standardized, and IETF QUIC (iQUIC), which is currently being standardized.
- gQUIC is expected to be replaced by iQUIC when it's approved, much as SPDY replaced HTTP/2.

Where HTTP
goes from here

The HTTP/2 specification was formally approved in May 2015, nearly 20 years after HTTP/1.0 was introduced and quickly replaced by HTTP/1.1. During this time, the internet has become an integral part of everyone's life, and the fact that HTTP/1.1 has lasted so well speaks volumes about the protocol. For a long time, however, the protocol stalled, and attempts to move it forward failed,[1] were limited to more accurately documenting HTTP/1.1, or added limited new functionality through HTTP headers.

Now that HTTP/2 is here and rapidly being rolled out across the internet,[2] where does HTTP go from here? How has HTTP/2 fared in the real world? Are the major problems with HTTP now solved? Will it be 20 years before the next major

---

[1] https://www.w3.org/Protocols/HTTP-NG/Activity.html
[2] https://w3techs.com/technologies/details/ce-http2/all/all

317

innovation of the protocol, or is a new phase of innovation in the internet leading to a much greater rate of change? This chapter attempts to answer these questions and make some educated guesses about how HTTP will evolve.

10.1   Controversies of HTTP/2 and what it didn't fix

HTTP/2 wasn't without its controversies, and more than a few people expressed concerns throughout the standardization process, especially as it approached its conclusion and ratification. Many arguments were made, some more vocal than others.[3] Arguments were made that SPDY shouldn't be used as the basis of HTTP/2 and that the privacy issues with HTTP weren't resolved. Also, arguments were made for and against enforcing encryption in the protocol. I discuss these, and numerous other, points of controversy in the following sections.

   Many of the criticisms were discussed on the *HTTP Working Group (HTTP-WG)* mailing list of the Internet Engineering Task Force,[4] as well as by the wider internet community on sites such as HackerNews,[5, 6, 7] SlashDot,[8] and The Register.[9] Many counterarguments were made.

   Now that the protocol has had some time in the real world and the future of HTTP is being discussed, it's worth reexamining these arguments to see which are still true and what developers can learn from them while considering the next iteration of HTTP.

10.1.1   Arguments against SPDY

HTTP/2 was heavily based on the SPDY protocol, proved in the real world by Google. SPDY was a practical upgrade that could be implemented and deployed on the internet. The success of SPDY led the IETF to look at upgrading HTTP,[10] and although the IETF didn't commit to SPDY alone, that protocol was a likely basis for HTTP/2. Many people complained that due consideration wasn't given to what HTTP/2 should be and instead concentrated only on how SPDY could become that new version.

WAS SPDY THE ONLY DE-FACTO OPTION FOR HTTP/2?

The HTTP Working Group's charter[11] stated the following with regard to HTTP/2:

> *There is emerging implementation experience and interest in a protocol that retains the semantics of HTTP without the legacy of HTTP/1.x message framing and syntax, which have been identified as hampering performance and encouraging misuse of the underlying transport.*

---

[3] https://lists.w3.org/Archives/Public/ietf-http-wg/2015JanMar/0043.html
[4] https://lists.w3.org/Archives/Public/ietf-http-wg/
[5] https://news.ycombinator.com/item?id=8850059
[6] https://news.ycombinator.com/item?id=9022470
[7] https://news.ycombinator.com/item?id=9066379
[8] https://tech.slashdot.org/story/15/01/09/0118226/http2—the-ietf-is-phoning-it-in
[9] https://www.theregister.co.uk/2015/02/18/http2_specification_approved/
[10] https://lists.w3.org/Archives/Public/ietf-http-wg/2012JanMar/0098.html
[11] https://datatracker.ietf.org/wg/httpbis/charter/

The Working Group will produce a specification of a new expression of HTTP's current semantics in ordered, bi-directional streams. As with HTTP/1.x, the primary target transport is TCP, but it should be possible to use other transports.

Work will begin using draft-mbelshe-httpbis-spdy-00 as a starting point.

That statement left little doubt that SPDY was to form the basis of HTTP/2. Although many people were impressed by SPDY's success, and few doubted that it was a good improvement over HTTP/1, many people felt that the IETF should have taken a wider look at how HTTP could be improved overall rather than rubberstamping this design. An arbitrary two-year timeline was proposed,[12] and some people felt that meeting such a timeline enforced SPDY as the only viable option.

Two other proposals were initially considered: Microsoft's HTTP Speed and Mobility proposal[13] (based on SPDY and WebSockets[14]) and the Network Friendly HTTP Upgrade.[15] Both proposals were similar in many ways to SPDY (hardly surprising, given the parameters under which HTTP/2 was defined) and concentrated on adding a binary framing layer and HTTP header improvements.

SPDY proved to work in the wild, however, and not only at Google. Many common web servers and web browsers supported SPDY, and many sites had already moved to SPDY or were in the process of moving to it. Facebook presented an early analysis of all three proposals[16] that endorsed SPDY and rejected the other two alternatives. It made sense for SPDY to form the basis, though it was changed and improved by the HTTP/2 Working Group during the standardization process. HTTP/2 isn't SPDY and isn't wire-compatible with it, though it shares a lot of ground.

The main concern was that an opportunity had been missed to go beyond SPDY. SPDY was designed to address one major problem with HTTP/1—performance—and though it performed that task well, it didn't address other concerns about HTTP, such as cookies. Given that previous upgrades such as HTTP-NG had failed, in large part because the scope grew too large and there were no practical ways of introducing it into the wild, moving forward with the one practical implementation was hardly a bad thing. SPDY was the original impetus for upgrading HTTP, and if the next version of the protocol hadn't been heavily based on it, we'd likely still be on HTTP/1.1 today.

SPDY AND GOOGLE

Another area of concern was that SPDY was primarily the result of one company: Google. Whereas other websites small and large also used SPDY (including Yahoo!, Twitter, and Facebook), it was owned and defined by Google. Some people expressed concern that Google, already a powerful presence on the web, was pushing its own

---

[12] https://lists.w3.org/Archives/Public/ietf-http-wg/2012OctDec/0003.html

[13] https://tools.ietf.org/html/draft-montenegro-httpbis-speed-mobility

[14] https://blogs.msdn.microsoft.com/interoperability/2012/03/25/speed-and-mobility-an-approach-for-http-2-0-to-make-mobile-apps-and-the-web-faster/

[15] https://tools.ietf.org/html/draft-tarreau-httpbis-network-friendly

[16] https://lists.w3.org/Archives/Public/ietf-http-wg/2012JulSep/0251.html

protocol, and, therefore, its agenda on the larger web community. Some mistrust of Google is due to its dominance on the internet, as there's mistrust of all companies that have a large presence in their fields. This situation is especially true for Google, given that it makes much of its money through web advertising, which has privacy and tracking implications. HTTP/2 was notable for not trying to address the privacy problems that many people saw as a larger problem with the protocol. I don't believe that ignoring the privacy issues of HTTP was nefarious, however, and understand that Google saw performance as the priority to solve.

This argument, however, missed the key value of standardizing SPDY into HTTP/2: removing single-company dependency while allowing the web community at large and the primary internet standards community (IEFT) to review and improve the protocol. Google continues to be one of the main innovators on the internet and has created many other advances in web standards, some of which (such as QUIC; see chapter 9) are discussed in this book. Ignoring Google's innovations or trying to work around them seems churlish if those innovations are beneficial.

10.1.2 *Privacy issues and state in HTTP*

Another controversy for HTTP/2 was privacy, especially regarding HTTP cookies. Cookies are often cited as one of the biggest problems with HTTP, due to their security and privacy implications. HTTP was designed to be a stateless protocol, and in most ways it still is, even under HTTP/2. Any request you make to a server is, in theory, unrelated to any previous or future request.

The reality, however, is that modern applications and websites need state. When you add something to your basket while shopping Amazon, you don't want to have to keep adding it. When you log in to internet banking, you don't want to have to log in again for every subsequent action (at least, for a short period). Therefore, because HTTP offers no way to associate a request with other requests, there was a need to add state to the protocol, and because connections weren't always persisted or reused, it couldn't be done at a connection level.

Various methods can be used to tackle this state dilemma in HTTP. URLs could be added with session ID parameters (such as http://www.example.com?SESSIONID= 12345), but these parameters are ugly, confusing, and full of security risks due to sharing or bookmarking URLs with session IDs. HTTP cookies[17] were conceived as the answer. Cookies are small pieces of information stored on the browser, which are sent by the browser with every subsequent request. With cookies, it's possible to have a session identifier or other preference or setting that works with HTTP. HTTP cookies have had a bad name recently, but HTTP cookies are neither good nor bad, and the alternatives (such as URL parameters) often introduce bigger problems.

There are many reasons why HTTP cookies are seen as being bad, including the following:

---

[17] https://tools.ietf.org/html/rfc6265

- They allow tracking for advertising purposes (or worse!).
- They're insecure by default.
- They're sent with every request.

COOKIES AND THIRD-PARTY TRACKING

Cookies can be used not only by the site being loaded, but also by any resource loaded by a web browser for that site. So-called *third-party cookies* are possible when a website (such as www.example.com) loads content from an advertising site (such as adwords.google.com) and sets a cookie that can be used on other websites (such as www.example2.com). This cookie also references the third-party advertising website (adwords.google.com), as shown in figure 10.1.

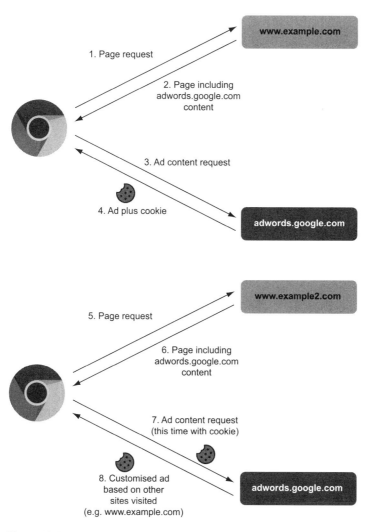

Figure 10.1 How third-party cookies allow tracking across sites

A relevant advertisement can be displayed on the subsequent website based on the user's browsing history, but often without that user's knowledge. As a result, the European Union (EU) implemented the so-called cookie law, under which websites had to inform users that they were using cookies, as shown in figure 10.2.

Figure 10.2   Cookie banner on the UK Government website

Web users, particularly in the EU, had to click to hide a rather pointless "This website is using cookies" message on every website they visited, because most websites were using cookies. An even stricter requirement in the General Data Protection Regulations (GDPR) came into effect in 2018 and has led to even bigger onscreen warnings about cookies. Many users see this warning as another pop-up window to click through to get to the content they want, often without realizing that the GDPR is pro-consumer legislation that aims to give back to consumers control of their data.

HTTP COOKIES AND SECURITY

Another problem is that HTTP cookies are insecure by default. Although options were added to make them more secure (such as Secure[18] and HttpOnly[19] flags), these options require programmers to set them explicitly when creating cookies. Even then, programmers can't always prevent those cookies from being overwritten by insecure cookies, so this solution is only a partial one. Studies at the time of this writing show that approximately 8% of cookies are set with these attributes,[20] showing that the vast majority of cookies use the insecure defaults.

This situation is bad because cookies that store session identifiers offer full access to an account, so getting a hold of a cookie is almost the same as having the username and password. For this reason, you'd think that cookies would be restricted (and they can be made restricted), but by default, they aren't.

Cookies for a site are sent on both HTTP and HTTPS requests, unless the Secure attribute is used when the cookie is created. Because of the performance cost of

---

[18] https://tools.ietf.org/html/rfc6265#section-5.2.5
[19] https://tools.ietf.org/html/rfc6265#section-5.2.6
[20] https://github.com/mikewest/http-state-tokens#a-problem

HTTPS (which for the most part isn't a problem anymore), only some login or check-out pages commonly used HTTPS, with the rest of the site available only in HTTP, but this arrangement exposes cookies that weren't explicitly set with the Secure attribute to being sent (and potentially read) over unsecured HTTP traffic. Similarly, any piece of JavaScript loaded on a page (such as the handy script that makes your page look good, adds a commenting system, or puts a cool widget on your page) has access to the cookies unless the HttpOnly flag is set when the cookie is created.

Even if you use all these protections, it's possible for the Secure, HttpOnly cookie to be overwritten by a malicious user who can fake an HTTP request. Cookie prefixes[21] have been proposed to prevent this problem by requiring, for example, a cookie with a name starting with __Secure to have the Secure attribute. Again, this solution requires buy-in from website owners (to use) and browsers (to enforce).

HTTP COOKIES ARE SENT WITH EVERY REQUEST

Cookies are sent with every subsequent request—a blessing in terms of simplicity, but a curse in many other ways. Although requests to your internet banking service to check your balance or move funds should require session information to be sent, requests for the logo or other static resources shouldn't need this information, yet the browser happily sends them anyway. This situation has security implications, especially for cross-site request forgery attacks,[22] with the risk of leaking information by sending unnecessary data with each request. A SameSite attribute[23] has been proposed to prevent cross-site requests that include cookies, but this attribute isn't a default and requires understanding to implement.

Other types of privacy tracking methods are often named cookies even if they aren't HTTP cookies. *Flash cookies,* which are implemented in Flash instead of HTTP, or *super cookies,* use other fingerprinting methods[24] to track users and can also be used to implement *zombie cookies,* which return even after cookies are cleared. All these variations further damage the reputation of cookies, especially as they circumvent any controls provided by the browser that allow users to manage cookies.

SHOULD HTTP/2 HAVE ADDRESSED THE PROBLEMS WITH HTTP COOKIES?

Although HTTP cookies are viewed as being negative because of their privacy and security implications, no viable alternative has been proposed. Cookies aren't inherently evil or dangerous; only the use of them can be. Alternatives that allow the addition of state to HTTP such as URL parameters and local storage[25] have similar flaws and give users less control, and they haven't been given the privacy and security oversight that cookies have.

---

[21] https://tools.ietf.org/html/draft-ietf-httpbis-rfc6265bis#section-4.1.3

[22] https://www.owasp.org/index.php/Cross-Site_Request_Forgery_(CSRF)

[23] https://tools.ietf.org/html/draft-ietf-httpbis-rfc6265bis#section-5.3.7

[24] https://nakedsecurity.sophos.com/2018/03/20/apple-burns-the-hsts-super-cookie/

[25] https://dev.to/rdegges/please-stop-using-local-storage-1i04

Some people say that HTTP/2 should have addressed this problem with state and implemented a more secure, less privacy-invasive solution. No one has come up with a better solution than cookies, despite frequent attempts to tackle the problem.[26] Any such solution would need to support traditional HTTP cookies as well or risk not gaining any traction. HTTP is stateless, and although HTTP/2 has added some concepts of state at the networking level (such as stream states and HPACK dynamic table state), at an application level it's still stateless. An HTTP message sent on one HTTP/2 connection may be slightly different from one sent on another HTTP/2 connection at a binary level (due to header compression, for example), but it's still the same stateless HTTP message to the higher-level application.

Some innovations in cookies have been made, as described earlier in this chapter, and maybe HTTP/2 could have enforced them rather than making them optional, as under HTTP/1. But enforcement would have created barriers to adoption, which is why the HTTP/2 charter expressed the desire to retain the semantics of HTTP/1 and change only the transport layer.

In the future, developers may want to implement a better state management system for HTTP than cookies. But there's no reason to hold back the next version of HTTP because all the problems with the current version can't be solved.

10.1.3 *HTTP and encryption*

Like state, encryption wasn't initially a design principle for HTTP; it was added after the fact with HTTPS. HTTPS wraps regular HTTP messages in an encrypted form before they're sent and unwraps them after they arrive, and for the most part, it works. Previously, there were concerns about the cost of SSL/TLS certificates and the performance of encryption and decryption, but those cost issues have mostly been engineered out with cheap (or even free)[27] certificates and as compute power has improved,[28] though the initial connection still incurs a performance penalty, as discussed in chapter 9.

SHOULD ALL OF HTTP BE ENCRYPTED?

The main concerns about HTTPS are the complexity of initial setup and management, the reliance on third-party certificate authorities (CAs) to provide recognized certificates,[29] and the fact it's not ubiquitous. The last point was a bone of contention while HTTP/2 was standardized. Many people felt that the next version of HTTP should be available only in a secure version (HTTPS) and that the unsecured HTTP world should be left in the past. Other people felt strongly that encryption was unnecessary in many cases and shouldn't be mandated in the protocol. Ironically, these people were often the same people who complained that HTTP/2 didn't improve privacy enough by addressing cookies.

---

[26] For example: https://github.com/mikewest/http-state-tokens
[27] https://letsencrypt.org/
[28] https://istlsfastyet.com/
[29] https://www.howtogeek.com/182425/5-serious-problems-with-https-and-ssl-security-on-the-web/

OPPORTUNISTIC ENCRYPTION

An alternative to full HTTPS encryption, which requires both encryption and authentication (through the use of third-party CAs), is *opportunistic encryption* for HTTP URLs. This technique encrypts the data in transport, but without any guarantees on authentication like the ones that HTTPS provides—that users are talking to the actual website rather than to someone pretending to be that website. Opportunistic encryption would be a step up from HTTP but not as strong as HTTPS; it could be deployed at protocol level, however, without the use of third-party CAs or any effort on the part of website owners.

HTTP/2 AND ENCRYPTION

In the end, after many arguments, no consensus was reached, and HTTP/2 was published with the ability to use both an encrypted (h2) and unencrypted (h2c) connection. The middle ground of using opportunistic encryption wasn't included.

The reality is a bit more one-sided. All web browsers (the primary clients of HTTP) decided to implement HTTP/2 only over HTTPS (h2), as discussed in chapter 3. This was done for ideological reasons (the main browser vendors stated their intention to move to an encrypted web)[30] and also for technical reasons; by using encrypted sessions, the new protocol could be introduced without any middleware internet networking infrastructure needing to know about this format. Microsoft was the only browser vendor that expressed interest in allowing unencrypted HTTP/2, but in the end, it shipped only the encrypted version, apparently after seeing interoperability issues when HTTP/2 wasn't used over HTTPS.

Firefox allows the use of the `Alt-Svc` header to fetch websites over alternative services, which has led to some vendors offering HTTP/2 for HTTP sites.[31] This method works for sites that have an HTTPS version but aren't ready to switch to it (such as to avoid mixed-content warnings). Firefox can use the `Alt-Svc` header to fetch the site over HTTPS (and HTTP/2) but present it as an HTTP site, which is opportunistic encryption with a twist.

Calls for HTTP/2 to be available only over HTTPS may have been premature. HTTPS use has jumped considerably over the past few years, but unfortunately, it's still far from universal. Chapter 6 stated that Firefox serves more than 70% of its web traffic over HTTPS, but that statistic is skewed by the larger players. When you look at the bigger picture, the numbers are less optimistic. The top 10 million websites still have slightly more than 40% of HTTPS use,[32] as shown in figure 10.3, though that figure also is trending upward. In 2015, when HTTP/2 was approved, only about 5% of sites used HTTPS by default.

Arguably, security (and performance, for that matter) is more important for larger sites, but there's still a way to go before HTTPS is a requirement for running a website.

---

[30] https://blog.mozilla.org/security/2015/04/30/deprecating-non-secure-http/ and https://blog.cloudflare.com/ opportunistic-encryption-bringing-http-2-to-the-unencrypted-web/

[31] https://blog.cloudflare.com/opportunistic-encryption-bringing-http-2-to-the-unencrypted-web/

[32] https://w3techs.com/technologies/details/ce-httpsdefault/all/all

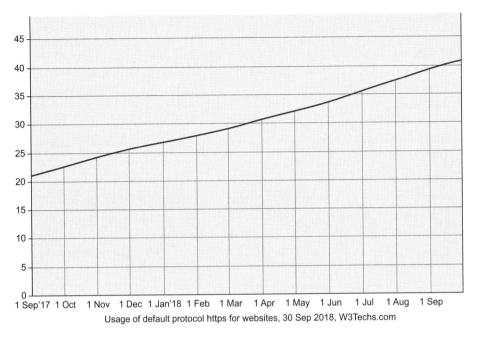

Usage of default protocol https for websites, 30 Sep 2018, W3Techs.com

Figure 10.3   HTTPS use on the top 10 million websites

For this reason alone, limiting HTTP/2 to HTTPS when it was standardized probably jumped the gun a little. There's a careful balance between using incentives to encourage adoption of good standards and adding another barrier to adoption.

The other use case to remember is internal, non-internet-facing traffic—both *intranet* sites and backend *application servers* fronted by a web server where HTTPS is offloaded. Intranet websites should be secured with HTTPS in the same way that external websites are, but this practice requires a level of commitment and infrastructure that isn't always present. The internet is only now moving to encryption, due in part to the risks of the open network it lives on. The closed internal network is often seen as being much less risky, and so encrypting intranet sites is often a lower priority. Use of HTTPS on intranet sites is likely to lag the internet HTTPS adoption for some time, especially for backend servers when a frontend web server is used to offload the HTTPS requirements. It's often seen as being unnecessary to encrypt between a web server and a backend application server, especially because of the extra effort required to manage HTTPS certificates on some application servers.

Internal-only sites often can't use commercial CAs (especially automated free CAs like Let's Encrypt) unless they expose themselves to the public internet or use a wild-card certificate, which is more expensive and not as easy to automate. Running an internal CA is often the answer, but internal CAs typically don't have the level of automation to allow automatic issuance and renewal of certificates. Finally, some web servers (particularly Java-based ones with a Java key store and IIS) require extra steps to install certificates, so even if you can automate certificate issuance, you need to look at how to automatically install and use certificates each time they approach expiration.

HTTP/2 isn't a requirement for a website, of course; you can view it as being an option for those who want speed gains, and this sort of advanced user is likely to be on HTTPS anyway. On intranet sites, latency shouldn't be as big an issue as on the public internet, so the benefits of moving to HTTP/2 are fewer. I showed in earlier chapters that there's no need to support HTTP/2 on backend servers at present as long as the edge server that visitors access is available over HTTP/2. Regardless, it makes little sense to try to invent a new version of the core protocol for the web when a large percentage of users would be unable to use it—up to 60% of the public internet at this writing and 95% when HTTP/2 was standardized. On private intranets, the percentages are likely to be much higher.

There's also the small matter of the growth of HTTP beyond websites and to the *Internet of Things (IoT)* domain, where certificate and HTTPS management are certainly more complicated. This area hasn't been sufficiently addressed even at this writing, though some proposals have been put forward, such as *HTTPS in the Local Network*.[33] Although IoT devices may not need the benefits of HTTP/2, it seems backward to force them to remain on HTTP/1 by insisting on encryption until this issue can be solved.

Ultimately, given the landscape when HTTP/2 was approved, it's not surprising that it wasn't standardized with an HTTPS-only requirement. Although there are good reasons to push for HTTPS as the norm, caution should be taken to push it in the right ways at the right time, and it was too early to do this for HTTP/2. QUIC decided to push for HTTPS only, which may make more sense because the landscape has changed in the three or four years between these two protocols, but many of the arguments for non-public-facing HTTP implementations still stand and haven't been adequately resolved.

10.1.4 Transport protocol issues

Other complaints were about the protocol itself at a transport level. Previously, HTTP didn't involve itself much at the transport layer other than saying that it was a stream of data preceded by a request (or response) line and HTTP headers. HTTP/2 changes this situation by introducing the binary framing layer.

LAYERING VIOLATIONS

As discussed way back in chapter 1, network protocols are often built in distinct layers. HTTP/2 stepped out of its traditional layer and took on many characteristics of TCP. Figure 10.4 shows the web stack and how it (roughly) maps to some of the OSI networking model layers, though there's some overlap. Layer 6, for example, doesn't map directly to any of these technologies, although HTTP allows communication of file formats.

---

[33] https://www.w3.org/community/httpslocal/

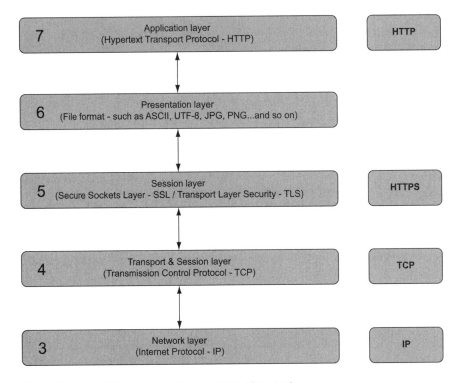

Figure 10.4   The OSI model and the web networking stack

HTTP/2 no longer maps only to the top Application layer, as HTTP/1 did; it manages many items traditionally considered to be the remit of the transport layer, such as multiplexing and flow control. Because HTTP/2 repeats rather than replaces the handling of these concepts in TCP, it's more like HTTP/2, supplementing what is traditionally thought of as HTTP. The new binary framing layer, therefore, spans several layers, as shown in figure 10.5.

Many people felt that this "layering violation" was a bad idea. Layering of protocols has allowed simpler implementations at each level and is generally seen as being a good thing. Although layering is never as clearly defined in the real world, and people can get too hung up on it (which isn't advisable),[34] the argument does have merit. In particular, the repetition of TCP concepts, while still being constrained by TCP limitations, leads to problems, as discussed in Chapter 9.

QUIC seeks to return a more defined layering between the application transport protocol (HTTP) and the network transport protocol (TCP and UDP), somewhat as shown in figure 10.6. In this model, HTTP/3 maps the HTTP frame types and shows how they should be used for HTTP traffic, but leaves the transport layer information

---

[34] https://tools.ietf.org/html/rfc3439#section-3

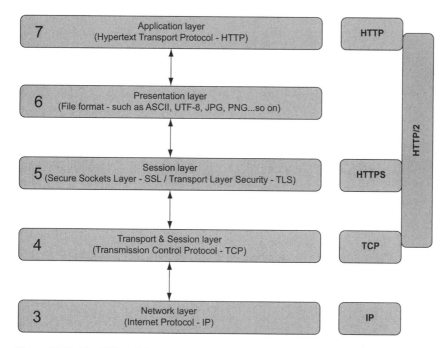

Figure 10.5 **The OSI model and the web networking stack with HTTP/2**

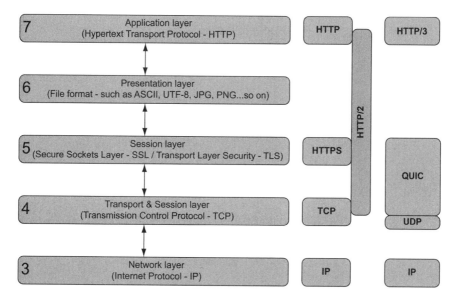

Figure 10.6 **The OSI model and the web networking stack with QUIC and HTTP/3**

(such as managing the multiplex streams) to QUIC itself. In other ways, QUIC arguably blurs the layers even more by merging parts of the TCP and HTTPS layers, but this arrangement perhaps makes sense. HTTPS was always mostly separate from HTTP, so it probably does belong more with the session and transport layers than the application layer.

TCP HOL BLOCKING

Chapter 9 explained how HTTP/2 multiplexing solved the HTTP head-of-line (HOL) blocking problem, but pushed it to the TCP level. Therefore, in certain lossy conditions, HTTP/2 is perhaps slower than HTTP/1. This problem was apparent from the start and was mentioned in the first HTTP/2 draft[35] (but removed from later drafts), which explained that the benefits of a single TCP connection outweigh the negative effects:

> *The use of multiple connections isn't without benefit, however. Because SPDY multiplexes multiple, independent streams onto a single stream, it creates a potential for head-of-line blocking problems at the transport level. In tests so far, the negative effects of head-of-line blocking (especially in the presence of packet loss) are outweighed by the benefits of compression and prioritization.*
>
> —HTTP/2 specification version 00

As you saw in chapter 9, QUIC aims to address this problem, but for most connections HTTP/2 was good enough. Holding out for the perfect solution would have needlessly delayed a useful upgrade, not to mention making the leap from HTTP/1.1 to QUIC and HTTP/3 a huge upgrade!

HTTP IS NO LONGER STATELESS

Another argument is that the protocol introduces state to core protocol HTTP for the first time. HTTP cookies, discussed earlier in this chapter, allow state to be transferred over HTTP but don't add state to the core protocol itself. The multiplexed nature of the protocol and stream IDs (chapter 4), the HTTP/2 state machine (chapter 7), and HPACK header compression (chapter 8) all add concepts of state to a previously stateless protocol without adding the one definition of state that HTTP users actually need: session state, as discussed in section 10.1.2. Although this choice was deliberate, it isn't as contradictory as it appears to be. Although state has been added to HTTP/2 at a connection level, at an overall HTTP level, it doesn't matter. The same HTTP request can still be made over a separate HTTP/2 connection, either in a parallel connection or later, and still conveys the same semantic meaning at the HTTP level. State is added to handle the multiplexed protocol and the header compression, but isn't used beyond those purposes. If the state gets muddled in any way, the connection can be torn down and reestablished, and the HTTP request can be attempted over the new connection with exactly the same issues and limitations as in HTTP (such as when it's safe to resend [idempotent]).[36] The stateful parts of HTTP/2 are no less or more

---

[35] https://tools.ietf.org/html/draft-ietf-httpbis-http2-00#section-4.3
[36] https://tools.ietf.org/html/rfc7231#section-4.2.2

important than the stateful parts of TCP that were always there. In fact, state has been added only to allow HTTP/2's streams to act more like TCP.

TOOLING FOR HTTP/2

The binary layering and the move from plain text also annoyed some people, as simple tools such as Telnet couldn't be used anymore; I used them in chapter 1 to show their use in HTTP. This complaint has little merit, however, because HTTPS encrypted connections suffer the same issues, and the toolset evolved to support HTTPS. Perhaps a better argument can be made that some HTTP-aware network devices (such as HTTP caches like Varnish) now need to implement more of HTTP to fully understand HTTP messages. But that argument hardly supports not evolving the protocol or letting infrastructure attempt to route HTTP traffic without fully understanding the details of the HTTP message.

IS HTTP/2 EVEN ABOUT IMPROVING HTTP?

Finally, most of the changes in HTTP/2 are at the transport level rather than what is traditionally thought of as HTTP level. Were enough improvements made at an HTTP level to warrant the HTTP/2 title, or should the protocol have been named HTTP/1.2, TCP/2, or HTTPS/2 instead? Further work in this area with QUIC seems to confirm that this layering perhaps shouldn't be considered to be part of HTTP. Ultimately, such an argument isn't productive. The new protocol contained breaking changes, so by any reasonable definition, it should be differentiated from the preceding version. Also, version numbers are cheap and used far too sparingly in many technology implementations. Moving to a version 2 after 20 years because it includes numerous breaking changes and isn't backward-compatible isn't unreasonable and in fact is the recommended path.

10.1.5 *HTTP/2 is far too complicated*

Another argument frequently put forward is that HTTP/2 is complicated. There's no doubt that this is the case, especially compared with the seemingly simple HTTP/1.1. The framing layer, its binary nature, and stateful protocol are tough concepts to get your head around compared with HTTP/1, let alone complex prioritization and header compression. You need a whole book to understand these concepts! Although that situation creates interesting work for technical authors, it's a real concern for the protocol. One of the main reasons for HTTP's success is its simplicity. The basic details of HTTP are in the one-page specification (if the page could be called a specification) of HTTP/0.9, and although HTTP/1.0 and 1.1 added to it, conceptually, HTTP is still easy to understand.

That isn't the whole story, however. Although HTTP/1.1 was easy for humans to understand, it was difficult to implement in software. All sorts of edge cases and extra processing are needed to ascertain the meaning of this unformatted, unstructured, text-based protocol. HTTP/2 seems to be a lot more complicated, but all those complexities can be automated fairly easily. This isn't to say that there won't be implementation errors or nuances in implementations that website developers won't need to work though (another reason for a book like this one), but that situation is true of any new technology and was especially true of HTTP/1. The complexities of HTTP/2, like those of HTTP/1, affect mostly low-level implementers such as web-browser and web-server developers, rather than higher-level web developers, and most of those low-level developers have argued that HTTP/2 is simpler to implement than HTTP/1.

Perhaps the main measure of whether complexity is an issue is the sheer number of implementations. The HTTP/2 home page lists more than 80 separate, active implementations.[37] Nearly all common web servers and web browsers support HTTP/2, and many supported it shortly after it went live. Although those implementations have had bugs and implementation issues, which may continue for some time, the speed of uptake suggests that these issues aren't serious problems. Note, however, that some parts of the specification (such as HTTP/2 push and prioritization) aren't present in every implementation because of the complexity involved.

It's hard not to argue that HTTP/2 is complex conceptually, which isn't as big a problem as you may think. In most cases, simplicity beats complexity (the Keep It Simple Stupid [KISS] principle), but HTTP/1 isn't as simple as it looks. Despite all the arguments that complexity doesn't matter, those who discover some obscure HTTP/2 implementation issue that takes them days to resolve will undoubtedly curse the complexity, and those of us who have been there and done that will sympathize!

10.1.6 *HTTP/2 is a stopgap*

HTTP/2 didn't attempt to resolve all the issues with HTTP. After years of stagnation, and with the proven use case of SPDY, the IETF HTTP-WG was keen to avoid getting stuck down rabbit holes, so many issues weren't fully resolved, and HTTP/2 was approved without consensus on some issues. This situation undoubtedly frustrated those who felt that some of the issues should have been resolved in HTTP/2, but the approach seems to be pragmatic.

HTTP/2 improved the performance of the protocol, removing some of the fundamental bottlenecks, so it was good to be launched and used in the real world. Nothing stops a future version of HTTP from further improving what this revision couldn't. In fact, additional ways to improve the protocol are being proposed through new settings and frame types.

QUIC aims to address some of the issues that HTTP/2 didn't resolve, such as TCP HOL blocking, more complete encryption, improved connection establishment, and connection migration. It could have taken another four years to incorporate these changes into HTTP/2, but there seemed to be no need for such a wait. When QUIC is standardized, it's likely to take longer to be implemented because it's even more complicated than HTTP/2. At a similar point in the standardization process, QUIC has fewer implementations than HTTP/2 did, probably due to the ease of migrating existing SPDY implementations to HTTP/2 implementations. But gQUIC

---

[37] https://github.com/http2/http2-spec/wiki/Implementations

hasn't been taken up in the same way. The move to UDP will also create challenges for an internet that has traditionally been almost completely TCP-based. Given that complexity, the fact that HTTP/2 is a stopgap and is making some progress is positive, not negative.

10.2 HTTP/2 in the real world

All those arguments were raised before HTTP/2 was formally standardized, but none was viewed as being serious enough to prevent or delay final standardization. Since then, HTTP/2 has been adopted quickly, with more than 30% of the top 10 million websites supporting it at this writing[38] (figure 10.7).

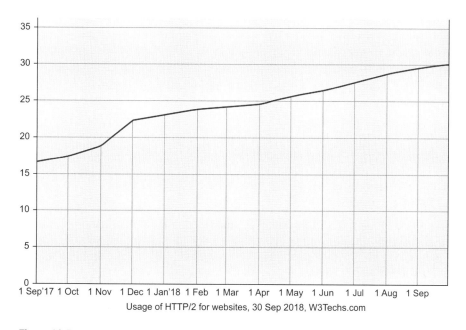

Usage of HTTP/2 for websites, 30 Sep 2018, W3Techs.com

Figure 10.7   HTTP/2 growth from September 2017 to September 2018

Even better, more than 55% of web traffic uses HTTP/2,[39] because large sites such as Google, YouTube, and Facebook support HTTP/2 and generate proportionally more traffic than smaller sites do. Based on these statistics, HTTP/2 has already proved to be a great success.

In addition, HTTP/2 has already been expanded, with new settings and frame types for enhancements to the protocol, such as *Alternative Services*,[40] the ORIGIN

---

[38] https://w3techs.com/technologies/details/ce-http2/all/all
[39] https://telemetry.mozilla.org/new-pipeline/dist.html#!cumulative=0&measure=HTTP_RESPONSE_VERSION
[40] https://tools.ietf.org/html/rfc7838

frame,[41] and *WebSockets over HTTP/2*.[42] Other proposals, such as *Cache Digests*,[43] seek to further extend HTTP/2, and many more suggestions are in the pipeline.

All in all, HTTP/2 has become a widespread part of the internet and continues to grow in both use and functionality. All the concerns discussed in this chapter, although not completely without merit, haven't proved to be big problems in real life.

Not everything has been a success, however. HTTP/2 push in particular has failed to make any particular impact so far, mostly due to the complexities of using it correctly (discussed in chapter 5), though lack of server-side support hasn't helped. Perhaps in hindsight, HTTP/2 push wasn't the panacea that some people thought it might be for performance. Maybe it should have been left out of the original HTTP/2 proposal and added as an optional frame later, if necessary. Some people are even calling for its removal from the specification, though that act seems to be a little premature.

Further, complications in implementing HTTP/2 show that HTTP/2 isn't as easy to switch on as you may like (not surprising for a major new protocol); neither is it a guaranteed performance boost. Most sites see performance improvements with a switch to HTTP/2, but some have seen a degradation in performance or haven't benefited as much as they thought they would. Getting the most out of any new technology takes good understanding. I expect HTTP/2 to continue to grow, at least until QUIC is released and becomes ubiquitous, but neither will replace HTTP/1 in many implementations any time soon, if at all.

10.3 *Future versions of HTTP/2 and what HTTP/3 or HTTP/4 may bring*

Now that HTTP/2 is out in the real world and use is growing, what can you expect from the next iteration of HTTP? Will it be HTTP/2.1 or HTTP/3?

10.3.1 *Is QUIC HTTP/3?*

QUIC takes the concepts of HTTP/2 to the next level, so is seen as the successor to HTTP/2, making it HTTP/3 by definition. In July 2018, one of the two chairs of the HTTP Working Group stated,[44] "I view QUIC as [HTTP/3] in most ways. . . hq is a logical successor to h2," and in November 2018, the HTTP Working Group agreed that the HTTP part of QUIC should be called HTTP/3 and move it (and QPACK) from the QUIC Working Group to the HTTP Working Group after publication.[45] The name HTTP/3 will not be formally registered until QUIC is ratified, so it is not guaranteed this is what HTTP/3 will be, but it is looking very likely at this writing.

QUIC is being positioned as a much larger, more generic Transport layer protocol however, intended for much more than HTTP, and HTTP/3 is only one use case for

---

[41] https://tools.ietf.org/html/rfc8336

[42] https://tools.ietf.org/html/rfc8441

[43] https://datatracker.ietf.org/doc/draft-ietf-httpbis-cache-digest/?include_text=1

[44] Patrick McManus (HTTP-WG co-chair), IETF 102 HTTPBIS meeting II (https://youtu.be/tQAfDmW0qlI?t=588)

[45] HTTP Working Group IETF 103 (https://youtu.be/uVf_yyMfIPQ?t=4956)

QUIC. In many ways, QUIC is the successor to TCP rather than HTTP/2, though some people take issue with the name TCP/2.[46] This is another reason the name HTTP/3 will be used to differentiate between the larger QUIC protocol and the HTTP part of this. This does not mean HTTP/2 is finished and will not evolve further, any more than HTTP/1.1 stopped being used once HTTP/2 came along—there are no plans to retire either HTTP/1.1 or HTTP/2, as many HTTP implementations will likely remain under TCP, using HTTP/2 or HTTP/1.1. However once QUIC becomes widely available, which will take some time, then HTTP/3 will represent the best version of HTTP and should be used where possible—hence the name.

10.3.2 *Evolving the HTTP binary protocol further*

Sidestepping the differences and future direction of the QUIC (h3) and TCP versions (h2/h2c), how should this new binary and multiplexed protocol be extended in the future?

In the past, HTTP headers enabled extension of the core HTTP protocol, depending on client and server use of these headers. HTTP/2 adds new abilities with new setting values and new frame types. The setting values[47] in particular allow new abilities to be discovered up front as the connection is established, which is much better than sending an HTTP header in the hope that the other side will understand it.

The protocol has been extended with the `ALTSVC`, `ORIGIN`, and (the proposed) `CACHE_DIGEST` frames. Other suggestions have been proposed, such as secondary certificates,[48] so a robust way exists of taking the protocol forward with new frame types.[49] There's no clear need for version numbering like HTTP/2.1 at this time, which is also why the HTTP Working Group dropped the minor version number and called the protocol HTTP/2 rather than HTTP/2.0.

10.3.3 *Evolving HTTP above the transport layer*

Although HTTP/2 and QUIC look at the lower-level transport layer of HTTP, what's being done at the higher level of HTTP? There's been a steady stream of new HTTP headers to control client and server behavior, but the HTTP semantics haven't changed much since HTTP/1.1, and HTTP/2 didn't bring any changes to this higher level.

As I mention earlier, one area of concern that keeps coming up is an alternative to HTTP cookies. So far, though, no proposal to replace them appears to be gaining traction.

Otherwise, HTTP has proved to be surprisingly robust at a higher level and has required clarification and tweaking rather than extension. Numerous extensions to HTTP are being worked on by the IETF Working Group,[50] the less-formal Web Platform

---

[46] https://github.com/HTTPWorkshop/workshop2016/blob/master/talks/quic.pdf
[47] https://www.iana.org/assignments/http2-parameters/http2-parameters.xhtml#settings
[48] https://tools.ietf.org/html/draft-ietf-httpbis-http2-secondary-certs
[49] https://www.iana.org/assignments/http2-parameters/http2-parameters.xhtml#frame-type
[50] https://github.com/httpwg/http-extensions

Incubator Community Group (WICG),[51] or as private outside interests—like SPDY and QUIC started as with Google. Most of these extensions can be implemented without fundamentally changing HTTP, instead using the extension methods already available (HTTP headers, HTTP/2 settings, or new HTTP/2 frame types).

NEW HTTP METHODS

What is perhaps most surprising is the fact that the main HTTP methods (GET, POST, PUT, DELETE, and so on) haven't been extended since HTTP/1.1. *Web Distributed Authoring and Versioning (WebDAV)*[52] introduced some new methods (including PROPFIND, COPY, and LOCK), and a few RFCs introduced others,[53] but the last one was registered in 2010 (BIND). On the whole, HTTP survives mostly on the four core methods introduced 20 years ago (mostly GET and POST, with some use of PUT and DELETE).

HTTP methods would be relatively easy to add, but there's been no need for them, and most requirements can be proxied through POST. The action variable in the following example conveys the necessary application-specific method (order this item), so doing the same in HTTP isn't necessary:

```
:method: POST
:path: /api/doaction

{
    "action": "order",
    "item": 12345,
.   "quantity": 1
}
```

Other HTTP implementations use HTTP headers to provide additional information, including the action to take:

```
:method: POST
:path: /api/doaction
action: order

{
    "item": 12345,
    "quantity": 1
}
```

After 20 years, I don't see an immediate desire for new HTTP methods. Although some new methods will undoubtedly be introduced in the coming years, I don't expect them to have a major impact beyond the applications for which they're introduced.

---

[51] https://www.w3.org/blog/2015/07/wicg/
[52] https://tools.ietf.org/html/rfc4918
[53] https://www.iana.org/assignments/http-methods/http-methods.xhtml

NEW HTTP HEADERS

The use of new HTTP headers has grown over time, and I expect it to continue to grow. HTTP/2 expressly forbids the use of new pseudoheader fields[54] that begin with a colon (`:method`, `:scheme`, `:authority`, `:path`, and `:status`), though these fields can be added with new specifications (such as the `:protocol` pseudoheader added with the Bootstrapping Websockets over HTTP/2 RFC).[55]

Other headers can be, and have been, added as applications see fit. The HTTP specification gives advice on considerations for new header fields,[56] showing that they're intended to be extended. There's an official registry of message headers[57] (including those used by HTTP), but applications use many headers without registering.

HTTP headers allow new functionality to be added easily, whether that functionality is additional information between the parties (such as "This response is using the XXX format"), hints (such as "FYI, I support the following formats"), authentication information (such as cookies), routing information ("This was forwarded from this IP address"), and much more. The applications at either end can act on the headers even if the HTTP infrastructure in between (such as an HTTP server or web browser) doesn't understand the header and blindly passes it on.

Using HTTP headers for security in particular has grown in the past few years. These headers are often sent from the website to the browser in responses as instructions to enable security features such as Content-Security-Policy (CSP)[58] and HTTP Strict-Transport-Security (HSTS).[59] Going the other way, there are proposals to provide more information to the server about the client (web browser or other), such as the Client Hints specification,[60] which should allow different content to be delivered based on what the client supports.

Many new headers will undoubtedly be added as HTTP use continues to grow and new features are added on the client and server sides. New HTTP headers haven't required and shouldn't require new versions of HTTP.

NEW FORMATS

Since the introduction of HTTP headers in HTTP/1.0, HTTP has supported different file formats and allowed different content encoding to be used by the HTTP protocol (like compression methods such as gzip and br). Again, HTTP is easy to extend in this area without the need for a new version number.

---

[54] https://httpwg.org/specs/rfc7540.html#PseudoHeaderFields

[55] https://tools.ietf.org/html/rfc8441

[56] https://tools.ietf.org/html/rfc7231#section-8.3

[57] https://www.iana.org/assignments/message-headers/message-headers.xhtml

[58] https://w3c.github.io/webappsec-csp/

[59] https://tools.ietf.org/html/rfc6797

[60] https://tools.ietf.org/html/draft-ietf-httpbis-client-hints

NEW STATUS CODES

HTTP status codes[61] are other ways of extending the functionality of HTTP. They don't require a new version, at least for new status codes within the rough groupings defined by the core HTTP specification,[62] as shown in table 10.1.

Table 10.1   HTTP status code groupings

Code	Type	Description
1xx	Informational	The request was received; the process is continuing.
2xx	Successful	The request was successfully received, understood, and accepted.
3xx	Redirection	Further action needs to be taken to complete the request.
4xx	Client Error	The request contains bad syntax or can't be fulfilled.
5xx	Server Error	The server failed to fulfill an apparently valid request.

HTTP status code 103,[63] for example, was introduced at the end of 2017 without requiring a new HTTP version. When 103 was first used, however, it revealed problems in many HTTP implementations (such as web browsers) that didn't expect to receive more than one HTTP response, due to the fact that 1XX informational responses hadn't been used much except under specific circumstances. Technically, this change was a nonbreaking change that didn't require a new version. But because it worked slightly differently from the existing status codes, many clients saw it as a breaking change until they corrected their implementations.

There's also the possibility of adding new categories (6XX, 7XX, 8XX, 9XX) without needing to extend the traditional three-digit response status code categories. In the 20 years that HTTP has been around, there's been no requirement to extend the status code categories, but extension may happen in the future; the scope is there.

10.3.4   *What would require a new HTTP version?*

Given all the ways of extending HTTP, it's perhaps unsurprising that the version of HTTP didn't change over the past 20 years. What would need to change to require a new version? The answer is that nobody knows at this point! The HTTP Working Group has brainstormed ideas,[64] and some areas of HTTP/2 weren't resolved (most of which are resolved under QUIC and HTTP/3). But at the moment, there's no firm idea about what the next version of HTTP beyond HTTP/3 might bring.

One thing is sure: like HTTP/2 and HTTP/3, the next major version needs to bring some breaking changes that aren't backward-compatible to warrant a major version-number upgrade. Whether these are changes in the wire format (as in HTTP/2),

---

[61] https://www.iana.org/assignments/http-status-codes/http-status-codes.xhtml#http-status-codes-1

[62] https://tools.ietf.org/html/rfc7231#section-6

[63] https://tools.ietf.org/html/rfc8297

[64] https://github.com/HTTPWorkshop/workshop2016/wiki/Future-of-HTTP#http3

changes in the underlying expectations of the transport (as in HTTP/3 moving to QUIC over UDP), or something else remains to be seen.

10.3.5 How future versions of HTTP might be introduced

The introduction of HTTP/2 provides more opportunities to extend the protocol and also introduces a path to introduce a new version with the use of ALPN or the other upgrade methods detailed in chapter 4. If a breaking change is required at some point, it should be easier to introduce, which ideally will lead to more innovation than has occurred over the past 20 years.

HTTP/3 also seeks to move away from TCP, and if it's successful, it opens new doors for moving to all-new underlying technologies in the future. Will developers use something other than TCP and UDP to deliver HTTP messages in the future? Will IP change? The answers are unclear, but this is a new age of advancement for internet protocols, and developers finally have the methods to introduce them.

10.4 HTTP as a more generic transport protocol

What about changes in HTTP use, and where might they lead the protocol in the future? The initial use case for HTTP was web pages, but there's a wide desire to use the popular HTTP beyond this use case. HTTP is a fairly easy protocol to understand and is widely supported, so many implementations and libraries exist. For HTTP/1.1, at least, it's easy to get a simple HTTP server or client with any software that allows reading or writing of a TCP channel (though as discussed earlier, the textual nature of HTTP/1.1 can lead to many problems that are initially concealed by this seeming simplicity).

HTTP is a protocol ripe for use beyond its original intention. In this ever-connected world, HTTP allows simple communication between separate systems in a standardized, well-understood way. From complex applications that use REST APIs or similar technology to IoT devices, HTTP is used within web applications and directly in nonweb applications.

Applications that want to use HTTP have several options:

- Use HTTP semantics and messages to deliver nonweb traffic.
- Use the HTTP/2 binary framing layer.
- Use HTTP to start another protocol.

I explore these options in the remainder of this chapter.

10.4.1 Using HTTP semantics and messages to deliver nonweb traffic

This method is the most common method of using HTTP outside web pages. API messages can be sent over HTTP in whatever format the client and server know to use (XML, JSON, or some proprietary format). Often, these HTTP-based APIs use common HTTP methods (GET, POST, PUT, and DELETE) to perform actions across services. The microservices architecture, for example, uses small independent services, for which HTTP is an excellent option. Other protocols can be modeled easily in HTTP (see the sidebar below).

DNS over HTTPS (DoH)

The Domain Name System (DNS) is a relatively simple protocol that usually involves fetching one record type from a central directory. Although DNS was traditionally its own proprietary format on a separate port (port 53), it could also be implemented with a simple `GET` request.

One reason to switch to HTTP is to use the encryption provided by HTTPS. In the past, DNS has been an unencrypted system, and attempts to add encryption led to complex protocols such as DNSSEC and DANE that have their own flaws and weaknesses, which are beyond the scope of this book. HTTPS is proven, secure (when configured correctly), and well supported. By putting an HTTPS interface on DNS, developers can solve the DNS encryption issue that they've argued about for decades. This system is known as DNS over HTTPS,[a] or DoH. (Try not to think of Homer Simpson.)

Developers could use TLS over the existing DNS messaging rather than move to HTTPS, and a separate specification exists for this purpose too,[b] but using HTTPS seems to be simpler to implement and allows the use of other benefits of HTTP. Those benefits include widely supported, proxy-friendliness use of HTTP/2 or QUIC in multiplex requests, and using HTTP/2 push to send back more than one response.

At this writing, Google[c] and Cloudflare[d] support DoH on the server side; Firefox has added support and started experimenting with it,[e] and has an excellent explanation of it.[f] The results are encouraging,[g] which shows the power of using HTTP for an application—even one that already has its own transfer protocol!

---

[a] https://tools.ietf.org/html/draft-ietf-doh-dns-over-https
[b] https://tools.ietf.org/html/rfc7858
[c] https://tools.ietf.org/html/rfc8484
[d] https://developers.cloudflare.com/1.1.1.1/dns-over-https/
[e] https://blog.nightly.mozilla.org/2018/06/01/improving-dns-privacy-in-firefox/
[f] https://hacks.mozilla.org/2018/05/a-cartoon-intro-to-dns-over-https/
[g] https://blog.nightly.mozilla.org/2018/08/28/firefox-nightly-secure-dns-experimental-results/

The IETF has published a specification, *On the Use of HTTP as a Substrate*,[65] which lists a set of recommendations and best practices to get the most out of using HTTP this way. Some applications diverge from the core HTTP specifications and use only part of the protocol, and this document doesn't attempt to forbid this divergence, but it points out why doing so may lose some of the benefits and learnings of using HTTP. HTTP has evolved the way it has for many reasons, some of which may not be immediately apparent, and this document tries to make these reasons clear for alternative users of the protocol.

---

[65] https://tools.ietf.org/html/rfc3205 but currently in the process of being upgraded so should soon be replaced by https://tools.ietf.org/html/draft-ietf-httpbis-bcp56bis

10.4.2 *Using the HTTP/2 binary framing layer*

The multiplexed binary framing layer introduces new options and reasons to use HTTP. Whereas HTTP may have been rejected due to its inefficiency in favor of direct TCP connections or perhaps WebSockets, HTTP/2 addresses many of these issues and becomes a contender. Google's new gRPC protocol (short for gRPC Remote Procedure Calls),[66] for example, uses the HTTP semantics and HTTP/2 binary framing layer[67] to implement a more efficient API based on protocol buffers,[68] rather than less efficient formats such as JSON. It's unlikely that Google would have chosen HTTP for this purpose without the improvements offered by HTTP/2.

Some people may want to use the HTTP/2 binary framing layer for non-HTTP traffic as a full duplex protocol rather than the client-initiated protocol that HTTP/2 is, with only constrained HTTP/2 push for server-to-client requests. At present, this feature isn't supported. Perhaps QUIC, being built from the ground up with use for other protocols in mind, is better suited to this purpose (or perhaps any such implementations will be back-ported into HTTP/2 over TCP). In the meantime, developers can use HTTP as a way to start another protocol, such as a true two-way protocol.

10.4.3 *Using HTTP to start another protocol*

The final option for using HTTP as a more generic protocol is to use HTTP at the start and then switch to another protocol. HTTP is a widely supported protocol and can be useful for masking other protocols to look like HTTP for wider network support, particularly over proxies and other intermediaries. The options include using the HTTP CONNECT method and upgrading the connection from HTTP (such as Web-Sockets). Both options start as HTTP and quickly diverge to another protocol. To outside observers, however, they may appear to be HTTP traffic.

HTTP CONNECT METHOD

Since HTTP/1.1, HTTP has had the CONNECT method, which allows the HTTP connection to be used as a proxy to tunnel through to an alternative server and port. This method is often used to allow an HTTP proxy to tunnel an HTTPS connection with syntax like this:

```
CONNECT example.com:443 HTTP/1.1
```

The syntax in HTTP/2 format is similar:

```
:method: CONNECT
:authority: example.com:443
```

---

[66] https://grpc.io/faq/
[67] https://github.com/grpc/grpc/blob/master/doc/PROTOCOL-HTTP2.md
[68] https://developers.google.com/protocol-buffers/docs/overview

This code creates a new connection from the HTTP server to example.com and allows messages to pass from the client to this server, as illustrated in figure 10.8.

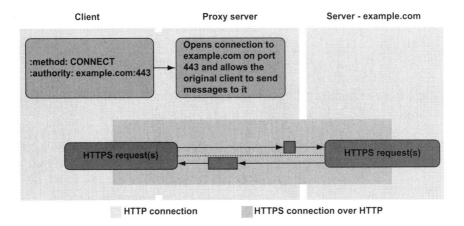

Figure 10.8 Using CONNECT to tunnel an HTTPS connection over an HTTP proxy connection

Note that this use of a proxy is separate from a man-in-the-middle proxy, which creates two separate HTTP connections. In this scenario, there's one HTTPS connection all the way through but over two TCP connections, so after the initial setup, it's as though the client were connecting directly to the end server.

The HTTPS connection isn't readable by the proxy because there's an end-to-end HTTPS connection, so this setup even allows HTTP/2 connections through an HTTP/1.1 proxy if the client and the server at either end support HTTP/2. See figure 10.9.

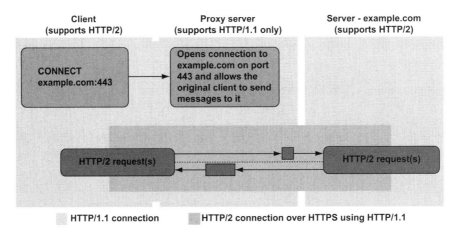

Figure 10.9 Using CONNECT to tunnel an HTTP/2 connection over an HTTP/1.1 proxy

The tunneled connection doesn't need to carry HTTP messages except for the initial message and can use any protocol. Figure 10.10 uses HTTP to connect to example.com on port 22 (used by SSH). Thereafter, any messages sent on this connection should be SSH instructions, not HTTP.

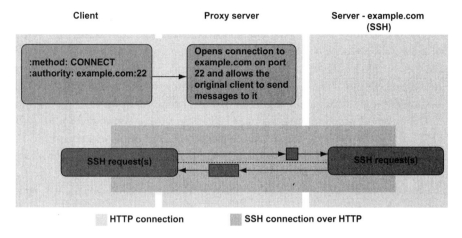

Figure 10.10 Using CONNECT to tunnel an SSH connection over an HTTP connection

Again, this setup can be useful to allow alternative protocols that might not be available directly from a system (assuming that they're available on the proxy server). All these examples show that HTTP can be used to allow other protocols to be introduced to environments. HTTP, therefore, can be used to introduce new protocols without worrying about networking infrastructure handling them, especially when HTTPS is used to hide the details from the proxy servers themselves. This process could be even more interesting over QUIC in moving from TCP to the lighter UDP protocol. At present, HTTP/3 doesn't support the CONNECT method without reverting to TCP, but proposals are already being raised for this purpose.[69] This setup requires a proxy server, and the client must be configured to connect via the proxy server.

UPGRADING THE CONNECTION FROM HTTP (SUCH AS WEBSOCKETS)

Yet another option is to use HTTP to start a connection and then upgrade that connection to an alternative protocol. WebSockets works this way. The handshake is illustrated below, using HTTP/1.1 syntax.

Client request (some other WebSockets header fields aren't included for simplicity's sake)

```
GET /application HTTP/1.1
Host: example.com
Upgrade: websocket
Connection: Upgrade
```

---

[69] https://tools.ietf.org/html/draft-pardue-httpbis-http-network-tunnelling

Server response

```
HTTP/1.1 101 Switching Protocols
Upgrade: websocket
Connection: Upgrade
```

Then the HTTP connection, still delivered over TCP ports 80 or 443, is converted to a WebSockets connection. WebSockets can be more efficient than HTTP for smaller messages, as there's no overhead for HTTP headers (which are much reduced in HTTP/2 thanks to HPACK but still have overhead), and it also allows full duplex communication. Using WebSockets can be useful, therefore, for real-time update applications such as chat, financial price applications, or sports updates.

This method isn't supported over HTTP/2 because it requires upgrading the whole HTTP connection, which doesn't make sense for a multiplexed connection in which only the stream should be upgraded. Therefore, WebSockets over HTTP/2 should use the CONNECT method[70] (with a slight variation to allow the protocol to be specified).

Client request (some WebSockets header fields aren't included for simplicity's sake)

```
:method = CONNECT
:protocol = websocket
:scheme = https
:path = /application
:authority = example.com
```

Server response

```
:status = 200
```

Thereafter, WebSockets data can be exchanged in either direction on that stream. The other HTTP/2 streams on that connection can continue to talk HTTP, other WebSockets communications, or even some other protocol that could be defined in a similar way. WebSockets opens many possibilities that the request-and-response nature of HTTP makes difficult. The same method could be used to switch to any other protocol, so I end this chapter with yet another way of using HTTP!

In this final chapter, I attempted to look to the future to see where HTTP goes from here. There's admittedly a lot of conjecture and little definitive information on what the next version of HTTP may look like, because at this stage, nobody knows. Two things you can be sure of are that HTTP will stay an important part of the internet and that its use will likely grow. At the beginning of chapter 1, I stated that "the World Wide Web was often incorrectly used interchangeably with the internet, [but] the continued rise of the Web, or at least HTTP which was created for it, may mean that soon it may not be as far off the truth as it once was." This chapter explains the various options that have allowed HTTP use to grow and that will continue to allow growth.

---

[70] https://tools.ietf.org/html/draft-ietf-httpbis-h2-websockets

By now, you should have a good understanding of HTTP/2 and the surrounding technologies. You've also discovered that although HTTP/2 offers many opportunities and potential speed improvements, it's not guaranteed to improve performance. Those who are looking for a quick fix may be somewhat dissatisfied, but HTTP/2 is still faster for most sites, and it's still in the early stages of use. QUIC and HTTP/3 will use the same concepts as HTTP/2 and take them to the next level. With the knowledge you've gained from this book, you should be well positioned to take advantage of QUIC. Even before QUIC comes along, there's still much to learn about HTTP/2 and how to use it best. But I hope that this book has given you the ability and interest to experiment further and watch the evolution of this interesting, widely used protocol. Happy experimenting!

Summary

- HTTP/2 had some controversies during the standardization process and a fair number of detractors. Those issues haven't hindered adoption of HTTP/2 in the real world and in most cases haven't proved to be as problematic as feared.
- HTTP/2 has been widely adopted in the real world and can already be considered a success for that reason.
- HTTP now consists of the HTTP/2 binary framing layer and the HTTP semantics that are sent via these frames.
- QUIC is seen as the natural successor to HTTP/2 and when this is published, the HTTP part of the QUIC specification will be called HTTP/3.
- HTTP has many methods for extending its use, and HTTP/2 adds more.
- HTTP can be used to transport other protocols.
- The future of HTTP looks bright!

appendix
Upgrading common
web servers to HTTP/2

This appendix covers upgrading some common web servers to enable HTTP/2 support in direct mode (A1) or as a reverse proxy (A2). The appendix is in no way intended to be a definitive reference for all web servers that support HTTP/2; you should refer to the documentation for your own web browser.

A.1   *Upgrading your web server to support HTTP/2*

In the following sections, I discuss how to install HTTP/2-compatible versions of common web servers and also how to configure them for HTTP/2 support. Note that this list is far from exhaustive and will change over time; it's meant to reflect some examples of setting up HTTP/2-compatible web servers. Each section repeats many steps, so skip to the section on the server you're most interested in.

> **Self-signed HTTPS certificates and certificate errors**
>
> Most of the examples in this appendix use self-signed SSL/TLS certificates (AKA HTTPS certificates). These certificates are supplied with the web server or created with an `openssl` command or the like. For a certificate to be recognized and trusted by a browser, it must be issued by a recognized certificate authority (CA). Each browser or operating system keeps a list of these CAs that it checks any certificates against. The dummy certificates that come with web servers (and those that you create in this appendix) aren't issued by a CA, and they're known as *self-signed certificates*. These certificates allow the site to run over HTTPS, but you get a warning from the browser because of the certificate. It's usually possible to skip through these errors and gain access to the site, but there are a few issues with using self-signed certificates even if you ignore the scary warning and the red padlock.

When clicking through certificate errors, however, Chrome and Opera don't use HTTP caching as a security feature,[a] so HTTP/2 push can't be used.

It's possible to add a self-signed certificate to the trust store of the computer so that the browser will recognize the certificate, display the green padlock, and resolve these errors. This technique is recommended for local development (via localhost). How you do it depends on your browser and operating system, but usually, double-clicking the certificate gives the option to do it.

If you're running a server with a real domain name, obtaining a real certificate is much preferred, because all browsers will recognize it without requiring an extra step to register it. This option isn't available for localhost or any nonprivate IP address (such as 127.0.0.1 or ::0).

***

[a]   https://bugs.chromium.org/p/chromium/issues/detail?id=103875#c8

A.1.1   *Apache*

Apache HTTP Server (AKA httpd) introduced HTTP/2 support in version 2.4.17 through the `mod_http2` module (called `mod_h2` when it was managed outside core Apache as a separate module).[1] It was marked as experimental until version 2.4.26. I recommend running the latest version of Apache (available at http://httpd.apache.org/), as this module was actively improved between those versions and beyond.

Apache supports HTTP/2 over HTTPS using ALPN and never implemented the older NPN method of negotiating SPDY/HTTP/2. Therefore, Apache requires at least OpenSSL 1.0.2 (or the equivalent) to enable HTTP/2 support even for browsers that still support NPN. Apache does allow HTTP/2 over plain-text HTTP connections (known as h2c), though this feature is of limited use because no browser supports it. Apache uses the nghttp2 HTTP/2 library as the basis of its HTTP/2 functionality and requires version 1.5.0 or later for full functionality at this writing.

HTTP/2 push is supported in Apache (covered in chapter 5). Apache also has the `mod_proxy_http2` module, which allows connections to backend systems over HTTP/2, though this module is still marked as experimental at this writing. As the "Do you need to speak HTTP/2 all the way through?" sidebar in chapter 3 discusses, speaking HTTP/2 all the way through to a backend connection often isn't necessary.

APACHE ON WINDOWS

Although using Apache on Windows on production systems perhaps isn't as common as it is on Linux, the Windows version is often used for development purposes. Compiling Apache from source for Windows is beyond the scope of this book. But if you're looking to get Apache up and running locally to experiment with HTTP/2, you can use prebuilt Windows versions from a variety of sources—unfortunately, not from Apache. Popular options for Windows versions include Apache Haus,[2] Apache

***

[1]   https://github.com/icing/mod_h2
[2]   https://www.apachehaus.com/cgi-bin/download.plx

Lounge,[3] and various XAMPP installations. These options are listed on the Apache website at http://httpd.apache.org/docs/current/platform/windows.html#down. You usually need to pick the type of Apache to use. Your choice depends on the following:

- *Which version of Visual C++ you want to use*—You may have to install Visual C++ Distributable (available from Microsoft). Be aware that Microsoft likes to refer to these distributables by year in some documentation and by version in other documentation. I list both types for ease of reference:
  - Visual Studio 2008: VC++ 9
  - Visual Studio 2010: VC++ 10
  - Visual Studio 2012: VC++ 11
  - Visual Studio 2013: VC++ 12
  - Visual Studio 2015: VC++ 14
  - Visual Studio 2017: VC++ 15

  You can see the versions you've installed in the Add or Remove Programs Control Panel of your Windows system. Installing a later version is easy, and I recommend choosing the latest version.
- *The architecture*—The choice is between 64-bit and 32-bit (aka x86). If you're running a 64-bit operating system, I recommend 64-bit Apache. If you're not running a 64-bit operating system, ask yourself why not, in this day and age! You can see the architecture by right-clicking My Computer (or My PC, in some versions) and choosing Properties from the contextual menu. In the resulting window, you should see the architecture listed below System Type.
- *The OpenSSL version*—You need 1.0.2 or later, but some sites offer builds against 1.1.0 or newer, and you may as well use the latest version where possible.

Here's how to install the Apache Haus packages with HTTP/2 support. Installing the others is similar:

1. Download the appropriate version, based on the preceding three choices, and unzip the folder to your preferred location (C:\Program Files\Apache\Apache24, for example).
2. Edit the conf\httpd.conf file to change this line

```
Define SRVROOT "/Apache24"
```

to your server location, for example

```
Define SRVROOT "C:\Program Files\Apache\Apache24"
```

Make sure that you don't end this line with a slash (C:\Program Files\Apache\Apache24\), and remember to include the path in quotes if it contains a space (such as Program Files).

---

[3] https://www.apachelounge.com/download/

3 Make sure that the mod_http2 module is activated and not commented out (with a hash before it):

```
LoadModule http2_module modules/mod_http2.so
```

4 Save the changes to httpd.conf, which may require administrator privileges if it's in the Program Files folder.

5 Start Apache, preferably from the command prompt so that you can see any errors:

```
cd "c:\Program Files\Apache\Apache24\bin"
httpd.exe
```

Following are some common problems that could prevent this command from working:

- An error message complains about a missing VCRUNTIME140.dll or a similar file, which indicates that you haven't installed the required Visual C++ redistributable, as discussed earlier in this appendix.
- The log file is set to read-only, so you see an error message about not being able to open the Error log. Right-click the C:\Program Files\Apache\Apache24\Logs folder, choose Properties from the contextual menu, and deselect the Read-Only option if it's selected.
- A Windows Firewall pop-up window asks you to give it access to this web server. You need to answer yes.
- An error message says you don't have permission to port 80 or port 443. Most likely, another program is using this port. Common culprits include World Wide Web Publishing Service (AKA IIS) in the Services application. (Stop this service and set it to Manual instead of Automatic if you don't use IIS, Skype, or another web server.)

6 When Apache is running, check http://localhost, where you should see the Apache Haus welcome page. Then try https://locahost, where you get a certificate error if you're using the default dummy certificate. Skip the certificate error, and you should see your page delivered over HTTP/2 if you open developer tools and add the Protocol column, as shown in figure A.1.

7 When you have Apache running manually and correctly, you can install it as a service to make stopping and starting easy and to have it start automatically when your machine restarts. Launch a command prompt as administrator, and run the following commands:

```
cd "c:\Program Files\Apache\Apache24\bin"
httpd.exe -k install
```

You should see the service on your Services screen. You can remove the service with the following code:

```
cd "c:\Program Files\Apache\Apache24\bin"
httpd.exe -k uninstall
```

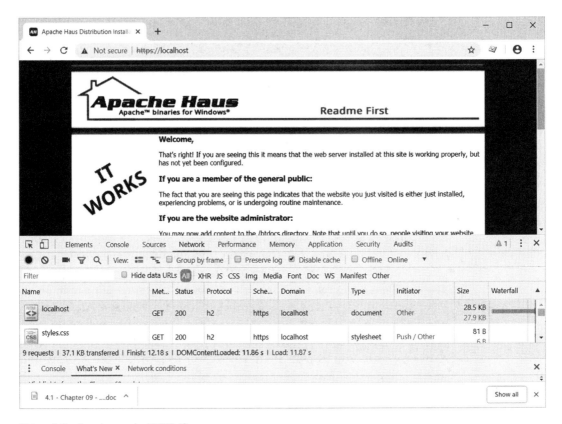

Figure A.1   Apache running HTTP/2

APACHE ON LINUX

Using HTTP/2 on Apache on Linux servers is more complicated, due to the older versions of Apache and the required software (discussed in chapter 3). You often have to install from source. I discuss one such method for Red Hat/CentOS in this section, but you need to adapt this method if you're running a different flavor of Linux.

Red Hat Enterprise Linux (RHEL) and CentOS, which it's based on, added OpenSSL 1.0.2 support in version 7.4, which solves one issue. But at this writing, they don't include a version of Apache with HTTP/2 support; instead, they include the older 2.4.6 version by default. Also, HTTP/2 isn't supported when Apache is using the prefork MPM (Multi-Processing Module),[4] which is often installed by default for compatibility reasons and can't be changed without recompiling.

Two semiofficial additional repos are available for Red Hat/CentOS:

- The Extra Packages for Enterprise Linux (EPEL) repo[5] is maintained by a Fedora special interest group and allows ease of installation of additional packages for

---

[4] https://serverfault.com/questions/383526/how-do-i-select-which-apache-mpm-to-use
[5] https://fedoraproject.org/wiki/EPEL

Red Hat/CentOS. Unfortunately, it doesn't include Apache, though it does include a more recent version of nghttp2 needed to enable HTTP/2 support in Apache.

- The Red Hat Software Collections (RHSCL) repo[6] is an officially maintained Red Hat repo that includes later versions of common software. Version 3.1 includes Apache 2.4.27, which includes HTTP/2 support provided that you're using RHEL/CentOS 7.4 or later. This repo installs an additional version of Apache (apache24) in a separate location (/opt/rh/httpd24/) with different configuration files and locations from normal, so it can take some getting used to. Also, because HTTP/2 is in active development, additional developments have occurred since version 2.4.27. These collections give you a semi-supported version, but may not be ideal, because they may be running older versions.

To get the latest version, you probably need to install from an unofficial location or install from source code. Neither method is ideal or to be chosen without careful consideration (see chapter 3).

With those warnings dispensed, and assuming that you still want to download from source, I'll show you how. The exact procedure depends on the version of RHEL/CentOS you're using. For versions before 7.4, you also have to install OpenSSL from source, as version 1.0.2 with ALPN support wasn't available. For 7.4 and later, some of the steps are easier because you can use the default version of OpenSSL:

1 Install all the dependencies required:

```
sudo yum -y install wget
sudo yum -y install perl
sudo yum -y install zlib-devel
sudo yum -y install gcc
sudo yum -y install pcre-devel
sudo yum -y install expat-devel
sudo yum -y install epel-release
```

2 Set up a directory for the software:

```
cd /tmp
mkdir sources
cd sources
```

For OpenSSL, you have two choices.

If you're using RHEL/CentOS 7.4 or later, you can use the packaged version of OpenSSL, which includes ALPN support:

```
sudo yum -y install openssl-devel
```

---

[6]　https://developers.redhat.com/products/softwarecollections/overview/

If you're using an older version or want the latest OpenSSL, you have to install it from source:

```
#Get it from http://openssl.org/source/
#For example:
wget https://www.openssl.org/source/openssl-1.1.1a.tar.gz
wget https://www.openssl.org/source/openssl-1.1.1a.tar.gz.asc
#Verify the package after download
gpg --verify openssl-1.1.1a.tar.gz.asc
#If you get a "Can't check signature: No public key" error
#then get the appropriate public key and verify again.
#For example:
gpg --recv-keys 0E604491
gpg --verify openssl-1.1.1a.tar.gz.asc
#Note you will see a WARNING that the key isn't certified
#with a trusted signature. This is expected and isn't covered here.
#Extract the file and compile it:
tar -zxvf openssl-1.1.1a.tar.gz
cd openssl-1.1.1a
./config shared zlib-dynamic --prefix=/usr/local/ssl
make
sudo make install
cd ..
```

3   Install nghttp2. Again, you can use the packaged version:

```
sudo yum install -y libnghttp2-devel
```

This version works for both RHEL/CentOS 6 and 7. If you want to get the latest version, because it has features you want to use, install from source (but note that no PGP key is included):

```
#Download and install nghttp2 (needed for mod_http2).
#Get it from https://nghttp2.org/
#Latest version here: https://github.com/nghttp2/nghttp2/releases/
#For example:
wget https://github.com/nghttp2/nghttp2/releases/download/v1.34.0/
nghttp2-1.34.0.tar.gz
tar -zxvf nghttp2-1.34.0.tar.gz
cd nghttp2-1.34.0
./configure
make
sudo make install
cd ..
```

4   Next, grab the signature keys needed to verify the Apache download:

```
#Download and install PGP keys used by Apache
wget https://www.apache.org/dist/httpd/KEYS
gpg --import KEYS
wget https://people.apache.org/keys/group/apr.asc
gpg --import apr.asc
```

5 Now you need to install the apr and apr-util development libraries. If you're using RHEL/CentOS 7.4 and the packaged OpenSSL (1.0.2), you can use the packaged versions:

```
sudo yum -y install apr-devel
sudo yum -y install apr-util-devel
```

If you want to use Openssl 1.1.0 or above or are using a version of RHEL/CentOS before 7.4, you should install from source:

```
#Download and install latest apr
#Note if using openssl 1.1.0 or above then need to be on APR 1.6 or above
#Get it from http://apr.apache.org/
#For example:
wget http://mirrors.whoishostingthis.com/apache/apr/apr-1.6.5.tar.gz
wget https://www.apache.org/dist/apr/apr-1.6.5.tar.gz.asc
#Verify the package after download
gpg --verify apr-1.6.5.tar.gz.asc
#Note you will see a WARNING that the key isn't certified
#with a trusted signature. This is expected.
#Install the package:
tar -zxvf apr-1.6.5.tar.gz
cd apr-1.6.5
./configure
make
sudo make install
cd ..


#Download and install latest apr-util
#Note if using openssl 1.1.0 then need to be on APR-UTIL 1.6 or above
#Get it from http://apr.apache.org/
#For example:
wget http://mirrors.whoishostingthis.com/apache/apr/apr-util-1.6.1.tar.gz
wget https://www.apache.org/dist/apr/apr-util-1.6.1.tar.gz.asc
#Verify the package after download:
gpg --verify apr-util-1.6.1.tar.gz.asc
#Note you will see a WARNING that the key isn't certified
#with a trusted signature. This is expected.
tar -zxvf apr-util-1.6.1.tar.gz
cd apr-util-1.6.1
./configure --with-apr=/usr/local/apr
make
sudo make install
cd ..
```

6 Finally, install Apache:

```
#Download and install apache
#For example:
wget http://mirrors.whoishostingthis.com/apache/httpd/httpd-
2.4.37.tar.gz
wget https://www.apache.org/dist/httpd/httpd-2.4.37.tar.gz.asc
#Verify the package after download:
```

```
gpg --verify httpd-2.4.37.tar.gz.asc
#Note you will see a WARNING that the key isn't certified
#with a trusted signature. This is expected.
#Extract the source code
tar -zxvf httpd-2.4.37.tar.gz
cd httpd-2.4.37
```

7 This step depends on whether you compiled openssl, nghttp, apr, and apr-util
   in the preceding steps. If you're using the system-installed versions of all these
   libraries, you can compile Apache as follows:

```
./configure --enable-ssl --enable-so --enable-http2
make
sudo make install
cd ..
```

If you used a local apr, apr-util, and openssl, you need to do the following to
use those versions:

```
./configure --with-ssl=/usr/local/ssl \
  --with-apr=/usr/local/apr/bin/apr-1-config \
  --with-apr-util=/usr/local/apr/bin/apu-1-config \
  --enable-ssl --enable-so --enable-http2make
sudo make install
cd ..
```

This code should install Apache to /usr/local/apache2.

8 Start Apache to see whether it works with basic HTTP:

```
sudo /usr/local/apache2/bin/apachectl -k graceful
```

If all is well, you should be able to visit your site over HTTP and see the default
"It works" page.

Getting HTTP/2 working requires a few more steps.

9 If you compiled OpenSSL or nghttp2, you need to edit the envvars file in the
   bin directory to load the paths for the local installations. If you're using the standard installs because you're using 7.4, skip to the next step:

```
if test "x$LD_LIBRARY_PATH" != "x" ; then
    LD_LIBRARY_PATH="/usr/local/apache2/lib:/usr/local/lib/:
    /usr/local/ssl/lib:$LD_LIBRARY_PATH"
else
    LD_LIBRARY_PATH="/usr/local/apache2/lib:/usr/local/lib/:
    /usr/local/ssl/lib"
fi
```

10 Uncomment the following modules from your httpd.conf file to load the SSL
    and HTTP modules, as well as the socache module required by SSL:

```
LoadModule socache_shmcb_module modules/mod_socache_shmcb.so
LoadModule ssl_module modules/mod_ssl.so
LoadModule http2_module modules/mod_http2.so
```

11 Add this line to include the SSL config:

```
Include conf/extra/httpd-ssl.conf
```

12 Add this line to show that the server prefers HTTP/2 (h2) first and then HTTP/1 and to enable logging:

```
<IfModule http2_module>
    Protocols h2 http/1.1
    LogLevel http2:info
</IfModule>
```

You can also add h2c to the Protocols line if you want to enable HTTP/2 over HTTP (and not require HTTPS), but this feature isn't supported by any browser and is of limited use.

13 Install an HTTPS certificate. Obtaining a certificate is beyond the scope of this book, so I show you how to use OpenSSL to generate a basic self-signed certificate. The browser won't recognize this certificate, but it'll work for some basic tests:

```
#Note the openssl command I'll use needs to be run as root
sudo su -
cd /usr/local/apache2/conf
openssl req \
    -newkey rsa:2048 \
    -x509 \
    -nodes \
    -keyout server.key \
    -new \
    -out server.crt \
    -subj /CN=server.domain.tld \
    -reqexts SAN \
    -extensions SAN \
    -config <(cat /etc/pki/tls/openssl.cnf \
        <(printf '[SAN]\nsubjectAltName=DNS:server.domain.tld')) \
    -sha256 \
    -days 3650
```

You should enter a correct subject and SAN for your server (shown as server.domain.tld in two places in the preceding code), but as the certificate won't be recognized anyway, this information isn't too important.

The default Apache config (in conf/extra/httpd-ssl.conf) expects the certificates to be called server.key and server.crt, but change the names as appropriate if you're using nondefault config.

14 Stop and restart Apache to pick up the new config. A graceful restart, which you'd normally do, isn't sufficient if you changed the envvars file in step 9:

```
/usr/local/apache2/bin/apachectl -k stop
```

Run the following command to ensure that all httpd processes have stopped:

```
ps -ef | grep httpd
```

Restart with the following command:

```
/usr/local/apache2/bin/apachectl -k graceful
```

15 Visit the site over HTTPS, and ignore the certificate error if you're using the self-signed test certificate from step 13 instead of a real certificate. You should see the page loaded over HTTP/2 (h2), similar to figure A.1, by opening developer tools and adding the Protocol column.

APACHE ON MACOS

Installing Apache on macOS is similar to installing it on Linux. First, check the installed version. The example commands are for macOS Mojave 10.14:

```
$ httpd -V
Server version: Apache/2.4.34 (Unix)
Server built:   Aug 17 2018 16:29:43
Server's Module Magic Number: 20120211:79
Server loaded:  APR 1.5.2, APR-UTIL 1.5.4
Compiled using: APR 1.5.2, APR-UTIL 1.5.4
Architecture:   64-bit
Server MPM:     prefork
  threaded:     no
    forked:     yes (variable process count)
```

This initially looks promising; you're using a recent version of Apache that has HTTP/2 support. You can see, however, that Apache has been compiled with the prefork version of Apache, which doesn't support HTTP/2. You have two options:

- Install from another package manager, such as Homebrew.[7]
- Install from source.

Neither option is ideal (see chapter 3).

Installing via Homebrew is simple and involves two commands:

```
/usr/bin/ruby -e "$(curl -fsSL https://raw.githubusercontent.com/Homebrew/
    install/master/install)"
```

```
brew install httpd
```

To check it, start Apache:

```
brew services restart httpd
```

Homebrew makes Apache available over ports 8080 and 8443 rather than the usual 80 and 443, so visit http://localhost:8080/ to see your new web server.

---

[7] https://brew.sh/

Configuring HTTP/2 requires editing the main configuration file

```
/usr/local/etc/httpd/httpd.conf
```

and making the following changes

1 Switch from prefork MPM to event MPM:

```
LoadModule mpm_event_module lib/httpd/modules/mod_mpm_event.so
#LoadModule mpm_prefork_module lib/httpd/modules/mod_mpm_prefork.so
```

2 Uncomment the following modules:

```
LoadModule socache_shmcb_module lib/httpd/modules/mod_socache_shmcb.so
LoadModule ssl_module lib/httpd/modules/mod_ssl.so
LoadModule http2_module lib/httpd/modules/mod_http2.so
```

3 Provide a server name (such as localhost):

```
#ServerName www.example.com:8080
ServerName localhost
```

4 Add the following config at the bottom:

```
<IfModule http2_module>
    Protocols h2 http/1.1
    LogLevel http2:info
</IfModule>
```

5 Set up an HTTPS certificate:

```
#Note the openssl command I'll use needs to be run as root
sudo su -
cd /usr/local/etc/httpd
cat /System/Library/OpenSSL/openssl.cnf > /tmp/openssl.cnf
echo '[SAN]\nsubjectAltName=DNS:localhost' >> /tmp/openssl.cnf
openssl req \
    -newkey rsa:2048 \
    -x509 \
    -nodes \
    -keyout server.key \
    -new \
    -out server.crt \
    -subj /CN=localhost \
    -reqexts SAN \
    -extensions SAN \
    -config /tmp/openssl.cnf \
    -sha256 \
    -days 3650
```

6 You should be good to restart Apache:

```
brew services restart httpd
```

Check https://localhost:8443/, and you should see the page served over HTTP/2.

Downloading from source is a little more convoluted and similar to the Linux setup:

1 Set up a directory for the software:

```
cd /tmp
mkdir sources
cd sources
```

2 Install the latest OpenSSL (or LibreSSL, if you prefer):

```
#Get it from http://openssl.org/source/
#For example:
curl -O https://www.openssl.org/source/openssl-1.1.1a.tar.gz
curl -O https://www.openssl.org/source/openssl-1.1.1a.tar.gz.sha256
#Verify the package after download by comparing these two values:
openssl dgst -sha256 openssl-1.1.1a.tar.gz
cat openssl-1.1.1a.tar.gz.sha256
#Extract the file and compile it:
tar -zxvf openssl-1.1.1a.tar.gz
cd openssl-1.1.1a
./config shared zlib-dynamic --prefix=/usr/local/ssl
make
sudo make install
cd ..
```

3 Install the nghttp2 module:

```
#Download and install nghttp2 (needed for mod_http2).
#Get it from https://nghttp2.org/
#Latest version here: https://github.com/nghttp2/nghttp2/releases/
#For example:
curl -O -L https://github.com/nghttp2/nghttp2/releases/download/v1.33.0/
nghttp2-1.33.0.tar.gz
tar -zxvf nghttp2-1.33.0.tar.gz
cd nghttp2-1.33.0
./configure
make
sudo make install
cd ..
```

4 Get apr, apr-util, and PCRE:

```
#Download and install latest apr
#Note if using openssl 1.1.0 then need to be on APR 1.6 or above
#Get it from http://apr.apache.org/
#For example:
curl -O http://mirrors.whoishostingthis.com/apache/apr/apr-1.6.5.tar.gz
curl -O https://www.apache.org/dist/apr/apr-1.6.5.tar.gz.sha256
#Verify the package after download
cat apr-1.6.5.tar.gz.sha256
openssl dgst -sha256 apr-1.6.5.tar.gz
#Install the package:
tar -zxvf apr-1.6.5.tar.gz
cd apr-1.6.5
./configure
```

```
make
sudo make install
cd ..

#Download and install latest apr-util
#Note if using openssl 1.1.0 then need to be on APR-UTIL 1.6 or above
#Get it from http://apr.apache.org/
#For example:
curl -O http://mirrors.whoishostingthis.com/apache/apr/
apr-util-1.6.1.tar.gz
curl -O https://www.apache.org/dist/apr/apr-util-1.6.1.tar.gz.sha256
#Verify the package after download:
cat apr-util-1.6.1.tar.gz.sha256
openssl dgst -sha256 apr-util-1.6.1.tar.gz
#Install the package:
tar -zxvf apr-util-1.6.1.tar.gz
cd apr-util-1.6.1
./configure --with-apr=/usr/local/apr
make
sudo make install
cd ..

#Download and install latest PCRE from version 8 branch
#note apache only works with PCRE 8 branch and not PCRE 10
#Get it from http://www.pcre.org/
#For example:
curl -O https://ftp.pcre.org/pub/pcre/pcre-8.42.tar.gz
#Install the package:
tar -zxvf pcre-8.42.tar.gz
cd pcre-8.42
./configure
make
sudo make install
cd ..
```

5 Install Apache:

```
#Download and install apache
#For example:
curl -O http://mirrors.whoishostingthis.com/apache/httpd/httpd-
2.4.37.tar.gz
curl -O https://www.apache.org/dist/httpd/httpd-2.4.37.tar.gz.sha256
#Verify the package after download:
cat httpd-2.4.37.tar.gz.sha256
openssl dgst -sha256 httpd-2.4.37.tar.gz
#Extract the source code
tar -zxvf httpd-2.4.37.tar.gz
cd httpd-2.4.37
./configure --with-ssl=/usr/local/ssl --with-pcre=/usr/local/bin/pcre-
config --enable-ssl --enable-so --with-apr=/usr/local/apr/bin/apr-1-
config --with-apr-util=/usr/local/apr/bin/apu-1-config --with-nghttp2=/
usr/local/opt/nghttp2 --enable-http2
make
sudo make install
cd ..
```

This code should install Apache to /usr/local/apache2.

6 Start Apache to see whether it works with basic HTTP:

```
sudo /usr/local/apache2/bin/apachectl -k graceful
```

If all is well, you should be able to visit your site over HTTP and see the default "It works" page on http://localhost, as shown in figure A.2.

It works!

Figure A.2   Default Apache "It works!" page on macOS

Getting HTTP/2 working requires a few more steps.

7 Uncomment the following modules from your httpd.conf file to load the SSL and HTTP modules, as well as the socache module required by SSL:

```
LoadModule socache_shmcb_module modules/mod_socache_shmcb.so
LoadModule ssl_module modules/mod_ssl.so
LoadModule http2_module modules/mod_http2.so
```

8 Add this line to include the SSL config:

```
Include conf/extra/httpd-ssl.conf
```

9 Add this line to show that this server prefers HTTP/2 (h2) first and then HTTP/1 and to enable logging:

```
<IfModule http2_module>
    Protocols h2 http/1.1
    LogLevel http2:info
</IfModule>
```

You can add h2c to the Protocols line if you want to enable HTTP/2 over HTTP (and not require HTTPS), but this feature isn't supported by any browser and is of limited use.

10　Next, install an HTTPS certificate. Obtaining a certificate is beyond the scope of this book, so I show you how to use OpenSSL to generate a basic self-signed certificate. The browser won't recognize this certificate, but it'll work for some basic tests:

```
#Note the openssl command I'll use needs to be run as root
sudo su -
cd /usr/local/apache2/conf
cat /System/Library/OpenSSL/openssl.cnf > /tmp/openssl.cnf
echo '[SAN]\nsubjectAltName=DNS:localhost' >> /tmp/openssl.cnf
openssl req \
    -newkey rsa:2048 \
    -x509 \
    -nodes \
    -keyout server.key \
    -new \
    -out server.crt \
    -subj /CN=localhost \
    -reqexts SAN \
    -extensions SAN \
    -config /tmp/openssl.cnf \
    -sha256 \
    -days 3650
```

You should give a correct subject and SAN for your server (shown as localhost in two places in the code), but the certificate won't be recognized anyway, so this information isn't too important.

The default Apache config (in conf/extra/httpd-ssl.conf) expects the certificates to be called server.key and server.crt, but change the names as appropriate if you're using nondefault config.

11　Stop and restart Apache to pick up the new config with the following command:

```
/usr/local/apache2/bin/apachectl -k graceful
```

12　Visit the site over HTTPS, and ignore the certificate error if you're using the self-signed test certificate from step 10 instead of a real certificate. You should see the page loaded over HTTP/2 (h2), similar to figure A.1, by opening developer tools and adding the Protocol column.

A.1.2　nginx

nginx (pronounced *Eengine-X*) introduced HTTP/2 support in version 1.9.5 through ngx_http_v2_module, which replaced ngx_http_spdy_module. I recommend that you run the latest stable version of nginx (available at https://nginx.org/en/download.html), as this module is still fairly new and was actively improved between 1.9.5 and the current version at this writing (1.14.2).

nginx doesn't support backend connections over HTTP/2 (nginx acting as a reverse proxy), and at this writing, there are no no plans to add this support.[8] nginx supports HTTP/2 over HTTPS using NPN and ALPN. As Chrome supports only ALPN, however, it's best to build nginx with at least OpenSSL 1.0.2 (or the equivalent) to enable HTTP/2 support for all browsers. nginx allows HTTP/2 over plain-text HTTP connections (known as h2c), though this feature is of limited use because no browser supports it.

NGINX ON WINDOWS

Unlike Apache, nginx provides Windows builds on its download page.[9] To get an HTTP/2 version of nginx running on Windows, do the following:

1 Download the latest stable version from the download page.[10]
2 Unzip the software wherever you want to install it (such as C:\Program Files\nginx).
3 Start a command prompt as administrator, and start the nginx.exe executable:

```
cd C:\Program Files\nginx
start nginx.exe
```

If you get any errors like these, another web server is already listening on port 80:

```
nginx: [emerg] bind() to 0.0.0.0:80 failed (10013: An attempt was made
to access a socket in a way forbidden by its access permissions)
```

On Windows, this server usually is the World Wide Web Publishing Service/IIS, so go into Services and stop it. Skype can cause similar problems.

At this point, you should be able to view the default nginx page over HTTP (but not HTTPS), and it should be served over HTTP/1.1 when you open developer tools and add the Protocol column.

4 Next, create some HTTPS certificates. Unfortunately, this process is a little tricky on Windows, as unlike Apache, nginx doesn't include any dummy certificates in the default Windows download. The easiest option is to generate the certificates on a Linux server by using the command shown in the Apache on Linux section. If using a Linux server isn't an option, use an online service such as http://www.selfsignedcertificate.com/ to generate certificates. These certificates should be used only on test servers, not on production servers. Save the key in a file called cert.key in the conf directory, and save the certificate in a file called cert.pem.

---

[8] https://trac.nginx.org/nginx/ticket/923
[9] https://nginx.org/en/download.html
[10] https://nginx.org/en/download.html

5 Configure nginx by editing the main configuration file (such as conf/nginx.conf), uncomment the SSL host section, and add `http2` to the `listen` command:

```
# HTTPS server
#
server {
    listen        443 ssl http2;
```

6 Reload the nginx config by running the following command in your command line:

```
nginx -s reload
```

7 Visit the default website over HTTP/2. You may have to ignore certificate errors if you're using self-signed certificates, which the browser won't recognize.

NGINX ON LINUX FROM NGINX REPOS

nginx.org offers official nginx repositories for the major operating systems.[11] As of version 1.12.2, the stable repo is built against OpenSSL 1.0.2 with ALPN support where the operating system supports it, so you can install the repo on an RHEL/CentOS 7.4 machine by following these steps:

1 Install the nginx repo by creating the repo file by using an editor such as vi:

```
sudo vi /etc/yum.repos.d/nginx.repo
```

2 Add the config to the nginx.repo file.
   For RHEL 7 (7.4 minimum), use

```
[nginx]
name=nginx repo
baseurl=http://nginx.org/packages/rhel/7/$basearch/
gpgcheck=0
enabled=1
```

For CentOS 7 (7.4 minimum), use the same code but change `baseurl` as follows:

```
baseurl=http://nginx.org/packages/centos/7/$basearch/
```

nginx also has a mainline version that includes the latest fixes, but I don't recommend installing it on a production system.

3 Install nginx:

```
sudo yum install nginx
```

4 Start nginx:

```
sudo nginx
```

---

[11] https://nginx.org/en/linux_packages.html

5 Check the default page loads over HTTP by opening developer tools and adding the Protocol column.

6 To turn on HTTP/2, add a default_ssl.conf file:

```
vi /etc/nginx/conf.d/default_ssl.conf
```

7 Add the following to the default_ssl.conf file:

```
# HTTPS server
#
server {
    listen       443 ssl http2;
    server_name  localhost;

    ssl_certificate      cert.pem;
    ssl_certificate_key  cert.key;

    ssl_session_cache    shared:SSL:1m;
    ssl_session_timeout  5m;

    ssl_ciphers  HIGH:!aNULL:!MD5;
    ssl_prefer_server_ciphers  on;

    location / {
        root   /usr/share/nginx/html;
        index  index.html index.htm;
    }

}
```

8 Create an HTTPS certificate:

```
#Note the openssl command I'll use needs to be run as root
sudo su -
cd /etc/nginx/conf
openssl req \
    -newkey rsa:2048 \
    -x509 \
    -nodes \
    -keyout cert.key \
    -new \
    -out cert.pem \
    -subj /CN=server.domain.tld \
    -reqexts SAN \
    -extensions SAN \
    -config <(cat /etc/pki/tls/openssl.cnf \
        <(printf '[SAN]\nsubjectAltName=DNS:server.domain.tld')) \
    -sha256 \
    -days 3650
```

Replace server.domain.tld in both places with your domain name. You receive
a certificate error anyway, so don't worry too much about this part.

9 Reload the nginx config:

```
nginx -s reload
```

10 Load the page over HTTPS, and make sure that it's displaying HTTP/2 by opening developer tools and adding the Protocol column (refer to figure A.1).

NGINX ON LINUX FROM SOURCE CODE

Because the official packaged version of nginx is built against OpenSSL 1.0.2 for those platforms that support it (such as RHEL/CentOS 7.4), you shouldn't need to build from source. If you're on an older platform, follow these steps:

1 Install the dependencies:

```
sudo yum -y install wget
sudo yum -y install perl
sudo yum -y install zlib-devel
sudo yum -y install gcc
sudo yum -y install pcre-devel
sudo yum -y install expat-devel
sudo yum -y install epel-release
sudo yum -y install libnghttp2-devel
sudo yum -y install openssl-devel

cd /tmp
mkdir sources
cd sources
```

2 For RHEL/CentOS before 7.4, install OpenSSL from source as well:

```
#Install Openssl http://openssl.org/source/
#For example:
wget https://www.openssl.org/source/openssl-1.1.1a.tar.gz
wget https://www.openssl.org/source/openssl-1.1.1a.tar.gz.asc
#Verify the package after download
gpg --verify openssl-1.1.1a.tar.gz.asc
#If you get a "Can't check signature: No public key" error
#then get the appropriate public key and verify again.
gpg --recv-keys 0E604491
gpg --verify openssl-1.1.1a.tar.gz.asc
#Extract the file and compile it:
tar -zxvf openssl-1.1.1a.tar.gz
cd openssl-1.1.1a
./config shared zlib-dynamic --prefix=/usr/local/ssl
make
sudo make install
cd ..
```

3 Download and extract the latest stable version of nginx:

```
cd /tmp
mkdir sources
cd sources
#Download the lastest stable version
```

```
#Get it from https://nginx.org/en/download.html
#For example:
wget https://nginx.org/download/nginx-1.14.2.tar.gz
wget https://nginx.org/download/nginx-1.14.2.tar.gz.asc
#Verify download:
#nginx keys are here: https://nginx.org/en/pgp_keys.html
#Install them all like this:
wget https://nginx.org/keys/mdounin.key
gpg -import mdounin.key
#Then verify the package:
gpg --verify nginx-1.14.2.tar.gz.asc
#Note you will see a WARNING that the key isn't certified
#with a trusted signature. This is expected.
#Extract the file and compile it:
tar -xvf nginx-1.14.2.tar.gz
cd nginx-1.14.2
```

4 Configure the make script.

For RHEL/CentOS 7.4, in which you're using the system openssl, use the following:

```
#Configure and compile:
./configure --with-http_ssl_module --with-http_v2_module
```

For RHEL/CentOS before 7.4, you need to use the custom OpenSSL you installed:

```
#Configure and compile:
./configure --with-http_ssl_module --with-http_v2_module \
   --with-openssl=/tmp/sources/openssl-1.1.1a
```

5 Make and install the build:

```
make
sudo make install
cd ..
```

6 Start nginx:

```
sudo /usr/local/nginx/sbin/nginx
```

7 Test the basic HTTP site (but not HTTPS) by opening developer tools and adding the Protocol column.

8 Configure nginx for HTTPS and HTTP/2 by editing the main configuration file (such as /usr/local/nginx/conf/nginx.conf), making sure that the HTTPS section is uncommented, and adding the http2 option shown in bold:

```
# HTTPS server
#
server {
    listen        443 ssl http2;
```

9 Create an HTTPS certificate:

```
#The openssl command needs to be run as root so sudo to that
sudo su -
cd /usr/local/nginx/conf
openssl req \
    -newkey rsa:2048 \
    -x509 \
    -nodes \
    -keyout cert.key \
    -new \
    -out cert.pem \
    -subj /CN=server.domain.tld \
    -reqexts SAN \
    -extensions SAN \
    -config <(cat /etc/pki/tls/openssl.cnf \
        <(printf '[SAN]\nsubjectAltName=DNS:server.domain.tld')) \
    -sha256 \
    -days 3650
```

You should give a correct subject and SAN for your server (shown as server.domain.tld in two places in the code). But the certificate won't be recognized anyway, so this part isn't too important.

The default nginx config (in conf/nginx.conf) expects the certificates to be called cert.key and cert.pem, but change the names as appropriate if you're using nondefault config.

10 Reload the nginx config:

```
sudo /usr/local/nginx/sbin/nginx -s reload
```

11 View the default "Welcome to nginx" page over HTTP/2.

NGINX ON MACOS

You have two ways to install nginx on macOS:

- Install from another package manager, such as Homebrew.
- Install from source.

Neither option is ideal (see chapter 3).

Installing via Homebrew is simple and involves two commands:

```
/usr/bin/ruby -e "$(curl -fsSL https://raw.githubusercontent.com/Homebrew/
    install/master/install)"

brew install nginx
```

To check that works, start nginx:

```
brew services start nginx
```

Homebrew makes nginx available over ports 8080 and 8443 rather than the usual 80 and 443, so visit http://localhost:8080/ to see your new web server.

Configuring HTTP/2 requires editing the main configuration file

```
/usr/local/etc/nginx/nginx.conf
```

and making the following changes

1 Uncomment the following lines to add the HTTPS server, and add the `http2` directive to the `listen` line:

```
# HTTPS server
#
server {
    listen        8443 ssl http2;
    server_name  localhost;

    ssl_certificate        cert.pem;
    ssl_certificate_key    cert.key;

    ssl_session_cache      shared:SSL:1m;
    ssl_session_timeout    5m;

    ssl_ciphers  HIGH:!aNULL:!MD5;
    ssl_prefer_server_ciphers  on;

    location / {
        root    html;
        index   index.html index.htm;
    }

}
```

2 Set up an HTTPS certificate:

```
#Note the openssl command I'll use needs to be run as root
sudo su -
cd /usr/local/etc/nginx
cat /System/Library/OpenSSL/openssl.cnf > /tmp/openssl.cnf
echo '[SAN]\nsubjectAltName=DNS:localhost' >> /tmp/openssl.cnf
openssl req \
    -newkey rsa:2048 \
    -x509 \
    -nodes \
    -keyout cert.key \
    -new \
    -out cert.pem \
    -subj /CN=localhost \
    -reqexts SAN \
    -extensions SAN \
    -config /tmp/openssl.cnf \
    -sha256 \
    -days 3650
```

3 Restart nginx:

```
brew services restart nginx
```

4 Check whether the site loads over HTTP/2 at https://localhost:8443/.

If you prefer not to use Homebrew, downloading from source is a little more convoluted and similar to the Linux setup:

1 Set up a directory for the software:

```
cd /tmp
mkdir sources
cd sources
```

2 Install the latest OpenSSL (or LibreSSL, if you prefer):

```
#Get it from http://openssl.org/source/
#For example:
curl -O https://www.openssl.org/source/openssl-1.1.1a.tar.gz
curl -o https://www.openssl.org/source/openssl-1.1.1a.tar.gz.sha256
#Verify the package after download by comparing these two values:
openssl dgst -sha256 openssl-1.1.1a.tar.gz
cat openssl-1.1.1a.tar.gz.sha256
#Extract the file and compile it:
tar -zxvf openssl-1.1.1a.tar.gz
cd openssl-1.1.1a
./config shared zlib-dynamic --prefix=/usr/local/ssl
make
sudo make install
cd ..
```

3 Install nginx:

```
#Download and install nginx
#For example:
curl -O https://nginx.org/download/nginx-1.14.2.tar.gz
#Extract the source code
tar -zxvf nginx-1.14.2.tar.gz
cd nginx-1.14.2
./configure --with-http_ssl_module --with-http_v2_module \
    --with-cc-opt="-I/usr/local/ssl/include" \
    --with-ld-opt="-L/usr/local/ssl/lib"
make
sudo make install
cd ..
```

4 Start nginx as root. Note that when installing from source, you use the default ports of 80 and 443, which require root access to use:

```
sudo /usr/local/nginx/sbin/nginx
```

5 Test the basic HTTP site (but not HTTPS) by opening developer tools and adding the Protocol column.

6 Configure HTTP/2 by editing the main configuration file, using a text editor such as vi:

```
sudo vi /usr/local/nginx/conf/nginx.conf
```

Also uncomment the following lines to add the HTTPS server, and add the http2 directive to the listen line:

```
# HTTPS server
#
server {
    listen       443 ssl http2;
    server_name  localhost;

    ssl_certificate      cert.pem;
    ssl_certificate_key  cert.key;

    ssl_session_cache    shared:SSL:1m;
    ssl_session_timeout  5m;

    ssl_ciphers  HIGH:!aNULL:!MD5;
    ssl_prefer_server_ciphers  on;

    location / {
        root   html;
        index  index.html index.htm;
    }

}
```

7 Set up an HTTPS certificate:

```
#Note the openssl command I'll use needs to be run as root
sudo su -
cd /usr/local/etc/nginx
cat /System/Library/OpenSSL/openssl.cnf > /tmp/openssl.cnf
echo '[SAN]\nsubjectAltName=DNS:localhost' >> /tmp/openssl.cnf
openssl req \
    -newkey rsa:2048 \
    -x509 \
    -nodes \
    -keyout cert.key \
    -new \
    -out cert.pem \
    -subj /CN=localhost \
    -reqexts SAN \
    -extensions SAN \
    -config /tmp/openssl.cnf \
    -sha256 \
    -days 3650
```

8 Restart nginx to pick up the new configuration:

```
sudo /usr/local/nginx/sbin/nginx -s reload
```

9 Check whether the site loads over HTTP/2 at https://localhost/.

A.1.3 *Microsoft Internet Information Services (IIS)*

HTTP/2 support was added in IIS 10, introduced in Windows Server 2016 and Windows 10. IIS supports HTTP/2 only over HTTPS. IIS 10 has HTTP/2 turned on by default, so if you're running Windows Server 2016 or later with HTTPS, you're probably already using HTTP/2 if you have an HTTPS site. If your server is earlier than Windows Server 2016, the only option is to upgrade the whole server. It's not possible to install IIS 10 with HTTP/2 support on older Windows machines.

For Windows 10 desktop machines, you may need to enable the IIS Management Console on the "Turn Windows features on or off" screen (available from the Start option by searching for *Windows features*), as shown in figure A.3.

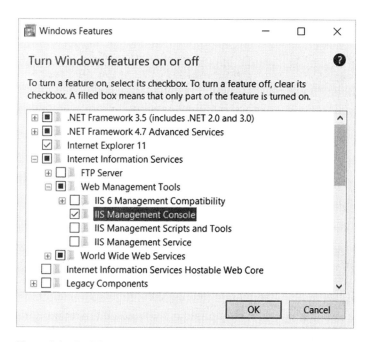

Figure A.3   Enabling the IIS Management Console

When this console is enabled, you should be able to configure the site as usual in the following location: Control Panel\All Control Panel Items\Administrative Tools\Internet Information Services (IIS) Manager.

After you've installed an HTTPS certificate (not covered here), you should be able to load the default website over HTTP/2.

A.1.4   Other servers

Other servers can be installed in a similar fashion. The important points are to check for HTTP/2 (and which version it was added in), to check which version of OpenSSL (or similar) it was built with, and to enable HTTP/2 and HTTPS. The HTTP/2 Implementations page[12] lists over 50 servers that support HTTP/2 at this writing.

A.2   Setting up HTTP/2 via a reverse proxy server

If upgrading your main web server to support HTTP/2 isn't possible, or if you want to test HTTP/2 without making any changes in your current setup, you may want to set up a reverse proxy in front of your web server to enable HTTP/2 support. In the following sections, I provide basic instructions for Apache and nginx.

In both these examples, the reverse proxy uses HTTP/1.1 to communicate with the backend server. Apache allows the use of HTTP/2 via the `mod_proxy_http2` module. At this writing, the module is still marked as experimental,[13] and there are few benefits for proxying backend connections over HTTP/2 at this time (see the "Do you need to speak HTTP/2 all the way through?" sidebar in chapter 3), so that use case isn't covered here. The following examples allow Apache or nginx to handle HTTP/2 communication and leave the backend server using HTTP/1.1.

A.2.1   Apache

For Apache to act as a proxy server, you need to enable HTTP/2 as detailed in the preceding section and to enable the following modules in the main configuration file:

```
proxy_module
proxy_http_module
```

You can enable these modules by uncommenting or adding the appropriate Load-Module lines in the main config file (httpd.conf or apache.conf) or by using a2enmod for Ubuntu-based systems.

Then you add the proxy config (assuming that the web server you want to proxy to is on localhost port 8080):

```
ProxyPreserveHost On

# Proxy all requests to localhost port 8080
ProxyPass / http://127.0.0.1:8080/
ProxyPassReverse / http://127.0.0.1:8080/
```

This code passes requests directly to the backend server by using the Ipv4 loopback address (127.0.0.1). You can also use the Ipv6 loopback address (::1) if you prefer. Either option is preferable to the localhost name, which requires a needless DNS lookup.

---

[12] https://github.com/http2/http2-spec/wiki/Implementations
[13] https://httpd.apache.org/docs/trunk/mod/mod_proxy_http2.html

The application may need to be configured to act with a proxy server in front of it. Any links that it produces, for example, should reference the proxy port (80/443), rather than the actual port it's running on (8080 in this example). Because reverse-proxying application servers is common, many applications make configuring this server easy with a Base URL or similar option. If the backend server doesn't provide this option, Apache allows you to use the proxy_html_module to rewrite HTML dynamically to replace links automatically (such as replacing http://www.example.com:8080 with https://www.example.com).

A.2.2 *nginx*

nginx works in a similar manner to Apache, with the following config:

```
location / {
    proxy_pass http://127.0.0.1:8080/;
}
```

Similar to the comment in the Apache section, the application server may need configuring to tell it that it's running behind a reverse proxy. If this configuration isn't possible, the ngx_http_sub_module can dynamically rewrite any URLs similarly to proxy_html_module for Apache.

index

Get Programming with JavaScript Next
New features of ECMAScript 2015, 2016, and beyond
by JD Isaacks

ISBN: 9781617294204
376 pages
$39.99
April 2018

Get Programming with JavaScript
by John R. Larsen

ISBN: 9781617293108
432 pages
$39.99
August 2016

For ordering information go to www.manning.com

MORE TITLES FROM MANNING

Angular Development with Typescript, Second Edition
by Yakov Fain and Anton Moiseev

ISBN: 9781617295348
560 pages
$49.99
December 2018

Angular in Action
by Jeremy Wilken

ISBN: 9781617293313
320 pages
$44.99
March 2018

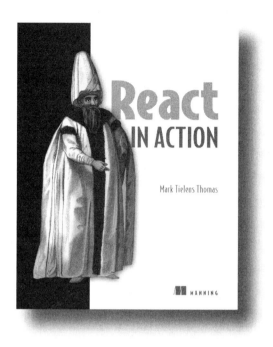

React in Action
by Mark Tielens Thomas

ISBN: 9781617293856
360 pages
$44.99
May 2018

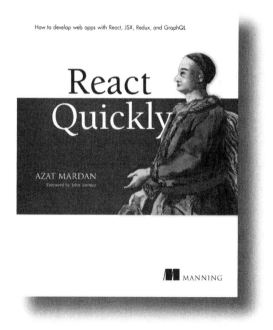

React Quickly
Painless web apps with React, JSX, Redux,
and GraphQL
by Azat Mardan

ISBN: 9781617293344
528 pages
$49.99
August 2017

For ordering information go to www.manning.com

MORE TITLES FROM MANNING

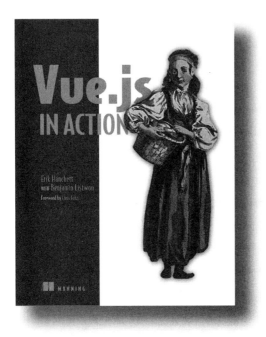

Vue.js in Action
by Erik Hanchett with Benjamin Listwon

> ISBN: 9781617294624
> 304 pages
> $44.99
> September 2018

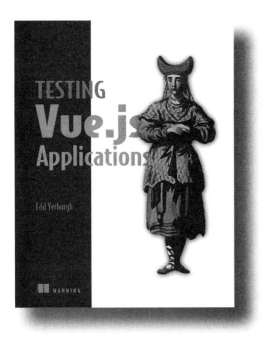

Testing Vue.js Applications
by Edd Yerburgh

> ISBN: 9781617295249
> 272 pages
> $44.99
> December 2018

For ordering information go to www.manning.com

OAuth 2 in Action
by Justin Richer and Antonio Sanso

ISBN: 9781617293276
360 pages
$49.99
March 2017

Securing DevOps
Security in the Cloud
by Julien Vehent

ISBN: 9781617294136
384 pages
$49.99
August 2018

For ordering information go to www.manning.com